SORLEY MACLEAN

CRITICAL ESSAYS

SORLEY MACLEAN

CRITICAL ESSAYS

Edited by

RAYMOND J. ROSS

JOY HENDRY

SCOTTISH ACADEMIC PRESS

EDINBURGH

Published by
Scottish Academic Press Ltd,
33 Montgomery Street
Edinburgh EH7 5JX

SBN 7073 0426 1

Typeset by the Tweeddale Press
Printed and bound in Great Britain by
Latimer Trend & Company Ltd, Plymouth

Dedication

By its very nature this book is in dedication to Dr Sorley MacLean, a tribute from us and from all the contributors to his life's work. We would like to add personal dedications to William Hendry and to Patricia Lovett.

CONTRIBUTORS

James B. Caird is a lifelong friend of Sorley MacLean, one of H.M. Inspectors of Schools, now retired, and author of many critical articles.

Robert Calder is a freelance writer, critic and poet.

Brendan P. Devlin is a novelist, literary critic in the Irish language and Professor of Modern Languages at St. Patrick's College, Maynooth, Ireland.

William Gillies, a native Gaelic speaker, is Professor of Celtic at the University of Edinburgh and edited the recently published *Ris a' Bhruthaich: The Criticism and Prose Writings of Sorley MacLean*.

Seamus Heaney is an Irish poet, critic, editor and broadcaster. He recently appeared in Timothy Neat's biographical film of Sorley MacLean, *Hallaig*.

Joy Hendry has been editor of *Chapman* since 1972, worked as a teacher for 7 years and is now a freelance writer and editor.

John Herdman is a novelist and critic.

Terence McCaughey worked on the Linguistic Survey of Scotland for 3 years and since 1964 has taught in the Irish Department of Trinity College, Dublin, and recently in its School of Biblical and Theological Studies.

Donald Archie MacDonald, a native Gaelic speaker, is a lecturer in the School of Scottish Studies, University of Edinburgh.

John MacInnes, a native Gaelic speaker, has written widely on Sorley MacLean and is a lecturer in the School of Scottish Studies, University of Edinburgh.

Aonghas MacNeacail, a native Gaelic speaker, is a Gaelic poet, critic and freelance writer.

Thomas Mac Síomóin is an Irish poet, freelance writer, editor and critic.

Raymond J. Ross, a founder editor of *Cencrastus*, poet and MacDiarmid scholar, works as a teacher.

Douglas Sealy worked as a teacher for 30 years, is Gaelic editor of *Books Ireland* and is well known as a critic of music and letters.

Iain Crichton Smith, a native Gaelic speaker, is a well-known Scottish poet, prose-writer and critic in English and Gaelic, and translator of Sorley MacLean's poetry.

Ronald Stevenson is a Scottish musician and composer who has set some of Sorley MacLean's lyrics to music.

FOREWORD

The idea for this book came out of the memorable celebrations held in Edinburgh for Sorley MacLean's 70th birthday in the autumn of 1981, organised by the John MacLean Society and *Chapman* magazine. As two of Scotland's younger generation of writers for whom the poetry of MacLean has had 'the force of a revelation', to quote Seamus Heaney's Introduction, we wanted to produce a more permanent and tangible tribute to Scotland's greatest living poet. It seemed incredible that no such book already existed, despite the widespread recognition MacLean nowadays receives.

Critical Essays on Sorley MacLean is intended both as a tribute and as a critical estimate, of interest both to the professional scholar and to the general reader. It has been a primary purpose of this book to make MacLean's writing more accessible to the non-Gael. We hope also that, in its critical function, the volume will serve to demonstrate why he is to be regarded as a major poet.

The book takes the form of a collection of specially commissioned essays, whose authors' talents are collectively well suited to cover the range of MacLean's life and work in a comprehensive manner. The essays hence deal not only with the major facets of his poetry, but examine also his work in other fields: his contribution to modern literary criticism; his agitation for a better deal for Gaelic in Scottish education; his rich family background, steeped in the best of oral and written Gaelic culture; his very fertile influence upon other poets. Nor have we ignored the human being behind the poetry, but have included a biographical essay and an essay from James B. Caird, a close friend and one of his own generation, on the man himself.

For reasons of space it was not possible to include essays in Gaelic. Quotations from the poetry, however, are given throughout in both Gaelic and English, the translations being the poet's own unless otherwise stated. The major exception is Douglas Sealy's essay 'Out from Skye to the World' in which the author has supplied his own translations, believing that 'the more translations the better'.

We are sensitive to the deep and genuine interest in the work of Sorley MacLean which exists furth of Scotland, and we hope the book will bring his work to the attention of even wider audiences in the USA, Canada, Europe, Australia, New Zealand and elsewhere. But it is the very special appreciation felt in Ireland which has given us the greatest inspiration in the making of this book. This is reflected in the very substantial contribution made here by Irish poets and critics.

Acknowledgements are due to Douglas Sealy for the beautifully drawn maps, and for compiling the 'Commentary on Placenames in MacLean's Poems'; and also to the other contributors — without whom this book would not be — for their equally enthusiastic response to the call to write; to Douglas Grant and the staff of Scottish Academic Press for encouragement and support throughout the preparation of the book. We would also like to thank the staff of the National Library of Scotland, particularly S. M. Simpson, for information and for access to material absolutely invaluable in the preparation of the book. To Mrs Valda Grieve and Michael Grieve we acknowledge thanks for permission to quote from correspondence between Hugh MacDiarmid and MacLean, and to Mrs Clara Young for permission to quote from correspondence between Douglas Young and MacLean.

Special acknowledgements must be made to Professor William Gillies of the Department of Celtic, Edinburgh University, for his many invaluable and meticulous contributions from the inception of the book right through to final publication, and to Dr Sorley MacLean himself, who has been consulted throughout and has helped untiringly, especially in providing material for the biographical essay. We hope that this book captures something of the generous spirit of the poetry.

Finally to those close to us, our respective families, we extend thanks for bearing with us during the many hours spent in compiling this book.

RAYMOND J. ROSS,
JOY HENDRY
Edinburgh, April, 1986.

Order of Contents

Illustrations

The line drawings on pages 44, 80, 90, 108, 126, 136, 164 and 184 are taken from the 1943 edition of *Dain do Eimhir* and are reproduced by kind permission of the artist, William Crosbie. The captions are the English titles of the poems to which they refer. The maps on pages 8, 52 and 154 are by Douglas Sealy and reproduced with his permission. The musical arrangement of 'Calbharaigh' reproduced on page 184 is by kind permission of Ronald Stevenson. The sketch of Sorley MacLean on the jacket is by John R. McWilliam, permission of Ronald Stevenson.

INTRODUCTION

What the Polish poet Stanislaw Baranczak has written about his compatriot, Czeslaw Milosz, applies with equal force to the achievement of Sorley MacLean:

> A writer can be great only when he is truly himself; and the more himself he is, the more is he true to the horizon that happens to encircle him, to the times in which he is born. But his loyalty to his own world of experience, which is a source of his writing, is also a barrier between him and a reader who has grown up in different circumstances, in a different "native realm".

One of the functions of this book is the removal of such a barrier, and scholars and critics with a specialised knowledge of Sorley MacLean's "native realm" will be in a better position than I am to explicate and amplify the signals transmitted by his loyal and deeply schooled imagination. My purpose here is to express my response as a reader who has been greatly rewarded by reading his poetry as I picked it up on the *ad hoc* equipment of my own receiving station.

It is often late, by chance, and with sudden delight, that we find those poets who later become vital to us. I knew Sorley MacLean by reputation before I felt his authority. His renovation of a poetic tradition, his cross-fertilization of love and politics, of metaphysical technique and traditional Gaelic modes, of 'dán díreach' and personal destiny — I knew about all this at second hand; it was part of that store of useful literary information that accumulates at the back of the literary mind like respected, unread books on the bookshelf. But then, in the early seventies, two things occurred which made the spark jump: I read Iain Crichton Smith's translations, *Poems to Eimhir*, and I heard MacLean himself read his own poems in the original Gaelic.

To take the translations first, since they were my first exposure: opening the book was like opening the door on a morning of sea-filled brightness; there was a feeling of unspecifiable freedom and intensity. The voice in the poems was at once unleashed and stricken. There was a tremendous sense of capacity, of emotional lift-off, a boldness and ardour that had a high romantic voltage; yet there was also a deeply modern guilt, a self-castigating intelligence which stuck like a hook in the throat of rapture:

> The love begotten by the heart
> is a love that dances in its chains
> when it embraces intellect —
> love of the scrutinizing brain.

> And the stone that's always broken
> by the assiduous mind

> becomes a bright entire stone
> made harder by each new wound.
>
> ('An Sgian')

Lines like these came through so strongly that I almost forgot I was reading a translation: curiosity about a respected name was obliterated by the impact of the thing itself. Poem after poem went home to that first place of recognition where once a poem has visited it can never afterwards be denied or forgotten.
Again, the perfect pitch of:

> I walked with my intelligence
> beside the muted sea:
> we were together, but it kept
> a little distance from me

gave way to the pressure of history and conscience:

> I who avoided the sore cross
> and agony of Spain,
> what should I expect or hope,
> what splendid prize to win?

Such lines were both sustenance and example to somebody hugging his own secret uneases about the way a poet should conduct himself at a moment of public crisis — for I first read them in the days of the heavy bombing campaign in Belfast, a town I had left in order to make some more deliberate commitment to the life of poetry.

At any rate, the effect of reading these invaluable translations was to string a new chord in my poetic ear. I could recognise a Yeatsian ring in some of Crichton Smith's handling; I could hear the tuning fork of Donne's or maybe Marvell's quatrains behind the melody of some versions, but this did not stop the sure vibration of the note that would sound from now on at the mention of Sorley MacLean's name.

And then I heard the voice of the man himself speaking the poems in Gaelic. I was lucky to be on the stage of the Abbey Theatre when Sorley and Norman MacCaig came to Dublin to read at the launching of their excellent poetry records which were being put out by Claddagh Records: my job was to read some of the translations (this time by Sorley MacLean) but my interest was in hearing the Gaelic. Again, this had the force of revelation: the mesmeric, heightened tone; the weathered voice coming in close from a far place; the swarm of the vowels; the surrender to the otherness of the poem; above all the sense of bardic dignity that was entirely without self-parade but was instead the effect of a proud self-abnegation, as much a submission as a claim to heritage. All this constituted a second discovery, this time of the true climate of his linguistic world.

Reading 'Hallaig' on that occasion, in the poet's own English, and hearing it in the deep lamenting register of the Gaelic, extended and confirmed my sense of him as a major figure. This was the song of a man who had come through, a poem with all the lucidity and arbitrariness of a vision. On the one hand, it rose like a mist over the ancestral ground in which this poet's tap-root is profoundly lodged, a poem of almost familial intimacy arising out of a naturally genealogical imagination, embodying all the fidelities implicit in the Irish word 'dúchas'. On the other hand, by its nonchalant beauty, its feeling of being absolutely 'given', it belonged to the world of Eliot's 'Marina', Rilke's Orphic sonnets, indeed to the metamorphic world of Orpheus himself. It held fast to a field of indigenous obsessions, but its effect was not merely to celebrate indigenous ground: it opened that "nailed and boarded" window of the first line in such a way that a sense of loss became a sense of scope, and what might have been a pious elegy became a rich and strange ode to melancholy, insofar as the curve of its feeling rehearses something similar to what Keats is touching on in the lines:

> Ay, in the very temple of Delight
> Veil'd Melancholy has her sovran shrine,
> Though seen of none save him whose strenuous tongue
> Can burst Joy's grape against his palate fine.

'Hallaig' is a key poem because it is about haunting and loss and this mood is a persistent one all through the work, as is the theme of love and wounding: which arrests the fluent dreamscape at the end of the poem. The bullet from the gun of love

Buailear am fiadh a tha 'na thuaineal
a' snòtach nan làraichean feòir;
thig reothadh air a shùil 'sa' choille:
chan fhaighear lorg air fhuil ri m' bheò.

Will strike the deer that goes dizzily,
sniffing at the grass-grown ruined homes;
his eye will freeze in the wood,
his blood will not be traced while I live.

The dimensions of the poem are all the more fully revealed if it is seen in relation to another mysterious lyric by Thomas Hardy which also exposes us to a sort of hallucinatory experience:

> One without looks in tonight
>   Through the curtain-chink
> From the sheet of glistening white;
> One without looks in tonight
>   As we sit and think
>   By the fender-brink.
>
> We do not discern those eyes
>   Watching in the snow;
> Lit by lamps of rosy dyes
> We do not discern those eyes
>   Wondering, aglow,
>   Fourfooted, tiptoe.

Hardy's poem is tender and purely uttered, but its furtive domesticity is the opposite of the shimmer of community that pervades 'Hallaig'. And Hardy's shyly quivering deer, by its very living credibility, is less absolutely a poetic presence than the heraldic, yet vulnerable, beast that is conjured by MacLean. 'The Fallow Deer at the Lonely House' has an exquisite suggestiveness of its own but I wish to claim that by comparison MacLean's poem stands out as a much greater epiphany, a kind of condensed symbolist epic. The naming of people and places gives it a foundation in history and a foothold in bardic tradition, but there is also a visionary objectivity about the point of view whereby the sorrowful recognitions are transposed into a paradisal key. Indeed, the perfect commentary on 'Hallaig' comes from another oracular poem about time and memory. In these lines from 'Little Gidding' Eliot, having declared that the use of memory is "for liberation — not less of love but expanding/Of love beyond desire" continues:

History may be servitude,
History may be freedom. See, now they vanish,
The faces and places, with the self which, as it could, loved them,
To become renewed, transfigured, in another pattern.

The emotional air of 'Hallaig' is as clear as the sky after a storm, but we encounter more dramatic and turbulent weather in *Dàin do Eimhir*. I am thinking in particular of a poem like 'An Tathaich' (Poem LVII; translated as 'The Haunting' in the Canongate selection and also translated by Iain Crichton Smith), but the whole sequence is charged with pent-up force. The face behind the poems is no artistic makeshift but keeps closing in like a hound of heaven. There is a driven quality in the writing itself, as if the poetry is leaping from one invention to the next like a man leaping for his life from ice-floe to ice-floe. This work will survive comparison with the very highest examples of the haunting face in literature. If the Beatrice of Dante's *Commedia* is more cosmologically centred, at once more densely allegorical and diaphanous, the Beatrice of the *Vita Nuova*, being closer to the moment of encounter in Dante's life, is closer to the muse of the Eimhir poems. MacLean's tone is more disconsolate and tragic, however: the trauma of the actual experience has set the needles trembling. Again, the Eimhir poems share what we understand to be a characteristic of the early Italian love poetry, a feeling of language rejuvenated by the discovery of new ranges for itself, as if something fallow had been touched by something marvellously fertile and a whole new culture of the spirit flourished overnight. As in the fairytale where the beanstalk darkens the window in the morning, fear and miracle spring from the one root in *Dàin do Eimhir*.

To invoke Dante, is, of course, mightily honorific, and to honour MacLean mightily is part of the purpose. But there is another reason as well. Like an increasing number of his readers, I cannot possess fully — and hence cannot be fully possessed by — the language in which these poems are written, yet I have just enough Irish to hear them from the inside and hence feel an unease in aligning them too patly with the tradition of English poetry — Hardy, Keats and Eliot notwithstanding. This is indeed one way to shoe-horn them into the contemporary literary consciousness, one way of giving readers familiar bannisters to hold as they climb to the bare place at the centre of the work. Yet it sets the controls just that bit off. English love poetry, even the poetry of Donne which by its pounce and reach is recognisably akin to MacLean's, still leads the reader to a more composed and accommodating relationship with the social world of possible feelings and manageable destinies. Donne is less distressed if equally animated by the shock of feeling. The whole undertow of doom which can subsist even in MacLean's most felicitous lyric gesture — say a poem like 'Am Mùr Gorm' — is exactly what tends to be missing in English lyrics. Something sensed beyond the pane of translation, an extra dimension of fear and need seems to course the veins of the Gaelic rhythms and perhaps this is why poetry from other languages, moods arising out of other emotional geographies, are helpful in trying to say exactly what MacLean does for us. Reading a poem like 'An Tathaich', I find myself thinking of the spectral presence in Alexander Blok's *The Twelve*, swirling along in a blizzard of apprehensions where the historical moment and the personal dilemma storm into the mind in a single blast.

Still, spiritual geology may be more important than emotional geography. If Beatrice is candidly a figure who mediates between the heavenly and earthly worlds,

Eimhir does so covertly. The woman in the poems resolves at a symbolic level tensions which would otherwise be uncontainable or wasteful. She is neither an escape from the world of moral decision nor an obliteration of it; she is neither an emblem of heavenly certitude nor a substitute for it. Yet she fills a necessary space in a mind that is ravenous for conviction. It is as if Hopkins had fallen in love at the moment of "the terrible sonnets" and his poems, instead of being "cries like dead letters sent/To dearest him who lives, alas, away", became cries to the loved one which neither relieved nor resolved his fear of the abyss or his doubts about his commitment, but which made them current in the world of erotic feeling rather than in the world of prayer.

In a way, MacLean's relation with his landscape is erotic too, because the language of his poems of place has an amorousness and abundance about it which springs from the contemplation of the beloved contours. Contrary to the notion of the poet as one who gives to airy nothings a local habitation and a name, MacLean begins with names and habitations. He has an epic poet's possession of ground, founders, heroes, battles, lovers, legends, all of them at once part of his personal apparatus of feeling and part of the common but threatened ghost-life of his language and culture. But to feel intensely within this first world of tradition is also to feel an imperative to become its custodian, and it is impossible to separate the potency of Sorley MacLean's art from this function of keeping and witnessing, being "true to the horizon that happens to encircle him". Without needing to proclaim the significance of his role — as MacDiarmid did constantly, for instance in 'Island Funeral' — MacLean establishes a conscience not only for the Gaelic nation but for the world which would diminish the integrity of that nation and thereby diminish its own.

There is nothing antiquarian or archival about this drive. We need only compare the way the names of mountains, waters and woods animate his poetry with the way the names of places and characters are put to work in the writings of David Jones in order to see how purely poetic, how non-programmatic, how free from the whiff of the scholar's midnight oil are the topographical and mythological elements in MacLean's work. Jones often intended to instruct his audience in what they should know if they were to be true Britons, he had a design for his work and a design upon his reader, and his writing suffers from the submerged righteousness of his mission. The strain of his counter-cultural effort shows up at times as an excess of exotic data that remains illustrative rather than emotionally naturalised, and sometimes its tone strikes us as eccentric in the common pejorative sense of the word rather than in its definitive etymological sense.

Jones's zeal was evangelical, MacLean's responsibility is druidic. He stands at the centre, if near the end, of a world he embodies. Hence the effortless rhapsody of poems like 'Ceann Loch Aoineart' and 'Coilltean Ratharsair' thrives on the same nutrient love of place as the more personal love-poems like 'A' Bhuaile Ghréine' and 'Tràighean'. In all of them an urgency to name springs from a sense of crisis, either personal or communal. They return to hallowed spots and exemplary names with the same intent as Yeats when he repeated the roll-call of his Olympians: in order to resist the erosion of certain values, to maintain the dignity and continuity of a style of life and a way of feeling and behaving characteristic of the poet's caste. If this solidarity results in both poets finding political positions which are ideologically opposed — Yeats defending the Big House and privilege, MacLean sending his prayers to the Red Army fighting on the Dnieper — it also exposes important resemblances. Like Yeats, MacLean has a haughty, chivalrous mind, fortified by a consciousness of ancestry, shadowed by a tragic sense of an ending. If he declines to draw his own profile in his poems as heroically and representatively as Yeats did, he nevertheless inherits a position within his own culture and within the world of poetry that resembles Yeats's: "Man is in love and loves what vanishes" is a motto to which the Gaelic poet could also assent.

When Sorley MacLean addresses Yeats directly, however, the accusation which Yeats thirsted for (at least once) is forthcoming:

Fhuair thusa 'n cothrom, Uilleim,	You got the chance, William,
an cothrom dha do bhriathran	the chance of your words,
on bha a' ghaisge 's a' bhòidhche	since courage and beauty
's an croinn bhratach troimh do chliathaich.	had their flagpoles through your side.
Ghabh thu riutha air aon dòigh,	You acknowledged them in one way,
ach tha leisgeal air do bhilean,	but there is an excuse on your lips,
an leisgeal nach do mhill do bhàrdachd	the excuse that did not spoil your poetry,
oir tha a leisgeal aig gach duine.	for every man has his excuse.

('Aig Uaigh Yeats')

In the previous stanza the socialist and fighter, James Connolly, is invoked, and Connolly is, of course, one of MacLean's Olympians, in that his socialism, his patriotism and his execution as a result of committed action have exemplary force. Yeats indeed wrote the poem 'Easter, 1916' but Connolly died in the event, and hence in spite of the triumph of his art, Yeats is still found guilty of holding back. Yet there is a note of collusion as well as accusation at the end, and it seems to me that, thirty years after his poem about not going to Spain (already quoted), MacLean is finding a double in the figure of the self-excusing Yeats: both of them are racked between the command to participate and their covenant with a non-participant muse.

In the meantime, however, MacLean had been a soldier and had gone through that initiation in danger without which every man feels incomplete, and in 'Dol an Iar' (first published in the 1977 selection) he writes a retrospective poem which takes him from his native island, through the remembered duel between love and honour, through desert warfare, into a sense of universal brotherhood and back into the deep, first resource of ancestry. At bottom it is reminiscence, in essence it is a conspectus of his poetic world:

Agus biodh na bha mar bha e,	And be what was as it was,
tha mi de dh' fhir mhór' a' Bhràighe,	I am one of the big men of Braes,
de Chloinn Mhic Ghille Chaluim threubhaich,	of the heroic Raasay MacLeods,
de Mhathanaich Loch Aills nan geurlann,	of the sharp-sword Mathesons of Lochalsh;
agus fir m' ainme — có bu tréine	and the men of my name — who were braver
nuair dh' fhàdadh uabhar an léirchreach?	when their ruinous pride was kindled?

But this genealogical line is not only a source of rhetorical defiance, it is an image which is as vital to the roots of his poetry and the validity of his language as that source which Yeats calls, in 'The Circus Animals' Desertion', "the foul rag and bone shop of the heart".

In one sense, all MacLean's ladders start where his whole being is first vested, in the Gaelic language itself, and what is inestimable about his achievement — artistically and politically — is the extent to which it has sounded the Gaelic note through the world at a moment when it might have been presumed to be growing less than audible. In another sense, his ladders start in the particular life he has lived and the particular choices he has made. But whether we locate the origins of the art in the linguistic deposit or personal experience, when we come to live with his poetry's unique rigours and bonuses we can only assent to Ezra Pound's salutary distinction that "there are works of art which are beautiful objects and works of art which are keys or passwords admitting one to a deeper knowledge, to a finer perception", in the grateful knowledge that Sorley MacLean's are of the second sort. What was unlooked for has grown indispensible.

SEAMUS HEANEY

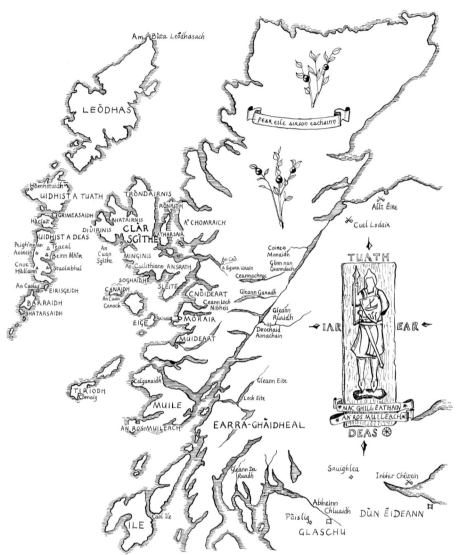

LEÒDHAS

Am Bùta Leòdhasach

Tòmhstaidh
UIDHIST A TUATH
TROÒNDAIRNIS
RÒNAIDH
GRIMEASAIDH
BHATAIRNIS
A' CHOMRAICH
Hàclait
DIÙIRINIS
CLÀR
UIDHIST A DEAS
SGITHE
RATHARSAIR
Peigh'nn'an
An
Aoireinn
Cuan
Teacal
MINGINIS
Coire
Sgithe
Beinn Mhòr
Monaidh
An Cuilithionn AN SRATH
An Càd
Cnoc
Glinn nan
Sgurr Unain
Hàllainn
Staolabhal
Geannachnoc
Ceannachnoc
An Caolas
EIRISGEIDH
SOGHAIDH
Gleann Garadh
CANAIDH
SLÈITE
BARRAIDH
Am Cuan
CNÒIDEART
Bhatarsaidh
Canach
Ceann Loch
Gleann
Nibheis
Rùaidh
EIGE
Àrisaig
MÒRAIR
Drochaid
Aonachain
MUIDEART

Calgaraidh
Gleann Eite
TIRIODH
Loch Eite
Canaig
MUILE

AN ROS MUILEACH
EARRA-GHÀIDHEAL

Gleann Da
Ruadh
Saughlea
Inbhir Chéitein
Abhainn
Chluaidh
Pàislig
DÙN ÉIDEANN
Caol Ìle
GLASCHU
ÌLE

Cuil Lodair

Fear eile airson eachainn

TUATH

IAR   EAR

MAC GHILL EATHAIN
AN ROS MUILEACH

DEAS

INNSE GHALL agus MÒR-
THÌR ALBANN

FICHEAD MILE

Sorley MacLean: the Man and his Work

The year 1970 was a turning point in the literary career of Sorley MacLean, the man who, only ten years later, had become internationally known as a major poet and his work accepted as comparable with major works in any language. Yet to talk about the literary career of a Gaelic poet is misleading, for what career is there for a poet writing in a language many say is dying and only 80,000 people in Scotland speak? Although most of his poetry was written before 1970, it was appreciated only by a few inside the Gàidhealtachd, and some enthusiasts outside it. Sorley MacLean began to emerge from that obscurity in 1970, with the appearance of *Lines Review* 34, a special issue devoted entirely to his work and, more significant still, the publication by Reprographia of a volume entitled *Four Points of a Saltire*, containing a substantial selection of the work of four poets: Stuart MacGregor, William Neill, George Campbell Hay and Sorley MacLean.

Poets are seldom slow to recognize the worth of a poet: Douglas Young in the Forties did everything he could to promote the poetry of Sorley MacLean; other Gaelic writers such as Iain Crichton Smith had long valued his work, but it was the uncompromising claims made in the preface to *Four Points of a Saltire* by Tom Scott, fellow poet but non-Gael, which marked a watershed in MacLean's poetic career. In his preface, Scott places him in the same rank as Hugh MacDiarmid and Edwin Muir:

> How many people know that the best living Scottish poet, by a whole head and shoulders, after the two major figures in this century, Edwin Muir and Hugh MacDiarmid, is not any of the English writing poets, but Sorley MacLean? Yet he alone takes his place easily and indubitably beside these two major poets: and he writes only in Gaelic . . . That Sorley MacLean is a great poet in the Gaelic tradition, a man not merely for time, but for eternity, I have no doubt whatever . . . If MacLean is not a major poet, then I do not know what major poetry is.

For the first time in Gaelic since 1943, and the first time ever in English, a large body of his poetry was readily available.

MacLean was born in 1911 in Osgaig, a small township on the island of Raasay off the east coast of Skye, lying between Skye and the mainland peninsula of Applecross, just north of Kyle of Lochalsh. His family on both sides were very talented, and, most important, they were tradition bearers who passed on to MacLean the Gaelic tradition in song, music and poetry from many parts of the Gàidhealtachd. His father's family were native to Raasay, but before that almost certainly lived in North Uist and perhaps originally came from Mull, the home of the MacLeans. His paternal grandmother, who lived with the MacLean family until her death when the poet was about twelve years old, was one of the Matheson family who had moved to Staffin in Skye when they were deprived of their land at Lochalsh in the eighteenth century. She preserved a great store of songs and traditional lore not only from her own immediate background, first of Staffin, then Portree and the Braes of Trotternish, but also from her family's background on the mainland, in Lochalsh and Kintail. Much of this traditional lore MacLean absorbed from her during her stay with the family. Among the Nicolsons, on his mother's side, were three fine singers, with a wide range of songs from all parts, two pipers and a bard. The voice of Angus Nicolson, his uncle, earned great praise from Professor Sidney Newman. From his paternal aunt, Peggie, he learned much of the native traditions from all over the Highlands, especially in song. His own father and his father's brother were both pipers.

Much of MacLean's inspiration as a poet comes from this incredibly rich background, steeped in the best of the Gaelic tradition. It figures as a constant backcloth to his poems, as he acknowledges in *Chapman* 16:

> I think that the first great 'artistic' impact on me was my father's mother singing some of the very greatest of Gaelic songs, and all in her own traditional versions.

It was chiefly the words, and the very subtle, intricate rhythms and *tempi* of these songs which made an impact on him, so much so that he remembered the words of songs he liked after only one hearing. This matched well with his brother John, who had a wonderful memory for the tunes of these songs, and for pibroch; together these brothers preserved both the words and the music of their vast inheritance in the Gaelic tradition. Bards figure among his ancestors on both sides. MacLean's father had an extraordinary sensitivity for the Gaelic language, sung or spoken, in its phonological and semantic variations between dialects, its rhythms, nuances and associations — a sensitivity he conveyed to his son. His father also had a wide knowledge of Gaelic poetry and, when young, MacLean would often witness long arguments between his father and his maternal uncle, Alexander Nicolson, on the relative merits of the main figures in Gaelic poetry, Duncan Macintyre, William Ross, Alexander MacDonald, Rob Donn, Iain Lom and others. So MacLean grew up in an environment rich in all aspects of the Scottish Gaelic tradition, an environment which furnished him with the basis for both the structure and content of his poetry: the importance to MacLean of this inheritance cannot be overestimated.

Sorley MacLean was educated at the local Raasay primary school, then at Portree High School in Skye, along with the rest of his family, two sisters and four brothers. His mother, Christina, and his father, Malcolm, survived on the proceeds of a small croft and a tailoring business. The family gave up the croft to move to a better house, leaving them financially dependent on the tailoring business which, as the Depression grew nearer, became less and less prosperous. MacLean's own generation turned out to abound in talent too; for example his brother Calum became one of Scotland's best folklorists.

An important part of MacLean's background is the history, not just of Raasay, but of the whole Highlands. Both Raasay and Skye have long histories which reflect the troubles of the Gaels through the centuries. Together with the rest of the Highlands, they experienced the Reformation and the impact of Calvinism, clan feuding, the Jacobite rebellions and subsequent persecutions, the Clearances, mass emigration and the constant shrinking of the Gaelic language in both power and influence. These historical factors were just as much present in MacLean's childhood as in the oral tradition. He knew many people whose memories went back to the Clearances: they had affected different parts of the Highlands and the bitter tragedy was keenly felt by everyone. History and poetry came together in the figure of Mary MacPherson, Màiri Mhór nan Oran — Great Mary of the Songs, who was one of the main influences on MacLean. As Bard of the Land League Movement, her work was much appreciated in Skye, particularly by MacLean's maternal uncle, Calum Nicolson, because of her protests about the Clearances and her championing of the people in their distress. This is also present in MacLean's work, in which an important theme is the historical and political position of the Gael.

The situation of his people, immediately of Skye and Raasay, but ultimately of the whole of Scotland and beyond, deeply affected MacLean. Not only were the Clearances a living memory, but MacLean grew up surrounded by visible evidence of them eveywhere — ruined crofting townships, people crowded onto infertile strips of land near the sea where they had to suffer the most meagre of existences, often in unhealthy conditions because of overcrowding. MacLean's mother's family lived in Braes, which was one of these coastal districts into which the population had been herded. Raasay itself had suffered clearances between 1852 and 1854, within the memory of some who were still alive when the poet was young. The experience of the Clearances bred a strong radical tradition in which the Clearances and Toryism were seen to be connected. This radical movement found expression in the Land League of the 1880s, culminating in the Battle of the Braes in 1882 in which MacLean's grandfather's brother took part. All this was a living, vital part of MacLean's childhood and a strong influence in his youth.

The Island of Raasay is a stronghold of Free Presbyterianism, a movement which seceded from the Free Church of Scotland in 1893. This could have been an excessively repressive force in MacLean's childhood, but his family were not as strictly orthodox as some, believing in it "at the level at which human beings can believe in it and continue sane" (*Chapman*, 16). Indeed, MacLean's poetry owes much to the length, eloquence and range of vocabulary in the Free Presbyterian sermons.[1] On a personal level, perhaps, the love of song and the Gaelic cultural tradition which was so deep in his family moderated the sternly rigorous influence of religion.

Childhood seemed to be happy for MacLean, who did well at school, particularly in History, Latin, Gaelic and English. No doubt his ability in History had something to do with his acute awareness of the history of his own people. On a more mundane level, reading material on Raasay was limited, and many of the books available were historical: MacLean, an avid reader, had read the whole of Thomas Carlyle's *French Revolution* and complete histories of Scotland and England by the time he was twelve. Of several of his teachers, and in particular of the Headmaster of Portree Secondary School, a Latin Teacher, Tait, and the Head of English for most of his time there, a woman called MacKenzie, he speaks very highly, remembering them with gratitude and affection. Later, when MacLean became a teacher himself, he used the teaching he had received at Portree as a model, such was its quality. It was at school, too, that the family passion for the energetic game of shinty found expression. While standards in both the arts and languages at Portree were extremely high, those in Maths and Science were not so well developed; but this accorded well with the predilections of MacLean and his brother John, both of whom went to Edinburgh University because neither Maths nor Science was required in the Open Bursary Competition there. Glasgow University, the natural focus for many Gaels, was out of the question since they did not shine at scientific subjects, but excelled in the humanities, John at Latin and Greek, Sorley at English and History.

At university, MacLean had to decide which course to follow. He had been advised in his final year at school to study history because of his aptitude for it and because it was a better qualification for the higher echelons of the Civil Service. However, history did not attract MacLean as a study, nor did the Civil Service as a career. The choice for him was between Honours English Language and Literature, and Honours Celtic. Regretfully, MacLean rejected the Celtic option: openings in this field were few and almost all the posts available then were filled with young incumbents. Perhaps even more important for MacLean was the fact that Celtic is an academic discipline and he may already have begun to feel that he was not primarily an academic; furthermore, his emerging passion was literature. Throughout his teens, he had been an eager reader of poetry, of Gaelic poetry and nineteenth-century English romantic poetry, Shelley and Wordsworth. In fact, one of his reasons for taking English was that he cherished a youthful ambition to write a book on Shelley whose *Prometheus* he admired, partly because of Shelley's humane socialism. All MacLean's instincts were leading him in the direction of literature. The realization that he was not by nature an academic grew throughout his four years at Edinburgh University; even on the English course, there was a large proportion of material in which he had no real interest and had simply to suffer for the sake of the qualification. This was one of the factors in his choice, after graduating with First Class Honours in English, not to go to Oxford to do post-graduate work, as Herbert Grierson, his professor, was urging him to do. Instead, he chose teaching as a career and took the post-graduate teaching diploma at Moray House College of Education, in Edinburgh. He had hoped during that year to take Honours Celtic as an extra, with the blessing of Professor Watson of the Celtic Department, but, unfortunately, Moray House's unbending bureaucracy frustrated this intention. In 1934, he began his first appointment as teacher of English at Portree High School.

It was while MacLean was at Edinburgh University that he met two men whose influence on him was to be seminal: James B. Caird and George Elder Davie. Quite apart from the close friendship which grew up between the three men, Caird and Davie each made an invaluable and unique contribution to the poet's intellectual life. It was Caird who, during this period, first uttered the 'heresy' of suggesting that "Milton was as great a poet as Donne, or Yeats as great a poet as Eliot". With Herbert Grierson, the great modern champion of John Donne, as Professor of English that was heresy indeed to many undergraduate minds. But for MacLean, this evidence of original thought greatly attracted him to Caird. Although MacLean later came to have the highest regard for Yeats's work, at that time he ruefully remarks, "I did not listen to him on Yeats enough to get past the early Yeats".[2] In Caird, MacLean came up against a man of extremely wide culture and learning, astonishing in someone so young. In an interview with Aonghas MacNeacail, he describes Caird as a man who "even then combined a tremendous knowledge of literature — English, Scots, French, Latin and Greek, as well as Russian in translation — with what I considered a very unusual sensibility". Indeed, MacLean thought that Caird "ought to have been Professor of Literature but circumstances and lack of worldly wisdom prevented that".[3] In fact, Caird later became one of H.M. Inspectors of Schools and an influential man in Scottish letters.

While Caird provided MacLean with a great 'literary stimulus', George Davie provided an equally great 'intellectual stimulus'. Davie, another undergraduate, was remarkable for his "historical knowledge of all kinds of things Scottish and his fundamental interest in ideas and immense range".[2] Davie had the deepest understanding of the entire gamut of Scottish culture — philosophy, theology, educational theory, of Scottish contributions to science and mathematics, as well as an understanding of art and literature. Most importantly, Davie's perception of Scottish philosophy set it firmly in the larger European theatre, and he was able to make connections between elements in Scottish thought and that of not only mainstream European thinking, but also of the more obscure elements, such as phenomenology, largely ignored by English philosophers. This range and depth is clearly visible in Davie's famous book *The Democratic Intellect,* which is probably the most important book ever written on the principles and development of Scottish thought, particularly in relation to the Scottish universities in their struggle to maintain an independent intellectual tradition against the more powerful, if not always intellectually superior, academic movements in England. Not only did Davie influence MacLean intellectually, but he was an extremely valuable source of ideas for Hugh MacDiarmid.

At no time in his youth was MacLean conscious of an ambition to become a poet, but it was almost certainly his love of Gaelic songs and poetry, Gaelic and otherwise, which led him to write his first poems, most of which were parodies, at the age of fourteen or fifteen. A crucial, if surprising factor, is MacLean's tone-deafness. He freely describes himself as a traditional Gaelic singer *manqué*: "Even to this day, I sometimes think that if I had been a singer I would have written no verse".[2] It is curious that both MacLean and Yeats, whom he much admires, were unable to sing, being relatively tone-deaf, yet both could produce poetry with an extraordinary quality of verbal music. But MacLean's need was not just to produce music, as the singer does, but also to create it, as he conjectures: "but perhaps if I had been a singer I would have tried to create original melodies".[2] His only outlet was the creation of verbal music in lyric poetry.

It is said that many young poets instinctively begin writing by imitating the techniques of established poets to whose work they are drawn. Perhaps this phenomenon was at work in the young MacLean when he was writing mainly parodies. Later in his teens, in common with many other poets, it was the first stirrings of love which provided the impulse to write poetry, in both Gaelic and English. Until he left school, he had no knowledge of modern poetry, but at university he fell under the influence of Eliot and Pound, an influence which found its way into his writing in English, but not so much his Gaelic writing. By the time he was twenty, he had written a good deal of poetry in both languages, but was becoming more and more dissatisfied with his English poetry, which seemed to him to lack both passion and depth:

> When I was at the university I came to realize that my English verse, which was mostly imitative of Eliot and Pound, was over-sophisticated, over self-conscious, and that what I had written in Gaelic was better in the sense that it was more myself.[4]

One English poem from that period survives, published in a small pamphlet, *Private*

Business, edited by David Daiches and published by the English Literature Society
of Edinburgh University in 1933.

East Wind

The air is chill, and a little rain
has left the moist cold tincture on the grass,
but drops have left the window pane
through which I watch the grey clouds pass
on Glamaig's wizened, dark-scarred face;
and eastern gusts, the surly black, efface
the tender blue and silver of the sea
to ripples of their own chill dreariness:

Full of the whole world's bitter weariness,
even of the soul, the spiral flame
that ever mounts encurl'd
on all the earthly images of praise and shame
pointing its snake tongue to some other world.

As John MacInnes has pointed out,[5] MacLean's poetry transcends Romanticism,
particularly in its symbolic and totally unsentimental use of landscape: the
beginnings of this, and of MacLean's pessimism, the signs of his intellectual and
emotional range, of his surrealistic imagery, are all there, even in this English poem.
It is fitting that in the same pamphlet is an early poem by Robert Garioch called
'Technical Notes' in which he defends the use of Scots in his poetry:

Burns fand emotion, coupin mice,
an Wordsworth saw religion in a stirk,
Gode warks in maist dumfoonrous weys,
A've kent folk even seek it in a kirk!

Wha'll blame me, syne,
ir slate this clarty dialect o mine?

A camel in the desert'll
slorp drumly watter oot a dub;
a man whaw'd write in Edinbro
maun seek his language in a pub.

A like it fine,
this bonny clarty dialect o mine.

As with MacLean's poem, the hallmark of the mature Garioch is clear in this short
poem.

In part at least, it was a political decision for Sorley MacLean to write in Gaelic,
his first language. No doubt in his mind at the time was the fact that he had studied
English, not Celtic at university, and the rejection of English as the language of his
own poetry assuaged his guilt over this earlier choice. It was a political decision in
that he gave the most positive support he could to his native language, culture,
traditions and way of life, all of which was and is still under threat from the powerful
political and economic forces of our capitalist society. MacLean's purity of motive in
this choice is underlined by the fact that he knew well that only a handful of people
would ever be capable of fully understanding his work in the original, and that he

was much less likely ever to see his work in print than any writer of comparable work in English. But the choice was also a perfectly natural one given his love of Gaelic song and poetry and his sensitivity to the Gaelic language. He remarks: "My ear's defect in pitch seems to me now to have been compensated for by a painful sensitivity to what I felt faults of rhythm and time".[2] That sensitivity could only operate fully in a Gaelic medium. For a poet like MacLean, with his love of sound and rhythmic subtleties, Gaelic is the natural language to write in, using his finely tuned ear for rhythm and melopoeia to the full. English, compared as a language to Gaelic in this respect, is arid and tuneless, heavily reliant on abstractions and rhythmically crude, its symbolism mainly visual. MacLean explains this in a letter to MacDiarmid: "My stuff, like most Gaelic verse, has a sensuousness chiefly of the ear. Now, as far as I can see, recent English poetry concentrates on a jungle of bristling, more or less surrealist imagery which strikes the eye".[6] Gaelic verse also has riches in rhyme and form which English cannot rival. It is as well to be aware of what is lost when poetry is translated from Gaelic into English. For many reasons, the decision to write in Gaelic rather than English was entirely the right one.

In the summer of 1933, during his final year at University, Caird and Davie introduced him to the work of Hugh MacDiarmid in *Scots Unbound, Sangshaw, Pennywheep* and, later, *A Drunk Man Looks at the Thistle* and *To Circumjack Cencrastus.* Such was MacLean's admiration of the early lyrics for their "under-the-skin awareness and auditory magic . . . which I consider as quite unrivalled and unapproached in the British Isles at present",[6] that he almost stopped writing himself, feeling that the nearest to the "unattainable summit of the lyric"[2] had been achieved. MacLean's obsession with the lyric was, initially, a direct influence from his Gaelic background in poetry and song, but it was also due to the literary influence in his teens of Blake and Wordsworth, as well as Shelley; Blake because of his close approximation to song in his short poems, and Wordsworth because of the lyric peaks in his poetry, particularly in *The Prelude,* which entranced MacLean because of its "expressions of a sensitivity to certain impressions from external nature".[2] MacLean's devotion to the lyric was confirmed and given philosophical consolidation when he discovered that Benedetto Croce "didn't believe in the long poem, that he considered it fundamentally a series of flats interspersed with lyric peaks. That I took to because it fitted in with my own predilections".[7] MacDiarmid's lyrics also confirmed MacLean's own convictions that "the lyric is the summit of all poetry",[2] but he clearly denies that they had any direct influence on his own poetry:

> I wouldn't say that these lyrics of Hugh MacDiarmid influenced my own poetry much though they had a kind of catalytic influence, because, as I think you will agree, that of all poetry, and I mean all poetry that I know, they are the most inimitable and the most difficult to follow in practice and imitate, but they had this tremendous influence on me and confirmed my belief in the supremacy of the lyric and the lyrical nature of poetry.[7]

Perhaps MacLean's use of the word 'influence' here is misleading. That MacDiarmid made a great *impact* on MacLean is clear; undoubtedly, knowledge of MacDiarmid and his work helped to sustain MacLean in his own writing. It is further tempting to see MacDiarmid as a linguistic influence on MacLean. In many ways the two poets were in similar positions, and achieved similar things. MacDiarmid revivified Scots, dragging it out of the nineteenth century (some might

say the eighteenth) into the twentieth, and using it to express a truly modern world
view and sensibility. As Iain Crichton Smith, John MacInnes and many others have
said, MacLean did the same for Gaelic and Gaelic poetry, which, until his poetry
appeared, was stuck in a nineteenth-century idiom, inward and backward looking in
content, sentimental and trapped in its own literary conventions. Both poets were
technical innovators in their use of language and poetic form. It is mistaken,
however, to see MacLean in any sense as following in MacDiarmid's footsteps,
remarkable though it is that at more or less the same time two Scottish poets should
provoke similar changes in the poetry of Scotland's two minority languages. There
was no direct, 'causal' influence at work: those who wish to provide explanations
may summon up the *Zeitgeist,* which probably furnishes as good an explanation as
any. The facts bear this out: MacLean was not aware of the work of Hugh
MacDiarmid until 1933, but, by 1931 he had already written 'A' Chorra-
ghridheach' and *Dàin do Eimhir* I[7], and in 1932 he wrote, 'A' Chiall 's a Ghràidh'.
Shortly after writing 'A' Chorra-ghridheach', he took the decision to write only in
Gaelic because he felt that poem to be so much better than anything he had done in
English. MacLean writes: "I was committed to Gaelic poetry before I had read a
single poem by MacDiarmid".[2] The word 'committed' must be understood in its
fullest sense here.

Sorley MacLean and Hugh MacDiarmid first met in 1934, while MacLean was
still studying at Moray House. A friendship arose between them almost immediately
and continued until MacDiarmid's death in 1978. It is not surprising that the two
men were strongly drawn to each other considering the similarity of their positions.
Each held the other's work in high regard, and, because they were working in
different traditions, there could be no question of rivalry between them. The first
fruit of their friendship was their co-operation on the translation of the Gaelic poems
by Alexander MacDonald, the 'Birlinn Chloinn Raghnaill' and 'Moladh Móraig',
and of Duncan Bàn MacIntyre's 'Ben Dorain'. When MacDiarmid's translation of
the 'Birlinn' appeared in *The Modern Scot,* MacLean wrote congratulating him for
capturing the spirit of the original better than any other translation. Gaelic scholars
were less positive in their response, which MacLean characterised as "piddling
pedantry"[8] and roundly dismissed their criticisms, reassuring MacDiarmid:

> You need not be perturbed by anything that the Gaelic scholars may say.
> Which of them in Scotland has produced a piece of criticism worth
> mentioning? The best of them are good grammarians not literary men. And
> which of them has produced a verse translation of a Gaelic poem that is not
> beneath contempt?[9]

MacLean described MacDiarmid's translation of 'Ben Dorain' as "wonderfully
good", but not on the whole so good as that of the 'Birlinn', since he failed to
"recapture the Gaelic rhythms – an impossible task".[10] There is a suggestion here
that MacLean is being generous in his estimation of these translations, no doubt
feeling that MacDiarmid's efforts, in spirit at least, deserved higher praise than
more scholarly works.

By 1935 MacDiarmid was living in isolation on Whalsay, Shetland, where
MacLean visited him in August of that year; his hospitality was returned two years
later when MacDiarmid stayed with MacLean during a visit to Raasay to gather
material for his book *The Islands of Scotland.* Their intention was to collaborate on
an anthology of Gaelic poems with English translations, a project which never came

about, partly because of MacDiarmid's subsequent ill health. These two men made a great impact on each other, something of which is visible in MacLean's letter to MacDiarmid, thanking him for the present of a small volume of selected poems:

> It is indeed a present to be proud of. I had long thought how imposing such a collection, comprising short lyrics from your longer poems as well as from the short lyric collections would be, but I was greatly struck when I saw the book itself. I realised that I had not fully appreciated the effect of the juxtaposition of such great lyrics.[11]

Although at first MacLean rated the lyrics in *Sangshaw* more highly than those in *A Drunk Man Looks at the Thistle,* he came to appreciate the latter much more in time. His reason was that he considered it to be

> the greatest long poem of the century that I have read, . . . because along with the subtlest and most daringly imaginative, the most organic and marvellously sustained use of symbolism, it has the variety that has something for most natures. It converted me to the belief that the long medley with lyric peaks was the form for our age.[2]

Here we can see how from MacLean's reading of *A Drunk Man* came the idea which led to his writing 'An Cuilithionn' four years later – an attempt, like *A Drunk Man,* to maximize the force and scope of the lyric.

Sorley MacLean was one among many millions of people who, in the Thirties, were unable to do what natural inclination might have led them to because of the Depression. While his brother John went to do post-graduate work in Cambridge, he did not go to Oxford, partly because he had rejected the academicism, but chiefly because family circumstances dictated the need for him to have a stable income. His father had given up the croft in 1931, and although it was never an important factor, the family missed its financial contribution. His father's tailoring business, faced with the declining economic situation, became increasingly less profitable. When, in 1934, MacLean took up his first teaching post in Portree Secondary School (now Portree High School), his salary helped to provide for his family and finance the education of his younger brothers and sisters.

Because Portree Secondary School catered for pupils from all over Skye, some teachers had to be resident in the Elgin Hostel, where pupils boarded during the week. MacLean, one of the teachers in the hostel, had to be on duty there every second night, a task he found both unrewarding and onerous:

> If I have to stay here (Elgin Hostel) much longer, I shall be extinguished completely. I can read but that is about all. I cannot get the necessary concentration for doing any real work. I suppose a teacher has sooner or later to recognize the fact that he cannot use what talents he has, however modest they are.[12]

That ominous note gives the first indication of the heavy toll of MacLean's talents and energies that teaching was to take. For a young teacher, the work is particularly strenuous and MacLean, as always, was more than diligent. He was lucky, though, at Portree, to have the companionship of one of his university friends, Jack Stuart. MacLean had met Stuart through his brother, Ellis Stuart, with whom MacLean had played shinty at university. Jack Stuart, in turn, had introduced MacLean to Robert Garioch, again during MacLean's undergraduate days. MacLean held Jack

Stuart in the highest esteem, and his presence at the school in Portree helped to make life bearable for him. Shortly before Stuart left Portree to go to Aberfeldy, MacLean wrote to MacDiarmid:

> I myself am being asked for an interview for a job at Tobermory, Mull and if I get it I shall take it . . . I do not like the idea of leaving Skye but things have changed for the worse in the school of late. However I really do not know what is to happen. Of course I shall never get a fellow like Stuart to teach with again and without him I am afraid of the prospect of Portree school.[13]

In January 1938, MacLean was appointed teacher of English at Tobermory Secondary School, where he felt as ever the heavy burden of teaching, the difficulty of writing under these circumstances, and the great intellectual isolation. But these were not the only frustrations for MacLean at that time. He has always seen himself essentially as a frustrated man of action, as more of a politician than a poet. This impulse first showed itself at the age of twelve, when he claims he "took to the gospel of Socialism" and saw himself as

> primarily an idealist democratic revolutionary and I fancied my future role in life as a politician helping to change the world, rather than as a scholar or a poet. 'Negative capability' I understood but it was not for me.[2]

Exactly how this change came about he describes in a published discussion.[14] He had been telling one of his uncles about the history being taught at school, regurgitating the text books' exaltation of Disraeli over Gladstone on the issue of imperialism and his uncle had exclaimed: "The bloody Tories, who did the Clearances!" MacLean adds, "I saw red from then on". From that moment also, the connection between the capitalist landlords and Toryism was clearly established in his mind. MacLean's youthful socialism accounted in great part for his admiration of both Shelley and John MacLean. The latter was also an admirer of Shelley and influenced the young MacLean more than any other literary figure. The poet had met several people in his youth who had known John MacLean and had regarded him as a hero and a saint; thus he came to have the highest respect both for John MacLean's political thought and for the man, whom he says "was the last word in honesty and courage. He was a terrific man."[14] Sorley MacLean's instinctive leaning towards the political figure as exemplar is expressed in a letter to MacDiarmid asserting that "names like Lenin, Connolly, John MacLean are more to me than the names of any poets".[15] Perhaps behind this is the implicit recognition that poetry, no matter how powerful, can do comparatively little to change the world. It also accounts for the frustration MacLean was feeling in Mull.

In the interview with Aonghas MacNeacail, MacLean describes his 'native' politics as a "kind of pretty left-wing radicalism focussed on what was happening in the Highlands". His socialism, however, was neither naïve, nor over-idealistic; to him, it was simply the most advanced and morally superior social and political theory yet evolved, and as such, he owed it his strongest support. Of the failure of Communism to live up to socialist ideals, MacLean says "Communism is an affirmation of humanity, however it has been debased or perverted". Fascism, on the other hand, he condemns as "an affirmation of cruelty, the desire for power . . . the denial of *all* humanity".[14] MacLean often refers to himself as a 'natural pessimist', someone too sceptical to believe wholeheartedly in any system. This 'natural pessimism' MacLean believes was probably engendered by my religious upbringing and a hatred of elitism, social elitism and all that made me equate what was happening then to the politics I had learned from the traditions of the Land League, and especially the traditions in Braes.[3]

MacLean's belief in political systems may be inhibited by profound scepticism, but his pride in his ancestry, and in the struggles on behalf of the crofting community by the "big men" of Braes, is quite without reservation. Equally 'native' to MacLean as a Scot, as a Gael, as a poet concerned with the culture of his country, is Scottish Nationalism, which MacLean supported alongside his socialism. There have been times when MacLean has felt very drawn towards nationalism as the best hope, for Scotland at least, but for the most part he has lacked belief in it as an ultimate force for change.

MacLean's strong political convictions were such that the impulse to action was irrepressible; but his family circumstances, the necessity of teaching, and the restrictions arising out of the public role of a teacher as well as the exacting nature of the job, prevented him from taking any direct political action. This frustration is expressed in an undated letter to MacDiarmid in the late Thirties, in which he agrees with MacDiarmid's 'special line' on Scotland, John MacLean's marxist view, and tells him that he has been "reading nothing but Marxism in which I am considerably more proficient than I used to be". This was the nearest to expression of political involvement available to him at the time, as he goes on to complain:

> Of course the position of a school teacher is intolerable – the matter of getting anything done – but I fear that for the present at least I shall have to abide it. I can only try to sail as near the wind as I can.[16]

It is worth noting that MacLean's marxism was not naïve or sentimental, as some critics have supposed, but both educated and informed.

Although MacLean relinquished Calvinism in favour of socialism at an early age, Calvinism continued to make a profound impact on him, influencing his thought as well as his language. This is examined in detail in Terence McCaughey's article in this volume, which shows that religious symbolism and reference abound in his poetry. His religious background is responsible for his 'natural pessimism' because "if you are brought up in a church which seems to say that the bulk of humanity are going to suffer an eternity of physical as well as mental torture, it is very difficult not to be a pessimist".[3] This condemnation of the bulk of humanity, and, of course, the bulk of Free Presbyterians, made Calvinism for him a terrible religion. The other aspect of this doctrine, that only a few, the 'Elect', will be saved, is also responsible for MacLean's hatred of social elitism, of any elitism, and for his disapproval of MacDiarmid's "arty attitude to politics"[17] and his apparent dismissal of the mass of people in A Drunk Man and elsewhere. MacLean also rejected this doctrine on more personal grounds. He complains to Douglas Young that only a few of those he loved would be 'saved' and that "salvation without them is a desolate prospect". His 'lost' friends were infinitely preferable to the 'saved'. Moreover, hardly anyone in his family seemed to show any "potentiality for salvation". He goes on:

> I dislike most of the obvious 'elect' not because of their good fortune but because most of them were unloveable people and I regarded their preoccupation with salvation much as I regard the careerist at present. . . and Christ's attraction was modified by the early realization that his earthly

suffering was nothing because he was not properly human.[18]

The Christian God may not have appealed much to MacLean, but the devil did evoke a certain sympathy in him as he explains to Douglas Young:

> I was never a 'converted' sinner who had experienced 'conviction of sin, repentance into life, effectual calling and sanctification' as Muir probably was in some ways. I had experienced conviction of sin and still do but not against a Seceder God or any other God but merely against my own aspirations.

The connection between the Christian God and the political establishment is obvious to MacLean, who says of himself, "I have never been on the side of the established angels".[19]

It cannot be supposed that MacLean altogether condemns and rejects his religious background: the truth is much more complex. He has complained that many people in Scotland, particularly in the Lowlands, criticize Calvinism out of ignorance. For instance, many quite wrongly associate Calvinism with smugness, self-righteousness and hypocrisy. MacLean claims that Free Presbyterianism is such a terrifying religion, so many souls being doomed, that smugness and self-righteousness were rare among the flock; even the 'Elect' were full of self-torture, wondering whether they were or were not of the 'Elect'. He finds it difficult to hate as a religion because he has known so many wonderfully good people who adhered to it, some of whom he has thought of as almost saints. Paradoxically, the terrifying nature of Calvinism has positive effects, in particular the fact that it brings people up against the cruelties of the world and in doing so prepares them better for life. In this respect, MacLean regards Calvinism as more intellectually honest than many other religions which paint a rosier picture of this life or the afterlife.

MacLean was very alone in Mull, and living there sharpened his awareness of the tragedy of the Gaels, because the island had suffered so badly from the Clearances. Mull, he says, "nearly drove me mad", it was such a "heartbreaking place"[14] for anyone named MacLean, the most common name on Mull until the Clearances. In 1938, there were almost no original Mull families on the island, a fact which greatly upset MacLean. The traumatic Mull experience, in fact, spurred him into poetry:

> I believe Mull had much to do with my poetry: its physical beauty, so different from Skye's, with the terrible imprint of the Clearances on it, made it almost intolerable for a Gael, especially for one with the proud name of MacLean.[2]

Out of MacLean's time on Mull comes 'Ban-Ghàidheal', one of his most moving poems, which describes the personal toll of the Clearances on many Highland women and men:

Is thriall a tìm mar shnighe dubh	And her time has gone like a black sludge
a' drùdhadh tughaidh fàrdaich bochd;	seeping through the thatch of a poor dwelling:
mheal ise an dubh-chosnadh cruaidh;	the hard Black Labour was her inheritance
is glas a cadal suain an nochd.	grey is her sleep to-night.

So far, the conflicts and frustrations felt by MacLean, in the years at Portree and Mull, have only been examined in general terms, but there were specific political causes for those frustrations. While MacLean could have no straightforward belief in socialism as the remedy of the world's problems, he could have a completely uninhibited fear of the rise of fascism which he observed in Europe from 1933 onwards. Probably his greatest preoccupation, from 1933 to 1945, was his hatred of and opposition to fascism. The advent of the Spanish Civil War, in July 1936, only confirmed his worst fears, that fascism would predominate in Europe, that creed which he regarded as the "denial of all humanity". Jack Stuart, his colleague at Portree Secondary School, wanted to go to Spain to fight with the International Brigade, and asked MacLean to go with him. With his family dependent on his salary, for the education of the younger members, it was impossible for MacLean to agree to this, but had he not been so committed, there is no doubt that he would have fought in Spain. His conduct in the Second World War bears this out.

Contrary to the impression given in some of MacLean's poetry, and by some critics, it is simply not true that MacLean did not go to Spain because of his love for a woman: he did not meet that woman, an Irish woman, until more than a year after the outbreak of the war. There was another woman, a Skye girl, to whom he had been strongly attracted in 1934-35, but the circumstances and his feelings had soon changed. This affair was not intrinsically serious enough to produce that pitch of conflict. In reality, it was outside factors, not internal conflict, which prevented him from fighting in Spain; the decline of his father's business, his mother's illness in 1936 and the need to help his father maintain and educate his younger brothers and sisters were very real, practical circumstances. MacLean's hankering after political action was no doubt symptomatic of a general wish to be politically involved, and, after the summer of 1936, this was compounded by the frustration of wishing to fight in Spain, yet not being able to do so.

The chronology of the poems backs this up: *Dàin do Eimhir* I was written in Raasay in August or September 1930[9], but the first and last verses were added in December 1939. Although it features in Iain Crichton Smith's *Poems to Eimhir* translations, it has been omitted from *Reothairt is Contraigh*. The girl referred to by the poem is neither of the women mentioned earlier. The line "What do I care for battles of their making" may foreshadow the famous conflict of later poems, but more probably it is simply a statement of the commonplace sentiment that his own feelings are more immediate to him at that moment than problems created by others which the poet feels have nothing to do with him, remembering that many battles are petty affairs which would have been better unfought. Most likely, the girl is a personification of the ideal object of desire, perhaps a symbol of his love for Raasay, for the Western Isles, his love specifically for a people, a culture, a way of life, a language which is disappearing. In this poem, the poet's passion has not yet reached its fiercest pitch, but is still latent, waiting for the right circumstances to bring it into full play. I cannot but see this poem as a description of the scene, a backcloth of landscape for the meditation in 'Gaoir na h-Eòrpa' (*Dàin*, IV). 'A Chiall 's a Ghràidh' (*Dàin* II) was written in Edinburgh in 1932. It explores, in abstract form, the conflict between reason and emotion and anticipates the later effect of this conflict on the poet:

is reub e friamh mo chré	and it tore the root of my being,
'gam sguabadh leis 'na shiaban.	sweeping me with it in its drift.

The conclusion of the poem, the reconciliation, is too easily achieved, and oddly hopeful for MacLean:

Is thubhairt mo thuigse ri mo ghaol:	And my intellect said to my love:
cha dhuinn an dùbailteachd:	duality is not for us;
tha 'n coimeasgadh 'sa' ghaol.	we mingle in love.

Perhaps that ending illustrates both the nature and, curiously, the limitation of intellect, which can glibly provide a reconciliation when none is, in reality, possible. In 'Am Buaireadh' (*Dàin,* III) the conflict, or turmoil, is described in much more specific terms, contrasting the poet's response to the suffering of the world, which made less of an emotional impression on him than "The glint / of her smile and golden head", at which his "stubborn heart leaped". The poem ends:

Agus chuir a h-àilleachd sgleò	And her beauty cast a cloud
air bochdainn 's air creuchd sheirbh	over poverty and a bitter wound
agus air saoghal tuigse Leninn,	and over the world of Lenin's intellect,
air fhoighidinn 's air fheirg.	over his patience and his anger.

In this poem, the woman is largely idealized, but at the time of writing (Portree, November or December 1935) he had in mind the Skye girl, who never had reason to suspect that MacLean had a strong, if transient feeling for her. The poem expresses, very dramatically, the obsessive turmoil into which such an experience, and especially an unrequited love, can throw any human being. What MacLean is condemning himself for is the extent to which the turmoil overcomes him, even to the extent of overshadowing his political and moral awareness; in this state he feels, temporarily, that all else is trivial. This is, in fact, not an unusual experience. In the background, heightening both the dramatic tension of the poem and the personal tension of the poet, is the ever-growing influence of fascism in Europe. The Spanish Civil War, of course, cannot figure, since it had not started when the poem was written.

The woman in 'Gaoir na h-Eòrpa' (*Dàin,* IV) is an Irish woman whom he met in Edinburgh while attending a Celtic Congress in August 1937. On this occasion, MacLean's passion was certainly stronger, and not at all transient. As with the girl in Portree, she knew nothing whatsoever about MacLean's feeling for her, which he kept to himself because he believed that one of his friends wished to marry her. Therefore, he felt he had no right to interpose his feelings between them. His decision not to act upon his feelings was confirmed by the fact that she seemed to be a pious Catholic, from a pious family, and to be conservative in politics. At the time, during the Spanish Civil War, MacLean was very negative about catholicism because he believed most Catholics were pro-fascist, supporting Franco. As with the first affair, the fact that this also was unrequited served to intensify the emotion felt, if for no other reason than that the affair relies on the imagination of the individual, becoming more urgent and powerful for being unfulfilled and therefore untempered by emotional release in real experience. This is all the more true when the person concerned tends, like MacLean, to be obsessive. Ironically, in December 1939, she married a man who gave up his Jesuitical training and became something of a socialist. This is referred to in the poem 'An Roghainn':

a bheil e fìor gun cual	is it true you heard
thu gu bheil do ghaol geal àlainn	that your beautiful white love
a' pòsadh tràth Di-luain?	is getting married early on Monday?

This poem dates from the summer of 1939, *before* MacLean heard that the wedding was to take place. It reflects on his decision, or choice, not to go to Spain. Because MacLean "followed only a way / that was small, mean, low, dry, lukewarm", because he "did not take a cross's death / in the hard extremity of Spain", he did not deserve "the radiant golden star", that "thunderbolt of love", fit only for those who, unlike him, had a "whole spirit and heart". This is an emotional impasse, a kind of self-crucifixion, from which he cannot escape. Having admitted to himself that his desire for a woman is greater than his desire to fight for a political ideal, he no longer deserves "the one new prize of fate", and, in preferring the woman, loses her. In 'Reic Anama', MacLean takes his argument one stage further: because the woman he loves has such "grace" and a "proud spirit", and in spite of her ability to forgive him for committing the "black blasphemy" of selling his soul for her love, she is forced to reject him for it. The remarkable aspect of this poem is its conclusion, in which the poet abandons himself completely to his feelings, even in the knowledge that they are also his doom:

Uime sin, their mi rithist, an dràsda,	Therefore, I will say again now,
gun reicinn m' anam air do sgàth-sa	that I would sell my soul for your sake
dà uair, aon uair air son t' àilleachd	twice, once for your beauty
agus uair eile air son a' ghràis ud,	and again for that grace
nach gabhadh tu spiorad reicte tràilleil.	that you would not take a sold and
	slavish spirit.

What emerges from this poem, and others, is that MacLean never quite comes to terms with the strength of his passion. All he can do is abandon himself to it; his intellect is incapable of dealing with it. This is important to remember when considering 'An Roghainn' and 'Urnuigh', both of which have helped to create the misconception that when confronted by the choice between his love for a woman and the fight in Spain, MacLean chose the former.

In 'Urnuigh', the poet scrutinizes his own "half-flayed" nature and concludes that he is condemned to persist as a spirit which is not "one-fold", that he will never have the purity and heroism of Cornford. In fact, this is purely an idealized conflict. MacLean never had the choice of whether to go to Spain or not: he had to stay to help provide for his family. The conflict is real enough, however, in the poet's imagination. It lay between his passion for the Irish woman and his political and moral duty as he saw it, remembering that his great political obsession during this period was the need to root out fascism, to oppose it whenever and wherever possible. It was clear to MacLean that if Franco won in Spain, then the way was open to Hitler and Mussolini to mount a fascist take-over of Europe, and that not only Europe, but the new Communist state of the U.S.S.R., about which MacLean was then very hopeful, was endangered. For someone already impelled by natural inclination towards the role of man of action, and one imbued with the traditional Gaelic esteem for heroism as one of the most important and admirable of human qualities, and cowardice, moral or physical, as one of the most despicable vices, the only course was to become directly involved in the Spanish conflict. MacLean is asking himself the hypothetical question: what would I do if I had a clear, free choice between this woman, and fighting in Spain? Being only too aware of the strength of his passion, he fears he might have chosen the woman:

Mo bheatha-sa a' bheatha bhàsail	My life the death-like life
a chionn nach d' fhail mi cridhe mo	because I have not flayed the heart of my
shàth-ghaoil,	fullness of love
a chionn gun tug mi gaol àraidh,	because I have given a particular love,
a chionn nach sgarainn do ghràdh-sa	because I would not cut away the love
	of you,
's gum b' fheàrr liom boireannach	and that I preferred a woman to crescent
na 'n Eachdraidh fhàsmhor.	History.

This stance amounts to cowardice, and is morally reprehensible in MacLean's eyes. He acknowledges to himself that there is a real, if hypothetical, conflict there, and that the choice is not one which could be made with a whole heart and mind. There is always the "shadow", the "faintness" which obscures the dictates of the moral intelligence.

MacLean seems to subscribe to Kierkegaard's idea that "purity of heart is to will one thing", in condemning his heart for being "half-flayed" and longing for a unity of reason and emotion, as he concludes in 'Urnuigh':

chan eil mo chaomhachd ris an Nàdur	I do not feel kindly towards Nature,
a thug an tuigse shoilleir shlàn dhomh,	which has given me the clear whole understanding,
an eanchainn shingilte 's an cridhe sgàinte.	the single brain and the split heart.

It seems paradoxical that his "clear whole understanding" cannot cope with his emotional passion. It is this conflict, inspired by the Irish woman, which dominates more than half of *Dàin* IV-XXII, written in 1938 and the first half of 1939. These poems are not ordered chronologically.

In 'Gaoir na h-Eòrpa', which dates from the spring of 1938, the sheer strength and quality of the poet's passions, the emotional on the one hand, and the political (his anguish in the face of political reality and human suffering) on the other, and the poet's moral sensibility and integrity, force him into making this hypothetical choice and into condemning himself for lack of moral integrity and single-heartedness. No doubt this ruthless morality stems partly from his Free Presbyterian background. The question posed in 'Gaoir na h-Eòrpa':

Dé gach cuach de d' chual òr-bhuidh	What every lock of your gold-yellow head
ris gach bochdainn, àmhghar 's dórainn	to all the poverty, anguish and grief
a thig 's a thàinig air sluagh na h-Eòrpa	that will come and have come on Europe's people
bho Long nan Daoine gu daors' a' mhór-shluaigh?	from the Slave Ship to the slavery of the whole people?

is not answered. But the dramatic, almost flamboyant way in which the question is put, leads one to feel that the poet would, recklessly, value the lock of gold-yellow hair more than the fate of humanity in the grip of fascism. However, what the poem also suggests is that MacLean's depth of feeling for both of these is unquestionable; his political anguish is as ineluctable as his love; but the fact that he can imagine himself in conflict here leads him to condemn himself morally, to suffer guilt at his own weakness and lack of courage. There is, of course, another kind of courage evident here — to take a conflict which is theoretical, not actual, and one which is extremely intimate, and to expose this inner struggle in the public medium of poetry. What emerges clearly is the uncompromising nature of MacLean's moral judgement, in placing himself in such a self-compromising dilemma. Finally, just as the conflict is idealized, we cannot assume that the object of MacLean's passion is anything other than idealized also. In a real sense, it does not matter which real woman the poet has in mind. Summing up this period, MacLean has said:

> From 1936 to 1939 I became, if a poet, a very different one from what my pre-1936 writings indicated. My mother's long illness in 1936, its recurrence in 1938, the outbreak of the Spanish Civil War in 1936, the progressive decline of my father's business in the thirties, my meeting with an Irish girl in 1937, my rash leaving of Skye for Mull late in 1937, and Munich in 1938, and always the

steady unbearable decline of Gaelic, made those years for me of difficult choice, and the tensions of these years confirmed my self-expression in poetry, not in action.[2]

Although MacLean had to suffer the frustration of not being able, for the reasons outlined earlier, to develop a relationship with the Irish woman, the experience was, on the whole, an inspiring and happy one. Years later, MacLean described her as being "as noble hearted as she is beautiful". Much less happy, however, was the experience he had with the Scottish woman, whom he had met briefly when she was in her teens, then again in Edinburgh in 1939. In August or September, 1939, he began to feel strongly attracted to her, and by December 1939 had committed himself by declaring his love for her. Her response gave him to understand that because of an operation she had been left incapable of enjoying a full relationship with a man. This took MacLean by storm. Having declared his feeling for her, he could do nothing but have the most passionate sympathy for her, being acutely aware of what he saw as her tragedy, and, ultimately, his also. Her subsequent confessions to him that their friendship served as a deterrent to suicide only increased his sympathy and feeling of responsibility towards her. This, and the difference between her situation and that of the Irish woman, is clearly described in 'An Dithis':

Tha sinn còmhla, a ghaoil,
leinn fhìn ann an Dùn-éideann,
is t' aodann suaimhneach còir
a' falach leòn do chreuchdan.
Tha agamsa mar chuibhrionn dhiot
ceann grinn is colainn reubte.

We are together, dear,
alone in Edinburgh
and your serene kind face
hides the hurt of your wounds.
I have as my share of you
a beautiful head and a torn body.

Is beag mo thruaighe-sa a nochd
seach olc do cholainn creuchdaich,
ach le do thruaighe-sa tha m' ghaol
air dhol 'na chaoir ghil leumraich,
a' losgadh am bruaillean mo chinn
mo chuimhne air an téile,
air té nas rathaile 's nas bòidhche
's i pòsda thall an Eirinn.

My misery is small tonight
beside the evil of your wounded body,
but with your misery my love
turns to white leaping flame,
burning in the turmoil of my head
my memory of the other,
of a more fortunate and more lovely one
who is married over in Ireland.

This predicament heralded what MacLean later described as two years of tragedy and it accounts for the tragic note of the poems in that section of *Reothairt is Contraigh* called 'The Haunted Ebb', stemming from the period from December 1939, when he learned of her situation, until August 1941. The woman who figures in these poems is the Scottish woman.

MacLean came to Edinburgh in January 1939 partly because he knew the war was coming and wanted to spend the remaining time there, in closer contact with national and political events. Also, he had the chance of a post at Boroughmuir High School, which had the full range of secondary teaching, from the first year to sixth year, and could offer greater scope than Tobermory, which had only first year to third year. For a few months, MacLean lived an isolated life in digs in Polwarth, but before long, he fell in again with Robert Garioch, whom he had first met during his undergraduate years at university. Garioch invited him along to weekly meetings in the Abbotsford Bar in Rose Street, where a number of poets met, including Sydney Goodsir Smith. MacLean and Smith soon became very friendly, as did MacLean and Garioch. MacLean held both men in great esteem: Smith for his intelligence and range of humour from rapier wit to sheer buffoonery, which he enjoyed for its own sake, and Garioch for his quieter, more intellectual wit. MacLean and Garioch began their collaboration on *Seventeen Poems for Sixpence,* which Garioch printed on his hand press, and which first appeared in January 1940. It contained eight poems by MacLean: four later published in *Dàin do Eimhir,* as nos. III, IV, XIV and XXIX ('Am Buaireadh', 'Gaoir na h-Eòrpa', 'Reic Anama' and 'Coin is Madaidhean-allaidh'), a section from 'An Cuilithionn' and three other poems ('A' Chorra-ghridheach', 'Trì Slighean', dedicated to Hugh MacDiarmid, and 'An t-Eilean'). Garioch's work was represented by six poems in Scots, two in English, and a translation into Scots of *Dàin,* III, 'Am Buaireadh':

> I never kent sic glaumerie
> nor stauchert frae sae stark a stound
> at thocht of Christ's dule on the yird
> or millions of the mappamound.
>
> I hae taen nae sic thocht of haiveral dreams,
> mirk-wrocht mirligoes of gleid
> as my dour hert hankert for the smool
> of her smile, and the glint of her gowden heid.
>
> The shadow frae her beauty lay
> owre puirtith and a waesom scauth,
> and the warld of Lenin's intellect,
> his pouer of patience and his wrath.

A second, corrected edition, appeared a couple of months later. The review of this volume in *New Alliance,* June/July 1940, hailed it in positive, if cautious terms: "One would like to think that this is an epoch-making book; it is certainly a very admirable and pleasant one".

'An Cuilithionn', which MacLean began writing in Edinburgh in the Spring of 1939, stemmed from an idea which he had had the previous year in Mull of writing "a very long poem, 10,000 words or so, on the human condition, radiating from the history of Skye to the West Highlands to Europe and what I knew of the rest of the world".[2] The poem ranged from "the most direct political utterance to varying degrees of symbolism".[20] Being an extended lyric, it was undoubtedly inspired by the structure of *A Drunk Man,* and this was one of the reasons why MacLean dedicated it to MacDiarmid. But MacLean was never happy with the way 'An Cuilithionn' was developing. To MacDiarmid, he described it as

> a crude, declamatory poem but certain passages manage to sound fairly well in Gaelic. (In translation) the crudity is painfully apparent and such few graces as it has in the Gaelic are conspicuously absent.[21]

The 'crudity' lay partly in the political statements made, some of which were too optimistic or propagandist for MacLean to support for long, in the symbolism itself and in the rather cumbersome nature of the poem's intellectual content. The war prevented him from publishing what there was of it, and by the end of the war he had lost his respect for the Soviet Union, and no longer wanted it published. MacLean stopped writing the poem abruptly when the affair with the Scottish woman turned

into a traumatic experience, after her confessions in December 1939, and instead
began the series of lyrics in 'The Haunted Ebb'. MacLean's reservations apart, the
published fragments show that 'An Cuilithionn' was by no means a total failure.

September 1939, of course, saw the beginning of the Second World War, and
MacLean lost no time in applying to join the army, but, as a volunteer, he would
have lost all his teaching salary. This would have affected his family, whom he was
still helping to support, so he waited until he was conscripted in September 1940,
when he was enlisted in the Signals Corps. In the meantime, he was able to
contribute to the war effort by teaching evacuees in Hawick, between October 1939
and June 1940. At last, he had the chance to fight the fascism which he had opposed
for years, but his reasons for joining up were double-edged, as he explained to
Douglas Young:

> I always knew he (Hitler) would attack Russia and that was my main reason
> for wanting to join up in September 1939 and my acquiescence in my own
> conscription in September 1940.[22]

Not that the state of affairs in the U.S.S.R. provided much ground for hope, as he
earlier commented to Young, "putting it bluntly, I think that all we can hope for is
that people like the Scots do the best that is left for themselves in a very bad
world".[23] That world, for MacLean, included both Stalin and the state of Western
Capitalism. No doubt MacLean would agree with C. S. Lewis when he said that in
the Second World War we were simply defending the bad against the worse. In the
same letter to Young, MacLean expresses his fear of the "humanist core" of
socialism and communism in using systems for military purposes. The difference
between communism and capitalism seemed to him to be that the aims of
communism were "less ignoble than the real capitalist aims". MacLean's position
on the war is best expressed in a letter to MacDiarmid written from Catterick Camp,
Yorkshire, where MacLean did much of his army training:

> My fear and hatred of the Nazis (is) even more than my hatred of the English
> Empire. My only hope is that the British and German Empires will exhaust
> each other and leave the Soviet the dominating influence on the oppressed
> people of all Europe including Britain and Germany . . . The only real war is
> the class war and I see my own little part merely as one that contributes to the
> mutual exhaustion of the British and German Empires. I support the British
> Empire because it is the weakest and therefore not as great a threat to Europe
> and the rest of the world as a German victory.[24]

For MacLean, then, the U.S.S.R. was the "greatest, perhaps the only hope of
Europe's working classes", but he could not entertain much hope, even in ordinary
people:

> I know all this sounds fantastic when I look round here and see the vile, cast
> iron, bourgeois class rule in the British army and I am full of despair when I see
> here how very willing great masses of humanity are to be slaves if that serves
> their immediate private interests. When I consider N.C.O.'s as a class I am
> filled with complete despair. The content and willing slave is the base of
> everything.[25]

MacLean's pessimism in respect of his faith in human nature was deepened by the
war, and afterwards, events in Poland in 1944 led him to abandon all hope in the

U.S.S.R. as the potential saviour of Europe's working classes and all hope in the Communist Party in general. This abandonment MacLean traces to a long conversation he had in 1944 with Sydney Goodsir Smith, in which Smith, after long and ruthless argumentation, convinced MacLean of the need to turn against the Soviets because of their behaviour towards the Polish people in particular. In 1946 MacLean admitted to MacDiarmid that he was "utterly at sea in politics these days, having for the past year, or even year and a half, come to the conclusion that the Communist Party is no use for me"; he added that he had been "shaken by the Polish rising" and had gone back to "social democracy and swithering between Labour and S.N.P.".[26]

Supporting the British Empire and Western Capitalism did not come easily to MacLean. With people whom he respected, like Douglas Young and George Campbell Hay resisting the authorities by refusing, as political objectors, to participate in the war effort, MacLean could not help but feel in conflict about his position, although intellectually he was quite clear about where he stood. He found it profoundly discomfiting that he enjoyed "the advantage of having all the scabs, liars and humbugs on my side".[27] He had no faith in the political judgement of those "damned fools" in the Communist Party and the Nationalist Party who claimed that the war had nothing to do with Scotland. That contempt extended to writers like Auden, whom he attacks for "saving his art" in America. However, he found it hard to condemn Young for his attitude, mistaken though he believed it to be:

> Still, with one of us in gaol and the other in the front line, I think we are in the only really honourable places a man can be in a war![28]

On joining up in 1940, MacLean was sent to Catterick in Yorkshire for military training, from which, he admits, he benefited by becoming physically fit; and in many ways he found army life not so intolerable as one might have expected. In October 1940 he wrote to Young that here he was a 'unit' of the British forces and reacting not at all as expected; he "liked the rude physical exertion and the feeling of becoming fit and hardy in body". The lack of privacy seemed not to bother him, as he wrote: "I have, I think, the capacity of covering myself with a tough shell". He also escaped the kind of victimization many suffer in the army because

> probably being a little tough I am not a subject for ragging of any kind, but I could imagine a more sensitive person having a bad time.[29]

He did have time in the evenings for reading and writing letters, but little poetry was written during this period, chiefly because of the effects of the affair with the Scottish girl. At one point he tried to learn Greek, but had only a limited success, admitting ruefully to Young, "I am not a facile linguist".[30] At least army training allowed him to "clear my system of complications in private life".[31]

MacLean made that statement in a letter to Young in December 1941 and, while it is no doubt true up to a point, it belies the reality that between December 1939 and August 1941 MacLean was suffering a great spiritual and emotional crisis. The army may have helped to take his mind off the situation, but he continued to be profoundly affected by it. In December 1940, he wrote to Young:

> I talked to you of feeling my private affairs irreparably gone wrong but don't be alarmed about that. That has been my normal condition for a few years now. It is merely due to an obsession with a woman and regrets I cannot overcome. I

am afraid that I am one of those weaklings who have one love affair that upsets their whole lives. No doubt many a bourgeois philistine is in the same predicament . . .[32]

Here MacLean was, despite being still very much in the throes of the 'predicament', trying to make light of it to Young. Looking at this period in retrospect, in November 1941, he was able to be more straightforward, although he never disclosed the cause of the crisis, and said that he had suffered an experience which

> has nearly driven me mad and not until July of this year did I become anything like normal and even yet I have very frequent moods that approach the suicidal . . . That explains the relative drought of my poetry from the early months of 1940 until July of this year. Had it not been that now and again I had moments free from the terrible fears which I had I could not have written anything . . . but these moments of freedom were very rare, whether I was alone or in company.[33]

In January 1941, he had written to Young that he was "very well physically, not so well mentally, and poetically quite dead".[34] By August of that year, he was saying that his poetry was recovering from a year's blight and by November that he had never been more full of poetic ideas, but these came to nothing because he could not concentrate and the ideas never had the chance to simmer. Finally, in December 1941, he was sent to Egypt on active service.

Gradually, while in Egypt, MacLean's state of mind improved, and he began to achieve a greater degree of serenity of mind. His mind turned to the war itself and the ordinary people caught up in it. In 1940, he had written to Young:

> For the ordinary man, workers or petty bourgeois, who does not mind whether he can express himself or not, I think fascism or ordinary capitalist conditions make little difference and now when things like Coventry and Hamburg are the rule, I feel for him, whether workers or petty bourgeois, with a sympathy I never before had.[35]

In Egypt, he became concerned with the plight of the ordinary soldier, irrespective of nationality, forced to fight in a war the origins of which were so remote from him and outwith his control. In October 1942, he wrote to Young about the first dead man he came across, who was a young German boy. Seeing his inglorious death made him ashamed of his "many foolish generalizations" about the need to wipe out fascists, and he realised that the ordinary soldier is not "any kind of an 'ist' at all". This experience gave rise to one of MacLean's finest war poems, 'Glac a' Bhàis':

An robh an gille air an dream a mhàb na h-Iùdhaich 's na Comunnaich, no air an dream bu mhotha, dhiubh-san	Was the boy of the band who abused the Jews and Communists, or of the greater band of those
a threòraicheadh bho thoiseach àl gun deòin gu buaireadh agus bruaillean cuthaich gach blàir air sgàth uachdaran?	led, from the beginning of generations, unwillingly to the trial and mad delirium of every war for the sake of rulers?
Ge b'e a dheòin-san no a chàs, a neoichiontas no mhìorun,	Whatever his desire or mishap, his innocence or malignity,

cha do nochd e toileachadh 'na bhàs   he showed no pleasure in his death
fo Dhruim Ruidhìseit.   below the Ruweisat Ridge.

Both MacLean and his fellow Scot, Hamish Henderson, have contributed greatly to
the body of twentieth-century poetry which exposes war for the ghastly, inhuman
thing it is.

In order to understand MacLean's spiritual and emotional state during 1942, and
to see its effects on his poetry, it is necessary to examine his affair with the Scottish
girl, since this was probably the most important factor during these years, no matter
how much military drilling or the experience of active service may have helped to
divert MacLean's attention from it. MacLean has never been a habitual writer, but
his poetry has almost entirely been inspired by some emotional crisis. That
precipitated by the Scottish girl was the most remarkable of all. During the last three
months of 1939, MacLean wrote *Dàin do Eimhir*, XXIII-XXXVI, which are
arranged chronologically, as are all the poems subsequently, plus a substantial part
of 'An Cuilithionn'. The trauma which followed the Scottish girl's disclosure of her
medical state late in December 1939 caused the writing of 'An Cuilithionn' to stop
abruptly and another set of the *Dàin do Eimhir* poems began. By March 1940,
MacLean had written *Dàin do Eimhir*, nos. XXXVII-LV and by spring or summer
had completed 'Coilltean Ratharsair' (which superseded 'An Cuilithionn'); after
that, no more poems were written for a year until late June and early July 1941, when
he wrote *Dain* LVI-LX.

The woman referred to or addressed in these poems (chiefly those of 'The
Haunted Ebb' section of *Reothairt is Contraigh*) variously combines with an ideal of
Scotland or the Scottish Muse. But some of the poems refer directly to the girl and,
bearing in mind the tragedy which seemed to have befallen her, certain symbols and
images in MacLean's poetry of that period become clear: the "mutilated body" of
'Uilleam Ros is Mi Fhìn'; the obsessive love from which he cannot escape in 'An
Tathaich'; the idea of drowning in sharpness and the "power of mutilation" in
'Crìonnachd'; the "golden banner" laid to the ground in 'Aithreachas'; the cutting
symbolism in 'An Sgian' and the "grey stake of misfortune" in 'Camhanaich'. One
of the most direct references is in the short poem, 'Muir-tràigh':

Chan eil mi strì ris a' chraoibh nach   I am not striving with the tree that will not
                              lùb rium   bend for me,
's cha chinn na h-ùbhlan air géig   and the apples will not grow on any
                            seach geug: branch;
cha shoraidh slàn leat, cha d' rinn   it is not farewell to you; you have
                        thu m' fhàgail: not left me.
's e tràigh a' bhàis i gun mhuir-làn   It is the ebb of death with no floodtide
                            'na déidh.   after it.

Marbh-struth na conntraigh 'nad   Dead stream of neap in your tortured
                        chom ciùrrte   body
nach lìon ri gealaich ùir no làin,   which will not flow at new moon or at full,
anns nach tig reothairt mhór an t-sùgraidh   in which the great springtide of love
                                                                          will not come -
ach sìoladh dùbailt gu muir-tràigh.   but a double subsidence to lowest ebb.

One of the remarkable features of this sequence of poems is the astonishing
emotional range and the subtlety with which this range is perceived. Despite the
tragedy, there are defiant moments: for example, in 'Am Boilseabhach', "I would

proclaim you queen of Scotland/in spite of the new republic'', or in 'Fo Sheòl', where the poet's feeling is suffused with memories from previous times.

The two years of tragedy gave way to two years of perplexity when, late in July 1941, MacLean was led to discount what he had earlier believed, and was told a story which seemed very different from the previous one. At first his response was one of bewilderment, but gradually out of that perplexity emerged a strong feeling of anger at his own quixotic folly. This discovery put an end to the poetic blight, and in 1942-43 he wrote a good deal about the affair seen in retrospect, most of which has not been published. However, the experience changed him: his writings after 1942 have a world-weary air, as if he has suffered a loss of primal innocence, or an expulsion from Eden into a rather sordid wilderness. It also turned him against his own poetry, as he confessed to MacDiarmid in a letter which shows that he was still not at peace because of his private life, even in 1942:

> I have probably increased in wisdom and honesty with myself but I think it will be many years before I can make poetry out of that and nowadays I am always finding my own stuff false, shallow and meretricious and frequently I question the value of most poetry.[37]

At that time, while he was in Egypt in 1942, there was no shortage of ideas for poetry, but he lacked faith in and enthusiasm for their realization and was becoming more impatient with certain aspects of his own character. For example, he felt himself lacking in discipline, tending to waste time and devoid of any habits of intellectual organisation and economy. These tensions emerge in his letter to MacDiarmid, written in March 1942:

> I am again pretty full of poetic ideas and rhythms but the nature of my duties precludes my having the time to let poetic ideas simmer and take shape. I always hanker after a restrained, calm manner that would express depth and not fire, a manner that would belie an intensity of matter, something that would suggest or be in the same way like the greatest art of Mozart and of the MacCrimmons, and I look with disgust at much of my own too patent subjectivity. But of course, all art is subjective; the problem is to camouflage the subjectivity so that it doesn't offend others, to become universal or apparently universal in one's subjectivity. . . . I try to avoid writing anything now as it reminds me of the *joie-de-vivre* I had during the last two months of 1939, and makes me feel that all my best stuff is the product of a drunkenness that won't return and that if I can write any more it will only be the dreich poetry of 'wisdom'. I liked my drunken idolatry.[38]

In October of the same year he writes that he is filled with "shame and disgust" when he thinks about his own poetry, which is "only rarely". Indeed, so completely did he turn against his own poetry that it spilled over to affect his appreciation of other poets. Donne, whom he had greatly liked, appeared to him now as aridly intellectual; and Shakespeare, whom he had described one year earlier as one of the greatest English poets, became a "sycophantic bugger";[39] and instead of Shakespeare's sonnets, which he acknowledges as one of the most important English influences on his work, being uppermost in his mind, it was Shakespeare's "very limited humanity" and his "private faults of toadyism"[40] which dominated.

Most moving of all of his writing from this period, and the most effective summary of MacLean's feelings about himself and his poetry is the following declaration which he made to MacDiarmid, probably in February 1942:

> I have not done anything since September or October and I know now that, if I
> am ever to write any more verse, it will be very different from what I have
> written, that it must be less subjective, more thoughtful, less content with its
> own music, and above all that I must transcend the shameful weakness of petty
> egoism and doubts and lack of single-mindedness that now disquiets me in
> much of my own stuff. Terrible things happened to me between 1939 and 1941
> and my own poetry was a desperate effort to overcome them and that left its
> marks. But now I think I have overcome all that and if I survive this fracas, I
> will certainly cut away everything that deters me from a complete devotion to
> my political beliefs, which are now more uncompromising and far more
> single-minded than ever. I shall try to do what I can to follow as closely after
> your single-mindedness and dis-interestedness in those two things as I can.[41]

So the effects of the disastrous affair with the Scottish woman permeated all
aspects of MacLean's life, turning him against poetry, and making him indifferent as
to whether he survived the war. For four years of his life, he was in love with, or
obsessed by this woman, and unable to form a serious relationship with any other. It
was not until 1945, when he visited the Irish woman in Dublin, that he completely
overcame his obsession. Simply being with the Irish woman, who was spiritually far
superior to the other, and her husband and three children, had the purgative effect of
exorcizing him of the obsession. The Irish woman, however, knew nothing of this,
nor of how, eight years earlier, MacLean had entertained such feelings for her,
feelings which had achieved such remarkable expression in his poetry.

MacLean may have had a premonition, in September 1939, that he would survive
the war, but he almost did not, being wounded three times. The third time, on 2
November 1942, during the Battle of El Alamein, MacLean was seriously injured
when a land mine exploded near him and many of the bones in his feet and heels
were broken. The following nine months were spent recovering gradually in military
hospitals, which at least afforded him plenty time for reading and writing, until his
discharge from Raigmore Hospital, Inverness, in August 1943.

It is ironic that MacLean should have turned against his own poetry at a time
when, at the insistence of Douglas Young, a volume of his poetry, his first solo
publication, was in preparation. A good deal of the correspondence between
MacLean and Young is concerned with the arrangements for the publication of
MacLean's book, which finally appeared in November 1943 under the title *Dàin do
Eimhir agus Dàin Eile*. MacLean was extremely grateful to Young, whose belief in
MacLean as a poet was such that he would spare no effort to try to help him and to
bring his work to public notice. MacLean also had great admiration for Young,
whom he describes as being "of an aristocratic mind and temperament", more so
than anyone else he knew. Yet, although they agreed about much, MacLean never
felt with Young the same sense of "political kinship", that "intimate feeling of
closeness politically" that he felt for MacDiarmid and Muir. MacLean also felt a
gap between himself and George Davie and George Campbell Hay, men he liked
and respected immensely, but neither of whom, he believed at the time, had
"experienced poverty or nearness to it". He explains his reaction further in a letter to
Douglas Young:

> Why do I immediately sense a sort of political kinship with people as different
> as Muir and Grieve, but not with you, Davie, Deorsa etc. I think it is a class

question. Neither you, nor Davie nor Deorsa nor Robert MacIntyre are really
of my 'class' and hence I have never immediately felt that intimate feeling of
closeness politically with you . . . though probably I should intellectually
agree less with either Muir or Grieve on most questions than I would with
you.[42]

Apart from helping to organize the publication of *Dàin do Eimhir*, Douglas Young
had also published in 1943 a volume of poems entitled *Auntran Blads*, containing
several translations into Scots of MacLean's poems and dedicated to MacLean and
George Campbell Hay. Here is Young's translation of *Dàin do Eimhir*, XXXIV:

> When I am talkan o the face and natur
> and the whyte spreit o ma whyte dear cratur,
> ye'd aiblins say I'd never seen
> the muckle mire wi ma blind een,
> thon hideous flow, reid and broun,
> whaur the bourgeoisie slounge and droun.
>
> But I hae seen frae the Cuillin's hicht
> baith shitten puirtith and glory licht;
> I've seen the sun's gowden glitter
> and the black moss o soss and skitter,
> I ken the ingyne's wersh smert
> mair nor the gley delyte o the hert.

In 1944, MacLean met Renee Cameron, to whom he was immediately attracted,
but history repeated itself in that he was led, quite mistakenly, to believe her to be
engaged to a man he knew. Not until a year later did MacLean learn of his mistake,
and their marriage took place on 24 July 1946. MacLean's happiness and the peace
of mind which he derived from this relationship are evident in the poems 'Lights'
and 'A Girl and Old Songs', both clearly written with Renee Cameron in mind.

When MacLean was formally discharged from military service, he returned to
teaching, first of all at Boroughmuir in Edinburgh where, in 1947, he was promoted
to the position of Principal Teacher of English. He remained at Boroughmuir until
1956, and would have been content to stay there indefinitely, because he was happy
in the school, and extremely fond of the pupils there. However, he longed to return to
the Highlands, to be again part of a Gaelic-speaking community. The easiest way to
do so was to seek promotion. In 1956 he was appointed Headmaster of Plockton
Secondary School in Wester Ross, where he remained until his retirement in 1972.

Although MacLean came to like teaching, it had certain drawbacks as an
occupation. There were also advantages in that it took him out of himself and
hardened him to a certain extent. It also enabled him to work with literature,
although there was, for him as for all teachers, the danger of a coarsened sensibility
because of having to work at such a low level. However, teaching demands a high
level of nervous energy which is constantly expended in order to keep discipline,
even with the best behaved pupils. MacLean found that teaching took a great deal
out of him, leaving him desperately tired in the evening. Another difficult problem
for him was the necessity of teaching to an exam syllabus, which demands restricting
the material taught to a fairly narrow field, especially for the less able pupils. At
Plockton, the size and location of the school meant that MacLean was constantly
searching for new teachers and for accommodation for them. MacLean had to make

up for the frequent vacancies or absences in the staff by teaching a large part of the curriculum himself in order to fill in the gaps. This left the normal administrative duties of a headmaster to be done in his own time at home in the evening, in addition to the teacher's normal burden of evening correction. What he had initially thought would be a less onerous post — being Headmaster at Plockton instead of Head of English at Boroughmuir — turned out to be not so at all.

The decline of Gaelic has always profoundly disturbed MacLean, and teaching in Plockton brought him face to face with the problem. The situation of Gaelic, as he saw it, is summarized in a letter to Douglas Young:

> The whole prospect of Gaelic appals me, the more I think of the difficulties and the likelihood of its extinction in a generation or two. A highly inflected language with a ridiculous (because etymological) spelling, no modern prose of any account, no philosophical or technical vocabulary to speak of, no correct usage except among old people and a few university students, colloquially full of gross English idiom lately taken over, exact shades of meanings of most words not to be found in any of its dictionaries and dialectically varying enormously (what chance of the appreciation of the overtones of poetry, except among a handful?) Above all, all economic, social and political factors working against it and, with that, the notorious moral cowardice of the Highlanders themselves . . .[43]

This illustrates another facet of MacLean's character: a ruthless realism coupled with a willingness to fight on the losing side. Despite this knowledge, MacLean used his influence as headmaster to push for the establishment of a Learners' paper in the Scottish Certificate of Education examinations. This aspect of MacLean's work is considered in detail by Aonghas MacNeacail in this volume.

It was inevitable that his poetry would suffer. MacLean now had a wife and three daughters to support, and the necessity of teaching meant that he had little energy left to write in the years 1943-72. Even week-ends did not provide much respite, because it would usually take until Sunday for new ideas to come and he would rarely find time to write them down before Monday morning destroyed the beginnings of creative activity and the possibility of intellectual continuity. MacLean concludes his autobiographical essay in *Chapman* 16 by referring to this problem:

> Some say that the habit of writing grows on one and that, once it is formed, it is not easy to eradicate. That may be true of most writers, but I think its truth depends on the chances of life. The chances are very much against the twentieth century Gael, who has always to make a living in other ways, and too often he has to do it by what must be one of the most exhausting of all ways, school teaching.

Despite the rigours of teaching, however, MacLean did write some extremely fine poems during this period, although not, one suspects, as many as he might have done in other circumstances. Among these is the wonderful 'Hallaig' which first appeared in 1954, and which encapsulates the history and situation of the Gaelic people. As John MacInnes writes:

> The Gaelic sense of landscape, idealized in terms of society, and the Romantic sense of communism with Nature merge in a single vision, a unified sensibility.

'Hallaig' synthesises the manifold variety of the modern Gaelic mind — a poem both sophisticated and simple and innocent.[44]

As well as 'Hallaig', the sixties saw the composition of 'Am Botal Briste', 'Curaidhean', 'Eadh is Féin is Sàr-Fhéin', 'Palach', 'Dà Dhòmhnallach', and the very moving 'Cumha Chaluim Iain Mhic Gill-Eain'. In the 1970s MacLean was mainly writing longer poems: 'Uamha 'n Òir'[45] and 'Screapadal'.[46] Both poems, but especially the former, show that MacLean still has great poetic power.

The publication of *Four Points of a Saltire* and *Lines Review* 34 in 1970 heralded a new era for MacLean whose poetry, always appreciated by those closely involved in Scottish literature, suddenly became more widely available and much more widely appreciated. In 1971, a volume of translations by Iain Crichton Smith entitled *Poems to Eimhir* appeared which greatly increased the quantity of MacLean's work available in English. Cuthbert Graham, reviewing this volume for the *Aberdeen Press and Journal*, wrote that these poems express "personal misery transmuted here into poetry of compelling power and exactitude of utterance".[47] He also quotes Iain Crichton Smith's statement that MacLean has opened "Gaelic poetry out to the world beyond purely parochial boundaries".[48] In 1973, Claddagh Records produced *Barran agus Asbhuain, Poems by Sorley MacLean read by himself.* Accompanying the record was a text of the poetry in both Gaelic and English, and notes by Iain Crichton Smith in both Gaelic and English (with an Irish translation by Máirtín Ó Direáin). The production of this record occasioned the article by Iain Crichton Smith which appeared shortly after in the *Glasgow Herald*, in which Smith explains the quality of MacLean's poetry in this way:

It is the work of the whole man, exposed, suffering, joyous, often in despair. But, more than that, this joy and despair, this turmoil has been transformed into art and therefore does not remain a brutal residue to poison the psyche but it is truly out there for others to use. It is this final triumph that one salutes. [49]

However successful MacLean's work seemed to have become, the problems inherent in being a Gaelic poet remained even in the 1970s. 'Uamha 'n Òir' was published in English translation, but the Gaelic original remained unpublished, and MacLean himself felt that no-one would want to publish it without the English version. Luckily, *Chapman* 15 published the poem in its Gaelic entirety (the English version was later published in *Chapman* 30). Most satisfying of all for MacLean was the appearance of *Reothairt is Contraigh, Spring Tide and Neap Tide, Selected Poems 1932-72* in 1977. This was extremely well received and widely reviewed. The reviews, which varied considerably in quality, are probably best summed up by Iain Crichton Smith:

When confronted by this kind of poetry, one can only marvel that it exists: criticism seems impertinent since there is so little to criticise. For this poetry is not simply verbalization: it is both words and music together, it is what one wants poetry to be.[49]

In the last ten years, MacLean's presence has been increasingly in demand at poetry readings and conferences all over Scotland and Ireland. Recognition of his work has spread to Europe, North America and England. In 1973, he began two years as Creative Writer in Residence at Edinburgh University, and from 1975-6 was Filidh at Sabhal Mór Ostaig, the Gaelic College in Skye. He has been awarded

Honorary Degrees by three universities: Dundee in 1972, the National University of Ireland in 1979, and Edinburgh University in 1980. The first Cambridge International Festival was an important event for MacLean. I was fortunate enough to be present at his first reading. The audience was packed by people who had come not to hear him, but other, better known, English poets. The entire company was astounded by his poetry, the like of which they had never heard before, despite the language difference. Unlike many poetry gatherings, the atmosphere was electrifying; the readings he gave were certainly the high point of the festival. MacDiarmid expressed his opinion of MacLean's status as a poet in a letter written the year before he died:

> You (MacLean) have always been over-indulgent about my poetry and too modest about your own. There is, I think, no doubt about you and I being the two best poets in Scotland . . . By definition, every good poet has something that is *sui generis* — something that is his alone and couldn't be done by anyone else. Like can only be compared with like. Your work and mine is utterly different, so it is rubbish to say . . . which of us is greater. [50]

MacLean's poetry undoubtedly ranks among the best in modern Europe because of the unrestrained and fearless passion with which he greets every experience, from the most obviously significant to the most apparently trivial. In it a remarkable human being opens the most intimate aspects of his nature to ruthless moral scrutiny, to an extent which even most poets fail to achieve. Here we see the anguish and the joy of an individual whose sensibility responds on a universal level to all the important issues of modern humanity with an understanding which stems from an awareness of the history of his own people and people everywhere. It is outstanding on account of its intellectual and emotional range, its combination of emotional sensitivity and rigorous intellectuality in a uniquely Gaelic synthesis.

It is somehow characteristic of the man that one of the deepest satisfactions of this past decade for him is the development of his daughters, Catriona and Ishbel into fine Gaelic traditional singers, and Mary into an artist.

Although now compelled not to undertake too much work, MacLean leads a very hectic life, between conferences, poetry readings and festivals; but even now, in his seventies, he is continuing to write poetry.

JOY HENDRY

NOTES

1. John MacInnes, "A Radically Traditional Voice", *Cencrastus*, 7, Winter 1981-82, p.14.
2. "On Poetry and the Muse", *Chapman*, 16, Summer 1976.
3. Angus Nicolson, "An Interview with Sorley MacLean", *Studies in Scottish Literature*, 14, 1979.
4. Catalogue to National Library of Scotland exhibition on Sorley MacLean, 1981, p.14.
5. John MacInnes, "Sorley MacLean's 'Hallaig', a note", *Calgacus*, 2, 1975.

6. Letter from Sorley MacLean to Hugh MacDiarmid, 25 May 1940, Edinburgh University Library (E.U.L.).
7. "An Interview with Sorley MacLean", *op. cit.*
8. Letter from Sorley MacLean to Hugh MacDiarmid, 8 Feb. 1935, E.U.L., *loc. cit.*
9. Letter from Sorley MacLean to Hugh MacDiarmid, undated, 1935, *ibid.*
10. Letter to MacDiarmid, 13 June 1935, *ibid.*
11. Letter to MacDiarmid, 4 Jan. 1935, *ibid.*
12. Letter to MacDiarmid, 20 Dec. 1936, *ibid.*
13. Letter to MacDiarmid, 8 Nov. 1937, *ibid.*
14. Sorley MacLean, "Poetry, Passion and Political Consciousness", *Scottish International*, 10, May 1970, p.14.
15. Letter to MacDiarmid, 25 May 1940, E.U.L., *loc. cit.*
16. Letter to MacDiarmid, undated, *ibid.*
17. Letter from Sorley MacLean to Douglas Young, 23 Nov. 1940, National Library of Scotland (N.L.S.), *Acc. 6419.*
18. Letter to Young, 7 Sept. 1941, *ibid.*
19, Letter to Young, 11 Sept. 1941, *ibid.*
20. Letter to MacDiarmid, 10 Jan. 1940, E.U.L., *loc. cit.*
21. Letter to MacDiarmid, 12 May 1940, *ibid.*
22. Letter to Young, 11 Sept. 1941, N.L.S., *loc. cit.*
23. Letter to Young, 6 Dec. 1940, *ibid.*
24. Letter to MacDiarmid, 8 Mar. 1941, E.U.L., *loc. cit.*
25. Letter to Young, 27 Oct. 1940, N.L.S., *loc. cit.*
26. Letter to MacDiarmid, 16 Jan. 1946, E.U.L., *loc. cit.*
27. Letter to Young, 25 May 1941, N.L.S., *loc. cit.*
28. Letter to Young, 6 Oct. 1942, *ibid.*
29. Letter to Young, 1 Oct. 1940, *ibid.*
30. Letter to Young, 14 June 1941, *ibid.*
31. Letter to Young, 18 Dec. 1941, *ibid.*
32. Letter to Young, 6 Dec. 1940, *ibid.*
33. Letter to Young, 9 Nov. 1941, *ibid.*
34. Letter to Young, 11 Jan. 1941, *ibid.*
35. Letter to Young, 6 Dec. 1940, *ibid.*
36. Letter to Young, 27 Oct. 1942, *ibid.*
37. Letter to MacDiarmid, 15 Mar. 1942, E.U.L. *loc. cit.*
38. Letter to MacDiarmid, 30 Mar. 1942, *ibid.*
39. Letter to Young, 6 Oct. 1942, N.L.S., *loc. cit.*
40. Letter to Young, 27 Oct. 1942, *ibid.*
41. Letter to MacDiarmid, 23 Feb. 1942 (date uncertain), E.U.L., *loc. cit.*
42. Letter to Young, 11 Sept. 1941, N.L.S., *loc. cit.*
43. Letter to Young, 15 June 1943, *ibid.*
44. "Sorley MacLean's 'Hallaig', a note ", *op. cit.*
45. *Chapman*, 15, Spring 1976.
46. *Cencrastus*, 7, *op. cit.*
47. Cuthbert Graham, "Poems to Eimhir", *Aberdeen Press and Journal*, 11 Sept. 1971.

48. *Poems to Eimhir,* translated by Iain Crichton Smith, Northern House, Newcastle on Tyne, 1971.

49. Iain Crichton Smith, "Major Gaelic Poet in a European Context", *Glasgow Herald,* 27 Oct. 1973.

50. Iain Crichton Smith, Review of *Reothairt is Contraigh, Glasgow Herald,* 21 April 1977.

51. Letter from Hugh MacDiarmid to Sorley MacLean, 27 Jan. 1977, E.U.L., *loc. cit.*

Sorley MacLean: a Personal View

It has been my privilege to have known MacDiarmid in the 1930s, before he had received the recognition due to him, and, at the same period, to have got to know men of such diverse personalities, views and talents as Fionn MacColla, Robert Garioch and Sorley MacLean, all of whom became my close personal friends. The old *Freeman* office at the top of India Buildings in Edinburgh's West Bow was a cementing influence. It was here that I first met MacDiarmid and MacColla, both of whom contributed a weekly column to the paper, and it was here too that I came across Robert Garioch. My friend, George Davie, who had an unerring nose for such things, had spoken to me of "a young Edinburgh teacher called Sutherland, who was making effective poetic use of the language of the Edinburgh streets". These were the days of 'Fi'baw in the Street' and 'The Masque of Edinburgh'.

At least two of these *Freeman* contacts were to become connected with Sorley MacLean. He himself would agree with me that it was George Davie and I who first introduced him to *A Drunk Man Looks at the Thistle*. I cannot remember whether it was in Sorley's digs or in George's that we spent a whole evening reading and discussing the poem with him. I think it was George who introduced him to MacDiarmid in the flesh. The results we all know: the interaction of these two major poets was of very great importance for Scottish poetry. Sorley's relationship with Garioch was not as close as that with MacDiarmid, but they liked, respected and appreciated one another. Their first published work in book form was *Seventeen Poems for Sixpence,* a joint production issued in 1940 by the Chalmers Press (a handpress operated by Garioch). It was a splendid gesture of Scottish cultural identity in a dark period when it was threatened by eclipse.

But it was at Edinburgh University that I first got to know Sorley. He had graduated a few years before me, and, when I met him, in my second year, he was doing teacher training at Moray House. Again I think it was George Davie who introduced me to Sorley. Like his elder brother, John, who was a distinguished classical scholar, and was later to translate *The Odyssey* into Gaelic hexameters, Sorley had a reputation for scholarship, having graduated with First Class Honours in English. He was also a perfervid Gael and a man of strong socialist convictions. I felt that he had absolute integrity and intellectual honesty, but, at the same time, too trusting and generous a nature. His glowing idealism and passionate commitment to a cause reminded one of Shelley, particularly the Shelley of 'Prometheus Unbound', who, indeed, was one of the earliest influences on his development. When he was aflame with enthusiasm for an idea or a poem, he was one of the most eloquent people I have ever met. In company he sat in silence, brooding over something or other (he had little gift for small talk), until a chance remark on a subject that touched him would arouse his interest. He would rise to his feet, his eyes would flash, and a torrent of rhythmically cadenced, magnificent language would pour forth: a kind of vatic fury would possess him.

At that time our discussions would range widely over politics, both national and international. These were the days of Hitler, "the brute and brigand at the head of Europe", and of the dreary, pusillanimous Chamberlain government. We were both affected by the myths of 1916 and 1917 and were both interested in and sympathetic to Irish nationalism, although I was struck by Yeats's quoting the old Fenian, O'Leary's remark that there were certain things a man must not do for his country. Pearse and Connolly played a prominent part in our discussions. Connolly, the socialist, above all appealed to Sorley's imagination, an appeal that has lasted, as his moving poem on the National Museum in Dublin shows. It is appropriate that in later life Sorley should have been honoured by the National University of Ireland.

We differed in our attitudes towards Scottish independence. At that time I was in favour of any non-fascist movement in that direction, whereas Sorley was committed primarily to a socialist remedy. The outbreak of the Spanish Civil War moved him profoundly. In more than one of his earlier poems he upbraids himself for not playing a hero's part in that conflict. He pays tribute to the poets, Julian Bell, John Cornford and Lorca who perished in it.

The conflict with fascism had its lighter moments. I remember vividly one summer evening in Edinburgh when Sir Oswald Mosley was holding a rally in the Usher Hall. He had brought a contingent of thugs, euphemistically called stewards, to deal with any opposition. A group of about a dozen members from the Celtic Society of Edinburgh University, including Sorley and myself, went along to the meeting. Most of them were stalwart six-footers. At one point in the proceedings Sorley rose to his feet to ask the question, "What about your socialist pledges?" (Mosley had been a Minister in a Labour Government). Immediately four or five blackshirts materialized at the end of the row in which we were sitting, with the aim of forcibly ejecting Sorley. All the Celtic stalwarts rose to their feet and glared menacingly at the 'stewards', who at once retreated. Later there were wild scenes outside the hall, when a collection of irate citizens, including the inevitable shawlie wives from the Old Town, hurled insults and threw stones and pieces of lead piping at the buses that were to convey the blackshirts back to England. How far they were motivated by nationalism and how far by socialism it is hard to say.

As for literature, we ranged widely over Greek, Latin, French, English and Scottish poetry. Coming to more modern times we talked about Yeats, Eliot, Valéry, Pound, Lawrence, MacDiarmid, and the emerging MacSpaundy group, although Sorley's crofter radicalism, nourished on memories of the Battle of the Braes and Glendale, was poles removed from the affected English public school communism of these gentlemen. But we nearly always came back to MacDiarmid and Yeats, to whose work we were passionately devoted. Yeats's despairing love for Maud Gonne and the magnificent lyrics in which he expressed it particularly moved Sorley. In a sense they anticipated the anguished lyricism of some of his own love poetry, where he apostrophises his beloved, "You are the fire of my lyric – you made a poet of me through sorrow". In one poem, indeed, he equates her with Maud Gonne and with Deirdre, Eimhir and Gràinne. Sorley had written some verses in English – influenced by contemporary models – but he was dissatisfied with these, and was considering expressing himself in the language he had known before he had acquired any English and in which he still thought – Gaelic. He disapproved, however, of the facile lyricism and patterned nostalgia of much nineteenth century and early twentieth century Gaelic verse. What he was to achieve was both a step forwards – he brought Scottish Gaelic literature into the twentieth century – and a return to earlier models – in the use of a syllabic verse form.

I regretted my ignorance of the language, since it meant that I was cut off from a major part of Scotland's cultural heritage. For many an evening Sorley would read aloud to me, expound and give a literal translation of poems by Iain Lom, Alexander MacDonald, Duncan Bàn Macintyre and William Ross. He had a great deal to say, too, about the anonymous lyrics of the sixteenth and seventeenth centuries. My debt to him in this respect is incalculable. My eyes were opened to a whole new cultural dimension. Given the right audience Sorley was an inspired and inspiring teacher. He did a great deal for the teaching of Gaelic as Headmaster of Plockton High School. His continued and eventually successful struggle to introduce the Learners' Paper in the S.C.E. examination (along with the late Donald Thomson of Oban) is only one example of his activity in this direction. We must not ignore, either, the help he gave Hugh MacDiarmid in his translations of MacDonald's 'Birlinn of Clan Ranald' and of Macintyre's 'Praise of Ben Dorain', not to mention the other Gaelic poems which were included in MacDiarmid's *Golden Treasury of Scottish Poetry*. His achievements both as Gaelic poet and propagandist for Gaelic culture have been recognised by his fellow Gaels, in that he has been accorded the almost unique distinction of having been elected for a second time Chieftain of the Gaelic Society of Inverness.

Sorley's first teaching appointment was to his old school, Portree High School. In June 1935, after I had sat my finals in English at Edinburgh, I spent a week or so in Skye. It was my first experience of the West Highlands. I was full of anxious anticipation as the train wound around Duncan Bàn's shapely Ben Dorain, and as later I gazed out at the white sands of Alexander MacDonald's Morar and came in sight of the jagged impatient scrawl of the Cuillin against the dark grey slate of the sky. At the week-end he and I visited his home in Raasay. Raasay has played an important part in his life and poetry. His most formative years were spent there, and it forms the setting for some of his deepest and most personal poems, such as 'Hallaig' and 'Coilltean Ratharsair'. We were rowed across from Braes in Skye by Sorley's father and some of his friends. That night we attended a ceilidh in the house of his grandfather, a venerable patriarch with the liveliest eyes I have ever seen and the most infectious laugh I have ever heard. The night was spent in song and story, and I counted myself privileged to be there. It was a revelation of a way of life, a culture, that had persisted despite forces inimical to it, throughout untold centuries. For Sorley comes of a race of 'tale-bearers', transmitters of an incomparable oral tradition of song, of story, of historical memories. As well as MacLean he has Matheson and Nicolson blood, and he has an amazingly detailed knowledge of Skye, Raasay, and the Lochalsh area; of places, of houses, of the people and their forebears, down to the remotest genealogical ramifications. All of this, allied to scholarship, has made him the formidable figure he is. To go round Skye in his company is a rich experience. To him the sixteenth century is as real and vivid as the present day. This feeling emerges very clearly in that elusive poem, 'Hallaig':

Tha iad fhathast ann a Hallaig | They are still in Hallaig,
Clann Ghill-Eain 's Clann MhicLeòid, | MacLeans and MacLeods,
na bh'ann ri linn Mhic Ghille-Chaluim | All who were there in the time of Mac Ghille-Chaluim

Chunnacas na mairbh beò. | The dead have been seen alive.

But Sorley was not the only member of his family to be distinguished for his command of the Gaelic oral tradition. His younger brother Calum was one of the finest collectors of his generation of folk-lore and traditional tales both in Ireland and in the Western Isles of Scotland. He also wrote an original and stimulating book on the Highlands. One of the finest of Sorley's later works is the moving and tender elegy he wrote on Calum. In this poem the terms of reference, the values, are peculiarly, almost tribally, Gaelic: it might have been composed at any time during the past five centuries.

Later, when we were both teaching in Edinburgh, Sorley would read and translate his as yet unpublished poems to my wife and me in our flat in the New Town. We realised that these were no ordinary productions. In their blend of passion and intellect, their striking imagery, they bore the unmistakable imprint of poetic genius of a high order. When war broke out, he left pencilled translations of some of them with us: they are now in the National Library of Scotland. When news came of our call-up we spent an uproarious evening in the company of James Carmichael Watson and others. Watson was Professor of Celtic at Edinburgh and the editor of the poems of Mary MacLeod. Soon afterwards he enlisted in the Royal Navy and was killed in a torpedo attack – a tragic loss to Celtic scholarship.

Our ways parted. I served in the United Kingdom and Europe. Sorley was posted to the Middle East, to the same theatre of war in which Garioch was captured to spend dreary years in prison camps. Sorley was severely wounded at El Alamein. There were anxious months in which we did not know what had happened to him. Fortunately the late Douglas Young and the Reverend John MacKechnie arranged for the publication of his poems. *Dàin Do Eimhir* appeared in 1943, and it proved to be one of the most important works to be published in Scotland in this century.

Sorley was invalided out of the Army and resumed teaching in Edinburgh, where I saw a fair amount of him during my last year in the Forces, when I was stationed at Scottish Command H.Q. Later still, when I taught at Peebles, we met frequently. By this time he had taken one of the best decisions of his life; he married Renée Cameron of Inverness. They complement one another. With her sense of humour, sound practical sense and sunny disposition, combined with an appreciation of the finer things of life, she is the perfect wife for Sorley.

During those Edinburgh years he saw a great deal of his fellow-poet, Sydney Goodsir Smith. Indeed for a time Sorley and Renée shared a house in Craigmillar Park (immortalised in 'Under the Eildon Tree') with the Smiths. Every time I saw him Sorley was full of amusing stories about Sydney – "the Auk" – whose unconventional ways and witty conversation intrigued him.

Years later, when Sorley was back in the Highlands, as Headmaster of Plockton High School, our paths crossed once more. I was Her Majesty's Inspector of Schools for Ross and Cromarty, and, of course, Plockton was in my District. It was then that I realised fully the extent of his work for Gaelic education, and his dedication to the interests of his pupils. In many ways he followed the pattern of the old-fashioned Scottish dominie, capable of teaching, and teaching well, a variety of subjects. Staffing problems led to his taking classes at one time or another in English, History, Latin, French and Gaelic, in addition to the normal administrative duties attached to his post. He was a fearless fighter for what he considered to be the best interests of his pupils, undeterred by the authority of county councils and their representatives, or even, on occasion, the Scottish Education Department. But unlike the old Scots dominie, he was not only interested in the "lad (or lass) o pairts". He was particularly helpful and sympathetic to pupils who had difficulty with their studies or had personal problems.

But these activities took their toll. There were years when the poetic impulse seemed to have dried up. Towards the end of his teaching career, however, and in the years of retirement, when he settled in Skye in a house (under Glamaig and facing Raasay) which had been inhabited by one of his ancestors, there has been a magnificent reflorescence of poetry, much more meditative, reflective and abstruse, less turbulent, than the early lyrics.

Official recognition followed. He became Writer in Residence at Edinburgh University. He has received Doctorates from three universities. He has taken part in poetry readings in Scotland, England, Ireland, on the Continent, and in Canada and the U.S.A. He is referred to respectfully (and this is a rare achievement for a Scottish writer) in 'quality' magazines and papers south of the Border. Throughout it all he has retained his integrity and – I use the term in a favourable sense – his admirable simplicity.

In some respects he is like the great Provencal poet, Mistral, although Mistral does not have the same astonishing lyrical power. They resemble one another in their attachment to their roots, familial and topographical, in their interpretation of the spirit and traditions of the countryside that had nurtured them, and in their successful use of a minority language in a declining state. It is a miracle that a language spoken by a handful of people in a remote corner of Scotland, at the north-western extremity of Europe, should have been the medium of expression of the greatest living poet in the British Isles.

J. B. CAIRD

'The Heron'

A Poet's Response to Sorley Maclean

In this essay I would simply like to say something about what the poetry of Sorley MacLean has meant to me, and what as Gaelic poets we can learn from it.

Let me begin with a biographical note. The first time I ever came across *Dàin Do Eimhir*, was when I was given the Gaelic prize in Fifth Year in the Nicolson Institute, Stornoway, in 1945, by an unusually enlightened Gaelic teacher. I think it would be fair to say that though the poems were new to me (the ambience, however, was familiar to me, at least from the angle of the Spanish Civil War, since I had by then read some Spender and Auden in *Penguin New Writing*) I was overwhelmed by the combination of music and imagery that I found in the book, and indeed it is the volume of poems to which I have returned most often, long after I sensed in Auden and Spender flaws which I did not find in MacLean.

I think it would be worth mentioning that I had been studying Gaelic literature in school and though I admired the love poetry of William Ross, there was little else at that time that seemed to me to be alive with the resonance that a young poet looks for. Later, of course, I have come to admire the masculine, executive power of Iain Lom, the harmonious observation of Duncan Bàn Macintyre, the surrealistic strangeness of, for instance, the storm scene in the 'Birlinn' of Alexander MacDonald. But in the fresh youthfulness of seventeen when the world appears new each day it was not such qualities that I was particularly looking for. I was searching for the throb of the contemporary that I found in a poet like Auden, with his marvellous ability to make the quotidian appear magical.

It was not this exactly that I found in MacLean's work, for MacLean's poetry is not intellectual in the way that Auden's is. However it has the same authority, that confidence which cannot be faked, which is present in all major poetry. This is presumably what is meant by that phrase in the Bible, "for he spoke with authority": someone who knows exactly what he is talking about and does so in unforgettable language. It was an authority which I had not heard often in the Gaelic poetry that I was reading at school and certainly not in the Gaelic poetry of the nineteenth century which avoided facing real issues and withdrew into sentimentalism. Whichever poem one looked at in *Dàin Do Eimhir* one had no sense of hedging, or of hesitation, but rather one felt the thing as it was, the voice of a whole man. On the whole, the poetry I had read until then was occasional, as this was too, but in a different way. I suppose one could say that the Spanish Civil War and a love-affair brought it into being, and in that sense it was occasional, but not as, say, William Ross's poetry was occasional, for side by side with great poems in his work one would find the frivolous and the plain bad. There was something undeviating about MacLean's whole book, *Dàin do Eimhir*: the volume seemed to compose a single poem, the record of a mind and heart engaged in work that was essential to

them, and written too in varying forms which seemed suitable to the twentieth
century. I had never before seen in Gaelic poetry a verse like the following:

Choisich mi cuide ri mo thuigse	I walked beside my reason
a-muigh ri taobh a' chuain;	out beside the sea:
bha sinn còmhla ach bha ise	we were together but it was
a' fuireach tiotan bhuam.	keeping a little distance from me.

Nor again had I read in Gaelic anything like the surrealistic 'Coin is Madaidhean -
allaidh' or for that matter anything like the image of his loved one putting on a
helmet. Gaelic poetry in my experience simply was not like that. And I think also
that the strange and eerie drawings in the book by William Crosbie had a great deal
to do with my response. They seemed to speak of a new consciousness, and even now
as I look at them they remind me of the discoveries of Picasso which I did not then
know about, and to suggest something of the sensation of being on a new frontier
which is found in the poems themselves.

Now it cannot be said that I could rationalise in this way at that time, but my
response was capable of sensing in advance of total understanding a new and
extraordinary poetry. I can see now, however, that MacLean was in fact more
traditional than I had thought: for instance in his use of a litany of adjectives as in
'Gaoir na h-Eòrpa': "Girl of the yellow, heavy yellow, gold yellow hair", a technique
widely used in earlier Gaelic poetry.

Nor is it the case that MacLean has ever been, as I have already said, an
omnivorous autodidact, as Auden and MacDiarmid were (although he is the most
scrupulous of scholars). That is to say, he did not seem particularly interested in the
wide range of European thought and ideas, and when he does philosophise or refer to
Freud, for example, he does not seem to me to have quite the same power as he has
when he is writing the passionate, obsessive lyric. Thus, I did not find in his poetry
the perhaps extraneous scholarship of Auden, nor indeed what one might call
intellectual fodder.

The poetry is in the passion for, unlike Auden, MacLean does not have the gift of
making poetry out of intellectual disquisition. His poetry needs the resonance of
passionate commitment to become memorable and this I think can be seen clearly in
'An Tathaich', where he wrestles with the idea of the mortality of his loved one in a
rather pedestrian fashion:

Ciod e an ceathramh seòl-tomhais	What is the fourth dimension
a bheir an àilleachd so fa chomhair	that will bring this beauty to the keen
	perception
sùla, reusain no aon chàileachd	of eye, reason, or any sense
thar fàsaichean glomhair?	over the wastes of the abyss?
Is dé a' chàil thar chàiltean	And what sense beyond senses
a mhothaicheas an àilleachd	will perceive their beauty when neither eye
nuair nach nochd sùil no cluas i,	nor ear will show it,
blas, suathadh no fàileadh...	not taste nor touch nor smell...

The whole poem has an unrelenting, almost plodding, quality which is wholly
untypical of MacLean and this is also true of the later poem, 'Eadh is Féin is
Sàr-Fhéin'. He is much happier when philosophising if he can find a central image
which will generate the poem as in 'A' Chorra-Ghridheach':

Thàinig corra-ghridheach ghiùigeach,	A demure heron came
sheas i air uachdar tiùrra,	and stood on top of sea wrack:

phaisg i a sgiathan dlùth rith'	she folded her wings about her side
a' beachdachadh air gach taobh dhith.	and took stock of all around her.
'Na h-aonar ri taobh na tuinne	Alone beside the sea
mar thuigse leatha fhéin 's a' chruinne,	like a mind alone in the universe,
a ciall-se mar chéill an duine,	her reason like man's —
cothachadh lòin meud a suime.	the sum of it how to get a meal.

MacLean's mind, in other words, does not have the intellectual play of Auden's, but it has a deeper, more obsessive seriousness: one always feels that he is involved and not playing on the surface of things like the Northern Lights.

MacLean is always obsessively concerned with a particular loved person and this brings him much closer to a Donne or a Catullus than to an Auden. Whereas one feels that Auden is not concerned with making an existential choice, one always knows from the agony of MacLean's poetry that this is exactly what he is doing. For instance in 'An Roghainn' he writes:

Cha do lean mi ach an t-slighe chrìon	I followed only a way
bheag ìosal thioram thlàth,	that was small, mean, low, dry, lukewarm,
is ciamar sin a choinnichinn	and how then should I meet
ri beithir-theine ghràidh?	the thunderbolt of love?

MacLean is never merely abstract. He is always writing about a specific person, to whom he has committed his whole personality; MacLean makes a 'life choice' in a way that Auden does not.

So, what I did find in MacLean was an intense and strongly focussed power, combined with what was extremely attractive to a youth of seventeen, iconoclasm. I remember that at about that time I had been quite rightly ticked-off for writing a series of spoof 'In Memoriam's' for the school magazine, based on ones which I had seen in the local newspaper. I suppose that I must have been rebellious to a certain extent, especially with regard to the narrow religion in which I had been brought up. This religion composed the funereal and eternal sabbaths of my youth, when a single day lasted as long as a week. The clean, unapologetic lines of a poem like the following spoke to me immediately. Here was a man who said what he thought without prevarication:

> My eye is not on Calvary nor on Bethlehem the Blessed, but on a foul smelling backland in Glasgow where life rots as it grows, and on a room in Edinburgh, a room of poverty and pain: where the diseased infant writhes and wallows till death.

I heard the same note at the beginning of 'Ban-Ghàidheal':

> Hast thou seen her, great Jew, who art called the one Son of God?

It was liberating and astonishing that a Gaelic poet should write: "Christ's cross of crucifixion has been nailing Europe's heart for two thousand years, tearing the wounded spirit."

For myself I did not have the courage to say such things from the heart of a Presbyterian island. The words did not seem to be attacking religion so much as passing it by, assuming its irrelevance. There was a casual mastery in the negligence of the saying.

It seems to me that MacLean's attitude towards religion is one of contempt since it does not deal with the real problems of poverty and the paradoxes on which the human mind is impaled. The movement, which seems to me to be almost wholly

intellectual, of Auden from Freud and Marx to Christianity is not a course that
MacLean has taken. The abstractionism of Auden, his hunger for ideas, his attempt
to erect Love into a sort of metaphysical God, is much more superficial than
MacLean's inward Highland knowledge of what Christ has meant to the woman
with the creel.

Thus, this iconoclasm attracted me, but above all the passion and power of the
love-poems appealed to me, as love poems of this order must appeal to a
seventeen-year-old who is at all interested in poetry and who at that age sways
between idealism and desire. The poems had the bitter-sweetness of love and
melancholy, and perhaps if the story had had a happy ending they would not have
been so interesting. There was, too, an *hauteur*, a Byronic touchiness and pride,
which I admired. Sometimes they showed sunny happiness as in the lines:

Air dara tobhta 'n fhuaraidh   On the second thwart to windward,
shuidh thu, luaidh, 'nam chòir   darling, you sat near me,
agus do ròp laist' cuailein   and your lit rope of hair
mu m' chridh 'na shuaineadh òir.   about my heart, a winding of gold.

Sometimes they showed a cutting terseness:

Sgatham le faobhar-roinn gach àilleachd   Let me lop off with a sharp blade every grace
a chuir do bhòidhche 'nam bhàrdachd.   that your beauty put in my verse.

And sometimes too they showed conscious arrogance as in "I gave you immortality,
but what did you give me?" *(Dàin do Eimhir,* no. XIX).

Altogether they appealed to the adolescent because of their iconoclasm, their
emotional odyssey, their mastery and cleanness of form, and above all, of course,
because of the fact that they had been written in Gaelic and were Gaelic in essence.

Shortly after Maclean writes

Choisich mi cuide ri mo thuigse   I walked with my reason
a-muigh ri taobh a' chuain   out beside the sea

he also writes

An sin thionndaidh i ag ràdha: Then it turned saying:
a bheil e fìor gun cual   is it true you heard
thu gu bheil do ghaol geal àlainn   that your beautiful white love
a' pòsadh tràth Di-luain?   is getting married early on Monday?

In that verse there is the simplicity and directness of Gaelic song, and the specificity
of "early on Monday", shows that he is talking about a real event.

For in this sense MacLean's poetry is simple ("Simple, sensuous, and
passionate"); it has no real ambiguities. Once one knows the background, the
references to Spain, to the political figures of the time and to Gaelic history, there are
no problems such as are created by Eliot. It is true, for instance, that a poem may be
built up on the ambiguity of a word like 'ciall' (which can mean both 'love' and
'wisdom' in Gaelic), or that there may be paradoxes as in

Mar riutsa tha m' irisleachd   With you my humility
co-ionann ri m' uaill   is equal to my pride,
agus tha m' ùmhlachd is m' àrdan   and my submission and pride
'nan ceòl-gàire buan.   are a permanent laughter of music.

But in no real sense is MacLean difficult. This is quite simply poetry which has been beaten out on the anvil of circumstance. There do not appear to be any strategies or artifices. The perplexities of life speak through it.

And its great advantage is that it speaks from the heart of a living language, as MacDiarmid's poetry does not. It is the collision of that which had been done before with that which had not which gave the poetry its special resonance. Likewise a special resonance arises from the collision of the Presbyterian mind with the apparent liberation of communism. In only one poem, however, have I found the silliness of a 'poster' communism, when he writes:

> I will put a handle on the sickle of the moon and a steel-headed hammer
> over the feeble gold and through it; and let God call it blasphemy.

This silliness is quite untypical of MacLean who hardly ever writes a poem unless the thought has been deeply felt. And whereas Yeats, whom MacLean greatly admires, has at times a theatricality, this is never the case with MacLean: for MacLean it is what he says that is important, not how he says it. MacLean's output over the years has not been large simply because he will not allow himself to develop within aesthetic categories alone.

With regard to MacLean's influence on other Gaelic poets I had better say at this point that I do not consider my own Gaelic poetry, except perhaps for a few pieces, to inhabit the same air as MacLean's. I admit that many of them have been intellectual in precisely the way that MacLean's poetry is not: and that some of them have been conscious attempts to do something new, again in a way that MacLean's poetry is not. The best of MacLean's work, and especially 'Hallaig', is to me comparable to a somnambulant power, telling the deepest and barest truths about the Highlands, as if their desolations spoke through him.

In the Thirties, MacLean set himself at the centre of his time in a way that Highland poets have not succeeded in doing. That is to say he was aware of a historical process which lay beyond Highland frontiers, though it might also have been considered as a variation on the violence of Highland history itself. I am speaking, of course, of the Spanish Civil War. And, as I have written elsewhere, there is a sense in which the Spanish Civil War does not form the background to these poems, but is the protagonist. The test of whether or not to go to Spain was a deep test of who he was, and therefore a test of the quality of his love. The two things seem to me to be inextricably entwined:

Cha d' ghabh mise bàs croinn-ceusaidh	I did not take a cross's death
ann an éiginn chruaidh na Spàinn	in the sore extremity of Spain,
is ciamar sin bhiodh dùil agam	and how then should I expect
ri aon duais ùir an dàin?	the one new prize of fate?
Cha do lean mi ach an t-slighe chrìon	I followed only a way
bheag ìosal thioram thlàth,	that was small, mean, low, dry, lukewarm,
is ciamar sin a choinnichinn	and how then should I meet
ri beithir-theine ghràidh?	the thunderbolt of love?

There has always hovered in front of MacLean the mirage of the man of action, in the light of whose courage poetry does not seem to be a sufficient activity. But he was aware of the politicisation of love itself, in exactly the same way as Auden was when he wrote:

> Be Lubbe, be Hitler, but be my good daily, nightly.

(Except, of course, that MacLean would not sell his soul in this way since, as he himself says, his loved one would not accept such a soul, once sold.)

Nor is it just the Spanish Civil War that MacLean writes about, for some of his best poems are those set in Africa where he served during the Second World War. In doing this he was not alone, for some of Campbell Hay's best poems were also written about Africa, especially the very fine 'Bizerta'. Derick Thomson was to write about Budapest (and translate poems by Solzhenitsyn) and Donald Macaulay wrote about Turkey and NATO. But MacLean was, I believe, the first Gaelic poet to be centred in the events of his own time, precisely as Auden and Spender were, but I think with greater authenticity. Therefore, perhaps the most important thing that these Gaelic writers and myself learned from MacLean was not concerned so much with subject-matter, for his poetry is highly experiential, but rather was the confidence that one can write about themes of major concern in Gaelic.

But, and this is very important, in being at the centre of events MacLean never lost the sense of his own heritage, nor the tang of his own tongue. There is a sense in which Auden became a lesser poet when he went to America; there is a sense in which MacDiarmid became a lesser poet when he began to write in English and divorced his intellect from his feelings and succumbed to the Scottish disease of pedantry: this is not a charge that can be laid against MacLean, for he was always clear in his own mind what a poem was. Beyond these references to Lorca, Julian Bell, and the others there is the music of Gaelic, there is the example of the world from which he came. At a time when so many poets have styles but no resonance, voices but no depth, when in the end they seem strangely indistinguishable from each other; at a time when cleverness, which has nothing to do with poetry, flashes superficial resemblances of urban imagery, this is very important. In precisely the same way as MacDiarmid, MacLean became a great poet because he remained faithful to his roots, because he spoke from within his own culture. Anyone who reads his essays on Gaelic poetry will quickly realise that MacLean is a man who knows his poets, their limitations and their strengths, and has a true creative historical perspective. He is also proud of being a Gael. 'Hauteur' is a word that constantly recurs in his poetry. He has the values of the clansman, the emphasis on courage and prickliness, but also something that goes beyond that, and that is truthful speaking. He tells us about his own weaknesses, his own despairs, almost in spite of himself.

It is of course highly improbable that we will ever again see the precise conjunction that brought these poems into being: and therefore it is unlikely that we will have such a poet again in Gaelic. For the poems to have been produced one needed to have a sensitive, scholarly man aware of his own heritage, brought face to face with conflicts both political and personal which forced him to shed all sorts of protective devices and walk naked. It is as if a shift in consciousness occurred when these poems appeared: they moved Gaelic poetry on to a new plane, as MacDiarmid did with his lyrics. They should serve us as shields against parochialism and prove that by dealing with subjects outside the Gaelic world we do not have to abandon that which is specifically Gaelic in our work. While 'making it new' MacLean was operating from a traditional base. The confidence to absorb the material was, of course, a result of the pressure and may not be found often, but it is an ideal that one should not neglect.

I do not mean to lay down the laws for Gaelic poets nor to say that they must deal with contemporary issues outside their own world; but merely to say that it can be done and has been done by MacLean and other poets who followed him. A Gaelic poet *can* stand by a corpse in Africa and in writing about a dead German soldier, he can bring the weight and power of his own tradition to such a poem. One of the weaknesses of Gaelic poetry in the past was the narrowness of subject-matter but this need no longer be the case. *Dàin do Eimhir* proved once and for all that Gaelic poetry is capable of dealing with subject-matters which do not solely belong within its own geographic borders: a Gaelic poet can in fact be mentioned on the same level as the best poets of his time. This is enormously liberating, enormously bracing. And it is what *Dàin do Eimhir* did.

IAIN CRICHTON SMITH

Rudha Hùnais
Sròn △ Bhiornaill
Mol Steinnseil Stamhainn
Lìonacro

TRÒNDAIRNIS

RÒNAIDH
Uamha 'n Fhuamhaire

Liondail
BHATAIRNIS
Ròmasdal △ An Stòr

Boraraig
Aodann △ Bhàn
RATHARSAIR

Gleann △ Dail
An t-Aigeach
Dùn Bheagain
Càsteal Bhròchaill

An Eist Fhiadhaich
Port-rìgh
Screapadal
A' CHOMRAICH

DIÙRINIS
Cruachan An t-Inbhir
An Carn
An Eaglais Bhrèige

Suidh Fhinn
Beinn △ Balachuirn
Dùn Cana

Bràcadal
Beinn △ Dùnabhaig
Hallaig

Beinn △
Oskaig △ An Leac
Geusto
Duagraich
Clachan Na Feàrnaibh

Uamha 'n Òir
Loch △ Am
Aoighre
Corcal
Am Ploc

Rudha nan Clach
Port
Beinn Lì △ Bràigh
Craig Dallaig

Talasgar △
MINGINIS
SCALPAIDH
Druim Bhuidhe

Apriseal
An Clachan

Am Bioda Rua
△ Scarral Mosgaraidh
Loch Aills

Bràighe
Grùla △ An Màm
Ceann Loch

Aoineart
Mararaphlainn Aoineart

Brunnal
△ Sgurr nan Gillean
Srath Shuardail

AN CUILITHIONN

Sgurr Alasdair △
Blàthbheinn
AN SRATH

Garsbheinn △

Rudha an Dùnain
An
Aird △ Loch
Mòir Shlaopain

SÒGHAIDH

Dùn Sgàthaich

An Cuan Canach
SLÈITE

CANNA
Aird Shlèite

CNÒIDEART

RUM

Ceann
Loch
Nibheis

MÒRAIR
TUATH

Arasaig

IAR
EAR

EIGE

DEAS

AN T-EILEAN SGITHEANACH

CLÀR THOMHAIS MÌLE 12

Out from Skye to the World:
Literature, History and the Poet.

In 1940 those who were in touch with the Gaelic world would have felt a tremor of some intensity, for that year saw the publication of *Seventeen Poems for Sixpence,* a collection which contained eight characteristic poems in Gaelic by Sorley MacLean; but it was not till 1943 that the eruption occurred which permanently altered the landscape of Gaelic literature. In *Dàin do Eimhir agus Dàin Eile* (Poems to Eimhir and Other Poems), nearly a hundred pages of poetry burst out of the restrictions imposed by two centuries of inbreeding, and the energies that had lain dormant in the Gaelic language for so long arose like "ròs geal bristeadh fàire" (a white rose breaking the horizon).[1]

The craft of the professional poets of the fifteenth, sixteenth and seventeenth centuries, the passion of the anonymous seventeenth-century folk songs, the vehemence of Iain Lom (late 17th century), the vigour of Alasdair Mac Mhaighistir Alasdair (18th century), and the delicacy of Donnchadh Bàn (18th century) are some of the varied strands which meet in *Dàin do Eimhir* and were joined, for the first time, with the main European tradition, partly mediated through late Elizabethan literature.

The sixty poems of the Eimhir series are full of a tortured introspection like that expressed by John Ford (c.1586—?) in the following lines:

> I have too long suppressed my hidden flames
> That almost have consumed me; I have spent
> Many a silent night in sighs and groans;
> Ran over all my thoughts, depised my fate,
> Reasoned against the reasons of my love,
> Done all that smooth-cheeked virtue could advise,
> But found all bootless: 'tis my destiny
> That you must either love, or I must die.[2]

Few have more persistently "reasoned against the reasons" of their love than has MacLean, and nobody in Gaelic. The Gaelic poets had accepted love or suffered it, or sometimes treated it like a courtly toy. Nobody had ever expressed his thoughts about the whole extraordinary business in Gaelic until MacLean, who had discovered the poetry of Yeats, Baudelaire and Blok, was driven by his "hidden flames" to express himself in a manner as extravagant as that of Baudelaire's lines:

> J'implore ta pitié, Toi, l'unique que j'aime,
> Du fond du gouffre obscur où mon coeur est tombé.
> C'est un univers morne à l'horizon plombé
> Où nagent dans la nuit l'horreur et le blasphème . . .[3]

MacLean lacks Baudelaire's hot-house sensuality, but his passion and wealth of language transformed Gaelic poetry.

The transformation had been a long time in coming. W. J. Watson's *Bàrdachd Ghàidhlig, Specimens of Gaelic Poetry 1550-1900* (first published 1918) included as one of its most recent examples a 152-line poem about Niagara Falls by Rev. D. B. Blair (1815-93). The climax of the poem, if it can be said to have one at all, is probably the thirty-fifth verse:

Is 'n uair bhiodh tu 'nad sheasamh làimh ris,	When you're standing beside it,
B'amhlaidh thartar	the noise is like
Is mìle carbad air cabhsair	a thousand waggons on a causeway,
'Nan deann dol seachad.	rushing past.

The thirty-eighth and final verse boldly states that since the author is unable to list all the wonders, he will stop. Even the editor feels he ought to apologize, for he adds in a note: "The sudden ending is a feature not uncommon in Gaelic poetry. Compare the ending of Duncan MacIntyre's 'Beinn Dòbhrain'." Gaelic, it seemed, was not a language for formal concision or a language that would foster thought.

Nicolas Lenau (1802-50), a contemporary of Rev. Blair, also wrote a poem about the Niagara falls. He put more thought into eight verses than the Scottish divine could muster in thirty-eight. Lenau was not noted, however, for philosophical or speculative power: he was a poet of weeping-willow trees and of the melancholy moods of nature:

> Den der Wandrer fern vernommen,
> Niagaras tiefen Fall
> Hört er nicht, herangekommen,
> Weil zu laut der Wogenschall.
>
> Und so mag vergebens lauschen,
> Wer dem Sturze näher geht;
> Doch die Zukunft hörte rauschen
> In der Ferne der Prophet.[4]

Gaelic poetry in the 1930s had yet to catch up with Lenau, not to mention Baudelaire, Blok and Yeats.

The spiritual affinity between MacLean and Baudelaire is most obvious in their use of the symbol of the abyss. Baudelaire's 'gouffre' becomes, in MacLean's Gaelic, "an slochd sgreataidh", the loathsome pit that swallows up man's aspirations; " 'na shlocan sgreagach fuaraidh gun chur", the chill, rocky, untilled pit that drains the generosity of youth; and "crithich an uamhais"[5], the frightful quagmire from which the soul can hardly escape. The pit has its physical embodiment in the marsh of Mararaulin, north of the Cuillin hills at the head of Glen Brittle:

. . . chunnaic mi bho àird a' Chuilithinn	I saw from the height of the Cuillin
gathadh glòir is breòiteachd duilghe:	a flash of glory and a grievous frailty;
chunnaic mi òradh lainnir gréine	I saw the golden glitter of the sun
agus boglach dhubh na bréine:	and the black and filthy marsh:
's eòl dhomh seirbheachd gheur an spioraid	I know the sharp bitterness of the spirit
na's fhèarr na aoibhneas luath a' chridhe.	better than the swift joy of the heart.

In *Dàin do Eimhir,* as in Baudelaire's *Les Fleurs du Mal,* more than one cycle of love-poems can be discerned. In *Selected Poems 1932-1972* these love-poems are conveniently divided into four sections: it seems likely that the Eimhir of the title subsumes what Thomas Campion called "a fair pomp of glittering ladies". The two most important sections or cycles are 'An Roghainn' and 'An Tràigh Thathaich'. 'An Roghainn' is inspired by a fair-haired woman who is an image of unattainable beauty: 'An Tràigh Thathaich' is inspired by another woman who causes him the most bitter anguish, as is clear from the poems 'An Dithis' and 'Aithreachas' which were originally *Dàin do Eimhir*, XLVI and XLVII, but withheld from publication until 1970, since the poet's wounds were still raw in 1941 when a publisher was being sought for *Dàin do Eimhir*.

The title poem of 'An Roghainn' combines a Baudelairean sophistication with the directness of the Gaelic songs that MacLean heard in his youth. The quatrain form, the outwardly dry tone, and the divided self in conversation are remarkably akin to Baudelaire's 'Toute Entière' [6] where the poet and his other self discuss the beloved who dazzles like the dawn and consoles like the night:

> Le Démon, dans ma chambre haute,
> Ce matin est venu me voir,
> Et tâchant à me prendre en faute,
> Me dit: 'Je voudrais bien savoir . . .

MacLean walks "with his reason" by the sea:

Choisich mi cuide ri mo thuigse	I walked with my reason
a-muigh ri taobh a' chuain;	out beside the sea.
bha sinn còmhla ach bha ise	We were together but it was
a' fuireach tiotan bhuam.	waiting a little away from me.
An sin thionndaidh i ag ràdha:	Then it turned saying:
a bheil e fìor gun cual	Is it true you heard
thu gu bheil do ghaol geal àlainn	that your beautiful white love
a' pòsadh tràth Di-luain?	is to marry early on Monday?

The matter-of-factness of the first four lines suddenly breaks into words that are reminiscent of the old song:

'S olc an sgeul a chuala mi	I heard bad news
Di Luain an déidh Di-Dòmhnaich,	on the Monday following the Sunday,
Sgeul nach bu mhath lium e —	news that brought me no pleasure—
Mo leannan dol a phòsadh.[7]	my sweetheart was going to be married.

The 'choice' of the title is that between a woman and a war, between love of a human and love of humanity, but the alternative turns out to be false, for not going to the war means losing the woman. Only an heroic love is worthy of the name. In the context of the Spanish Civil War, during which the poem was written, a declaration of love became, in effect, a political declaration. The 'I' of the poem does not declare for either the woman or the war, but follows what MacLean calls the 'low way':

Cha do lean mi ach an t-slighe chrìon	I followed only the small mean way,
bheag ìosal thioram thlàth.	the way that is low, dry and meek,
Is ciamar sin a choinnichinn	and how then should I meet
ri beithir-theine ghràidh?	a thunderbolt of love?

MacLean dramatizes a dilemma of love versus politics that must have worried many at the time. The autobiographical elements in a poem do not make it an autobiography and MacLean cannot have identified himself wholly with the 'I' of the poem, for in 'Trì Slighean' he writes that he could have followed the mean, dry, low way but did not, because of his passionate involvement:

B'urrainn, mur b'e am fiaradh	I could have, were it not that my mind
a chuireadh 'nam aigne dà bhliadhna	had been given its bent during these two years
le m' dhùthaich fhìn is càs na Spàinnte,	by my own country and the plight of Spain,
cridhe feargach is nighinn àlainn.[8]	by my passionate heart and by a beautiful woman.

It was, in fact, the economic circumstances of his family that prevented MacLean from going to Spain, but the emotional tensions of 'The Choice' ring true, and are concentrated in the final verse:

Ach nan robh 'n roghainn rithist dhomh	But if I had the choice again
's mi 'm sheasamh air an àird,	and were standing on the headland,
leumainn á neamh no iutharna	I would leap from heaven or hell
le spiorad 's cridhe slàn.	with a whole heart and spirit.

Such a leap from a headland would usually be *to* heaven or hell: Baudelaire, in 'Le Voyage', wished to plunge into the abyss, careless whether he would come to heaven or hell. But MacLean is referring to the ecstasies and torments of love and sees that only by abandoning them, by leaping *from* them, can his heart and spirit become whole. The final verse affirms an heroic resolution, but the phrase "If I had the choice again" betrays a subconscious fear that one's second choice might be no different from the first. There are no second chances in life. It is this hint of uncertainty behind the resolution that gives the poem much of its poignancy.

When MacLean was in Mull in 1938, an island closely associated with the history of the Clan MacLean, he wrote a poem called 'Ban-Ghàidheal' which is filled with passionate indignation about the plight of those who had to spend their lives at the "dubh-chosnadh" (the black labour), a term which means not only hard outdoor work, but work in lieu of rent. 'Blackwork' in the sense of working for the landlord without wages had existed for at least three centuries.

The poem plainly expresses MacLean's *animus* against landlords and clerics, in this case those of the Established Church of Scotland, who were mostly drawn from the landlord class. The Established Church, or Kirk, was in effect a tool of the landlords and its ministers were ready to interpret the destruction of communities carried out by the landlords or their agents as instances of God's wrath against a sinful generation. In the first quarter of the nineteenth century, many of the highland chiefs made a fortune out of seaweed which was burnt into kelp and sold as manure, but the poem is not without its contemporary applications.

After the crash of the Wall Street Stock-market in 1929 and the succeeding economic recession that reached Europe at the start of the Thirties, the struggle for existence changed from being a cliché into a painful reality. The course of history appeared to confirm Marx's prediction of the imminent collapse of capitalism, but hopes of the millenium were shaken by the outbreak of the Spanish Civil War in 1936. Few had any idea of the complexity of Spanish internal politics and the war appeared to be a straightforward struggle between socialists and fascists. The general strike which was organised by the socialist trade union, the Unión General de Trabajadores, in 1934, had culminated in the armed rising of the Asturian miners which so terrified the Bourgeoisie that Spain's hereditary enemies, the Moors, were called in to crush it. This episode might be considered the first battle of the Civil War and it certainly left its mark on MacLean, who writes with a feeling of envy about:

am mèinear Spàinnteach a' leum ri cruadal   the Spanish miner leaping into danger
is 'anam mórail dol sìos gun bhruaillean.   and his proud soul going down purposefully.

MacLean felt a special sympathy for the Englishman, John Cornford, who went to fight against the rebel army in Spain three weeks after the Civil War began, and whose poem beginning:

> Heart of the heartless world,
> Dear heart, the thought of you
> Is the pain at my side,
> The shadow that chills my view.
>
> The wind rises in the evening,
> Reminds that autumn is near.
> I am afraid to lose you,
> I am afraid of my fear . . .

indicated a struggle between private love and public duty that paralleled MacLean's. Cornford later wrote that he had gone to Spain "with the intention of staying a few days, firing a few shots, and then coming home" and his father claimed that in Spain John had found an escape from 'personal responsibilities'. Doubtless, like many others, his motives were not of the purest, and not, at first, untainted by naive romanticism, but once involved he realized that "You can't play at civil war".

MacLean's long poem 'Urnuigh', which is about the necessity, and difficulty, of purifying the Spirit before one can attain one's goal, refers to the verses above.

Bha seo aig Cornford òg 'na ghaisge,   Heroic young Cornford felt this:
eagal smuain a ghaoil bhith faisg air   he was afraid to think of his love at his side
nuair bha an Spàinn 'na latha-traisg dha;   when Spain had become a fast-day for him;
eagal a challa air an duine,   the man was afraid of his loss,
eagal an eagail air a' churaidh.   the warrior was afraid of his fear.

Another hero of the times was Dimitrov, who is mentioned in Cornford's 'Full Moon at Tierz', as well as in 'Urnuigh'. Cornford writes:

> Three years ago Dimitrov fought alone
> And we stood taller when he won.
> But now the Leipzig dragon's teeth
> Sprout strong and handsome against death,
> And here an army fights where there was one.

Georgi Dimitrov was a Bulgarian Communist who was arrested in 1933 on the trumped-up charge of having set fire to the Reichstag buildings. He conducted his own defence at his trial in Leipzig, making a fool of Goering, his prosecutor, which explains the reference in 'Dol An Iar':

. . . Dimitrov air bialaibh cùirte   Dimitrov facing the court,
    a' bualadh eagail le ghlag gàire   defeating fear with his hearty laugh.

Dimitrov found sanctuary in Russia, from where he returned after the war to become leader of Communist Bulgaria.

The poems, not more than six, in which MacLean mentions Spain, are not 'Civil War Poems', but poems about mental conflict; 'An Roghainn' is the most concise and effective; 'Urnuigh' is the most complex and anguished. The title 'Urnuigh' indicates in Gaelic a specifically religious prayer, and the language used in the poem is full of Biblical echoes, but the poem works by continually disappointing one's expectations of what a prayer should be: "co-chomunn dìomhair an anama ri Dia trìd Chrìosd" (the soul's mysterious association with God through Christ) in the words of Rev. Dr Norman MacLeod (1783-1862)[9]. The first stanza contradicts the psalmist's "God is our refuge and strength" by asserting that there is no refuge, but at the same time it admits that the request has not the sincerity of a true prayer, thus creating the paradox of an unbeliever making a prayer he knows to be inefficacious:

A chionn nach eil dìon ann
agus a chionn nach eil m' iarrtas
ach 'na fhaileas faoin sgialachd,
chan eil ann ach: dèanam làidir
M' aigne fhìn an aghaidh àmhghair.

Because there is no refuge
and because my request
is only a vain shadow of a fiction, there is
only:
let me strengthen my own mind against
anguish.

The anguish was caused by the rising of 1934 and renewed by the Civil War of 1936 in which Cornford purified himself— "Spain had become a fast-day for him" — and also by the recession of the Thirties which had raised the spectre of "a' ghort air na raointean" (the famine in the fields). It was a political and economic situation in which it must have seemed natural to many to seek guidance in prayer. MacLean asks despairingly:

Ach saoil sibh an dèan mi ùrnuigh
ri m' spiorad fhìn an aghaidh m' ùidhe,
stad mo chridhe, dalladh shùilean?
An guidh mi do ghaol bhith air a shracadh
á friamhaichean mo chridhe thachdte?

But do you think I will pray
to my own spirit against my desire,
stoppage of my heart, blinding of eyes?
Will I beg that love of you be torn
from the roots of my strangled heart?

The poet as hero can make the choice between "bàs 'sa' bheatha bhiothbhuain no beatha bhàsail" (death into eternal life or a death-like life): the young Cuchulainn preferred a hero's reputation to a single day of life, but the poet as lover would take "the deathly life": " 's gum b'fheàrr liom boireannach na 'n Eachdraidh fhàsmhor" (for I preferred a woman to History in its course).

The poet knows, in the words of Christopher Caudwell, that "The Spanish People's Army needs help badly; their struggle, if they fail, will certainly be ours tomorrow . . ."; he knows that only by completely stripping his heart of the softness of his love will he be able to stand for his political ideals against the horsemen (marc-shluagh) of death and famine that have been released, not by the opening of the seals of the Apocalypse, but by the betrayal of the cause of the people. And so he prays, but although he prays to no God he is impelled to describe his prayer as blasphemous:

'S e 'n ùrnuigh seo guidhe na duilghe,
an guidhe toibheumach neo-iomlan,
guidhe cam coirbte an tionndaidh,
an guidhe gun dèan mi guidhe,
gun ghuidhe 'n t-susbaint a ruigheachd.

This prayer is the sorry difficult plea,
the blasphemous incomplete plea,
the crooked corrupt plea of turning,
the plea that will allow me to plead
without pleading to reach the substance.

God is without "variableness or shadow of turning",[10] but MacLean prays to his own spirit which is not "one-fold" (aon-fhillte) as though striving to follow the Biblical injunction: "Purify your hearts, ye double minded".[11]

He cannot allow his prayer for wholeness to be granted for that would be to blaspheme against his love: her cause is as urgent and pure as the cause of Spain. And the prayer ends as it began, with a rejection of divine intervention and a despairing acceptance of the flawed nature of humanity.

A chionn nach cuirear coire air diathan,	Because the gods are not to be blamed,
nach eil ach 'nam faileas iarraidh,	for they are only a reflection of our longing,
agus a sheachnadh an duine Crìosda,	and to avoid the man called Christ,
chan eil mo chaomhachd ris an Nàdur	I do not feel friendly towards Nature
a thug an tuigse shoilleir shlàn dhomh,	who gave me my sound clear understanding,
an eanchainn shingilte 's an cridhe sgàinte.	my single-minded brain and my torn heart.

MacLean has described how he became a Socialist in his early teens. He was brought up on Raasay in the tradition of the Free Presbyterian Church which seceded from the Free Church of Scotland in 1893. The Free Church itself had seceded from the Established Church in the great Disruption of 1843. Calvinism did not encourage dissent, but it certainly bred it. And when MacLean felt that the Free Presbyterians were not supporting the tradition of dissent, he 'seceded' and became a socialist.

Given his strong socialist convictions it is little wonder that he should have felt impelled to write "a very long poem, 10,000 words or so, on the human condition, radiating from the history of Skye to the West Highlands to Europe and what I knew of the rest of the world". This poem, 'An Cuilithionn', was begun in 1939, but work on it ceased in the same year due to the experiences which gave rise to the poems in 'An Tràigh Thathaich', the fourth section of the Selected Poems. The few parts of 'An Cuilithionn' that have been published show the poet, standing on the Cuillin Hills, and looking over Skye, whose great promontories of Duirinish, Waternish and Trotternish lie on the water like the wings of a great dead bird, and he recalls "eachdraidh chianail an eilein àlainn"[13] (the sad history of the beautiful island).

The saddest part of that history was the Clearances. When the clan system was destroyed after the Rising of 1745 and the Battle of Culloden, the relationship between chief and clansmen, which had been based on ties of kinship, degenerated into a merely economic relationship of landlord and tenant. The anglified chiefs evicted their tenants without pity or scruple in order to turn their holdings into more profitable grazing land for sheep, and deer forests.

Even before the 'Forty-five, MacDonald of Sleat and MacLeod of Dunvegan had sold some of their people, including some of their relatives, as indentured servants for the Carolinas in 1739. The ship onto which they were driven was named Long nan Daoine, or the Ship of the People. This first slave-ship to carry people from the Hebrides is recalled with bitterness in Part VI of 'An Cuilithionn' in the words of a Highland girl who was forced into slavery:

Fhuair mise diachainn gun fhaochadh	I endured hardship without cease
bho 'n latha chuireadh mi air Long nan Daoine	from the day I was put on the Ship of the People.
Bha mi 'n Geusdo a' buain maoraich	I was in Gesto gathering shellfish
an uair a ghlacadh mi 's mi 'm aonar.[14]	and I was seized, being alone.

The ship is also mentioned in 'Gaoir na h-Eòrpa' where it can be taken as representative of slave-ships in general. The girl who was kidnapped in Gesto is said to have been met by a Highlander in the King's army in America who asked her the time. She could not understand his English or his French, but when he spoke in Gaelic she replied: "am crodhadh chaorach mu dhà thaobh Beinn Dubhagraich" (It is the time one folds the sheep on the slopes of Ben Duagraich).

Emigrant ships left Skye in the 1770s carrying about 2,000 people, but after 1792, known as Bliadhna nan Caorach or The Year of the Sheep, evictions increased and whole communities were 'cleared' to make way for sheep. In 1846 the last MacGille Chaluim, or MacLeod of Raasay, sold the island of Raasay to an Edinburgh man who shipped 129 families to Australia and banished others to the small bare island of Rona. In Mull of the MacLeans the population was reduced by half between 1821 and 1881. Not until 1882, after the Battle of the Braes (Blàr a' Chumhaing) in Skye, was it decided to set up a Commission to listen to the complaints of the crofters. The evictions ceased, but the prophecy of Mary MacPherson (1821-98) was never fulfilled:

'S tillidh gineal na tuatha	The country folk
Rinneadh fhuadach thar sàile	who were driven overseas will return
'S bidh na baigearan uasal	and the beggarly gentry
Air an ruaig mar bha iadsan.	will be expelled as *they* were.
Féidh is caoraich 'gan cuibhleadh,	Deer and sheep will be wheeled around
'S bidh na glinn air an àiteach . . .	and the valleys will be reinhabited . . .
'S théid na tobhtachan fuara	the cold ruined houses
Thogail suas le ar càirdean.	will be rebuilt by our kinsmen.

The emigrants did not return and pine forests took the place of deer as deer had taken the place of sheep, for trees had become more profitable than deer or sheep.

The episode of the girl from Gesto is followed by the most traditional of MacLean's poems, a gentle lyric in praise of Skye, in simple strophic form, much used by the seventeenth-century poets Iain Lom and Mary MacLeod.

Am Bràcadal	In Bracadale
nam bruthach cas	of the steep slopes
nan cluaintean glas', tha m'ùidh;	and green meadows is my desire.
am Minginis	in Minginis
as grinne slios,	of the fairest mountainsides
as guirme pris, mo rùn.[16]	and greenest bushes is my love.

Much of 'An Cuilithionn' is over-rhetorical, praising heroism and denouncing the exploitation of the poor with excessively simplistic fervour. The Cuillin hills stand for heroic struggle, the marsh at their base for the sickness of the world that neither Christianity nor socialism has been able to cure, let alone prevent. The conclusion of the poem is an apocalyptic rendering of the eternal quest for "an nì do-ruighinn" (the inaccessible thing), the quest that appears in many guises throughout his poetry. Heart, brain and intellect are all engaged on this quest and feed on man's impetuous blood:

Ròs dubh a' Chuilithinn ghuinich	The black rose of the sharp-wounding Cuillin,
dearg le fuil cridhe 'n duine;	red with the blood of man's heart;
ròs ciar na h-eanchainne glaise	the dim rose of the grey brain,
dearg le tuar na fala braise;	red with the hue of the impetuous blood;
ròs geal tuigse nan saoi	the white rose of the philosophic intellect
dearg leis an fhuil gun chlaoidh,	red with the unoppressed blood;

ròs dearg treuntais nan laoch   the red rose of hero courage,
thar mullach shléibhtean 'na chaoir . . . [17]   aflame above the mountain summit.

It is likely that the form of 'An Cuilithionn' — "a long meditative rant interspersed
with lyrics" — was inspired by Hugh MacDiarmid's *A Drunk Man Looks at the
Thistle* (1926) but MacLean's poem, as far as one can judge by the less than 400
lines that have been published, lacks the wealth of reference and metaphor and the
extraordinary variety and flexibility that make the former such a stimulating, and
indeed amusing, poem. MacLean's tone verges on the strident, as does Pablo
Neruda's in his immense poem on the history of Chile, *Canto General*. Neruda's
poem, written in the 1940s, also makes man's exploitation of man one of its main
themes, and has as its central symbol the heights of Macchu Picchu, an emblem as
meaningful in its context as the Cuillin in the poetry of MacLean. There are fine
things in 'An Cuilithionn', as there are in *Canto General*, but the quieter passages
can be more effective than the noisy ones. The episode of the girl from Gesto has
many parallels in *Canto General,* as in the following extract:

. . . a unos señores trabaja,   she works for some gentry,
   lavándoles, pues, la ropa.   doing their laundry.
   Hambre pasábamos, capitán,   We suffered hunger, captain,
   y con una varilla golpeaban   and they beat my mother
   a mi madre todos los días.   with a switch every day.
   Por eso me hice minero.   So I became a miner.
   Me escapé por las grandes sierras . . . [18]   I ran away over the high mountains . . .

'An Cuilithionn' is a *Canto General* in embryo, and in its unabridged form is likely
to have suffered from Neruda's faults of inflated language and gigantism. The
worthiest propaganda does not make the best poetry, as can be seen in
MacDiarmid's doggerel:

> In short, any utterance that is not pure
> Propaganda is impure propaganda for sure! [19]

It is to the Presbyterian tradition that we must look to find one of the most
powerful influences on the poetry of MacLean, whether as socialist or love-poet.
MacLean dismisses the Church, but the use of religious terminology comes
naturally to him for he was brought up in one of the strictest Calvinist sects and his
language has much in common with that of Dugald Buchanan[20]. The nightmare
quality of Buchanan's 'Là a' Bhreitheanais' (The Day of Judgement) has many
parallels in MacLean's poetry and the lines on the resurrection of the unrighteous
from the "sloc" (pit) could have suggested MacLean's:

. . . boglach oillteil ghrànda   . . . the ugly loathsome morass
's am bheil a' bhùirdeasachd a' bàthadh . . . [21]   where the bourgeoisie are drowning . . .

in *Dàin do Eimhir*, XXXIV. Buchanan writes:

Dùisgear na h-aingidh suas 'nan déigh,   Then will the wicked be roused up,
Mar bhéisdean gairisneach as an t-sloc;   like hideous monsters out of the pit;
'S o ifrinn thig an anama truagh   and their pitiful souls will come from hell
Thoirt coinneamh uamhasach d'an corp.   to make the horrible rendezvous with their
                                              bodies.

'N sin labhraidh 'n t-anam brònach, truagh[22]   Then the wretched mournful soul

R'a cholainn oillteil, uamhar, bhreun . . .   will speak to its foul, loathsome and repulsive
                                                flesh . . .

and certainly the apparition in MacLean's 'An Trom-laighe' has also risen from
such company in the pit:

. . . straon an ceann oillteil   . . . the loathsome head started
bho chùl a' bhalla 'n clisgeadh;   suddenly from behind the wall
is rinn na cràgan ciara   and the long foul dark fingers
fada bréine mo sgòrnan   seized my throat in a rapid grip.
a ghlacadh an greim obann.

Likewise Buchanan envisages the fires of the Last Day, "Mar fhalaisg ris na
sléibhtibh cas" [23] (like a moor-burning racing up the steep mountains); and
MacLean had once hoped to see "the brittle fire-wood of money" going up in smoke
— "b'e falaisgir an àigh" (It would have been a splendid moor-burning).

The eternities of religion and the eternities of love are often expressed in similar
terms; the vast desert of time called eternity is for MacLean a "cuan gun tràghadh"
(an unebbing sea) and, for Buchanan, a "chuain ata gun tràigh". Both show a like
intentness in attempting to measure it. Buchanan writes:

Ged àir'mhinn uile reulta néimh,   Though I counted all the stars of heaven,
Gach feur is duilleach riamh a dh'fhàs,   each grassblade and leaf that ever grew,
Mar ris gach braon ata sa' chuan   along with every drop that is in the sea
'S gach gaineamh chuairticheas an tràigh;   and each grain of sand the shore collects;
Ged chuirinn mìle bliadhna seach,   though I lived a thousand years
As leth gach aon diubh sud go léir,   for each one of them all,
Cha d' imich seach de'n t-sìorruidheachd   no more of vast eternity would have passed
                                  mhóir
Ach mar gun tòisicheadh i 'n dé. [25]   than if it had begun yesterday.

MacLean, with his great love of place, localizes the image in 'Tràighean':

Agus nan robh sinn cuideachd   And if we were together
air tràigh Chalgaraidh am Muile,   on the shore of Calgary in Mull,
eadar Alba is Tiriodh,   between Scotland and Tiree,
eadar an saoghal 's a' bhiothbhuan,   between the world and the everlasting,
dh' fhuirichinn an sud gu luan   I would stay there till the last day
a' tomhas gainmhich bruan ar bhruan.   measuring sand grain by grain.
Agus an Uidhist air tràigh Hòmhstaidh   And in Uist on the strand of Homhsta
fa chomhair farsuingeachd na h-ònrachd,   facing the vastness of the solitude
dh' fheithinn-sa an sud gu sìorruidh   I would wait there eternally,
braon air bhraon an cuan a' sìoladh.   the sea diminishing drop by drop.

When Buchanan speaks of God hidden away even from the angels "Far nach ruig
sùil no smuain 'na chòir" [26] (where neither eye nor thought can reach him), he
might be speaking of those depths where MacLean sees all human beauties
vanishing away in his poem 'An Tathaich':

Dé 'n t-sùil a nì am faicinn   What eye can see them
no chluas a nì an claisteachd   or what ear can hear them
's iad air turus faondraidh   as they go on an exposed straying course
bharr smaointean aigne?   beyond a mind's thoughts?

Buchanan, like MacLean, castigated landlords who were "a' feannadh" [27]
(flaying) the tenants, and the warrior in his poem of that title, as well as struggling

against the lusts of the flesh, fights against "gach bochdainn 's dòruinn ta san t-saogh'l" [28] (every poverty and pain in the world), a phrase that would be very much at home in 'An Cuilithionn'.

The poems written about the Spanish Civil War belong to the cycle of the fair-haired Irish woman; a short poem called 'An Dùn-Eideánn 1939' may mark the transition between that cycle and the cycle of the other, the Scottish woman. The poet writes that, despite the murderous commotion in Germany and France, he will remember two evenings he spent in the same house:

Am bliadhna roghainn na h-Albann	This year the flower of Scotland,
An nighean ruadh, clàr na gréine;	the red haired girl with the sunlit forehead;
'S a' bhòn-uiridh an nighean bhàn,	and the year before last the fair-haired girl,
Roghainn àlainn na h-Eireann.[29]	the beautiful flower of Ireland.

Spain and those two years of questioning have passed; now the war has come and the Scottish girl, the girl of 'The Haunted Ebb' poems, has raised her face which in the poem 'Crìonnachd' has the power "chur caochlaidh air conn" (to kill reason) and has taken possession of the poet.

This Scottish 'Eimhir' breaches the defences of the poet's heart, attacks him with his own weapons of love, destroys his peace of mind, and upsets the proportions of his world, and yet he cannot do without her. He describes what she has done in 'Am Mùr Gorm' and in its final verse marvels at the strange co-existence of love, reason and poetry:

Agus air creachainn chéin fhàsmhoir	And on a distant luxuriant bare summit
chinn blàthmhor Craobh nan Teud,	there grew the blossoming Tree of Strings,
'na meangach duillich t' aodann,	and among its leafy branches your face,
mo chiall is aogas réil.	my reason and the appearance of a star.

'The Tree of Strings' or 'The Harp Tree' is the title of one of the greatest compositions for the Highland bagpipe and its title is so evocative that it tempted MacLean to unite manifold expressions of the human predicament in one long poem, to which 'Am Mùr Gorm' might have served as a coda. In the poem 'Craobh nan Teud',[30] the tree that flourishes on the bare summit feeds on the poverty and suffering of humanity and the rustling of its leaves becomes music and poetry. The music is above all that of the two Patricks: Patrick Mór MacCrimmon and his son, Patrick Og MacCrimmon, who were hereditary pipers to MacLeod of Dunvegan between 1640 and 1730. Patrick Mór composed the famous pibroch 'Cumha na Cloinne' (Lament for the Children) when his family died of fever; Patrick Og founded the school of piping at Boreraig. The beautiful pibroch 'Maol Donn' (The Brown-Polled Cow) is attributed to a MacCrimmon and known in English as 'MacCrimmon's Sweetheart'. These two laments are not only woven into 'Craobh nan Teud' but also into the opening of Part II of 'An Cuilithionn':

Air Sgurr Dubh an Dà Bheinn	On the Black Pinnacle of the Two Bens
thàinig guth gu m' chluais a' seinn,	a voice came singing to my ear,
Pàdraig Mór 's a cheòl ag caoineadh	Patrick Mor with his music lamenting
uile chlann a' chinne daonna.	all the children of the human race.
Agus feasgar air a' Ghàrsbheinn	And one evening on the Garsven
bha ceòl eile ann a thàinig,	there was another music that came,
Maol Donn agus ùrlar sàth-ghaoil	Maol Donn and its theme of the fullness of love
a' bristeadh cridhe nan fonn àluinn.[31]	breaking the heart of the beautiful tunes.

The poetry mentioned in 'Craobh nan Teud' is above all that of the Blind Harper, Ruairi Dall MacMhuirich (Roderick Morrison) who lived from around 1646-1725 and would have known both MacCrimmons. His celebrated 'Song to MacLeod of Dunvegan' [32] laments the decay of the old Gaelic customs and reproves the young chief for deserting his homeland and aping English ways. Not only were the Highland chiefs no longer the patrons and protectors of musicians and poets, but they also ill-treated their tenantry in order to raise the extra money needed for their new way of life. The song takes the form of a dialogue between Echo and the poet:

Chaidh Mac-alla as an Dùn	Echo had left the Castle
an am sgarachdainn dùinn ri 'r triath;	when we parted from our chief;
's ann a thachair e rium	I then met him as he
air seacharan bheann is shliabh;[32]	wandered over mountains and moorland.

The poet ends by asking Echo to bear a message to the young chief, telling Roderick MacLeod to remember the example of his father who had never allowed Dunvegan castle to be without music and song.

MacCrimmon and the Blind Harper are not the only voices in 'The Tree of Strings'. They are joined by O'Rahilly (1670-1726), the Irishman who wrote the noble 'Gile na Gile' (Brightness of Brightness), a vision of Ireland personified as a beautiful woman waiting to be rescued by the Stuart Pretender; and by William Ross (1762-90), celebrated for the Gaelic Songs he wrote about his unhappy love-affair. There is also the voice of an anonymous poet, speaking for Deirdre, who describes the places in Scotland where she found happiness before returning to Ireland with Naoise and his two brothers:

Glend Eitci! O'n Glend Eitci!	Glen Etive!
Ann do togbhus mo chét tig;	There I raised my first house,
Alaind a fidh iar néirghe	beautiful are its woods in the morning,
Buaile gréne Glend Eitchi . . .	Glen Etive, the fold of sunlight . . .
Glend Daruadh! O'n Glend Daruadh!	Glen Da Ruadh!
Mo chen gach fer da na dúal;	My love to everyone who inherits it;
Is binn guth cuaich ar craib cruim	sweet is the cry of the cuckoo on the bending branch
Ar in mbinn os Glend Daruadh.[33]	on the summit above Gleann Da Ruadh . . .

Homer joins the company with a glimpse of Priam prostrating himself before Achilles in order to beg for his son's body; so do Shakespeare and Baudelaire. The latter expresses his sympathy for the Parisian prostitutes in their old age and decrepitude — alone and disregarded, though, their names were once in everybody's mouth: "Dont autrefois les noms par tous étaient cités". "Les Petites Vieilles" he called them in the poem of that name. The last poet to be mentioned is Alexander Blok (1880-1921), for he alone of those mentioned foresaw the spiritual destiny of Russia — "ar-a-mach mór dearg an duine" (the great red revolution of man). It is true that Baudelaire had been a socialist, but after the repression of the Parisian revolt of 1848 he lost his interest in politics.

It was a risky course to bring all these names together in one poem, but it succeeds, firstly because MacLean has used the all-embracing 'Tree of Strings' as his dominating image, and secondly he has imbued all these figures with a slant of his own: they have all become honorary Celts. It is possible that he feels closest to the Blind Harper to whom "the Echo came unsought, blind Roderick agitated by the pricks of humiliated pride":

's am Mac-talla thàinig gun shireadh
gu Ruairi Dall is e air iomairt
le àrdan tàmailte 'ga bhioradh.[35]

They are brothers in pride as well as poetry. The unsought Echo, the "faodail" or treasure that is chanced on by accident, is inspiration, one of the gifts of the 'Tree of Strings'. MacLean has told us how three poems came to him[36] "gun shireadh" (without seeking): 'Na Samhlaidhean', 'Coin is Madaidhean-Allaidh' and the conclusion of 'An Cuilthionn' came to him in his sleep and had only to be written down, headlong inspirations in which words take wing, unencumbered. Here are the last two lines of 'Na Samhlaidhean':

Falbhaidh iad 'nan ròs air sléibhtean	They will go, a rose on the mountains
far bheil grian nam bàrd ag éirigh.[37]	where the sun of the poets is rising.

'Craobh nan Teud' ends, as did 'Am Mùr Gorm', with the apparition of a face among the branches. The poet sees the face and the tree as two in one, so inseparable have love and poetry become to him. And yet — only the tree is eternal, the face will fade, and "Cinnichidh an ròs gun chluaine dh' aindeoin tiormachd ghlas nam fuaran" [38] (the truthful rose will grow in spite of the grey dryness of the springs).

Another long poem with a central symbol is 'Coilltean Ratharsair', and here the woods provide an even richer symbol than the single tree, with their many-coloured, symbolic helmets and their restless intricacy. On Iona there is an ancient slab bearing an effigy of MacLean of the Ross of Mull, wearing a saffron shirt and a pointed mediaeval helmet. One of MacLean's ancestors, "Ruairi Beag a' chlogaid dhrìlsich" (Little Roderick of the glittering helmet), who is mentioned in the 'Elegy for Calum MacLean', was one of those whose steel helmet well became him, as the old songs used to say:

Clogad cruadhach 's suaicheantas dearg ort

Dhan maith thig clogaide cruadhach.[39]

He was Roderick Matheson (fl.c.1600-30) from Glas na Muclaich in Lochalsh, and Mary Matheson, MacLean's paternal grandmother, was descended from him. So a helmet well becomes Sorley MacLean, but the helmets bestowed by the Woods of Raasay, though they glitter, are not made of steel. Instead, they are helmets of "sharpness", of "tranquillity", of "temptation" and of "pride": "the strange pride of the MacLeans";[40] the pride that was "a battlement on the excess of my love" [41]; the pride that led the MacLeans to their "léirchreach", their destruction, and not only at Inverkeithing.

'Coilltean Ratharsair' is an extraordinary and mysterious poem. The opening is a richly assonantal and rhythmically hypnotic paean to the woods which are seen as that rare and precious object of desire — "an leug fhaodail dhrithleannach" (the sparkling jewel chanced on by accident). As in a later poem, 'Eadh is Féin is Sàr-fhéin', the woods appear to stand for all the rich, unworked material that lies in the bottom of the poet's mind, the humus of the imagination.

Suddenly, after 88 lines, rhythm and mood change and a face troubles the quietness of the woods. The rest of the poem maintains a shifting equilibrium between the "many-coloured waulking" of the woods and, across the water, the pinnacles of the Cuillin, no longer hard and inaccessible, but crumbling on an unsteady base. Snakes appear beneath the foliage, now that the Cuillin is no longer a barrier, and Actaeon is seen, pursued not by his own hounds but by "an triùir bhan-dia chuimir rùisgte" (the three shapely naked goddesses) who can only be Hera, Athene and Aphrodite — wealth, wisdom and love. In this transformation and jarring conflation of the myths of Diana bathing and of Paris presenting the Apple of Discord, Actaeon is pursuer as well as pursued and the torment externalized in the myths is back in the poet's mind. The goddesses fade back into the woodland of which they are an emanation, and when the vision of beauty is gone the Cuillin is seen to be "prann, briste, an sloc sgreataidh" (crumbled and broken, in a disgusting pit). The poet is voicing his dissatisfaction with the symbol of the Cuillin: it cannot help him to believe with "feoil, eanchainn 's le cridhe" (flesh, intellect and heart) that there is something beautiful and accessible that will not succumb to time, a theme which links the poem with 'An Tathaich' in 'The Haunted Ebb' poems; nor can the Cuillin suggest any answer to the despairing question:

Dé fàth bhith toirt do nighinn	Why give a woman
gaol mar ghormadh speur	love like the skies becoming blue
ag éirigh as a chamhanaich	as they rise out of the dawnlight,
gu lomnochd ri gréin?	nakedly facing the sun?

Every reason, one might reply: but if the love is not reciprocated then there is no simple answer. 'The Woods of Raasay' is a forerunner of those later poems of despair, 'An Ceann Thall' and 'A' Bheinn air Chall', where human endeavour is seen to be without hope and without direction. In 'An Ceann Thall', even the idyll of Deirdre and Naoise, and Naoise's brothers Aillean and Ardan, "ceathrar ainmeil a' bhròin" (the sorrowful four famous ones), is seen to be tainted:

Seo an t-àite mu dheireadh	This is the final place
an déidh bòsd curanta do spéis,	after the valorous vaunting of your hope,
an ceann thall far nach eil tilleadh	the further end where there is no returning,
ach bristeadh cridhe 's uaill gheur.	only heartbreak and bitter pride.

A group of very personal poems appeared in *Lines Review* 34, some of which were originally parts of *Dàin do Eimhir*, and the rest date from 1941. Among them are 'Aithreachas', 'Am Barr Glas', and 'Ma Théid Mi Suas Do 'n Bhail' ud Shuas'.

The last ('Ma Théid mi Suas do 'n Bhail' ud Shuas') is a quotation from 'Oran an Amadain Bhòidhich' (The Song of the Handsome Fool). The poem and its story are to be found in Sinclair's *An t-Oranaiche* (p.522). A young man fell in love with his father's milkmaid. His mother, displeased, waited till the milkmaid had gone to wash herself in the river and then told her son that she had seen a beautiful white duck in the water. The young man took his gun and shot his sweetheart in error.

The first lines of the poem reverse the movement of the old song:

Chaidh mi sìos do 'n bhail' ud shìos	I went down to the town below
is binn mo bhàis 'nam làimh.	with my death-sentence in my hand.

In the old song the youth was the cause of the girl's death; the reversal in the poem implies that the girl would be the cause of the poet's death, though equally without deliberation. The 'death-sentence' refers to two crimes, for neither of which the poet was responsible: the crime that caused the loved one's misery and the crime of Nazism.

The extraordinary efflorescence of poetry caused by his love for 'Eimhir' had come to an end. His love had withdrawn like a spring-tide, though not without leaving its wrack behind.[42] MacLean took a traditional verse from a song about

'John MacLean holding off his passion for the Campbell woman':

Cha bhi mi 'strìth ris a' chraoibh nach lùb leam	I will not be striving with the tree that will not bend for me
Ged chinneadh ùbhlan ar bhàrr gach géig;	though apples should grow on the tip of each branch;
Mo shoraidh slàn leat ma rinn thu m' fhàgail,	if you have left me I bid you farewell,
Cha d' thàinig tràigh gun mhuir-làn 'n a déigh[43]	there was never an ebb that was not followed by flood

and changed its meaning from proud resignation to bleak despair, in the poem 'Muir-tràigh', written in 1941.

Chan eil mi strì ris a' chraoibh nach lùb rium	I am not striving with the tree that will not bend for me
's cha chinn na h-ùbhlan air géig seach geug;	and the apples will not grow on any of the branches;
cha shoraidh slàn leat, cha d'rinn thu m'fhàgail:	I do not bid you farewell, you did not leave me:
's e tràigh a' bhàis i gun mhuir-làn 'na déidh.	it is the ebb of death that no flood follows.

In the original song each verse is an almost independent unit, but in MacLean's second and last verse he works out the relevance and implications of the symbol, and the regular rhythm of the first stanza becomes stumbling and distorted.

Even when MacLean is not deliberately refashioning an old song, as in 'Muir-tràigh', or in Part IV of 'An Cuilithionn', where he adapts some lines of a song by the nineteenth-century Skye poet, Norman Nicolson,

'S gann gu 'n dìrich mi chaoidh	I shall hardly ever again climb
Dh' ionnsuidh frìthean a' mhonaidh . . .	to the hunting grounds of the moorland,
Gabhail sealladh air na sléibhtean	gazing at the mountains
Far am bi na féidh a' fuireach[44]	where the deer are dwelling

by changing "féidh" (deer) to "reultan" (stars), he often seems to have the old songs in the back of his head. It is hard to read *Dàin do Eimhir* LX,

's ann fo chòta truagh an rìgh	my foolish heart leapt
a leum an cridhe gòrach . . .[45]	beneath the king's wretched coat

without being reminded of the many Scots who marched away in the regiments of the Hanoverian kings, most of them never to return, and of the songs they made.

Again, in 'Dol an Iar' an old song figures when MacLean expresses his lack of hatred for the enemy's soldiers in a striking image that recalls the savagery of the clan wars: an image that was frequently not merely an image but a terrible fact, as in the old song:

Dh'fhàg mi e air sgeir mhara	I left him on a sea rock
'S fhuil go frasach air an rò-shruth.[46]	with his blood pouring into the tide.

The image of the sea-rock had been used by Mary MacPherson (1821-98), when she had been unjustly sentenced for a theft she did not commit, a sentence which stung her into poetry:

'Nuair chaidh mise chàradh air sgeir gu' m bhàthadh,	When I had been placed on a skerry to drown
Le truaghan Bàillidh, gun ghràdh na chom;	by a wretched unfeeling magistrate,

Chuir thusa bàta, le sgioba 's ràimh dhomh   you sent me a boat with a crew and oars,
'Nuair dh' fhàg a' phàirt ud mi bhàn sa'   when that lot left me down in the mire.
                                        pholl.[47]

MacLean makes the image even more vivid:

Chan eil gamhlas 'na mo chridhe   I have no hatred in my heart
ri saighdearan calma 'n Nàmhaid   against the brave soldiers of the Enemy,
ach an càirdeas a tha eadar   but only the fellowship there is between
fir am prìosan air sgeir-thràghad,   men imprisoned on a tidal skerry,

a' fuireach ris a' mhuir a' lìonadh   waiting for the sea to flood
's a' fuarachadh na creige blàithe,   and cool the warm rock,
agus fuaralachd na beatha   and the chill of life
ann an gréin theth na Fàsaich.   in the hot sun of the Desert.

Another poem about the war in the desert, 'Curaidhean', describes the bravery of
an unnamed English soldier, who showed by his conduct in battle and his death in
action that he was the equal of those heroes of the past whose names have lingered in
memory or book. He has his place in MacLean's roll of honour along with Lannes,
MacLennan, MacBain, MacDonald and Alasdair of Glengarry, all of whom are
mentioned in the poem. Lannes was Napoleon's brave young officer from the
Pyrenees, who greatly distinguished himself at the storming of Ratisbon (now
Regensburg) in the Austrian campaign of 1809.

The others heroes of 'Curaidhean' are perhaps less well-known, even to Gaels.
MacLennan was standard bearer to the Earl of Seaforth who supported the
Covenanters at the battle of Auldearn on the Moray Firth in 1645. When the Earl
saw that Montrose and the Royalists were about to defeat the Covenanters, he
ordered a retreat. MacLennan spoke: "Cha deach a' bhratach seo riamh air ais an
làimh duine dhe mo dhaoine-sa, 's chan eil i dol air ais an diugh" (This banner never
retreated in the hand of any of my people and it is not retreating to-day).
MacLennan and his clansmen therefore stood their ground and were decimated.

Gill-Iosa (Gillies MacBain) killed fourteen at Culloden, surviving bayonet
wounds, sword wounds, and grape-shot. Isolated, he placed his back against a wall
and continued to fight until he was trampled down under the hooves of the English
cavalry.

The man in the ale-house when fists were being clenched ('n àm nan dòrn a bhith
'gan dùnadh) was Allan MacDonald of Kingsburgh, Skye, husband of the famous
Flora MacDonald; he was being attacked by members of the Martin family. He is
the hero of an old song 'M' eudail Ailein mac 'ic Ailein' (Dear to me is Allan,
grandson of Allan) in which the quoted line appears.[48]

The poem ends with a reference to Silis of Keppoch's elegy on Alasdair Dubh
MacDonald of Glengarry, hero of the battle of Sheriffmuir during the Jacobite
Rising of 1715, who died in the 1720s:

Alasdair á Gleanna Garadh,   Alasdair of Glengarry,
Thug thu an diugh gal air mo shùilean.[49]   you brought tears to my eyes today.

Silis of Keppoch would not have written an elegy on a private soldier, but MacLean
celebrates no clan chief: it was an insignificant English soldier who brought tears to
the poet's eyes. Death obliterates distinctions and heroism; it is not restricted to the
handsome, the noble or the flamboyant.

The later poem 'Aig Uaigh Yeats' is a tribute not only to Yeats's mastery of

language, but also to the heroism of Constance Markievicz and James Connolly.
MacLean, at the foot of Ben Bulben, remembers Yeats's lines:

> . . . long ago I saw her ride
> Under Ben Bulben to the meet,
> The beauty of her countryside . . .

But he also remembers the Irish legend of Diarmid and Gràinne and of how Diarmid
was slain by the enchanted boar on the mountain. The story of Diarmid's untimely
death is unforgettable, but the story of Constance Markievicz's espousal of the
revolutionary labour cause and her part in the 1916 Rising (she was second-in-
command of the detachment of Connolly's Citizen Army that held St. Stephen's
Green) means more to the socialist MacLean. He rebuts the criticism in Yeats's
'Easter 1916':

> That woman's days were spent
> In ignorant good-will.
> Her nights in argument
> Until her voice grew shrill.
> What voice more sweet than hers
> When, young and beautiful,
> She rode to harriers?

MacLean's second verse runs as follows:

An guth binn air slios Beinn Ghulbain	The sweet voice on the slope of Ben Bulben,
o'n aon bhial cuimir òg	coming from the one shapely young mouth,
a thug a chliù o Dhiarmad	has taken his fame away from Diarmid
on chualas e air Grìne,	because it was heard on a Green,
's e air fàs 'na sgread le bròn	though it had grown shrill with grief
agus leis an fheirg uasail	and with the noble anger
is leis na h-euchdan còire	and generous deeds
bu bhinn an cluais O Conghaile	that sounded sweet in the ears of Connolly
's an cluasan a sheòrsa.	and others of his kind.

So far the poem is straightforward, but the third and last verse brings up the
question of 'imcheist' (perplexity, doubt, anxiety) regarding the relationship
between the man of words and the man of action. In 'Meditations in Time of Civil
War', Yeats envied the soldiers who came to his door; and he was impelled, in
'Easter 1916', to praise the revolutionaries despite his lack of sympathy with their
ideals.

It is death that has produced the "terrible beauty"; it is the encounter with death
that puts the seal on heroism; MacLean, like Yeats, envies the men who have died
for their dream and, when he says that there is an excuse on Yeats's lips, he is voicing
his own failure to do more than write. And because human nature is flawed,
everyone has something that needs to be excused, not excepting those who choose
perfection in life rather than perfection in work. MacLean's poem itself is flawed: the
vivid image of the "croinn bhratach" (the flag-poles) would have been a better end
than the truism that everyone has an excuse.

MacLean's poem 'Làrach Eaglais' is written in remembrance of all the members
of the Clan MacLean who died at the Battle of Inverkeithing (20 July 1651) when
the Royalist army was defeated by Cromwell's troops under the command of
Lambert. Of 700 MacLeans fighting on the Royalist side, only 40 are said to have

survived, and there was no congregation left to attend their church in Mull. The seventeenth Chief of the MacLeans, Eachann Ruadh nan Cath (Red Hector of the Battles), after whom a noble pibroch was named, fell on the battlefield in spite of the efforts of his followers to protect him. Clansman after clansman leapt to his defence, shouting what was to become the battle-cry of the MacLeans: "Fear eile air son Eachainn" (Another one for Hector). Of one family of fifteen sons the only survivor was the poet Eachann Bacach (Lame Hector) who earned the epithet because of an injury sustained in the battle. His brother, Niall Buidhe, whom his mother had tried to keep from the fighting, was among the slain.[50] Eachann Bacach composed an elegy for the chief, but Sorley MacLean's poem is an elegy for the clan and ends:

Ach dé mu na ciadan eile	And what about the hundreds of others,
is ficheadan dhiubh cheart cho àrd	scores of whom were every bit as proud
anns an spiorad ri 'n ceann-cinnidh	in spirit as their chief
is ri bràthair a' bhàird?	or as the poet's brother?

History, and Scottish history in particular, is never far away, even in the love-poems, and many of MacLean's poems from the period 1945-1972 are crammed with historical references, as was 'An Cuilithionn' and the early 'An Soitheach'[51], written in 1934. Viewing the poetry as a whole, it would seem that the great burst of love-poetry found in *Dàin do Eimhir* was an accidental deflection of the poet's talents and that the more enduring passion was the cause of justice and equality among men, nourished by his resentment of the waste of lives and land that is still to be seen in Scotland today.

'An Soitheach' sums up some four centuries of Scottish history. The ship is a symbol of Gaeldom and the poet asks whether it will ever be seaworthy again, or find another captain. The energetic Alasdair MacMhaighistir Alasdair, who fought on the Jacobite side in 1745 and published his *Aiseirigh na sean Chanoin Albannaich* (The resurrection of the old Scottish language), a book of poems in Gaelic, in 1751, is dead and forgotten in Moidart. The old Bardic Poetry of the sixteenth and seventeenth centuries ("the shapely black one") and the great anonymous songs ("the fair one") are only visionary boats that went astray in the 'Celtic Twilight':

Té dhubh dhealbhach agus té bhàn,	A shapely black one and a fair one,
soilleireachd mara mu 'n cuairt orr'.	with the clarity of the sea around them.
Chunnacas, cha b' ann am bruadar,	A man was seen standing on a headland, and
duine 'na sheasamh air àird . . .	it was no dream . . .
Dhealbh e longphort anns na neòil dhaibh,	He formed a port in the clouds for them,
mheall e 'n té dhubh 's an té bhàn.	he deceived the black one and the white one.

But the men of the 'Celtic Twilight' were not responsible for the Clearances or for the spoliation of the country: the ship of Gaelic Scotland was not under their control. It sailed in English seas and under English skies and the dour followers of Calvin were at the helm.

Agus fear ùr ort nach b' eòl duit,	And there was a new man on you whom you did not know,
fear thug an sgoinn bho d' chùrsa,	a man who made your course purposeless —
an cruas dubh, an liath cheann lom,	the black hardness, the bald grey head,
's an Taghadh teann 'na shùilean.	and the doctrine of Predestination tight in his eyes.

Now that calvinism is losing its power, the ship is drifting directionless and no new crew is seen to sail it through the night towards the "camhanaich dhearg air fàire" (the red dawn on the horizon).

The anti-English theme is taken up again in 'Dà Dhomhnallach'. In the Scottish United Services Museum there is a picture which shows Colonel James MacDonald at the head of a detachment of British guardsmen, forcing shut the great wooden gates of the farmyard of Hougoumont against a press of French. Hougoumont was the Bastion of Wellington's right wing at the Battle of Waterloo and remained in British hands throughout the battle. MacDonald's heroism could be said to have saved the English and destroyed the Scots; for at home his elder brother Alasdair was busy clearing the tenants off the estates of Glengarry. Alasdair Ranaldson MacDonell, as he is usually known, was an absurdly theatrical Highlander; he was the inspiration for Fergus MacIvor in Walter Scott's *Waverley* which appeared in 1814, the year before Waterloo, and is best known in Raeburn's celebrated portrait in the Scottish National Gallery.[52]

The second MacDonald of the poem was Jacques Etienne Joseph Alexandre MacDonald, the son of Niall MacEachainn from South Uist, who had fled to France in 1746 on the same ship as Prince Charles Edward Stuart and had adopted the style of MacDonald.[53] Niall's son Jacques commanded the army of the Sambre-et-Meuse in the 1790s and on 7 July 1809, after the battle of Wagram, Napoleon made him a Marshal of France, saying: "Il y a longtemps que vous le méritiez". It was said of him that no stain of cruelty or faithlessness remained on him; and perhaps, if Napoleon had succeeded in invading England in 1805, MacDonald might have become Prince of Scotland, in addition to being Duke of Tarentum in Italy.

Nach bochd nach tàinig esan	It is a shame he did not come
Le Bonaparte a nall.	over with Bonaparte.
Cha togadh esan tuath	He would not have evicted the tenantry
Air sgàth nan caorach òraidh,	for the sake of the gilded sheep
'S cha mhò chuireadh esan gaiseadh	nor would he have blemished
Ann an gaisge mhóir Chloinn Dòmhnaill.	the great bravery of the MacDonalds.
Nach bochd nach robh esan	It is a shame that he was not
'Na dhiùc air Tìr an Eòrna	Duke of Uist
Is 'na phrionns' air Albainn.	and Prince of Scotland.

Jacques MacDonald did not declare for Napoleon in 1815. In 1825 he visited his relatives in Scotland and did not omit to call on that noted lion-collector, Sir Walter Scott. He made himself known to his father's friends in South Uist and before he departed from the island he took some soil from the ruins of his father's house and a potato from the field behind it.

An old man in Sutherland once said to Sorley MacLean's brother, Calum: "The soldiers came back from the wars and found the houses where they were born reduced to ashes and knew not where in the wide world their flesh and blood had gone. If Napoleon had come over, things would not have been as bad as that . .".[54] The man was ninety-three and the Clearances had hardly ceased when he was born: if clearances ever cease, anywhere.

In the visionary poem 'Hallaig', which is about the cleared townships of Raasay, time is frozen in a happier age;

Tha iad fhathast ann a Hallaig,	They are still in Hallaig,
Clann Ghill-Eain 's Clann MhicLeòid,	the MacLeans and MacLeods,

| na bh' ann ri linn Mhic Ghille-Chaluim: | all who were there in the time of MacLeod of Raasay: |
| chunnacas na mairbh beò. | the dead have been seen alive. |

Life continues as it did before "bristeadh cridhe an sgeòil" (the heartbreak of the tale), before the departure of the chief, before the Clearances, before the planting of the pine-woods — "chan iadsan coille mo ghràidh" (they are not the wood of my love) — but only in the poet's mind, inspired by love. The "grass-grown ruined homes" are all that are to be seen at Hallaig now. The poem is quiet, confident and inevitably elegiac in tone until the end when the energy that drove the dream is made explicit in a remarkable image:

's nuair theàrnas grian air cùl Dhùn Cana	And when the sun sinks behind Dun Cana
thig peileir dian á gunna Ghaoil;	an intense bullet will speed from Love's gun;
's buailear am fiadh a tha 'na thuaineal	and strike the deer of Time that is dizzily
a' snòtach nan làraichean feòir;	sniffing at the grass-grown ruins;
thig reothadh air a shùil 'sa' choille:	his eye will congeal in the wood:
chan fhaighear lorg air fhuil ri m' bheò.	his blood will not be traced while I live.

So intense is the poet's vision that the reader is persuaded that he can share it; but the last line shows that the vision is essentially the poet's own and cannot be wholly shared. As the poet's own epigraph states: "Tha tìm, am fiadh, an coille Hallaig" (Time, the deer, is in the wood of Hallaig), and he is there still, sniffing around, for only in the poet's imagination has he been killed. The Clearances did take place and their effects are irreversible.

To quote Keats, MacLean is one of

> . . . those to whom the miseries of the world
> Are misery, and will not let them rest,[55]

and socialism remains for him the only political movement that even has its sights in the right direction. In the mordant poem 'Am Botal Briste', however, he wonders whether all the sacrifices that have been made have in any way led to a better world. In 'A' Bheinn air Chall' the "heroism and endurance of the hundreds" symbolized by the Cuillin are ineffectual now, for the Cuillin is lost in the wood of the primitive, instinctive forces that can feed the imagination and the wood itself is out of control and is lost to us.

| Tha bheinn ag éirigh os cionn na coille, | The mountain is rising above the wood, |
| air chall anns a' choille th' air chall | it is lost in the wood that is itself lost. |

This poem, written in 1970, when the Vietnam War still had three of its fourteen years to run and the present conflict in Ulster was only a year old, still longs for that synthesis which had been recognized as an impossibility thirty years before in *Dàin do Eimhir* XXIII. In the latter poem it was seen that not even the art of Beethoven nor of the MacCrimmons could make an acceptable unity of the splendours and miseries of the world. It is impossible to conceive of an eternal mind that encompasses Belsen, the gangrene of South America and the purity of the snow on Sgurr Urain, 3,500 feet above Glen Shiel.

Socialism has not solved the world's ills, the vigour of youth is directed towards other ends and, as for religion, neither that of Dante nor that of Dugald Buchanan is better than a stumbling block, since their heavens are only open to an elite. Christ said to the other robber on the cross, the one who did not revile him: "This day shalt thou be with me in paradise"; but there was no word for Spartacus, the leader of the slave revolt against the Romans in 72 B.C., who died in battle and 6,000 of whose followers were crucified along the road from Capua to Rome. He lived before the Christian dispensation.

Despite defeat heroes persist, and MacLean cherishes their memory. They are solar flares that can cause no small disturbance on earth. One such was the Czech student, Jan Palach, who immolated himself in protest when the Red Army occupied his country in 1968 after the short-lived liberalization of the 'Prague Spring'. The Red Army which had once fought against fascism and capitalism, resisting Hitler's armies along the river Dnieper in 1941, defending Stalingrad on the Volga in 1942 and relieving Leningrad on the Neva in January 1944, after a siege of 900 days, was the new tyrant. This was a bitter draught for a poet who had once referred to it as the "Red Army of humanity". Among those lost on the lost mountain were the Paris Communards of 1871, slaughtered at the cemetery of Père Lachaise; the members of the pro-government troops who died in the Spanish Civil War in the Sierra Guadarrama; the Chinese Communists who retreated 6,000 miles from south-east to north-west China in 1934, and whose Long March might have been forgotten if they had not reached the suspension bridge over the Tatu Ho in the nick of time, crossing it under fire.

The poem 'Palach' opens gloomily enough, but there is a note of hope in the final couplet: "There is no text in my words; there are a dozen Palachs in France". Because, in 1968, there were risings in various centres of France, where workers and students were on the barricades together, MacLean imagined that there was no need for a text, or a sermon; the students had provided their own text in their actions. However, workers and students did not remain united for long, the risings were suppressed and subsequent May-day meditations will have pondered whether the French 'Palachs' had not burned themselves out to as little apparent effect.

Tha corra shamhla cnocaireachd	There is a ghost or two gloomily walking
mu 'n Bhealltainn seo fo ghruaim.	over the hills on this May-day.

The most recent poem of MacLean's that I have seen appeared in *Cencrastus 7*, (Winter 1981-82). It describes the beauty of Screapadal, a deserted township in the north of Raasay, which, like Hallaig, was cleared of its tenantry in 1846. It is impossible to forget the clearances in such places. However, the Sound of Raasay is the deepest stretch of sheltered water around the British Isles. For this reason it may be used for the testing of nuclear-powered submarines, and since now not only seals and sharks emerge from these waters, but also periscopes and conning-towers, it is impossible not to think of new 'clearances' which may destroy not only people but also the land of their nurture:

Ach 's e luingeas-fo-thuinn	But it is the submarines
Agus an luingeas adhair	and the aeroplanes
Agus an dadmun is an neodron!	and the atom and the neutron!
Chan e bhochdainn mhall chràiteach	The painful creeping poverty is not
An tiodhlac ach an léirsgrios obann	their gift; their gift is the sudden and complete destruction
A thuiteas as an iarmailt	that will fall out of the sky,
'S a dh'éireas as gach bruthaich	and will rise from every hillside,
'S a leanas ris gach lianaig àlainn	and will stick to every beautiful meadow
Eadar ceann a tuath na Creige	between the north end of the Rock

Agus a' choille ghiubhais   and the pinewood,
Eadar Screapadal 's an Caisteal.   between Screapadal and Brochel Castle.

'Screapadal' avoids the apocalyptic, but it is too diffuse for the urgency of its subject. There is a poem by Iain Crichton Smith which is more successful in getting the measure of the threat largely because it is concentrated in eight lines instead of one hundred and forty. It comes from his *Biòbuill is Sanasan-Reice* (Glasgow 1965):

Aig clachan Chalanais an dé   At the stones of Callanish yesterday
chuala mi té ag ràdh ri t'éile: I heard one woman saying to another:
'So far na loisg iad clann o shean'.   'This is where they burnt the children in
                                                                     early times.'

Chan fhaca mi druidhean anns na reultan   I did not see druids among the planets
no grian no gùn: ach chunna mi   nor sun nor robe; but I saw
ball breagha gorm mar nèamh a' sgàineadh   a beautiful blue ball like heaven cracking,
is clann le craiceann slaodadh riutha   and children with skin hanging to them
mar a' bhratach sna dh'iobradh Nagasàki.   like the flag in which Nagasaki was sacri-
                                                                     ficed.

MacLean prefers the meditative mode which is entirely suited to a long poem 'Uamha 'n Òir', the first three parts of which appeared in 1976, in *Chapman* 15.[56] The 'Cave of Gold' is at the end of Harlosh point in Loch Bracadale, about six miles south of Dunvegan Castle. Skye tradition narrates that one of the MacCrimmons marched into the cave playing the pipes and was never seen again. Words were put to the music:

Na minn bheaga 'nan gobhair chreaga,   The little kids will be goats of the crags
Mun tig mise, mun till mise   before I come, before I return,
Na minn bheaga 'nan gobhair chreaga   the little kids will be goats of the crags
Mun till mise á Uamha 'n Òir.   before I return from the Cave of Gold.

Na laoigh bheaga 'nan crodh dàra, . . .   The little calves will be cattle ready for
                                                                     breeding, . . .

Na mic uchda 'nam fir feachda, . . .[57]   the suckling sons will be men bearing arms,

It is also said that a woman sitting at the well of Tulach, near Harlosh, heard the piper's voice coming up through the water, singing

Mo dhìth, mo dhìth gun trì làmhan,   My loss, my loss, that I do not have three
                                                                     hands,
Dà làimh 'sa phìob, 's làmh 'sa chlaidheamh. two hands on the bagpipe and one on the
                                                                     sword.

Two further verses were handed down in MacLean's family and these include the line "'s i a' ghall' uaine shàraich mi" (It was the green bitch that overcame me) which plays an important part in the poem. The poem is built around these traditional verses which are the framework for a restatement of many of the themes of MacLean's work.

In Part I the MacCrimmon piper enters the cave, not rejecting, but deliberately turning his back on the beauties of external nature which have always meant so much to MacLean.

Chan fhac e 'ghealach buidhe mór   He did not see the moon, large and yellow,
Os cionn a' Chuilithinn 'na stad   pausing above the Cuillin while her foot-
                                                                     prints,

'S a lorgan 'nam buinn dhe 'n òr
Air leaghadh is 'nan sìol air sàl.
Chan fhac e h-éirigh air an Stòr.

coins of molten gold,
became seeds on the brine.
He did not see her rise above the Storr.

The piper entered the cave untroubled by those emotions and circumstances which dogged MacLean. The ninth verse, quoted below, may refer to the Blind Harper of 'The Tree of Strings', with whom MacLean emotionally identified himself, and the use of the distinctive word 'faileadh' which means to lose the hair and soft parts by maceration, steeping in water, or by putrefaction, instantly recalls 'Urnuigh' where the word is used six times.

Có eile dh' fhàgadh Dùis MhicLeoid?

Who else would have left the land of MacLeod?

'S gun e ri cosnadh an dìol-déirce,
'S gun e 'ga bhioradh leis an àrdan:
Ach rathail làidir sona òg,

He was not labouring for a beggarly reward,
nor was he being pricked by pride;
rather was he prosperous, strong, happy and young,

Gun fhaileadh le uisge na tàmailt
'S gun bhaobh an aithreachais air a thòir.

not steeped in the water of humiliation,
and not pursued by the Fury of remorse.

The word 'baobh', translated as Fury, comes from the Old Gaelic 'badb' which means the scald-crow, the shape in which the Celtic war-goddess appeared to men. 'Baobh' has come to mean a wicked, mischievous female but here MacLean has, mindful of the word's ancestry, succeeded in restoring much of its dignity.

It was not Calvinism that made the piper turn his back on the things of this life, nor yet the familiar dichotomy between heart and intellect. He was not a fanatic like 'Blind Munro', a fine fiddler who was converted to Evangelicism by an itinerant preacher in 1805 and became a stubborn enemy of Gaelic music and culture. Such was the power of Munro's oratory and such was the temper of the times that he persuaded his hearers to make an enormous bonfire of their fiddles and bagpipes at Snizort in Skye. 'Blind Munro' appears in this poem in the most explicit of MacLean's attacks on the Evangelical mind, which was more 'Calvinistic' than Calvinism itself in its hatred of pleasure. MacLean's piper is no Evangelical:

Cha robh a Dhall-san air an spiris
Eadar a chridhe 's eanchainn
A' maistreadh Nàduir le loinid
Ag cur a' bhainne 'na fhuil
Agus na blàthaich 'na h-eabar
Air bruaich shleamhainn an t-sluic.

His 'Blind one' was not perched
between his heart and brain,
churning up nature with a dash-stick,
turning the milk into blood
and the buttermilk into slush
on the slippery edge of the pit.

The pit is a familiar image: this piper is safe from it, but nowhere has he come across "an fhaodail" (the treasure found by chance). His search for what can only be found "gun shireadh" (without searching) has brought him to doubt its existence, so he leaves the upper world — perhaps the paradox will become comprehensible in the dark realms.

In Part II another piper enters the cave, playing the pipes but armed with the bleak weapons of despair and dogged defiance. This second piper knows no object for his quest and knows that his sacrifice will be of no avail: like the protagonist of an earlier poem he could be said to be carrying "binn a bhàis 'na làimh" (his death sentence in his hand). His music is the product of sour experience. Like the Blind Harper, he foresees the destruction of the old Highland way of life; like Marx, he fears the impossibility of escaping the dead hand of the past. As Marx puts it, "The tradition of all the dead generations weighs like a nightmare on the brain of the living" (*The Eighteenth Brumaire of Louis Napoleon*).

This second piper's adventure is only a gesture. His weapons are useless and only his musical art has any strength or validity; but even that is suspect, its ineffable sweetness a false pride, "A bhinneas do-labhairt 'na mhór-chuis". He might leave the name of hero behind him, there would be "seòrsa misneachd 'na dhìobhail" (a sort of courage in his loss), but that would be all.

In Part III, which is a veritable sixteen-handed reel of thoughts and metaphors, it is argued that though art may be an illusion, it may be the strongest thing we have, if enough single-minded passion has gone into its making and if the form can hold the passion in a permanence beyond death:

'S e an ceòl fhéin a rinn an strì . . .   It was the music itself that struggled . . .

An argumaid a bha 'na ghaoir,   the argument that was in its shrilling cry,
Ge lag, nas treas na'n laoch   though weak, was stronger than the strongest
                                                                                   hero

Bu treasa chunnacas air raon   that was ever seen on a battlefield
Ag gleachd ri gall' uaine 'bhàis.   wrestling with the green bitch of death.

Parts IV and V of 'Uamha 'n Oir' are still in progress: the actual cave is reputed to have an exit in another cave of the same name in the north of Trotternish, but no one has ever entered at one end and emerged from the other.

Despite its philosophical complexity — it is the most difficult of MacLean's poems — 'Uamha 'n Oir' is not an inward-looking work. It gathers up so many of the major themes in MacLean's work that even in its unfinished state, it is one of MacLean's finest poems.

In his essay 'Old Songs and New Poetry', MacLean asks whether beauty in poetry is relevant to the contemporary world. It may often seem that this world is hostile to the kind of poetry that MacLean writes, but there are witnesses of the power of such poetry to survive. Eugenia Ginsburg,[59] a woman of feeling and unquestionable courage, describes in her autobiography how the recital of poems by Blok and Pasternak helped to keep her sane in Stalin's prisons and concentration camps. And there are others to testify to such relevance.

In the age of the atom bomb, memorable poetry may well be more permanent than poetry that only lives on paper. And there can be few who have read the poetry of Somhairle Mac Gill-Eain in the original who have not stored some of it in their heart. It would be difficult to forget 'Hallaig':

Tha bùird is tàirnean air an uinneig   There are boards and nails on the window
troimh 'm faca mi an Aird an Iar   through which I saw the West,
's tha mo ghaol aig Allt Hallaig   and my love is at Hallaig stream.
'na craoibh bheithe, 's bha i riamh . . .   she has become a birch tree, and she has
                                                                              always . . .

because here, as in all MacLean's poems, there is not only a passionate involvement with the subject, but also great verbal and rhythmical skill. MacLean believes that to write poetry is, in Yeats's words: "to articulate sweet sounds together"; and those poets with whom he has felt a special affinity, Yeats, Blok and William Ross, are noted not only for their devotion to the unattainable beloved, but also for their attention to verbal music. The richness of literary and historical reference in MacLean's poetry locates it in time, but the poetry itself transcends the limitations of its material, and when MacLean makes the customary poetic claim to permanence it seems all the more credible because it is stated with a new music and with a new image, though it is inevitably less striking without the tone, diction and music of the original Gaelic:

Thog mi an calbh so	I have raised this pillar-stone
air bheinn fhalbhaich na tìme,	on the shifting mountain of time,
ach 's esan clach-chuimhne	but it is a monument
a bhios suim dheth go dìlinn . . .[60]	that will arouse interest for ever . . .

DOUGLAS SEALY

NOTES

The title 'Out from Skye to the World' is taken from an interview with Sorley MacLean which appeared in *Scottish International* 10, Edinburgh, May 1970, p. 10.

1. Unless otherwise indicated the poems may be found in *Reothairt is Contraigh* (Springtide and Neaptide): *Taghadh de Dhàin 1932-72* (Selected Poems 1932-72), Edinburgh 1977.
2. *Plays by Webster and Ford,* Everyman's Library, p. 279.
3. Baudelaire, *Les Fleurs du Mal,* Le Livre de Poche, 1972, p. 45.
4. Lenau, *Sämmtliche Werke,* Leipzig 1885, p. 84.
5. *D.E.,* p. 32.
6. Baudelaire, *op cit.,* p. 54.
7. K. C. Craig, *Orain Luaidh,* Glasgow 1949, p. 109.
8. *D.E.,* p. 82.
9. Norman MacLeod, *Caraid nan Gàidheal,* Edinburgh 1910, p. 497.
10. *James* 1, v. 17.
11. *Ibid.* 4, v. 8.
12. The lovers, in the order in which they appear in the poem, are: Deirdre; Maud Gonne MacBride; the girl from Cornaig in Tiree, heroine of an old song — there is a version in K. C. Craig, *op. cit,* p. 108; Young Margaret, heroine of an old song to be found in Archibald Sinclair's *An t-Oranaiche,* Glasgow 1879, p. 522; The Handsome Fool who was Young Margaret's lover; Una MacDermot and Thomas Costello whose story is in Douglas Hyde's *Love Songs of Connaught,* London/Dublin 1895, pp. 46-61; Emer, the wife of Cuchulainn; Grainne, the heroine of the Fenian Cycle; Helen of Troy; Marion, the beloved of the poet William Ross, see G. Calder, *Gaelic Songs by William Ross,* Edinburgh 1937; Audiart, see Ezra Pound, *Selected Poems 1908-1959,* London 1975, p. 17; Queen Maeve, the great queen of the Cattle Raid of Cooley; Major John MacBride; Naoise the lover of Deirdre; Donald MacDonald of Bohuntine who composed part of the song for Young Margaret; Bertrans de Born; Cuchulainn; Fionn and Diarmaid, the lovers of Grainne.

13. *Four Points of a Saltire,* Edinburgh 1970, p. 122. Extract from 'An Cuilithionn', Part I.
14. *Ibid.,* p. 124. Information about the girl from Gesto from Dr. S. MacLean.
15. D. E. Meek (ed), *Màiri Mhór nan Òran,* Glasgow 1977, p. 82.
16. *Four Points of a Saltire,* p. 125.
17. *Gairm* No. 72, Am Foghar 1970, Glasgow, p. 319. Translated in *Lines Review* 34, Edinburgh 1970, p. 17.
18. Pablo Neruda, *Canto General,* II, Buenos Aires 1955, p. 51.
19. Hugh MacDiarmid, *Complete Poems,* London 1978, p. 558.
20. Dugald Buchanan (1716-68), the perfervid Calvinist poet from Balquhidder in Perthshire.
21. *D.E.,* p. 32.
22. Dughall Buchanan, *Dàin Spioradail,* Glasgow 1946, p. 16.
23. *Ibid.,* p. 20.
24. *Ibid.,* p. 28 (cf. *R.C.,* p. 141).
25. *Ibid.,* p. 28.
26. *Ibid.,* p. 3.
27. *Ibid.,* p. 44.
28. *Ibid.,* p. 38.
29. *D.E.,* p. 83.
30. *D.E.,* p. 62.
31. Somhairle Mac Ghill-Eathain and Robert Garioch, *Seventeen Poems for Sixpence,* Edinburgh 1940, p. 10; cf. the poem 'Oidhche Chiùin' in *R.C.,* p. 41.
32. W. Matheson, *The Blind Harper,* Edinburgh 1970, p. 58.
33. Alexander Cameron, *Reliquiae Celticae,* II, Inverness 1894, p. 467.
34. *D.E.,* p. 68.
35. *D.E.,* p. 67.
36. Sorley MacLean, 'Poetry, Passion and Political Consciousness', interview in *Scottish International* 10, May 1970, p. 12.
37. *D.E.,* p. 29.
38. *D.E.,* p. 65.
39. Cf. Campbell and Collinson, *Hebridean Folksongs,* I, Oxford 1969, ll. 1242-45 and Ó Baoill, *Bàrdachd Chloinn Ghill Eathain, Eachann Bacach and other MacLean Poets,* Edinburgh 1979, pp. 200-201.
40. *Lines Review* 34, September 1970, p. 39.
41. *Contemporary Scottish Verse,* eds. MacCaig and Scott, London 1970, p. 165.
42. *Contemporary Scottish Verse, op. cit.,* p. 162. 'Cóig Bliadhna Fichead o Richmond'.
43. Archibald Sinclair, *An t-Oranaiche,* Glasgow 1879, p. 264. Sinclair's version is anonymous. Sorley MacLean gives the attribution to John MacLean in his essay, "Old Songs and New Poetry", in *Memoirs of a Modern Scotland,* ed. Karl Miller, London 1970, p. 127.
44. Sinclair, *op cit.,* p. 491. MacLean's adaptation is in *Lines Review* 7, January 1955, p. 10.
45. *D.E.,* p. 50.

46. A. Carmichael, *Carmina Gadelica,* VI, Edinburgh 1971, p. 7.
47. Màiri Nic a' Phearsain, *Dàin agus Òrain,* Inverness 1891, p. 157.
48. K. C. Craig, *op. cit.,* p. 68.
49. W. J. Watson, *Bàrdachd Ghàidhlig,* Stirling 1932, p. 128.
50. Colm Ó Baoill, *Bàrdachd Chloinn Ghill Eathain,* op. cit., pp. xliii-xlv, 196-199.
51. *D.E.,* p. 59. Reprinted with translation in *Four Points of a Saltire,* pp. 116-121.
52. For information about Alasdair Ranaldson MacDonell, see John Prebble, *The Highland Clearances,* Penguin Books, 1969, pp. 139-44, 273, 277.
53. Dr. S. MacLean informs me that Niall MacEachainn was a son of MacEachainn, Tacksman of Howbeg in South Uist, but that there is a tradition that he was really an illegitimate son of a daughter of MacEachainn and a MacDonald. He was a captain in the French army and an undercover agent of France.
54. Calum MacLean, *The Highlands,* London 1959 (reprinted Inverness 1975), p. 144.
55. Keats, *The Fall of Hyperion,* Book I, ll. 148-9.
56. A translation appeared in *Chapman* 30, 1981.
57. Frances Tolmie, 'Songs of Occupation from the Western Isles of Scotland', *Journal of the Folk-song Society* 16, London 1911, pp. 157-60.
58. *Memoirs of a Modern Scotland,* ed. Karl Miller, op. cit., pp. 121-135.
59. Author of *Into the Whirlwind,* London 1967, and *Within the Whirlwind,* London 1981.
60. *D.E.,* p.20.

The opinions and interpretations offered in my essay are, it goes without saying, solely my own, and I have preferred to make my own translations into English, because the more translations the better.

'*A Highland Woman*'

In Spite of Sea and Centuries:
An Irish Gael looks at the Poetry of
Somhairle Mac Gill-Eain

It would be gratifying to be able to report from Ireland that the appearance of *Dàin do Eimhir* in 1943 established Somhairle Mac Gill-Eain at once and for good in the esteem of Irish Gaelic speakers. The collection was indeed received favourably in the literary magazines of the time, without, it would appear, any marked awareness of the revolution in the Gaelic poetic tradition which was implicit in the work. At least, if such awareness there was, it largely failed to communicate itself to those of us who were reading our university courses in Celtic studies a decade later. Our exposure to Scottish Gaelic literature, in my view even then altogether too slight, hardly went beyond a ritual poem or two from Alasdair Mac Mhaighistir Alasdair and Donnchadh Bàn Mac an t-Saoir and whatever we cared to discover for ourselves in Watson's *Bàrdachd Ghàidhlig*. In one way, this failure was remarkable in that a new vitality was just then manifesting itself in Irish Gaelic literature: a new determination to break out of repressive traditional moulds and tackle the preoccupations of the mid-twentieth century, to win new audiences and treat new themes. A programme of which, one would have thought, the poetry of Somhairle Mac Gill-Eain should have come as a powerful and uncannily accurate fulfilment.

But of course, the Gaelic cultural tradition was then, as it still is, barely able to maintain itself by the constant efforts of a small minority. A fitful flame at best, and heavily dependent on coteries of university graduates, whose quickly-succeeding generations fail to pass on or refuse to pick up ideas and values just as in any other area of human society. And so, in one way or another, the name of Somhairle Mac Gill-Eain passed us by, we who were too young to have known his brother, Calum Iain, who had left such memories behind among folklorists and in the Conamara Gaeltacht. We were busy understanding and reducing to some sort of critical order the new harvest of poetry and prose in Irish, Máirtín Ó Direáin, Seán Ó Ríordáin and Máirtín Ó Cadhain, and were shamefully oblivious for the moment to the other branch of the Gaelic tradition beyond the Sea of Moyle.

For my own part, it was the hazard of a visit to Scotland that was to reveal to me the poetic world of Somhairle Mac Gill-Eain. On a spring evening in Kyle of Lochalsh with an hour to spare, my friend and guide among the glens and kyles of Wester Ross, Colm O'Boyle, chanced to remark that we were close to Plockton. So it happened that I walked on Talisker shore before I read 'Tràighean' and saw the "mùr eagarra gorm" of the Cuillin before experiencing what the alchemy of a powerful poetic imagination had made of them. All those landscapes in their stark spring majesty were fresh in mind when, back in the plains and rank hedgerows of

Leinster, I sat down to scan a copy of *Dàin do Eimhir,* its cramped typeface and grey wartime paper. The grey pages opened casements for me onto a land of what Poussin might call *délectation,* a country, to use the words of another Scottish Gaelic poet, "far an do bhuadhaich na Gàidheil" (where Gaeldom lived and throve).

For this Gaelic voice was above all alive, something which came to me with a sense almost of shock, since so many writers are awarded reputations in minority cultures and turn out to be more remarkable for effort than inspiration. This poetry was master of the element in which it soared and glided and stopped. Vast landscapes passed below its eagle eye, and homely detail was as clear to its glance as mountain ranges. It roved the worlds of past and present as easily as it did its native country, and woke echoes of the universal imagination in my memory of other lands and literatures, as though Pascal's eye had gleamed with recognition in

Lìonmhoireachd anns na speuran,	Multitude of the skies,
òr-chriathar muillionan de reultan,	golden riddle of millions of stars,
fuar, fad as, lòghmhor, àlainn,	cold, distant, lustrous, beautiful,
tosdach, neo-fhaireachdail, neo-fhàilteach.	silent, unfeeling, unwelcoming.

A solitary heron between the "frail beauty of the moon" and the "cold loveliness of the sea" becomes the vehicle of an intensity of contemplation, of an unsentimental, creative community. It recalls the early Irish lyrics of the Culdee monks, or the *sumi* drawings of those other practitioners of solitude and austerity, the Zen Buddhist monks of mediaeval Japan:

Mise mar riut 's mi 'nam ònar	I am with you, alone,
ag amharc fuachd na linne còmhnaird,	gazing at the coldness of the level kyle,
ag cluintinn onfhaidh air faolinn	listening to the surge on a stony shore
bristeadh air leacan loma 'n t-saoghail.	breaking on the bare flagstones of the world.

More intimately and poignantly still, there comes to an Irish Gael the dawning realization that the predominant accents of this voice are not foreign ones at all; they require little of that accommodation of ourselves to different assumptions, to values learned from a different kind of past, which is demanded by the more triumphant traditions of the great nations. Gaelic Ireland and Gaelic Scotland were of course a cultural continuum down to the seventeenth century and in spite of widely differing circumstances since then, the Gaelic speaker in both countries today looks back on the three centuries since then as a tale of harassment and contempt for Gaelic culture, of 'mìorun mór nan Gall', of the decline almost to elimination of Gaelic-speaking people.

Oddly enough then, the Irish Gael, particularly if, like the present writer, he comes from an Ulster background, is immediately drawn to that radical aspect of his social and political attitudes which are so evident a feature of the poetry of Somhairle Mac Gill-Eain. There exists, at least in Ireland, a widely-popularised stereotype of the Irish Catholic Gaelic speaker as obscurantist, exclusivist and unshakably conservative in social and political attitudes. I believe it to be a sustainable thesis that such is the case insofar as he accedes to and accepts the bourgeois values, which in Ireland have always been part and parcel of the cultural imperialism of English. However that may be, the Irish Gael knows himself to have an inheritance of exclusion and discrimination which has by no means disappeared in the politically independent Republic of Ireland. Memories of landlordism in rural Ireland or of the slums of pre-independence Dublin ensure a ready response to:

Chan eil mo shùil air Calbharaigh	My eyes is not on Calvary

no air Betlehem an àigh,	nor on Bethlehem the Blessed,
ach air cùil ghrod an Glaschu,	but on a foul-smelling backland in Glasgow,
far bheil an lobhadh fàis;	where life rots as it grows;

or again to the Highland woman's slavery in:

Am faca Tu i, Iùdhaich mhóir,	Hast Thou seen her, great Jew,
ri'n abrar Aon Mhac Dhé?	who art called the One Son of God?
Am fac' thu 'coltas air Do thriall	Hast Thou seen on Thy way the like of her
ri strì an fhìon-lios chéin? ...	labouring in the distant vineyard? ...
Chan fhaca Tu i, Mhic an t-saoir,	Thou has not seen her, Son of the carpenter,
ri'n abrar Rìgh na Glòir,	who art called the King of Glory,
a miosg nan cladach carrach siar,	among the rugged western shores
fo fhallus cliabh a lòin.	in the sweat of her food's creel.

And it is perfectly understandable that the *saeva indignatio* at what has been done to the poor and defenceless should express itself in a mistrust of churches which profess to love the Lord God with heart, mind and strength and forget the latter half of the great commandment. Or how could we fail to sympathise with the hunger for a better world of 'Am Boilseabhach'

nach tug suim	who never gave heed
riamh do bhànrainn no do rìgh;	to queen or to king;
nan robh againn Alba shaor,	if we had Scotland free,
Alba co-shìnte ri ar gaol,	Scotland equal to our love,
Alba gheal bheadarrach fhaoil,	a white spirited generous Scotland,
Alba àlainn shona laoch.	a beautiful happy heroic Scotland.

The passions aroused by the Spanish Civil War were of course long settled into history when my generation came to read *Dàin do Eimhir,* but the reflections of that drama in the poetry of Somhairle Mac Gill-Eain were profoundly instructive for us, if I may apply so detached a word to that intimate lyricism. The same must be said of those poems which came out of the author's experience of war in the Western Desert which we read in *Four Points of a Saltire.* They obliged us to recognize the obverse side of Irish independence and political neutrality; they armed us to make essential distinctions and establish priorities among the attitudes which have come to make up Irish separatism. One effect of those attitudes and of Irish history during the last half-century has been a certain self-absorption and introversion, not least in writing in Irish, and so it came to us with unusual freshness to hear a Gaelic poet say:

Oir chunnaic mi an Spàinn caillte,	For I have seen Spain lost,
sealladh a rinn mo shùilean saillte,	a sight that has made my eyes salt,

or to find names like James Connolly and Dimitrov, Lenin, Liebknecht and Garcia Lorca, rubbing shoulders in lines of Gaelic, even if some of them did not belong to our pantheon. I suppose, heaven help our narrow minds, it was even a matter for mild surprise that this poet who shared our mythology from the emigration of the nineteenth century back to the Sons of Uisneach should show himself concerned over a pair of Englishmen, Cornford and Julian Bell. And we were similarly compelled to reflect on the sovereign truth of the artist by a poem from the Second World War like 'Curaidhean' which did not hesitate to mention in the same breath the epic heroes of Auldearn and Culloden (no less!) and an obscure little English gunner who stood his ground. War, like art, has no room for comfortable prejudice.

For us, of course, the Great Famine had broken our people's patience with fighting the wars of Empire and not since Francis Ledwidge died in the mud of Flanders had our poetry expressed the pathos of men caught in wars not of their making; as Mac Gill-Eàin puts it:

a threòraicheadh bho thoiseach àl	led, from the beginning of generations,
gun deòin gu buaireadh	unwillingly to the trial
agus bruaillean cuthaich gach blàir	and mad delirium of every war
air sgàth uachdaran.	for the sake of rulers.

This, then, was a poet who refused to settle for the easy certainties of that kind of romantic nationalism which in Ireland we associate with the name of the Gaelic League, with the manicheism and self-indulgent pathos with which it tries to conjure the demons of our painful history. Mac Gill-Eain took another and more uncompromising stance. We could fully appreciate his satire of the 'fior-Ghàidheal', *mutatis mutandis*, in 'Road to the Isles':

Théid mi thun nan Eileanan	I will go to the Isles
is ataidh mi le m'bhaothalachd	and I will swell with my vapidity
mu bhruthan sìth an Canaidh 's Eige,	about fairy knolls in Canna and Eigg,
mu ghusgul ròn an Eirisgeidh,	about the voice of seals in Eriskay,
mu chlàrsaichean 's mu Eilean Bharraidh.	about harps and the Isle of Barra.

Ireland has had more than its share of this kind of thing, which in the popular mind sometimes tends to supplant a genuine sense of traditional values. But we whose culture is Gaelic had failed to fight it with this kind of irony, failed maybe to see our concern for our own culture in a wide-enough human context, as our share of the world-wide and everlasting struggle against the big battalions, against the mercenary and the hypocrite, the racist and the exploiter of others. Somhairle Mac Gill-Eain had proclaimed his change of course clearly enough, and in his own characteristic terms in 'Clann Ghill-Eain':

Chan e iadsan a bhàsaich	Not they who died
an àrdan Inbhir-chéitein	in the hauteur of Inverkeithing
dh'aindeoin gaisge is uabhair	in spite of valour and pride
ceann uachdrach ar sgeula;	the high head of our story;
ach esan bha 'n Glaschu,	but he who was in Glasgow
ursann-chatha nam feumach,	the battle-post of the poor,
Iain mór Mac Gill-Eain,	great John MacLean,
ceann is fèitheam ar sgeula.	the top and hem of our story.

The twentieth-century social revolutionary is the contemporary incarnation of a heritage of pride and courage which long found its outlet in the mythical memory of a battle against hopeless odds.

That the poet should turn so naturally and unaffectedly to an event of almost three centuries earlier is an aspect of the Gaelic mind which often seems puzzling to the Anglo-Saxon. (Even the largely de-Gaelicized Irish are still accused periodically of being obsessed by their past.) But to the Irish Gaelic reader it is an instinct which brings us a thrill of recognition and an impulse to clasp this man to us as one of our own in that solidarity to which he himself alludes in his moving elegy on his brother, enduring in spite of sea and centuries:

.... an fhéile	.... the humanity
Nach do reub an cuan,	that the sea did not tear,
Nach do mhill mìle bliadhna:	that a thousand years did not spoil:
Buaidh a' Ghàidheil buan.	the quality of the Gael permanent.

Nothing perhaps in the work of Somhairle Mac Gill-Eain makes a more powerful and immediate appeal to the Irish Gael than the full measure in which he possesses and is informed by the quality fundamental to so much of both branches of the Gaelic tradition. We both, I believe, call it *dùthchas* and it is a term as untranslatable as *virtù*, or *honnêteté*, or *gemütlichkeit* in their respective languages. In an effort to explain it in English, the Royal Irish Academy's dictionary of the common Old Gaelic languages uses such terms as "inheritance, patrimony; native place or land; connexion, affinity or attachment due to descent or long-standing; inherited instinct or natural tendency". It is all these things and, besides, the elevation of them to a kind of ideal of the spirit, an enduring value amid the change and the erosion of all human things, all the more cherished in cultures like ours with the unbearable pain of past overthrow and present decline, and the spectre of imminent dissolution.

This spirit pervades the poetry of Mac Gill-Eain and it is this which ensures him an enduring audience in Ireland and brings him at once into such intimacy with that audience. We find it in the homely sense of family which nerves him in the sand of Libya:

Agus biodh na bha mar bha e,
tha mi de dh'fhir mhór' a' Bhràighe,
de Chloinn Mhic Ghille Chaluim threubhaich,
de Mhathanaich Loch Aills nan geurlann,
agus fir m' ainme – có bu tréine
nuair dh'fhàdadh uabhar an léirchreach?

And be what was as it was,
I am of the big men of Braes,
of the heroic Raasay MacLeods,
of the sharp-sword Mathesons of Lochalsh;
and the men of my name – who were braver
when their ruinous pride was kindled?

Even if we are not immediately aware of how the men of Braes struggled for their land, or what precisely was the descent of Clann Mhic Ghille Chaluim, we recognize the note. It is perceptible in his sense of the value of one's own place, the *petite patrie*, which, like the gods in Patrick Kavanagh's well-known line, makes its own importance felt, as in 'Gleann Aoighre':

Tha eilean beag 'na mo chuimhne
's e 'na laighe air cuan deich bliadhna...

There is a little island in my memory,
lying on a sea of ten years...

Am feasgar ud air a' bhearradh
thuig mi an nì nach b' aoibhinn...

That evening on the ridge
I realised the unhappy thing...

a dh'aindeoin gach spàirn is dichill,
ged bhiodh Leathanaich is Leòdaich,
Clann Mhic 'Neacail is Clann Dòmhnaill
air tòir an agairt,

in spite of every struggle and persistence,
though MacLeans and MacLeods,
Nicolsons and MacDonalds,
were urging their claim,

nach fhaighinn-sa an nì a dh'iarr mi...

that I would not get the thing I wanted...

In a wider sense, it is to be found in the poet's profound attachment to the places and landscapes of the Gàidhealtachd, in the characteristically Gaelic pleasure in naming places, and consequently in the rich nomenclature of the Gaelic lands, which I at least feel is rivalled in picturesque, poetic or homely detail only by the Arabs. Think of a poem like 'Tràighean':

Nan robh sinn an Talasgar air an tràigh
far a bheil am bial mór bàn
a' fosgladh eadar dà ghiall chruaidh,
Rubha nan Clach 's am Bioda Ruadh...

If we were in Talisker on the shore
where the great white mouth
opens between two hard jaws,
Rubha nan Clach and the Bioda Ruadh...

And the eye of imagination summons reefs and headlands, rocky shores and whole islands, and vast seascapes to be the witnesses of his exaltation – Talisker and Prishal, Moidart, Mull and Tiree, and Scotland itself. The Gaelic reader must nurse his own wound that the true and meaningful names of these places, just as in Ireland, are condemned to survive only in barbarously mutilated forms. These places and landscapes are the constant correlative with which the poem translates his passion. His lady is dawn on the Cuillin and benign day on the Clarach and the distant Butt of Lewis is no adequate destination for his desire's journeying ('Camhanaich', 'Fo Sheòl'). Their names become the loving catalogue of the features of Skye and of the memories of human fellowship attaching to them, their warmth chilled by the realisation of the people's fate:

Eilein Mhóir, Eilein mo dheòin,	Great Island, Island of my desire,
Eilein mo chridhe is mo leòin...	Island of my heart and wound...
chan eil dòchas ri do bhailtean	there is no hope of your townships
éirigh àrd le gàire 's aiteas,	rising high with gladness and laughter,
's chan eil fiughair ri do dhaoine	and your men are not expected
's Ameireaga 's an Fhraing 'gam faotainn.	when America and France take them.
Mairg an t-sùil a chì air fairge	Pity the eye that sees on the ocean
ian mór marbh na h-Albann.	the great dead bird of Scotland.

This sense of landscape and attachment to place is closely bound up with human relations, not merely with personal memories of friends and of their company as in 'An t-Eilean', but with a profound awareness of the community extended not only in place but also in time; an awareness of all those who lived and strove and were buried in this earth, not as remote figures in a history-book but as part of one's own flesh and blood. It is this same instinct, for example, which made the Irish Declaration of Independence of 1916 begin "in the name of God and the generations who are gone before us". So Somhairle Mac Gill-Eain can contemplate a ruined church in the Ross of Mull and pass in a line to the battle of Inverkeithing and the memory of a three-hundred year old poem. Once again the Irish reader may have to brush up his Scottish history or may never have heard the tradition of the seven MacLeans dying with the shout of "Fear eile air son Eachainn!", but he will have no trouble in stepping across the centuries with the poet or sharing the pathos of that tragic pride.

Not for one moment is the poet's attitude to that past defined by the sort of unearned emotion with which even sympathetic outsiders have often looked at Gaelic history; what one might call the "All their wars were merry and all their songs were sad" syndrome. The last verse of the poem we have just mentioned brings that flight of fancy down to earth:

Ach dé mu na ciadan eile	But what of the hundreds of others
is ficheadan dhiubh cheart cho àrd	of whom scores were quite as high
anns an spiorad ri'n ceann-cinnidh	in spirit as their chief
is ri bràthair a' bhàird?	or as the brother of the bard?

The art of rigorous control of lyric emotion is, it seems to me, a characteristic which makes Mac Gill-Eain's poetry an authentic continuation of one of the most enduring aspects of the Gaelic tradition, whether Irish or Scottish. Time and again, we find the upsurge of feeling reined in by an adamantine detachment; the fervour of mediaeval religious verse by a detail of homely, almost homespun, realism; the glow of the *amour courtois* by a sudden twist of irony; the lyric intensity of folksong by an expression simple to the point of *naïveté*. All through Mac Gill-Eain's poetry we find this same elegance and distinction of spirit, and know ourselves to be in the presence of a poet whom we in Ireland would be glad to account with Ó Bruadair and Ó Rathaille among the aristocrats of lyricism.

Nor is Mac Gill-Eain himself ever in doubt about the worth of his poetic inheritance; he has no hesitation about coupling Dante and Dugald Buchanan, or the black ships

a sheòl Odysseus a nall á Itaca	that Odysseus sailed over from Ithaca
no Mac Mhic Ailein a nall á Uidhist.	or Clanranald over from Uist.

When he would call to his aid the mythic lovers of the past, they start to him from all tongues indifferently, from Ireland and Scotland, Homer and the troubadours:

Do m' shùilean-sa bu tu Deirdre	To my eyes you were Deirdre
's i bòidheach 's a' bhuaile ghréine...	beautiful in the sunny cattle-fold...
an Una aig Tómas Làidir,	Strong Thomas's Una,
Eimhir Chù Chulainn agus Gràinne.	Cuchulainn's Eimhir, and Grainne.
Bu tu té nam mìle long,	You were the one of the thousand ships,
ùidh nam bàrd is bàs nan sonn,	desire of poets and death of heroes,
's bu tu an té a thug an fhois	you were she who took the rest
's an t-sìth bho chridhe Uilleim Rois,	and the peace from the heart of William Ross,
an Audiart a bhuair De Born	the Audiart who plagued De Born,
agus Maoibhe nan còrn.	and Maeve of the drinking horns.

With ease and sureness he finds in old Gaelic literature the symbol which will most effectively embody his theme. The jealousy of the ageing King Conchobhar reaches into the grave to separate Naoise and Deirdre, his memory still haunted by the idyll of their dalliance in the Scottish glens about which Deirdre sang. How much more alive and unbroken is the long literary tradition of the Gaels for this poet than for anyone in Ireland!

Chan fhàg mi 'san aon uaigh iad	I will not leave them in the same grave
fad fin-shuaineach na h-oidhche,	for the whole long night,
a broilleach cìoch-gheal	her fair breasts
ri uchd-san mór geal	to his great fair chest
tre shìorruidheachd na h-oidhche,	throughout the night's eternity,
a bhial-sa r' a bial, r' a gruaidh	his mouth to her mouth, to her cheek,
air cho fliuch 's bhios ùir an tuaim:	for all the wet earth of the tomb:
b' fhaide 'n oidhche na 'n Gleann Da Ruadh,	the night would be longer than in Glen Da Ruadh,
bu luasgan cadal Gleann Eite;	sleep in Glen Etive was unrest;
bidh 'n oidhche fada, 'n cadal fòil,	this night will be long, the sleep tranquil,
gun dìth shùilean air na doill.	the blind will need no eyes.

It would of course be inadequate and unjust to conceive of Mac Gill-Eain's relationship to the Gaelic tradition purely in terms of a rehearsal of historical memories and legendary motifs and in the echoing of poetic conventions. What is most exhilarating is the realisation that for him the 'dùthchas' of which we have already spoken is not an inert endowment from his people's past, but a source of vitality, a renewal of hope, and a pledge of life. Seen in the ominous perspective of the present situation of both Gaelic languages, this is perhaps what stirs the deepest emotion in the Irish reader – the fulfilment, in art at least, of all that the Irish Revival movement from the Gaelic League on had hoped and worked for. Nothing less than the survival, the rejuvenation and triumphant restatement of the culture of a deprived and dispossessed people, of what Mac Gill-Eain himself calls

.... an nì do-ruighinn buailte
a dheilbh ar daoine anns an uaigneas,
as an anacothrom 's as a' bhuaireadh
gus na dhiùchd as am mìorbhail.

.... the unattainable stricken thing
that our people fashioned in obscurity
out of hardship and passion,
until there came out of it the marvel.

It is an effective answer to that nagging doubt so familiar to those who write in threatened languages like ours, and which Somhairle Mac Gill-Eain too expressed:

Chan fhaic mi fàth mo shaothrach
bhith cur smaointean an cainnt bhàsmhoir...

I do not see the sense of my toil
putting thoughts in a dying tongue...

ach thugadh dhuinn am muillion bliadhna
'na mhìr an roinn chianail fhàsmhoir,
gaisge 's foighidinn nan ciadan
agus mìorbhail aodainn àlainn.

but we have been given the million years,
a fragment of a sad growing portion,
the heroism and patience of hundreds
and the miracle of a beautiful face.

A typically Gaelic defiance, we would like to think, of what looks like hopeless odds. Eachann Ruadh nan Cath was no more dauntless at Inverkeithing.

This tragic pathos which haunts any thinking inheritor of the Gaelic past and lurks in Somhairle Mac Gill-Eain's poetry seems to me to achieve its *locus classicus* in the poem 'Hallaig', wherein, too, an unbroken courage faces the unthinkable, the disappearance of people and language and of all cultural freehold. For this reason the poem is an epitome of much of the specific attraction which the poet's work holds for Irish audiences. The outrage at injustice, held under iron restraint, is there; the burden of a history which tore a Gaelic people from their beloved places, from the loved faces of their friends and forebears; the 'tuaineal', the trauma, brought on by the contemplation of such wilful profanation of these holiest of human things; all expressed in a dream sequence which might itself be seen as a contemporary re-working of a Gaelic convention with a long history, the 'aisling', in an age which has seen a fresh significance in oneiric literature.

I would not have it thought, however, as a consequence of the preceding disquisition that the undoubted admiration in Ireland for Somhairle Mac Gill-Eain is based solely on the reflection in his work of preoccupations of our own, on a sort of Gaelic parochialism, as it were. Apart from the fact that many of these preoccupations are, it seems to me, our particular share of the pity and the pride of the human condition, this present consideration of our fellow-feeling is secondary, in the sense that it assumes and should be read against the primary achievement of a major lyric poet. The Irish Gael, too, is first caught and held by a poetry of private and public drama, by the golden love of 'Tràighean' and 'A' Bhuaile Ghréine' and 'Fo Sheòl', by the agonized love and remorse and the intimation of blight and death in 'Aithreachas' or the poems of 'An Iomhaigh Bhriste'.

This essay has chosen rather to dwell, with complacence and maybe self-indulgence, on those contingent things of our common inheritance which Somhairle Mac Gill-Eain has forged into a new permanence. For many of us still in Ireland, against all appearances, the remaking of the Gaelic tradition into new forms, perhaps even into the matrix of a new sense of communion, remains one of the profoundest and most lasting ways of binding up our many wounds, in Ulster, in

Eire, maybe for all I know in Alba too.

> On bha t' ùidh anns an duine....
> rinn thu Gàidheil dhe na Goill.

"Since your care was for the human being," wrote Somhairle of his brother Calum Iain, "you made Gaels of the Gall." When we in Ireland contemplate the resurrection of Gaelic culture accomplished in Somhairle Mac Gill-Eain's poetic *opus,* the renewed sense of ourselves which it provokes in us, we might echo: "You made Gaels of the Gaels too":

> "Rinn thu Gàidheil dhe na Gàidheil".

BRENDAN DEVLIN

'When I Speak of the Face'

Marx, MacDiarmid and MacLean

"The revival of Gaelic poetry in the twentieth century", writes Malcolm Chapman in *The Gaelic Vision in Scottish Culture*, "cannot be divorced from attempts to develop a specifically Scottish political consciousness". [1] For Chapman, the two important figures who 'loom large' in this context are Hugh MacDiarmid and Ruaridh Erskine of Marr. To those two names, we may surely add at least a third: that of Sorley MacLean whose *Dàin do Eimhir* (1943), it could be argued, provides justification in itself for the use of the term 'revival'.

The *Eimhir* poems, in the words of Iain Crichton Smith, "represent for the Gaelic psyche the first wholly unmistakable twentieth-century voice that speaks to it (though there have been others since)". [2] Or, as Donald MacAulay puts it:

After the publication of this book Gaelic poetry could never be the same again. At the time it seemed astonishingly new, and to some extent this sense of innovation remains, but now one tends to see it rather as renovation and recreation, a breathing of new life into the ancient art of Gaelic poetry. In the future, perhaps, it will be seen as the vital and incomparable link between the old style and the new. A great many of the virtues of this poetry are traditional ones, such as eloquence, passion, and intellectual inventiveness. [3]

This echoes MacDiarmid's comment in 1945, that MacLean's poetry "recaptures and renews some of the qualities of Gaelic classicism". [4] And, as MacAulay goes on to say, these traditional virtues are at the same time "at the service of humane and political ideas. The Gaelic world was interpreted in a new light, and the way was opened up for new topics and new methods of presentation". [5]

MacLean's significance in all of this is eminently comparable to that of MacDiarmid with regard, specifically, to Scots and, generally, to Scottish poetry. "With regard to quality alone," MacDiarmid himself had "no doubt" as to MacLean and himself "being the two best poets in Scotland today". [6]

In terms of "Scottish political consciousness", MacDiarmid's example was important to the younger poet. As he recently put it:

I do not pretend now that it was not of very great importance to me, and to people like me, in the early thirties that by far the greatest living Scottish poet was an uncompromising Socialist and Scottish Nationalist . . his union of poetic sensibility and spiritual and practical commitment was then to me, and still is, above all admiration. His very poverty was itself a proof of the greatness of his uncompromising commitment. [7]

However, it was not the nationalist, Erskine of Marr, who loomed large in Sorley MacLean's consciousness, but the republican socialist, John MacLean, regarded by MacDiarmid himself as also being "above all admiration". For MacDiarmid, John

MacLean was the "unbreakable spirit" and the "true tower" of Scotland's strength. For Sorley MacLean, he was not only "the battlepost of the poor" but, in family tradition, "a saint and a hero".[8]

MacDiarmid knew Erskine of Marr, publishing, for example, his one act play 'Fo Chromadh An Taighe' in the Scottish Chapbook of March 1923. At that time MacDiarmid was the local secretary in Montrose for R. E. Muirhead's Scottish Home Rule Association which, in alliance with Marr's Scots National League and Lewis Spence's Scottish National Movement, formed the National Party of Scotland in 1928. Marr had been an associate of John MacLean's towards the end of the latter's life (d. 1923) and although MacLean had no direct influence on the literary revival, in either Scots or Gaelic, it was his leadership and heroism that was to inspire the two poets.[9]

Despite suggestions to the contrary, MacDiarmid never knew the marxist schoolteacher, John MacLean.[10] Both poets came to know of him through reputation and the printed word. It was primarily through two of his uncles that the young Sorley MacLean was to learn of the significance of the 'Red Clydesider':

> I think it was very difficult to live in Glasgow at the time, and have any knowledge about what the working-class movement was without having this kind of mystique about John MacLean, because John MacLean became a legend pretty soon ... John MacLean was the great, ... the great man ... The name was greater than the knowledge...[11]

MacDiarmid was to claim John MacLean, albeit retrospectively, as a political forerunner to the Scottish Renaissance. The literary revival of the twenties, as Hamish Henderson put it, "cannot be disassociated from the growth to political maturity of the Scottish working classes during World War I".[12] For Sorley MacLean there was a special significance in all of this, as the most famous of Scottish marxists was a fellow clansman.

Sorley MacLean, then, stands in relation to the Gaelic revival in much the same way as does MacDiarmid to the Scots revival. Both brought their respective poetic media abreast of twentieth-century requirements and both sought to combine the political with the aesthetic. Much of MacLean's subject matter, embodying as it does a marxist outlook, is political, especially in those poems which are concerned with the rise of fascism, the Spanish Civil War, the Second World War and, most recently, the possibility of nuclear destruction.[13] His attitude is perhaps best summed up by the following statement:

> If 'committed', the poetry must be in some way confessional if it is to be true to the perpetual dilemma of the 'existentialist' choice. Iain Lom's famous words to Alasdair MacDonald, "You do the fighting and I'll do the praising", I consider disgusting, however expedient they might have been to the exigencies of the situation, and however wise they might have been in the long run. I could not have been an Iain Lom at Inverlochy or an Auden in America in 1939.[14]

Nevertheless, despite his admiration for MacDiarmid's uncompromising commitment, the idea of "the 'full-time' professional poet" was not for MacLean, although this had much to do with "long years of grinding school-teaching" and what he calls his "addiction to an impossible lyric ideal".[15] This combination of the committed and the confessional, coupled with his inability to go the whole way with MacDiarmid, on the one hand, and his refusal to acquiesce, on the other, are major elements in the complex from which his poetry was produced. This can be seen in the poem, 'Trì Slighean':

> Cha b'urrainn domh-sa cumail fàire
> air slighe chumhang nan àrd-bheann
> a nochdadh thar cridhe do bhàrdachd:
> agus, uime sin, Mhic Dhiarmaid,
> soraidh leat; ach nam bu mhiann leam
> b'urrainn domh an t-slighe chrìon ud,
> thioram, ìseal, leantuinn tiorail
> th' aig Eliot, Pound agus Auden
> Macneice, is Herbert Read 's an còmhlan:
> b'urrainn, mur b' e am fiaradh
> a chuireadh 'nam aigne dà bhliadhna
> le m' dhùthaich fhìn is càs na Spàinnte,
> cridhe feargach is nighinn àlainn.

I could not keep within sight of the narrow high-mountain road that was indicated across the core of your poetry: and, therefore, MacDiarmid, farewell: but, if I liked, I could comfortably follow that petty, dry, low road that Eliot, Pound, Auden, MacNeice and Herbert Read and their clique have: I could, were it not for the twist, put in my heart for two years by my own land, the fate of Spain, an angry heart and a beautiful girl.[16]

Much has been made of the confessional aspect of MacLean's poetry, specifically in relation to the 'beautiful girl', the Eimhir of the poems. One critic goes as far as to say that "MacLean's genuine poems are mostly love-poems".[17] But, as the above suggests, MacLean's poems are more complexly wrought than that. The straightforward love-poem, with or without remorse, is relatively rare. It is the unique combination of the elements mentioned above, if anything, that makes the poems genuine. Moreover, personalised criticism has done to death the traumatic love-affair business and has, especially with regard to the Spanish Civil War, been chronologically inaccurate.[18] Furthermore, to the best of my knowledge, the *Eimhir* of the poems is an *imaginative* embodiment compounded of at least three different persons.

The long and the short of this is that it was not a love-affair which prevented MacLean from going to Spain and it should be noted that he was keen to fight in the army after the outbreak of the Second World War. As he wrote to Douglas Young from Egypt in 1942, he would rather be in the front line (where he was) or in prison (where Young was) than "with Auden 'saving his art' in America or Spender doing likewise in London".[19] His commitment to action against the fascists is further illustrated in another letter to Young where he states, regarding MacDiarmid's conscript war-time employment:

I have only a hazy idea of what a bench-fitter is but it seems a strange job for the greatest poet in Europe. No doubt the English 'communist poets' of the Gollancz era are flourishing in the M.O.I. or some such haven of intellectual eunuchs.[20]

MacLean's commitment, then, should be beyond doubt and Eimhir should not be mistaken for an over-riding personal love. The upshot of this is that the tensions in MacLean's poetry are deeper and more complex than any putative rivalry between

the personal and the political. In a recent tribute to Hugh MacDiarmid he wrote of
MacDiarmid's influence:

> It was, however, inevitable that his power over us should temporarily lessen with
> the great acceleration of material urgencies from the beginning of the Spanish
> War in 1936 and through 1937, 1938 and 1939, when almost every month made it
> more likely that Fascism was going to conquer Europe and hold it down for
> generations. In the face of those probabilities both the golden lyric and the castle
> walls of the most impassioned and comprehensive philosophical poetry seemed
> frail defences, not much stronger than the Ivory Towers of the most self-indulgent
> escapists.[21]

That final sentence illustrates the deeper tension, perhaps even the central
paradox, on which much of his poetry is built: a tension between the active and
passive sides of his nature, between the frustrated moral activist (the politician) and
the lyricist of 'high seriousness'.

MacLean once said that he was, up until the end of the Second World War,
"fundamentally ... much more interested in politics than in poetry" and that, as a
young man, he did not have an ambition to be a poet:

> I didn't have an ambition to be a poet, but the Civil War affected me
> tremendously ... Because of certain circumstances, family circumstances, which
> were very difficult in my case, I couldn't go. I would have been the man ... who
> would have gone first, I think, before making poems because I think my political
> passion was far greater than what you could call aesthetic passion.[22]

That political passion might be best described as the passion of a moral activist,
since for MacLean politics means not so much the art of the possible but "a most
important part of moral philosophy".[23] It was primarily to the men of action rather
than to the men of words that he was drawn. As he wrote to MacDiarmid in 1940:
"Names like Lenin, Connolly, John MacLean etc. are more to me than the names of
any poets".[24]

Hence, the poetry of the Spanish Civil War was born out of frustration. MacLean
would have preferred direct action but, circumstances being what they were, his
political passion was directed into poetry, into the lyric of 'high seriousness' which
was what, incidentally, he valued most in the poetry of Hugh MacDiarmid: the
lyrics of *Sangschaw* and *Penny Wheep*:

> To me, the best of them were, and still are, the unattainable summit of the lyric
> and the lyric is the summit of all poetry, but they could not be followed even 'afar
> off' by me or anyone else. In them I saw a timeless and 'modern' sensibility and
> an almost implicit 'high seriousness' and an unselfconscious perfection of rhythm
> that could not be an exemplar because it was so rare.[25]

But, because of the strength of his political passion, MacLean could not have
written as MacDiarmid did in *To Circumjack Cencrastus*:

> Better a'e gowden lyric
> Than a social problem solved.

As he wrote to Douglas Young in 1940, as early as *A Drunk Man* he "had resented
an arty attitude to politics" in MacDiarmid's poetry.[26]

So, while channelling his political passion into poetry, MacLean nevertheless realisèd that this was no substitute for direct action, no matter how golden the lyric. Thus, it is simplistic to see the tension in MacLean's poetry deriving from the rivalry of a personal erotic love and a frustrated desire to act on behalf of mankind. Rather, as his tribute to MacDiarmid suggests, that tension derives from a deep commitment to the lyric of 'high seriousness' in the face of his realisation that poetry alone not only could not do much to bring about radical social change, but could only put up at best 'frail defences' against fascist (and, indeed, capitalist) 'probabilities'. This awareness must have been especially clear to him in the autumn of 1939 when western civilization itself seemed *in extremis.*

Nevertheless, MacLean was, as a poet, obsessed by the "impossible lyric ideal". This can be interpreted in several ways. In the first place, the obsession arose from the fact that MacLean was, or at least regarded himself as "a traditional Gaelic singer *manqué* ":

> Even to this day, I sometimes think that if I had been a singer I would have written no verse . . . very early in life I came to be obsessed with the lyric, first of all because of my unusually rich Gaelic background; with the lyric in the Greek sense of a marriage of poetry and music, and then, because I was not a musician, with the lyric in the Shelleyan and Blakeian sense of a short or shortish poem suggesting song even if it could never be sung ...[27]

Thus, the lyric ideal to which he became committed was "impossible" because, being neither singer nor musician, he could never effect, properly speaking, "a marriage of poetry and music". Consequently, he was drawn to the Shelleyan/ Blakeian lyric form:

> The kind of lyric in the modern sense is the nearest approach. In many ways I'm an absolutist and if I were to write a song it would have to be words out of which the melody rose like an exhalation, as it were.

But even with the "lyric in the modern sense" MacLean was confounded by the extraordinary success of MacDiarmid's early lyrics, and, although they had a "cathartic influence" on him, this was "not a thing that would lead to emulation and imitation".[28] His success "could not be an exemplar because it was so rare".

But the lyric ideal was "impossible" in another sense: for it could never satisfy the whole man, the moral activist as well as the poet. It is interesting to note here that as MacDiarmid deserted the golden lyric for an "impassioned and comprehensive philosophical poetry", so MacLean attempted something similar with his abortive long-poem, 'An Cuilithionn'. In a letter to MacDiarmid in January 1940 he describes the poem as:

> . . a medley of some 1,700 lines in 7 parts called *The Cuillin* and dedicated to yourself and to the memory of Alexander MacDonald. It varies from the most direct political utterance to varying degrees of symbolism. It works out from the history of Skye to a sort of contemplation of Scotland and the rest of Europe.[29]

In June 1940, MacDiarmid wrote to him:

> . . you must understand that the arrival of your poem is a tremendous event in my life — and its dedication to me an honour equivalent to (and because in poetry and in respect of a contribution to *Scottish* Literature even greater and more brain-seizing) than Sorabji's dedication to me of his stupendous *Opus Clavicembalisticum.*[30]

But MacLean had already decided that overall 'An Cuilithionn' was "a crude declamatory poem".[31] He had been inspired to write it by *A Drunk Man*. Where he could not hope to emulate MacDiarmid's lyric peaks he had hoped to create a similar "medley with the lyrics rising out of that".[32] His failure, in his own view, was attributable to the fact that he "didn't have the *vis comica* that MacDiarmid had so magnificently, so wonderfully".[33]

But it may be that even the long poem failed to satisfy the whole man. Certainly, his moral-political passion found *A Drunk Man* an inadequate model outwith the purely formal context. "There is a more serious flaw in the poem, a disrespect for the ordinary human creature, especially for the ordinary Scottish creature", although MacLean also draws attention to the poet's self-distaste or self-loathing (sgreamh dheth fhéin) "accompanying the contempt which he vents on others".[34]

So then, both the lyric form and the long poem were at best "frail defences" for the moral activist, and attempts to 'bolster up' the lyric form in a medley failed to satisfy the poet. But MacLean's desire to give the lyric an abiding substance and centrality that would satisfy his moral passion also led him to "put the people's anguish in the steel of my lyric" ('Sgatham') much as MacDiarmid, indeed, sought to embody "the flower and iron of the truth" ('First Hymn to Lenin') in his poetry. But the lyric ideal (and the lyric remained "the summit of all poetry" for MacLean) never finally satisfied, and his continuing dialectical argument with Eimhir was, in this sense, an argument with the lyric ideal itself. Thus is he haunted by his "unwritten poems" in 'Coin is Madaidhean-allaidh':

Coin chiùine caothaich na bàrdachd,	The mild mad dogs of poetry,
madaidhean air tòir na h-àilleachd,	wolves in chase of beauty,
àilleachd an anama 's an aodainn,	beauty of soul and face,
fiadh geal thar bheann is raointean,	a white deer over hills and plain,
fiadh do bhòidhche ciùine gaolaich,	the deer of your gentle beloved beauty,
fiadhach gun sgur gun fhaochadh.	a hunt without halt, without respite.

And while Eimhir's beauty may "cast a cloud / over poverty and a bitter wound / over the world of Lenin's intellect, / over his patience and his anger" ('Am Buaireadh'), the intellect and anger of the man of action remains unfulfilled in material or practical terms. MacLean is therefore deeply troubled by the "frail defences" of poetry of any sort, especially in his native language:

Chan fhaic ni fàth mo shaothrach	I do not see the sense of my toil
bhith cur smaointean an cainnt bhàsmhoir	putting thoughts in a dying tongue
a nis is siùrsachd na Roinn-Eòrpa	now when the whoredom of Europe
'na murt stòite 's 'na cràdhlot.	is murder erect and agony.

This sense of frailty as expressed in 'Chan Fhaic Mi...' is undoubtedly made more poignant for MacLean because of his fear that Gaelic may be "a dying tongue", but even the best of Scots and English lyrics serve only to demonstrate to him how impossible is the lyric ideal. As he once wrote:

What an unsatisfactory thing poetry is! Grieve's lyrics, at least the greatest poetry in Britain in our time, is at its greatest "of marginal content" as Davie has said. Yeats's great lyrics are just the splendid expressions of a weakling's moments of self-realisation, hopelessly tangled with his posturings, often just arrant nonsense.[35]

In 'A' Bheinn Air Chall', this impossible lyric ideal is represented by 'The Lost

Mountain' of the title. The "many-coloured images of our aspiration", the mountain which rises above the wood, are

air chall anns a' choille th' air chall . . .	lost in the wood that is lost . . .
a chionn 's nach téid na sràidean ciùrrte	since the tortured streets will not go
'sa' choille mhaoth an cochur rèidh.	in the wood in a smooth synthesis.

In other words, the poet asks, in what lyric ideal can the people's anguish be put; in what lyric ideal can the desired centrality and substance be embodied?

Dé 'n t-sìorruidheachd inntinn 's an cuirear	In what eternity of mind
Ameireaga mu Dheas no Belsen,	will South America or Belsen be put
agus a' ghrian air Sgurr Urain	with the sun on Sgurr Urain
's a bhearraidhean geàrrte 'san t-sneachda?	and its ridges cut in snow?

The question is imponderable rather than rhetorical. MacLean will not accept the golden lyric in preference to the social problem solved. He will not have "Paradise without the paradise of his own people" and so the poem closes with a vision not of the desired "eternity of mind" but of "Spartacus with his tortured army".

It should not then be surprising that throughout MacLean's poetry (and not just with reference to Spain) we are confronted with images of, and references to, heroic figures whose moral or political passion is evident through action. For example, in 'Ard-Mhusaeum na h-Eireann', MacLean contrasts the passive role of the poet with the deeds of James Connolly:

Cha d' rinn mise ach gum facas	I have done nothing but see
ann an Ard Mhusaeum na h-Eireann	in the National Museum of Ireland
spot mheirgeach ruadh na fala	the rusty red spot of blood,
's i caran salach air an léinidh	rather dirty, on the shirt
a bha aon uair air a' churaidh	that was once on the hero
as docha leamsa dhiubh uile	who is dearest to me of them all
a sheas ri peileir no ri béigneid	who stood against bullet or bayonet,
no ri tancan no ri eachraidh	or tanks or cavalry,
no ri spreaghadh nam bom éitigh.	or the bursting of frightful bombs.

In 'Aig Uaigh Yeats', while celebrating "the generous deeds/that were sweet in the ears of Connolly and in the ears of his kind", he compares his own passive role *qua* poet with that of Yeats. In 'Palach', the subject symbolizes the people's anguish through his self-immolation, but even here the poet feels that his words can only partially express his horror, sympathy, and sense of betrayal (regarding Russian communism):

Chan eil ceann-teagaisg 'nam chainnt:	There is no text in my words:
tha dusan Palach anns an Fhraing.	there are a dozen Palachs in France.

And that final dialectical thrust I take to be a reference to *les évènements* in Paris in 1968.

MacLean's own direct action in the North African Desert during the Second World War brought him face to face with death and personal heroism, as conveyed in the famous poem 'Curaidhean', which closes:

Chunnaic mi gaisgeach mór á Sasuinn,	I saw a great warrior of England,
fearachan bochd nach laigheadh sùil air;	a poor manikin on whom no eye would rest;
cha b' Alasdair á Gleanna Garadh —	no Alasdair of Glen Garry;
is thug e gal beag air mo shùilean.	and he took a little weeping to my eyes.

Moreover, as the equally famous poem 'Glac a' Bhàis' shows, MacLean's sympàthies were not reserved for his own comrades-at-arms. As he writes of the dead German boy:

Ge b'e a dheòin-san no a chàs,   Whatever his desire or mishap,
a neoichiontas no mhìorun,   his innocence or malignity,
cha do nochd e toileachadh 'na bhàs   he showed no pleasure in his death
fo Dhruim Ruidhìseit.   below the Ruweisat Ridge.

The poem follows closely his thoughts on the actual incident as described in a letter from the Middle East in October 1942:

> The first dead man I saw in action was a young German sitting in a pathetic attitude in a dug-out entrance. He made me ashamed of many foolish generalisations I had often made about the necessity for wiping out all Fascists. Probably he wasn't a fascist after all or, if he was, only of the kind the ordinary, politically unconscious man must be in every fascist country, but of course the ordinary man is never really a fascist in any fascist country, just as the ordinary Englishman is not an 'imperialist' no matter what even he thinks he is.[36]

Again, it is the people's anguish that he wishes to put into the steel of his lyric:

An robh an gille air an dream   Was the boy of the band
a mhàb na h-Iùdhaich   who abused the Jews   .
's na Comunnaich, no air an dream   and Communists, or of the greater
bu mhotha, dhiùbh-san   band of those

a threòraicheadh bho thoiseach àl   led, from the beginning of generations,
gun deòin gu buaireadh   unwillingly to the trial
agus bruaillean cuthaich gach blàir   and mad delirium of every war
air sgàth uachdaran?   for the sake of rulers?

It is, then, typically the 'poor martyrs' who are the subject of MacLean's political passion as expressed in his poetry. This is nowhere more apparent than in 'Am Botal Briste':

Tha 'm botal briste 's an ràsar   The broken bottle and the razor
an dòrn 's an aodann a' ghill' òig   are in the fist and face of the boy
neo'r-thaing Auschwitz is Belsen,   in spite of Auschwitz and Belsen
a dh' aindeoin na croiche ann an Sruighlea and the gallows in Stirling
agus na téile ann an Glascho   and the other one in Glasgow
is tìodhlacadh Mhic Gill-Eain.   and the funeral of John MacLean.

Tha na martairean ag éigheach   The martyrs shout
air gach taobh de dh' Abhainn Chluaidh,   on each side of the River Clyde,
's ciad O Conghaile 'n Eirinn,   and a hundred Connollys in Ireland;
's chan eil a choltas air Uladh   and Ulster does not show
gu'n do lean Wolfe Tone Rìgh Uilleam.   that Wolfe Tone followed King William.

Tha fuil dhòirte is feòil reubte   Spilt blood and torn flesh
mu na Tighean Seara 'g éigheach   shout about the Easterhouses
's a' mùchadh le sgreadan cruaidhe   and stifle with hard screeches
guth nam martairean truagha.   the voice of the poor martyrs.

This is not to say, of course, that MacLean's political passion is his poetry, although his poetry would not be what it is without that passion. Moreover, heroism is not always public or political: for example, in his elegy for his brother, 'Cumha Chaluim Iain MhicGhill-Eain':

'S tric a bhios mi foighneachd
Dhe mo chridhe fhìn
An e creideamh na Ròimhe
No cruadal annasach 'nad sheòrsa
A chuir do threuntas g' a àirde
Mar gum b' ann gun strì.

Often do I ask
of my own heart
if it was the creed of Rome
or a rare hardihood in your kind
that put your heroism to its height,
as it were without effort.

Is daor a cheannaich thusa 'n t-uabhar
A cheannaich sinne 'nad bhàs:
Fad cheithir bliadhna gun àrdan
Chleith thu do chinnt air do chàirdean
Cho faisg 's bha do bhàs.

You dearly bought the pride
that we bought in your death:
for four years without hauteur
you hid from your kind your certainty
that your death was so near.

Is daor a cheannaich sinne 'n t-uabhar
A mhiadaich le do bhàs:
Gu robh do threuntas 'na mhìorbhail
Air falach 'na do spòrs;
Gur tearc a chunnacas do leithid
Ann a leithid de chàs.

We dearly bought the pride that increased
with your death:
that your heroism was a marvel
hidden in your fun;
that seldom was seen your like
in such an extremity.

Thus, for MacLean, in a very real sense the personal and the political are subsumed under the moral and he has an abiding interest in the psychology as well as in the politics of heroism. What the lyric ideal is to his aesthetic passion, the heroic ideal is to his moral passion. But that is to subdivide the whole: for in the actual poetry the aesthetic and the moral passion are inseparable.

Moreover, in those poems where the personal and the political are presented as being, in one way or another, antithetical, they nevertheless form part of a dialectical unity which may be defined as a dialectic of moral questioning, if not of moral argument. Thus, in 'An Tathaich' he may write:

Ma tha Arm Dearg a' chinne
an gleachd bàis ri taobh an Dniepeir,
chan e euchd a ghaisge
as fhaisg' air mo chridhe,

Though the Red Army of humanity is
in the death-struggle beside the Dnieper,
it is not the deed of its heroism
is nearest my heart,

ach aodann a tha 'gam thathaich,
'ga mo leantuinn dh' oidhche 's latha,
aodann buadhmhor nighne
's e sìor labhairt.

but a face that is haunting me,
following me day and night,
the triumphant face of a girl
that is always speaking.

But in 'Gaoir na h-Eòrpa' he will ask:

Dé bhiodh pòg do bheòil uaibhrich
mar ris gach braon de 'n fhuil luachmhoir

What would the kiss of your proud mouth be
compared with each drop of the precious blood

a thuit air raointean reòta fuara
nam beann Spàinnteach bho fhòirne cruadhach?
Dé gach cuach de d' chual òr-bhuidh
ris gach bochdainn, àmhghar 's dòrainn
a thig 's a thàinig air sluagh na h-Eòrpa

that fell on the cold frozen uplands
of Spanish mountains from a column of steel?

What every lock of your gold-yellow head
to all the poverty, anguish and grief
that will come and have come on Europe's people

bho Long nan Daoine gu daors' a' mhór-   from the Slave Ship to the slavery of the
                        shluaigh?   whole people?

At the emotional, or empathetic, level, what unites the heroism of love (or personal
heroism) and the heroism of action (or political heroism) in the poetry is the shared
element of tragedy. As he puts it in 'An Iomhaigh':

Rinn mi ìomhaigh dhe mo ghaol;   I made an image of my love;
cha b' i an iomhaigh shocair   not the comfortable image
a chuireadh bàrd air sgeilpe 'n tùr   that a poet would put on a shelf in a tower,
ach té a chinneadh mór 'san Fhàsaich,   but one that would grow big in the Desert,
far am biodh an fhuil 'na bùrn.   where blood would be water.

The element of tragedy, or of what we might call 'tragic ambiguity', pervades the
poetry because the impossible lyric ideal is itself mirrored by what is an impossible
love ideal. By that I do not mean an 'ideal love', but a love ideal that derives from
moral passion and strives for an *absolute* attainment in terms both of private and
public sympathy and commitment in the face of inevitable human limitations. This
note of tragedy is perhaps nowhere more clearly expressed than in 'Coilltean
Ratharsair' where he writes:

Ged bheirteadh gaol cho coimhlionta   Though a love were given as perfect
ri gaisge 'n aghaidh chàs,   as heroism against circumstances,
gun athadh, gun teagamh, gun dòchas,   unhesitant, undoubting, hopeless,
goirt, crò-dhearg, slàn;   sore, blood-red, whole;
ged bheirteadh an gaol do-labhairt   though the unspeakable love were given,
cha bhiodh ann ach mar gun cainte   it would be only as if one were to say
nach b' urrainn an càs tachairt   that the thing could not happen
a chionn gun robh e do-labhairt.   because it was unspeakable.

In 'Coilltean Ratharsair', the "unspeakable love" represents the unattainable
absolute after which not only the poet's but humanity's moral passion is seen to
strive. Tragedy is inherent because although the absolute may remain 'unspoiled' it
is nevertheless "unattainable, lost". Indeed, the tragic element is emphasized
through the implication that the attainment of such would in itself spoil the
metaphysical prize:

Chunnacas mùr a' Chuilithinn leagte,   One has seen the Cuillin wall knocked
                                                                            down,
    prann briste, an slochd sgreataidh;   brittle, broken, in a loathsome pit,
    agus chunnacas an gaol singilt   and one has seen the single-minded love
    do-ruighinn, caillte, neo-mhillte.   unattainable, lost, unspoiled.

'S e gu bheil iad ag éirigh   It is that they rise
    as an doimhne thruaigh reubte   from the miserable torn depths
    tha cur air beanntan an éire.   that puts their burden on mountains.

Bochd mi-chinnteach am bonn   Poor, uncertain the base
    tha stèidheachadh Cuilithionn nan sonn.   on which the heroic Cuillin is based.

This 'tragic flaw' in the spiritual life of humanity is a recurrent theme in MacLean's
poetry, but it should not be thought of as simply referring to the poet's personal
experience. The notion of a tragic struggle against circumstance was one that
possessed MacLean long before any personal love-entanglement. Of his initial
conversion to socialism, in his early teens, for example, he wrote:

But the great Socialists for some time appeared to my inmost mind as splendid

Titanic humanitarians fighting a battle certainly lost. God was on the other side. At this stage the Titanic humanitarian was everything even if he were certain to be wrong. By far the greatest intellectual stirring in my teens was my first reading of Shelley's "Prometheus" and for years Shelley was almost everything to me.[37]

Moreover, the tragic consciousness which MacLean saw in socialism was never entirely lost to him, even in full adulthood:

> .. my Promethean view of socialism is an inversion of the career of the "saved" in the sense that it was a justification of the "lost", "damned" Promethean. I had to find a humanist, hence Promethean, substitute. I have never been on the side of the established angels. In my teens my socialism would have repudiated the "class war" utterly. My later communism or socialism is probably a fortifying or rather restatement of the Promethean non-class war boyish socialism in the light of my experience of the actualities of life.[38]

MacLean's Promethean view of socialism is apparent throughout his work, in his desire to put the people's anguish into his poetry and to embody "the voice of the poor martyrs". Given his over-riding political passion it is perhaps surprising how some critics have refused to accept MacLean's engagement with marxism at any profound level and have sought to limit it to a superficial or romantic attraction. Iain Crichton Smith, for example, sees "no evidence of much other than an emotional commitment" to communism in MacLean's poetry, and notes that, "In this he is unlike MacDiarmid who does give the impression that he has actually *read* some of the texts".[39] More recently, Duncan MacLaren has written:

> MacLean's Marxism was essentially of the romantic sort, clutched at as a coherent philosophy which diagnosed the main faults of the Scotland and Europe of his day and could advocate decisive ways of improving the situation. MacLean never became, like MacDiarmid and Cornford . . a communist poet. Marxism, tempered by Scottish nationalism, provided MacLean above all with a club with which to beat the bourgeois landlords and uncaring clerics who had contributed to the decline of his native society.[40]

But as much (or, indeed, as little) has been asserted of MacDiarmid's relationship with marxism, in any case.[41] With regard to questions of emotionalism and romanticism, it is perhaps as well to note here what MacLean wrote under the title 'Realism in Gaelic Poetry' as early as 1938:

> Lack of realism usually comes not from emotion but rather from a lack of emotion, whose place is taken by mere fancifulness, day-dreaming, wish-fulfilment, or weak sentimentality. In a person of any brain power at all, intensity of emotion conduces rather to an intense realization of reality. There is little doubt that perhaps the chief reason for this romantic escapism in the poets of England, France and Germany was the fact that nineteenth-century poetry, a product of the bourgeoisie, found the industrial capitalism erected by that class so sordid that poets had to eschew contemporaneity by an escape to the past or the exotic. In the twentieth-century escapist romanticism is at a discount, its place having been taken by the deliberate romanticizing of racism, brutality and irrationality fostered by fascist propaganda. This is the new and most terrible opium for the people ever devised. Its high priests, however, are politicians not poets. There is a limit to the depth to which a poet can sink.[42]

This is surely a lucid appraisal of what is (or should be) by now a critical commonplace. It should also serve to warn us away from a shallow appraisal of MacLean's creative engagement with marxist dialectics as, indeed, should the dialectical nature of much of his poetry. John MacInnes is much nearer the mark when he writes of the impact and nature of MacLean's poetry:

> Now, for the first time, the Renaissance mind, the classical values, and the sceptical modern temper are compounded with the mediaeval humours and virtues, and Gaelic poetry in one step moves triumphantly into the contemporary world.
>
> It was Marxism that provided at least one of the frameworks, perhaps the major one, within which these processes occurred. It gave the poet a coherent theory of history which enabled him to bring together, for instance, the Highland Clearances and the success of fascism in Spain in the thirties as related events in the same historical process.[43]

Or again:

> Marxism gave the form in which he was able to view the history of his own people in the context of world politics.[44]

I have sought to illustrate something of the dialectical nature of MacLean's poetry and to go some way towards 'placing' it with regard to contemporary figures like MacDiarmid and contemporary political and aesthetic pre-occupations. I would argue that the nature of both MacLean's creative and critical writings confounds Crichton Smith's argument that his involvement with marxist ideas is "debatable".[45]

Furthermore, MacLean was certainly well-versed in marxist texts. He first read Marx in his twenties and, despite his later disillusionment with Russian communism, still holds to the belief that "Marx made a few of the most valid generalizations that have ever been made about history".[46] In the mid-1930s he wrote to MacDiarmid from Portree:

> At present I am reading nothing but Marxism in which I am considerably more proficient now than I used to be and I am convinced that the special line you are taking with regard to the Scottish and communist question is the best especially in view of the great difficulty of striking at British Imperialism otherwise.[47]

That "special line" with regard to the Scottish and communist question was MacDiarmid's advocacy of what he called the "John MacLean line": in short, his advocacy of a Scottish Workers' Republic. While in a British uniform Sorley MacLean remained convinced that (and the words echo John MacLean's) "the only real war is the class war".[48] In these war years, moreover, he believed that the only thing which would save the Gaelic language would be the "quick setting up of a Scottish Soviet Republic which would eliminate the cash and profit and careerist motive more radically than Russia appears to have done . . you have to kill the careerist motive. That only a thorough Communism would do".[49]

There is, undoubtedly, a moral fervour in MacLean's socialism (and one that is not always apparent in MacDiarmid), but this should not be mistaken for emotionalism or romanticism. MacLean was enough of a scholar not only to do his homework, but also to think out very carefully his position as a revolutionary socialist regarding direct action against the Nazis. To MacDiarmid he wrote in

1941:

> I support the British just because I think it the weaker and therefore not as great a danger to Europe and European socialism as a German victory would be. I cannot therefore go the whole hog with yourself and Young and Hay though I must confess I find my present position involving me in very bad company politically. I cannot share the belief that Britain is likely to win and, as a result, the fear of a long Nazi domination of Europe is an obsession with me . . and I am afraid that if they knock out Britain they will knock out the Soviet later and thereby extinguish the greatest, perhaps the only hope of Europe's working classes. I cannot therefore view this war as I would have done the last war where Germany was more hopeful from the working class point of view than Britain was. I know hundreds of so-called Socialists are advancing this viewpoint merely to put a face on their cowardice and fear of any real Socialist activity but the certain fact that all the Dollans etc. are doing this cannot really alter my own obsessing fear and hatred of the Nazis.[50]

In opposition to MacLean's attitude, MacDiarmid had written to him in 1940:

> I note what you say about the War but do not agree. Although the Germans are appalling enough and in a short-time view more murderously destructive, they cannot win — but the French and British bourgeoisie can, and is a far greater enemy. If the Germans win they could not hold their gain long — but if the French and British bourgeoisie win it will be infinitely more difficult to get rid of them later. That is my point of view.[51]

MacLean made his position quite clear in several letters both to MacDiarmid and to Douglas Young in the war years and has repeated it several times since. In an interview published in 1979, he stated:

> I was convinced that it was necessary to fight to the end for the bad against the worst, and I had never time for what was considered a kind of Communist doctrine (it wasn't the official one) but it was that let the Nazis get power and the Fascists get power — after them us . . I couldn't agree with MacDiarmid in that.[52]

In *The Age of MacDiarmid* he wrote:

> I would not care to say how much MacDiarmid was sustained during those years, 1936 to 1939, by the Communist belief that Fascism was just the last kicks of Capitalism and that its triumph would be short-lived; and that therefore one ought not to be greatly concerned with the defence of a rotten pluto-democracy against a more brutal but a more short-lived kind of Capitalism. At any rate, this Communist doctrine was made irrelevant by the heroic examples of so many Communists in Spain and their devotion to a United Front . .

Spain, as MacLean says elsewhere, stuck in his throat, and in a Nazi victory he could see only the concentration camps. Whatever one makes of the opposing analyses of MacDiarmid and MacLean, not only is it obvious that they spoke the same political language, but a reasonable case could be made to suggest that MacLean had a firmer grasp of marxist ideas than did MacDiarmid. With regard to MacDiarmid claiming to be both a marxist and a Douglasite, MacLean has noted how impressed he himself was by Grassic Gibbon's apposite commentary:

> Lewis Grassic Gibbon had referred to Douglas Social Credit sarcastically as that

ingènious scheme being to the social revolution as child birth without pain, and even more intriguing, without a child![53]

MacLean, then, knew his Marx as well as his MacDiarmid. But, just as he (rightly) denied to Douglas Young that stylistically he was "one of Hugh's sons",[54] so he never fully embraced communism to the point, at least, of joining the Communist Party:

> I was never a member of the Communist Party because I was too sceptical to become either what you might call a materialist or an idealist in philosophy. I still am and I always was . .[55]

Or, as he puts it elsewhere:

> Munich made me very near being a Communist but not quite. Not quite, you see, because I was too much perhaps of a pessimist — maybe because of my type of religious upbringing — and also because philosophically I was fundamentally a sceptic.[56]

It is perhaps the case that MacLean's socialism is rooted in a moral abhorrence of the unco guid and his hatred of social élitism, but it would be wrong, especially given his acutely critical intellect, to reduce that to emotionalism or romanticism. Moreover, he was no more of a doctrinaire communist than was MacDiarmid. Like MacDiarmid, he was, and still is, a marxist intellectual and, as a poet, a dialectician of the first creative order. Like MacDiarmid, he is also (as the former put it) "fu' o' a sticket God", a failed God; the God of Christianity — as is only too apparent from poems like 'Ban-Ghàidheal', 'Calbharaigh' and 'An Crann Dubh'. MacLean is perhaps too much of a pessimist or sceptic ever to have given complete faith to a future, classless society, but that *vis comica*, whose presence in MacDiarmid he admired so much and whose absence in himself he lamented, is perhaps not entirely missing from his poetry. Central to MacLean's work, as to MacDiarmid's, is a celebration of the human spirit and its potentiality, and on at least one occasion the comic force breaks the surface. I refer to that wonderful dialectical *jeu d'ésprit*, 'Am Boilseabhach':

'S mi 'm Bhoilseabhach nach tug suim	A Bolshevik who never gave heed
riamh do bhànrainn no do rìgh,	to queen or to king,
nan robh againn Alba shaor,	if we had Scotland free,
Alba co-shìnte ri ar gaol,	Scotland equal to our love,
Alba gheal bheadarrach fhaoil,	a white spirited generous Scotland,
Alba àlainn shona laoch;	a beautiful happy heroic Scotland,
gun bhùirdeasàchd bhig chrìon bhaoith,	without petty paltry foolish bourgeoisie,
gun sgreamhalachd luchd na maoin',	without the loathsomeness of capitalists,
's gun chealgaireachd oillteil chlaoin,	without hateful crass graft;
Alba aigeannach nan saor,	the mettlesome Scotland of the free,
Alba 'r fala, Alba 'r gaoil,	the Scotland of our blood, the Scotland of our love,
bhristinn lagh dligheach nan rìgh,	I would break the legitimate law of kings,
bhristinn lagh cinnteach shaoi,	I would break the sure law of the wise,
dh' èighinn 'nad bhànrainn Albann thu	I would proclaim you queen of Scotland
neo-ar-thaing na Poblachd ùir.	in spite of the new republic.

But the poem is, for better or worse, atypical. The new republic was not to be, and the historical process from MacLean's point of view was anything but hopeful. With the people's anguish in the steel of his lyric, he wrote in 'An t-Eilean':

Chan eil dùil gum faicear pàighte
strì is allaban a' Bhràighe,
is chan eil cinnt gum faicear fiachan
Martarach Ghleann-Dail 's iad diolte;

chan eil dòchas ri do bhailtean
éirigh àrd le gàire 's aiteas,
's chan eil fiughair ri do dhaoine
's Ameireaga 's an Fhraing 'gam faotainn.

Mairg an t-sùil a chì air fairge
ian mór marbh na h-Albann.

It is not likely that the strife
and suffering of Braes will be seen requited
and it is not certain that the debts
of the Glendale Martyr will be seen made good;

there is no hope of your townships
rising high with gladness and laughter,
and your men are not expected
when America and France take them.

Pity the eye that sees on the ocean
the great dead bird of Scotland.

More recently, there has been little to alleviate this pessimism. MacLean's fear, as expressed in 'Screapadal', is a fear of the ultimate clearance which will render all ideals not only impossible but irrelevant:

Dh' fhàg Rèanaidh Screapadal gun daoine
Gun taighean, gun chrodh ach caoraich,
Ach dh' fhàg e Screapadal bòidheach;
R' a linn cha b'urrainn dha a chaochladh.

Thogadh ròn a cheann
Agus cearban a sheòl,
Ach an diugh anns an linnidh
Togaidh long-fo-thuinn a turraid
Agus a druim dhubh shlìom
A' maoidheadh an nì a dheanadh
Smùr de choille, de lianagan 's de chreagan,
A dh' fhàgadh Screapadal gun bhòidhche
Mar a dh' fhàgadh e gun daoine.

Tha tùir eile air an linnidh
A' fanaid air an tùr a thuit
Dhe mhullach Creag a' Chaisteil,
Tùir as miosa na gach tùr
A thog ainneart air an t-saoghal:
Peireascopan 's sliosan slioma
Dubha luingeas a' bhàis
A mharbh mìltean Nagasaki,
Bàs an teis mhóir 's na toite...

Rainy left Screapadal without people,
with no houses or cattle, only sheep,
but he left Screapadal beautiful;
In his time he could do nothing else.

A seal would lift its head
and a basking-shark its sail,
but to-day in the sea-sound
a submarine lifts its turret
and its black sleek back
threatening the thing that would make
dross of wood, of meadows and of rocks
that would leave Screapadal without beauty
just as it was left without people.

There are other towers on the Sound
mocking the tower that fell
from the top of the Castle rock,
towers worse than every tower
that violence raised in the world;
the periscopes and sleek black sides
of the ships of the death
that killed the thousands of Nagasaki,
the death of the great heat and the smoke...

It is against this possibility, as MacLean is only too well aware, that we have now to effect further meaningful developments of a specifically Scottish political consciousness. Part of that does necessitate an appreciation of the "frail defences" of poetic genius in its struggle to express the people's anguish, as it also necessitates a willingness for direct action. In these terms, it may well be that Sorley MacLean's poetry will be remembered above all for its deep and lasting expression of a genuine sense of struggle. That sense of struggle characterises MacLean's political and aesthetic passions. It is the hallmark of a genuinely revolutionary spirit.

RAYMOND J. ROSS

NOTES

1   Malcolm Chapman, *The Gaelic Vision in Scottish Culture*, London/Montreal 1978, p. 145.
2   Iain Crichton Smith, 'The Poetry of Sorley MacLean', *The Glasgow Review*, 4, No. 3, Summer 1973, p. 38.
3   Donald MacAulay, *Modern Scottish Gaelic Poems*, Edinburgh 1976, p. 54.
4   Hugh MacDiarmid, 'Six Scottish Poets of To-Day and Tomorrow', *Poetry Scotland*, 2, 1945, p. 69.
5   MacAulay, *op. cit.*, p. 54.
6   Letter from Hugh MacDiarmid to Sorley MacLean, 23 Jan. 1977.
7   Sorley MacLean, 'MacDiarmid 1933-44', in *The Age of MacDiarmid*, ed. P. H. Scott and A. C. Davis, Edinburgh 1980, pp. 17-18.
8   Letter from Sorley MacLean to Douglas Young, 7 Sept. 1941, National Library of Scotland (abbrev. N.L.S.), Acc. 6419.
9   Something of the general influence of John MacLean on the Scottish Literary Renaissance may be gauged from *Homage to John MacLean*, ed. T. Berwick and T. S. Law, Edinburgh 1979 (first pub. 1973).
10 This is implied in a letter from MacDiarmid to George Ogilvie in 1916. But MacDiarmid stated quite categorically to the late Morris Blythman ("Thurso Berwick"), Chairman of the John MacLean Society, that he never met John MacLean.
11 Angus Nicolson, 'An Interview with Sorley MacLean', *Studies in Scottish Literature*, 14, 1979, p. 33.
12 Hamish Henderson, 'Flower and Iron of the Truth: A Survey of Contemporary Scottish Writing', *Our Time*, 7, No. 11, 1948, p. 304.
13 Sorley MacLean, 'Screapadal', *Cencrastus*, 7, Winter 1981-82, p. 18.
14 Sorley MacLean, 'On Poetry and the Muse', *Chapman*, IV, No. 4, Summer 1976, p. 30.
15 *Ibid*, p. 31.
16 This English translation of 'Trì Slighean' (dedicated to MacDiarmid) is given by MacLean in a letter to Douglas Young, 15 April ?1942, N.L.S., Acc. 6419.
17 Denis Donoghue, 'A Vocation for Remorse', *TLS*, 9 Sept. 1977.
18 A. D. Mackie, for example, writes (*Scots Independent*, November 1973), that "MacLean's poetry is impregnated with a strong sense of guilt that his over-powering personal involvement with a woman held him back from participation in the fight for the Left in Spain". But, as MacLean points out in his interview with Angus Nicolson (see note 11 above), and elsewhere, "It wasn't a woman fundamentally that kept me from going, though there was one."
19 Letter to Young, 6 Oct. 1942, N.L.S., Acc. 6419.
20 Letter to Young, 27 April 1942, *ibid*.
21 *The Age of MacDiarmid, op. cit.*, p. 21.
22 Sorley MacLean, 'Poetry, Passion and Political Consciousness', *Scottish International*, 10 May 1970, p. 10.
23 *The Age of MacDiarmid, op. cit.*, p. 17.
24 Letter to MacDiarmid, 25 May 1940, Edinburgh University Library.
25 *Chapman, op. cit.*, p. 29.
26 Letter to Young, 23 Nov. 1940, N.L.S., Acc. 6419.
27 *Chapman, op. cit.*, pp. 25-28.
28 Raymond J. Ross, 'Sorley MacLean: a Bard to All People', *The Weekend*

Scotsman, 24 Oct. 1981.
29   Letter to MacDiarmid, 10 Jan. 1940, N.L.S. Acc. 6419.
30   Letter to MacLean, 5 June 1940, *ibid.*
31   Letter to MacDiarmid, 12 May 1940, *ibid.*
32   Sorley MacLean, 'Poetry, Passion and Political Consciousness', *op. cit.*, p. 11.
33   Raymond J. Ross, *op. cit.*
34   Sorley MacLean, 'Am Misgear agus an Cluaran', *Gairm*, 6, 1953, p. 151.
35   Letter to Young, 30 March 1942, N.L.S. Acc. 6419.
36   Letter to Young, 27 Oct. 1942, *ibid.*
37   Letter to Young, 7 Sept. 1941, *ibid.*
38   Letter to Young, 11 Sept. 1941, *ibid.*
39   Iain Crichton Smith, 'The Poetry of Sorley MacLean', *The Glasgow Review*, 4, no. 3, Summer 1973, p. 39.
40   Duncan MacLaren, 'The Shy Guru', *Q. Question*, 10 June 1977, p. 10.
41   John Wain, 'Beyond the Stony Limits', in *The Age of MacDiarmid, op. cit.*, p. 172.
42   Sorley MacLean, 'Realism in Gaelic Poetry', *Transactions of the Gaelic Society of Inverness*, 37, 1934-36, pp. 83-86. (A late addition to Vol. 37, this paper was actually delivered to the G.S.I. on 19 April 1938.)
43   John MacInnes, 'Sorley MacLean: the Harvest of his Genius', *The Weekend Scotsman*, 23 April 1977.
44   John MacInnes, *Scottish International*, December 1973.
45   Iain Crichton Smith, 'Major Gaelic Poet in a European Context', *Glasgow Herald*, 27 Oct. 1973.
46   Sorley MacLean, 'Poetry, Passion and Political Consciousness', *op. cit.*, p.15.
47   Letter to MacDiarmid, 21 Sept. ?1934-7, N.L.S., Acc. 6419.
48   Letter to MacDiarmid, 8 March 1941, *ibid.*
49   Letter to Young, 27 May 1943, *ibid.*
50   Letter to MacDiarmid, 8 March 1941, *ibid.*
51   Letter to MacLean, 5 June 1940, *ibid.*
52   Angus Nicolson, 'An Interview with Sorley MacLean', *op. cit.*, p. 30.
53   *Ibid.*, p. 31.
54   Letter to Young, 7 Sept. 1941, N.L.S., Acc. 6419.
55   Sorley MacLean, 'Poetry, Passion and Political Consciousness', *op. cit.*, p. 11.
56   Raymond J. Ross, 'Sorley MacLean: a Bard to All People', *op. cit.*

'The Choice'

Poet of Conscience:
The Old and the New in the Poetry of Somhairle
MacGill-Eain

My primary concern in this chapter is to consider the most enduring and the most universal aspects of the art of Somhairle MacGill-Eain, especially with regard to *Dàin do Eimhir* and his other love poetry. For it was within the conventions of the love-poem that he engaged himself with the greatest intensity in the solution of the problem which he defines as "how to find this suggestion of song or chant in poetry that satisfies the mixed, troubled modern mind, and carries what is implicit in the old-fashioned phrase, 'criticism of life' ".[1]

My first concern here will be to show how MacGill-Eain has tapped the power of the primal myth that has subtended the emotional and much of the artistic life of Europe for the last 800 years. The form in which this myth was incorporated and in which it has given artistic expression to Gaelic civilization is the main legacy to which MacGill-Eain is heir, and a very self-conscious heir at that. Secondly, I would hope to demonstrate how his assimilation of the conceits of the Gaelic love-song to the requirements of the Symbolist canon created new opportunities for the exercise of the poetic power of the former, opportunities which were exploited by him with genius and panache. Finally, I propose to explore the way in which the loss of a meaningful world and the consequent ontological, ethical and other ambiguities that are of the essence of modernity, pervades the work of MacGill-Eain, giving it a powerful contemporary and, indeed, universal relevance that must ultimately secure recognition for it in the forefront of European poetry.

But first, the myth. "Love and death, a fatal love", writes Denis de Rougemont in the opening salvo of his *Passion and Society,*

— in these phrases is summed up, if not the whole of poetry, at least whatever is possible, whatever is universally moving in European literature, alike as regards the oldest legends and the sweetest songs. Happy love has no history. Romance only comes into existence where love is fatal, frowned upon and doomed by life itself. What stirs lyrical poets to their finer flights is neither the delight of the senses nor the fruitful contentment of the settled couple; not the satisfaction of love, but its passion. And passion means suffering. There we have the fundamental fact.[2]

Here is the central conceit of *amour courtois,* the romance myth which became an internationally diffused sensibility, an emotional renaissance to which the concept of 'love' in the still current romantic sense may be ascribed and, by interconnection, the beginnings of modern poetry.

The assumptions on which this 'courtly-love' poetry is based are: the ennobling power of love (no sacrifice is too great for the lover to make), the elevation of the status of the beloved above that of the lover (his or her beauty and attributes being often divinized), and the equation of love with desire, ever-increasing desire, insatiable desire. Unrequitedness is central to the conceit; the condition is attended by pain or sickness, evidenced in the lover by a time-honoured symptomatology. The lover sighs, weeps and sickens unto death, but if he could receive a single kiss from his beloved he would be restored instantly to health. Thus, twelfth-century troubadour Jaufre Rudel de Blaye sings:

Colps de joi me fer que m'ausi,	I am stricken by joy which slays me,
Et ponha d'amor que.m sostra	and by a pang of love which ravishes
La carn, don lo cors magrira;	my flesh, whence will my body waste away;
Et anc mais tan greu no.m feri,	and never before did it strike me so hard,
Ni per nuill colp tan no langui,	nor from any blow did I so languish,
Quar no cove, ni no s'esca.	for that is not fitting, nor seemly.[3]

The elements of the romance myth, as just described, are of the very essence of the Gaelic love-song. Thus, for example, in 'Oran Gaoil d'A Leannan agus I Posadh ri Fear Eile' ('Love Song to his Darling on Her Marriage to Another'),[4] possibly composed by Maighistir Seathan (born about 1680 and a poet of the MacLean heartland of Mull), there is the mandatory unrequitedness in the very title of the song, and the ability of the loved one's kiss to heal, her superb beauty and the intensity of the poet's desire for her, in the following verse:

'S e shlànaich mo chreuchdan	What has healed my wounds
Pòg no dhà od' bheul cùbhraidh,	is a kiss or two from your fragrant lips
's gu bheil maise na feucaig	for the beauty of the peacock
Ann at eudann ga ghiùlan.	lies in your face;
'S mi nach iarradh de spréidh leat	I would seek no dowry with you
Air chruinne na gréine	of all the world under the sun
Ach t'fhaotainn á léinidh	but to have you in your shift
Le toil cléir agus dùthcha.	with the approval of clergy and community.

Anndra Mac an Easbuig (born about 1635) has similiar regard for the conventions in his song addressed to Barbra Nighean Easbuig Fullarton.[5] The lady's physical beauty is celebrated in the following terms:

Thugas gaol nach fàillinneach	I have given unfailing love
Do rìbhinn nan cuach fàmannach,	To the maiden of the waving locks
Gur bòidheach dualach àr-bhuidhe	Beautiful curled and golden yellow
Mar aiteal deàrrsaidh theud.	Like the shining gleam of harp strings.
A h-uchd nach crìon ri thaisbeanadh	Her bosom so smooth to see
Bheil dà chìoch cho tlachdmhora	With two breasts so delightful
Bhuin gach crìdh 'na *chaptive* leò	Which have taken all hearts captive
Fo ghlasaibh aice fhéin.	Imprisoned by her.

Her kiss has the power to heal:

Gur mils' a pòg na mealannan;	Her kiss is sweeter than honey;
'S i 's cinntich glòr gun aimideachd —	Her speech is most assured and free from foolishness —
Bheir brìgh a beòil 's a h-analach	The power of her lips and her breath
Neach anacrach o'n eug.	Can save those in agony from death.

Barbra rejects Mac an Easbuig's suit, and the poet is within predictable terms of reference when he concludes with "B'fhearr dhomh mura buainichinn thu Bhith 'san uaigh am péin" (Better for me if I failed to win you To be suffering in the grave).

The practice of ideal *amour courtois* constitutes, paradoxically, an asceticism, almost a religious passion; the Tantric yoga of India is a parallel. Accordingly, it is no surprise to hear de Rougemont speaking in this context of the achievement of "transfiguration" by courtly love, "a kind of transcendental state outside ordinary human experience, into an ineffable absolute irreconcilable with the world, but that they (the troubadours) feel to be more real than the world".[6]

The centrality of *amour courtois* to the art of Somhairle MacGill-Eain is stressed in 'A' Bhuaile Ghréine' ; indeed, the symbolic object of the poet's address, Eimhir, is defined exclusively within these terms:

Do m' shùilean-sa bu tu Deirdre	To my eyes you were Deirdre
's i bòidheach 's a' bhuaile ghréine;	beautiful in the sunny cattle-fold;
bu tu bean Mhic Ghille Bhrìghde	you were MacBride's wife
ann an àilleachd a lìthe.	in her shining beauty.
Bu tu nighean bhuidhe Chòrnaig	You were the yellow-haired girl of Cornaig
is Mairearad an Amadain Bhòidhich,	and the Handsome Fool's Margaret,
an Una aig Tómas Làidir,	Strong Thomas' Una,
Eimhir Chù Chulainn agus Gràinne.	Cuchulainn's Eimhir, and Grainne.
Bu tu té nam mìle long,	You were the one of the thousand ships,
ùidh nam bàrd is bàs nan sonn,	desire of poets and death of heroes,
's bu tu an té a thug an fhois	you were she who took the rest
's an t-sìth bho chridhe Uilleim Rois,	and peace from the heart of William Ross,
an Audiart a bhuair De Born	the Audiart who plagued De Born,
agus Maoibhe nan còrn.	and Maeve of the drinking horns.

A veritable galaxy of *femmes fatales* and tragic heroines this, both of Gaelic and other legends and of the more recent past. Maud Gonne to whom Yeats paid court ("Why should I blame her that she filled my days with misery" he wrote in 'No Second Troy'), for example, is cheek by jowl with Helen, De Born's Audiart (evidence of MacGill-Eain's sensitivity to the Provençal roots of his art), the tragic "nighean bhuidhe Chòrnaig" (killed by her brothers to prevent a marriage of which they disapproved) and with Úna Bhán of Tomás Láidir Ó Coisdeala's lament, one of the great tragic love songs of Ireland.

These particular symbols of intense emotional life and MacGill-Eain's aesthetic, in which primacy is assigned to 'emotion' rather than 'intellect', are of a piece. In a remarkable article, 'Realism in Gaelic Poetry',[7] the poet himself has set the matter straight for us. "The matter of a poem . . . must be contemplated emotionally", he writes. "The object contemplated may be hopeless love, a ship in the sea, the destiny of mankind, a deer on the mountain, the death of a hero or the ugliness of a reptile, a lost cause or a base success. The emotion may be love, reverence, awe, world-weariness, hatred, anger or disgust, and it may be apparent or latent . . . the emotion with which the object is contemplated, allied with the rhythm and tone which that emotion does much to suggest, has a completely transfiguring effect on the matter contemplated, but this transfiguration is not necessarily unrealistic, and in fact the greater the poem the greater is its realism in spite of this emotional and formal transfiguration". Emotion and realism are not seen as opposites, then; on the contrary: "Lack of realism usually comes not from emotion but from lack of emotion, whose place is taken by mere fancifulness, day-dreaming, wish-fulfilment, or weak sentimentality. In a person of any brain power at all, intensity of emotion conduces rather to an intense realization of reality".

The ideal of a purely cerebral, donnish, poetry is accordingly forsworn:

. . . ņam bu mhiann leam   . . . had I so wished
b'urrainn domh an t-slighe chrìon ud,   I could with ease have followed
thioram, ìseal, leantuinn tìorail   the way, trifling, mean and arid
th' aig Eliot, Pound agus Auden,   of Eliot, Pound and Auden,
Macneice, is Herbert Read 's an còmhlan: Macneice, and Herbert Read and their crew:
b'urrainn, mur b'e am fiaradh   could have, but for the twist
a chuireadh 'nam aigne dà bhliadhna   put in my intellect these two years
le m' dhùthaich fhìn is càs na Spàinnte,   by my own land and the travail of Spain,
cridhe feargach is nighinn àlainn.   a passionate heart and beautiful girl.[8]

It is entirely consistent with his announced aims that MacGill-Eain should further refine his poetic ideal to "dàintean 's am faighte singilt'/ buadhan an triùir 's iad fillte,/ dàintean 's am faicte chrois/ bh' air Yeats is Blok is Uilleam Ros" [9] (translated as, 'songs woven of great words/ like the high trinity of bards,/ songs containing the great cross/ of Yeats, Blok and William Ross", in Iain Crichton Smith's elegant translation of Poem XX in *Dàin do Eimhir*).[10]

Concerning the connection between MacGill-Eain and Yeats we shall say nothing here — the works and pomps of the latter being an essential part of English literary discourse and hence, we assume, familiar to the reader.

Uilleam Ross (1762-90), less known to non-Gaelic speakers, was the first major Scottish Gaelic poet to have left a substantial body of love-songs, thus securing a freedom and acceptability for the individual Gaelic love lyric in an area that had previously been mainly the preserve of non-professionals and the great anonymous. Biographical details are provided in the edition of his collected songs edited by George Calder.[11] Briefly, he seems to have incorporated the courtly ideal not only into his poetry but also into his private life. He became infatuated with Mór Ros, a girl he met in Stornoway, and although his songs indicate that the infatuation was on his side only, friends attested to an engagement between himself and Mór in which she invoked fire from heaven to consume her if she were unfaithful. For all that, she married a sea-captain not long afterwards and took up residence in his port, Liverpool. Regretting her choice, she wrote to Uilleam suggesting that they meet in Gairloch. He agreed, travelled as far as Stirling to meet her, but thought better of the whole idea and decided to retrace his steps. Reaching his father's cottage after a night in the open he took to his bed for the last time at the age of 28.

MacGill-Eain's praise of his work is nothing if not fulsome. "I myself consider William Ross's last song one of the very greatest poems ever made in any language in the islands once called British", he declares in 'Old Songs and New Poetry',[12] and later: "neither I nor anyone else can ever hope to persuade the non-Gaelic world that William Ross's last song is comparable in quality to the best of Shakespeare's Sonnets".

The generality of Ross's work, however, although undoubtedly sonorous, earthy, occasionally risqué and always easy on the ear, is all too often vitiated by *cliché*, by a too-ready resort to conventions that would have been 'old hat' to the older MacLean poets we have quoted previously. In 'Oran Gaoil na h-Oighe do Chailein' ('Song on the Love of the Maid for Colin'),[13] to take an example, the charms of the maid in question are recalled in terms that had lost their freshness centuries before Ross:

"Bha falt cama-lùbach, bòidheach,   Her hair cross-looped, pretty,
Bachlach, òr-bhuidhe, 'na dhuail,   Crook-like, golden, in curl,
Cas-bhuidhe, snìomhanach, fàinneach,   Crisp-yellow, twisted ringlets,

An neo-chàramh, mu'n cuairt —
"Do bhràghad sneachdaidh a b'fhìor-ghlain
Fo lic bu mhìn-dheirge gruaidh,
Gun innleachd bhàth, ach buaidh nàduir,
A' toirt gach bàrr dhut gun uaill!"

In a déshabillé whirl —
"Round thy snowy neck the purest,
'Neath cheek of pink hue,
No cosmetic but nature
Gives thee excellence true!"

Not a case where the poet is well-served by his translator, as anyone with a modicum of Gaelic will appreciate, but the point still stands. And most of Ross's more famous 'Oran Gaoil' ('Love Song')[14] is similarly constituted.

The cure-from-death-or-illness convention is found in the seventh verse of 'Oran Gaoil' and again in the final verse of 'Oran Gaoil do Chailin Araidh':

Bi'dh Diùcachan ag ùmhlachadh,
'S a' tuiteam air an glùinean dut,
A's ciùin-shealladh do ghnùis gile
Mar ùr-chasg o na bhàs dhoibh.

Dukes will be humbly pleasing thee
And falling on their knees to thee,
The look serene of thy face to see
From death a rescue new to them.[15]

'Oran Eile, air an Aobhar Cheudna' ('Another Song, on the Same Theme')[16] is a *tour de force*, however; loss of his lover and consequent depression leading to the death of his art and the foreshadowing of his own death are the matter of a poem whose intensity lends it wings. It concludes:

Cha dùisgear leam ealaidh air àill',
    Cha chuirear leam dàn air dòigh,
Cha togar leam fonn air clàr,
    Cha chluinnear leam gàir nan òg:
Cha dìrich mi bealach nan àrd
    Le suigeart mar bha mi 'n tòs,
Ach triallam a chadal gu bràth
    Do thalla nam bàrd nach beò!

I'll not wake a song of fine art,
    I'll not set a part to be sung,
I'll not raise a tune on the harp,
    Or hark to the laugh of the young;
I'll not climb the path of the steep
    With the leap that was mine heretofore,
But I'll reach there forever to sleep,
    The hall of the bards of no more.

With regard to Ross's love-songs it might have been thought that the poetic possibilities for expressing romantic passion had been exhausted, the few remaining permutations and combinations of a limited and ancient stock of images and metaphors having been pressed into service. Furthermore, their serviceability as models for modern Gaelic poetry is called into question by MacGill-Eain's general criticism of the traditional Gaelic love-song, "as poetry, the old Gaelic song has everything except our modern world and the far-ranging, uninhibited, troubled, explicit modern intellect";[17] a caveat which applies equally to the work of William Ross.

On balance, then, it is difficult to avoid thinking that MacGill-Eain's inclusion of the latter in his poetic Pantheon has less to do with his concern to find a poetic model appropriate to his concerns — we find few, if any, significant echoes of Ross in *Dàin do Eimhir* — than to find a symbol for Gaelic poetry and for a life determined by a grand and tragic romantic passion.

The question of possible motives behind MacGill-Eain's concern to give poetic expression to what appeared to be to all intents and purposes an outmoded conceit is one we will touch upon later; the point here is that such a project was at the core of his enterprise, and what could be designated the 'mediaeval' aspect of his achievement was nothing less than to have refurbished the whole rusted armoury of the love poet. MacGill-Eain's *amour courtois* is situated securely within a contemporary ambience and imagery. Thus, in 'Fo Sheòl' for example, Provençal unrequitedness is updated in an unexpected and bright new minting:

Bha 'm bàt agam fo sheòl 's a' Chlàrach
ag gàireachdaich fo sròin,
mo làmh cheàrr air falmadair
's an téile 'n suaineadh sgòid.

My boat was under sail and the Clarach
laughing against its prow,
my left hand on the tiller
and the other in the winding of the sheet
rope.

Air dara tobhta 'n fhuaraidh
shuidh thu, luaidh, 'nam chòir
agus do ròp laist' cuailein
mu m' chrìdh 'na shuaineadh òir.

On the second thwart to the windward,
darling, you sat near me,
and your lit rope of hair
about my heart, a winding of gold.

A Dhia nan robh an cùrsa ud
gu mo cheann-uidhe deòin,
cha bhiodh am Buta Leódhasach
air fóghnadh do mo sheòl.

God, if that course had been
to the destination of my desire,
the Butt of Lewis would not
have sufficed for my boat under sail.

In 'Am Boilseabhach' MacGill-Eain gives a neat twist to an old love convention wherein the beloved is preferred even to God by replacing the latter with the State, in this case a fantasized Scottish Republic.

The beauty of the beloved is evoked in conventional but striking terms in 'Camhanaich':

Bu tu camhanaich air a' Chuilithionn
's latha suilbhir air a' Chlàraich,
grian air a h-uilinn anns an òr-shruth
agus ròs geal bristeadh fàire.

You were dawn on the Cuillin
and benign day on the Clarach,
the sun on his elbow in the golden stream
and the white rose that breaks the horizon.

But in the epigrammatic 'An Òinseach' a modern unease concerning the 'shabby equipment' of language is reflected; all talk about 'beauty' is merely hot air which signifies nothing when beauty is apprehended in its concreteness:

Nuair thuirt thu nach robh bhòidhche
ach cosamhlach is le fàiling
's ann bha mise smaointinn:
saoil, òinseach àlainn
an cainte sin ri Naoise
nuair thaobh e Earra-Ghàidheal?

When you said that beauty
was only relative and with a defect
what I thought was:
think, lovely fool,
would that be said to Naoise
when he approached Argyll?

The poem brings Yeats's 'Politics' to mind:

> How can I, that girl standing there,
> My attention fix
> On Roman or on Russian
> Or on Spanish politics?
> Yet here's a travelled man that knows
> What he talks about,
> And there's a politician
> That has read and thought,
> And maybe what they say is true
> Of war and war's alarms,
> But O that I were young again
> And held her in my arms!

In 'Irisleachd' the elevated status of the beloved is stressed, and the healing convention is rescued from the mundane by the imagery that expresses it:

Fhuair mi faoisgneadh as a' chochull	I have burst from the husk
a rinn cor mo réis,	which my life's condition imposed,
is dhiùchd barr-gùc m' anama	and my spirit's blossom has come
bho arraban 'na léig.	out of distress an adamant.

The point could be repeated over and over again using other examples. And, again, it is simply that Somhairle MacGill-Eain has made courtly love 'news' again. In 'Tradition and the Individual Talent', T. S. Eliot has written, "The poet . . . must be quite aware of the obvious fact that art never improves, but that the material of art is never quite the same. He must be aware that the mind of Europe — the mind of his own country — a mind which he learns in time to be much more important than his own private mind — is a mind which changes, and that this change is a development which abandons nothing *en route*, which does not superannuate either Shakespeare, or Homer, or the rock drawing of the Magdalenian draughtsmen",[18] and the statement might well have been formulated with MacLean in mind who has neither 'superannuated' William Ross and his bardic forebears, nor yet flinched at expressing "the age's accelerated grimace".

Inclusion of Alexander Blok (1879-1921), the Russian Symbolist, in MacGill-Eain's triumvirate reflects the latter concern. It has much to do, I suspect, with the Gaelic poet's search for and legitimization of a method or theory within whose terms he could draw together both the disparate, variegated strands of his thought and experience and his knowledge of the 'great' songs into a poetic vehicle adequate to modern urgencies. "What is in question", he writes in 'Old Songs and New Poetry', "is whether there can be poetry, or any art, which is fully relevant to the modern world and which at the same time satisfies the instinct for what is called 'beauty' ".[19] In the same article he himself suggests a possible direction to be taken: "On the European front itself, it is this necessity for an intellectually satisfying content that remains art which has produced Symbolism, and Symbolism, in its manifestations in Blok, Yeats, Valéry, Rilke, MacDiarmid and Eliot, is the most impressive 'ism' that I know of in this century." [20]

The extent to which translations of Blok's work were available to MacGill-Eain during his most creative period (in the late 30s and early 40s) is unknown to the present writer, but there is no gainsaying the congruence of significant elements of the two sensibilities. Thus, Blok sings 'To the Muse':

> I cannot explain why, at daybreak,
> with my strength ebbing out like a wave,
> I did not go under but saw you
> and asked for the comfort you gave.
>
> I wanted us two to be enemies,
> so why did you give me a field
> full of flowers and a sky full of galaxies —
> the curse that your beauty revealed?
>
> Northern nights were never more treacherous,
> golden wine never more potent,
> gipsy love never more transient
> than your terrible embrace . . .

And there was a dark exaltation
in sacred things torn apart,
and, bitter as wormwood, this passion
was a wild delight to my heart.[21]

This poem parallels MacGill-Eain's 'An Dithis':

Is beag mo thruaighe-sa a nochd   My misery is small tonight
seach olc do cholainn creuchdaich,   beside the evil of your wounded body,
ach le do thruaighe-sa tha m' ghaol   but with your misery my love
air dhol 'na chaoir ghil leumraich,   turns to white leaping flame,
a' losgadh am bruaillean mo chinn   burning in the turmoil of my head
mo chuimhne air an téile,   my memory of the other,
air té nas rathaile 's nas bòidhche   of a more fortunate and more lovely one
's i pòsda thall an Eirinn   who is married over in Ireland

in the sense that unbidden love is their common stimulus. Likewise, the woman of
Blok's 'Accordeon':

Capricious, cunning woman,
dance! deceiving girl,
forever and ever poison
my godforsaken soul!

I shall go crazy and berserk,
raving that I love you,
that you are all the night, all dark,
that I am drunk on you . . .

that you have robbed me of my soul —
the soul you poisoned —
that I sing of you, you, girl,
songs without end[22]

and the woman of MacGill-Eain's 'Uilleam Ros is Mi Fhìn' are both transformed
into the matter of poetry:

On nach eil an còrr ri fhaotainn   Since no more is to be had,
is colainn mo ghaoil ghil air faondradh, and my fair love's body ruined,
is gun fheum — gun fheum saoghail,   and useless — without a use in the world —
's e chuir mo ghaol-sa gu laomadh   it's that that put my love to seed
leis a' bharrach fhaoin bhàrdachd   with the vain brushwood of poetry
's e mathaichte l' a colainn mhàbte.   manured with her mutilated body.

In MacGill-Eain, as in Blok, the real woman and object of the poet's passion is
transfigured into symbol. In *Poetry of This Age*, J. M. Cohen has the following to say
concerning Blok's Symbolism: ". . . its central figure, the Beautiful Lady, not only
embodies a living woman, . . . but stands also for the principle of Beauty, and for
[the mystical philosopher] Soloviev's idea of Sophia, the Divine Wisdom. It is very
difficult . . . to separate the several strands of his symbolism, and say with any
certainty that one poem is addressed to a woman, another to an idea, and a third to
his native country; in his multiple meanings he is a typically modern poet".[23] Like
considerations apply, roughly, to the case of Eimhir, and a like elusiveness. She is a
complex, multifaceted symbol serving to cohere meaning on many different and not
necessarily causally-connected levels, shade and emphasis varying with the poem,

but frequently standing for private passion, a principle that is seen in MacGill-Eain's ethical scheme of things as vitiating political action and public duty.

As this ethical dilemma is at the core of what is most intense and most moving in the art of Somhairle MacGill-Eain, the subject of Eimhir in this one of her many guises will be the subject of the rest of the essay.

In the early poem, 'A' Chorra-Ghridheach', MacGill-Eain's perception of his own ontological status, which stands in intimate relationship to the sphere of the ethical, is presented in terms of a 'Fall' myth; man is construed as falling from a state of grace or unity, symbolized by a heron, where thought and act are co-terminous ("lagh dìreach neo-cham corra-grithich" — the straight unbending law of herons) into a series of warring, psychic fragments or dualities.

M' aisling-sa air iomairt truaighe,	My dream exercised with sorrow,
briste, cam, le lainnir buairidh,	broken, awry, with the glitter of temptation,
ciùrrte, aon-drithleannach, neo-shuairce;	wounded, with but one sparkle;
eanchainn, cridhe 's gaol neo-shuaimh-neach.	brain, heart and love troubled.

In 'Gleann Aoighre', for example, the ideal, symbolized by "ceann sgorach Bhlàbheinn ceòthar, mùgach" (the rugged head of Blaven misty and morose) is posited over and against the concrete sensuality of "an t-ubhal coigreach, grinn, cùbhraidh" (the fragrant, delicate, exotic apple):

'S cha robh mo mhiann air na h-àirdean	And my desire had left the heights
o'n chunnaic mi an t-ubhal ùrar,	since I had seen the fresh apple,
an t-ubhal coigreach, grinn, cùbhraidh:	the fragrant, delicate exotic apple:
chan fhaighinn sàsachadh a' ghàraidh	I would not get the satisfaction of the garden
no aon fhurtachd air na h-àirdean	nor any comfort on the heights,
agus mo chàil air bhoile.	with the divisive passion of my spirit.

The poem is, plausibly, a poetic correlative of what the poet has referred to elsewhere as "my own lack of singlemindedness"; he has explained his failure to join the Communist Party in similarly revealing terms: "because I was too sceptical to become either what you might call a materialist or an idealist in Philosophy".[24] The consequences of such scepticism are listed in 'A' Chorra-Ghridheach':

Anfhannachd an strì,	Faintness in fight,
aognuidheachd am brìgh,	death pallor in effect,
gealtachd anns a' chrìdh,	cowardice in the heart
gun chreideamh an aon nì.	and belief in nothing.

The explicit nihilism of the last line quoted is not, on the evidence of 'Eadh is Féin is Sàr-Fhéin', assuaged by the siren voices of the various religious and secular creeds on offer. Rather, the heart scorns

bhith 'n crochadh air piotan ris an stalla	to hang from a piton against the rock-face
is fear mór 'na cheannard ròpa,	with a big man as rope-leader,
Calvin no Pàp no Lenin	Calvin or Pope or Lenin,
no eadhon bragairneach bréige,	or even a lying braggart,
Nietzsche, Napoleon, Ceusair.	Nietzsche, Napoleon or Kaiser.

Nor has the affective basis of MacGill-Eain's stance diminished throughout the years between 'A Chorra-Ghridheach' and the much later 'Creag Dallaig' where

Tha mo chridhe air a' bhearradh	My heart is on the ridge

agus leth dheth shìos,	and half of it down,
is mo cheann a' streap 's a' tuiteam	and my head climbs and falls
's an crochadh air sgeilpe chaoil,	and hangs on a narrow shelf,
is mo chasan gun aon taice	and my feet have no support
ach mo chridhe 's e fàs maol,	but my heart, which is getting blunt,
gun ghreim coise aig an eanchainn	and the brain has no foothold
gu ròp a leigeil sìos g' a thaobh.	to lower a rope to my heart.

Having said that, and judged it in the context of all of MacGill-Eain's hitherto published poetry, the appellation 'nihilism' has little to do with either his philosophy or poetry which is predicated on a view of the human condition intimately bound up with the concept of 'responsibility' in the sphere of the ethical.

If we are to take a risk here and assign a label to the sensibility that finds expression through *Dàin do Eimhir*, for example, 'existentialist' may fit the bill, or at least be a convenient heuristic peg on which to hang a few coats.

Nothing particularly exotic is being signalled by the use of the term here; the basic reference is to Plato's view of the human predicament, in which the soul is separated from its 'home' in the sphere of pure essences. Man is estranged from what he essentially is, existence in a transitory world contradicts his essential participation in the world of ideas. God and his sundry secular cognates are dead, no ultimate source of values exists, man is adrift in an indifferent universe. The congruence of this cluster of ideas with those expressed in the latest poems quoted in this essay is a point that needs no labouring.

An effective congruence underlying the ideational one can be inferred from 'Tràighean' where MacGill-Eain speaks of "building a rampart wall" "roimh shìorruidheachd choimhich 's i framhach" (against an alien eternity grinding).

My emphasis here is on the word 'alien', and the eeriness, incoherence, even hostility of the night sky evoked by 'Lìonmhoireachd'

Lìonmhoireachd anns na speuran,	Multitude of the skies,
òr-chriathar muillionan de reultan,	golden riddle of millions of stars,
fuar, fad as, lòghmhor, àlainn,	cold, distant, lustrous, beautiful,
tosdach, neo-fhaireachdail, neo-fhàilteach	silent, unfeeling, unwelcoming

is in resonance with the feelings of the horrified Roquentin of Sartre's *La Nausée* as he confronts elementary nature, shorn momentarily of labels and meaning. We need to qualify this by saying that in other contexts, as in 'Ceann Loch Aoineart', for example, the traditionalist breaks through and a deep sensual delight in nature and the description of nature is expressed with a panache and flair that recalls the work of Duncan Bàn MacIntyre and countless earlier Gaelic poets of Scotland and Ireland. But the impression made by those lines of 'Lìonmhoireachd is abiding.

In *The Courage To Be* the philosopher-theologian Paul Tillich writes of Existentialism as being expressed contemporaneously "in all classes of man's creativity", as permeating "all educated classes", and when he states that "Every analyst of present-day philosophy, art and literature can show their ambiguous structure: the meaninglessness which drives to despair, a passionate denunciation of the situation, and the successful or unsuccessful attempt to take the anxiety of meaninglessness into the courage to be oneself",[25] one is conscious of reading what amounts to the terms of reference for MacGill-Eain's artistic enterprise and, furthermore, the basis of a useful criterion by which to assess it.

"In our time the destiny of man presents its meaning in political terms", according to Thomas Mann. Somhairle MacGill-Eain would hardly disagree, and it was the overthrow of the Spanish Republic — "Oir chunnaic mi an Spàinn caillte, sealladh a rinn mo shùilean saillte" (For I have seen Spain lost, a sight that has made my eyes salt) — and two intense love-affairs that provided the events and experiences through which personal and artistic resolution would have to be sought. His problem in practical terms is expressed simply and graphically in Poem XVII of *Dàin Eile* (from *Dàin do Eimhir agus Dàin Eile*):

'N e d' mhiann bhith eadar sléisdean nighne	Is it your desire to be between a woman's thighs
's do bheul air blàth a cìochan,	and your mouth on the flower of her breasts,
's an t-Arm Dearg an éiginn áraich	and the Red Army in the travail of the battlefield
air a shàrachadh 's a riasladh?	conquered and trounced?

The choice was not part of some arbitrary pseudo-intellectual game for one whose left-wing alignment, nurtured on the radicalism of Braes and memories of the Skye Land League struggle, is expressed powerfully and unambiguously in poems such as 'Sgatham', 'Gealach Ùr', 'Dùn Éideann', and in a particularly explicit way in 'An Cuilithionn'. This is evident, for example, from the following segment of Part II:

Agus trom air suain na frìthe	And heavy on the slumber of the deer-forest
cruaidh-chàs is bochdainn nam mìltean	the hardship and poverty of thousands
de thuath is de mhith-shluagh na tìre,	of the tenantry and the common people,
mo chàirdean is mo chuideachd fhìn iad.	they are my kindred and my own people.
Agus ged nach d'rinn an càs-san	And though it was not their plight that made
gaoir ghoirt saoghail na Spàinne,	the bitter cry of the world of Spain,
agus ged nach d'rinn an dìol-san	and although their fate did not make
brat fala air aodann na h-iarmailt,	a cloak of blood on the face of the sky,
mar chunnaic Marlowe fuil Chrìosda	as Marlowe saw the blood of Christ
agus Leonhardt fuil Liebknecht;	and Leonhardt the blood of Liebknecht;
gus ged nach d'fhuaradh fios	and although information was not obtained
air oidhche-challa an sgrios	concerning the dread night of destruction
a lìon an saoghal le gal bròin,	that filled the night with sorrowful cry
call nan Asturaidheach 's an glòir,	the tragedy of the Asturians and their glory,
b'e an càs-san càs na tuatha 's nam bochd,	their plight was the plight of the tenants and the poor,
an cruaidh-chàs, a ghainne is an lochd	their hardship, the deprivation and the crime
bho 'n mhealladh mór-shluagh nan tìrean	by which the common people of the countries were deceived
le uachdarain, le stàt 's lagh sìobhailt,	by rulers, government and civil law,
agus leis gach seòrsa strìopaich	and by every kind of harlot
a reic an anam air a' phrìs ud	who sold her soul for that price
a fhuair gallachan an t-saoghail	exacted by the bitches of the world
bho 'n chàrn uachdarain am maoineas.	from what the rulers accumulated in wealth.[27]

The complexities and ambiguities inherent in a similar ethical dilemma are outlined by Sartre in his essay 'Existentialism'. "If God does not exist", he writes, "we find no values or commands to turn to which legitimize our conduct. So, in the bright realm of values, we have no excuse behind us, nor justification before us. We are alone, with no excuses". Thus the stage is set for the case of one of his students

who came to see me under the following circumstances: his father was on bad terms with his mother, and, moreover, was inclined to be a collaborationist . . .

His mother lived along with him, very much upset by the half-treason of her husband . . . the boy was her only consolation.

The boy was faced with the choice of leaving for England and joining the Free French Forces — that is, leaving his mother behind — or remaining with his mother and helping her to carry on. He was fully aware that the woman lived only for him and that his going-off — and perhaps his death — would plunge her into despair. He was also aware that every act he did for his mother's sake was a sure thing, in the sense that it was helping her to carry on, whereas every effort he made towards going off and fighting was an uncertain move which might run aground and prove completely useless; for example, on his way to England he might, while passing through Spain, be detained indefinitely in a Spanish camp; he might reach England or Algiers and be stuck in an office at a desk job. As a result, he was faced with two very different kinds of action: one, concrete, immediate, but concerning only one individual; the other concerned an incomparably vaster group, a national collectivity, but for that very reason was dubious, and might be interrupted *en route*. And, at the same time, he was wavering between two kinds of ethics. On the one hand, the ethics of sympathy, of personal devotion; on the other, a broader ethics, but one whose efficacy was more dubious. He had to choose between the two.

Who could help him choose? Christian doctrine? No. Christian doctrine says, 'Be charitable, love your neighbour, take the more rugged path, etc., etc'. But which is the more rugged path? Whom should he love as a brother? The fighting man or his mother? Which does the greater good, the vague act of fighting in a group, or the concrete one of helping a particular human being to go on living? Who can decide *a priori*? Nobody. No book of ethics can tell him.[28]

The fact that the actual circumstances that prevented MacGill-Eain from going to Spain related to, in his own words, "pure family economic terms" and that the Spanish War predated the *Dàin do Eimhir* love affairs,[24] make it reasonable to infer a parallel between the case described by Sartre and MacGill-Eain's actual situation. Thus, *Dàin do Eimhir* is, arguably, an imaginative, poetic synthesis of chronologically disparate elements of experience and feeling.

Motivational aspects apart, the poet faces his choice and its consequences, with all their emotional and philosophical ramifications, in 'Urnuigh' and in terms that recall the Sartrean and, by extension, the general existential *Weltanschauung*.

There is no court of higher appeal, "A chionn nach eil dìon ann" (Because there is no refuge), and the unified ethos of youth has been lost:

Chunnacas mùr a' Chuilithinn leagte,	One has seen the Cuillin wall knocked down,
prann briste, an slochd sgreataidh;	brittle, broken, in a loathsome pit,
agus chunnacas an gaol singilt	and one has seen the single-minded love
do-ruighinn, caillte, neo-mhillte.	unattainable, lost, unspoiled.

The centre has not held; in a universe without ultimate meaning, desire itself is only " 'na fhaileas faoin sgialachd" (the vain reflection of a story), of indeterminate cause, as the concluding verses of 'Coilltean Ratharsair' make clear:

Chan eil eòl air an t-slighe	There is no knowledge of the course
th' aig fiarachd cham a' chridhe	of the crooked veering of the heart,
's chan eil eòl air a' mhilleadh	and there is no knowledge of the damage
do 'n tàrr gun fhios a cheann-uidhe.	to which its aim unwittingly comes.
Chan eil eòlas, chan eil eòlas	There is no knowledge, no knowledge,

air crìch dheireannaich gach tòrachd	of the final end of each pursuit,
no air seòltachd nan lùban	nor of the subtlety of the bends
leis an caill i a cùrsa.	with which it loses its course.

The only possible prayer in the context of this intellectual and emotional vertigo is the atheistical or 'blasphemous' "dèanam làidir m' aigne fhìn an aghaidh àmghair" (let me strengthen my own spirit against agony):

An guidhe toibheumach neo-iomlan,	The blasphemous imperfect prayer,
guidhe cam coirbte an tionndaidh,	the crooked perverted prayer that turns back,
an guidhe gun dèan mi guidhe,	the prayer that I may pray
gun ghuidhe 'n t-susbaint a ruigheachd.	without praying to reach the substance.

The coupling of "neoinitheachd" (nothingness) with "bàs nan sàr-fhear" (the death of the great) in the second verse of 'Urnuigh' and, to make the message even more explicit, with "gach dòchas treun faoilidh le 'n sgarar sinn bho 'n bhàs aognuidh" (every brave generous hope by which we are separated from chill death) in the third verse, underlines MacGill-Eain's apprehension of the existential void that lies at the heart of the secular faiths to which, as we have seen, he is, nonetheless, emotionally committed.

All of this is in the context of an intense, personal, eschatological vision that recalls Yeats's 'The Second Coming' and Blok's 'The Scythians':[29]

Dé an t-eagal a bhios ormsa	What fear will I have
roimh thuiltean aognuidh an onfhaidh	before the chill floods of the surge
a nis on chuala mi am monmhar?	now since I have heard their murmur?
Theirear gum faicear trom-laighe	It is said that a nightmare will be seen,
am bàs 's a' ghort a' tachdadh aighir.	death and famine choking gladness.

The political dimension of this vision is fascist dictatorship. As indicated in 'Gaoir na h-Eòrpa', beauty and art offer emotional compensation of questionable legitimacy for failure to fulfil the duty of resisting oppression:

An tugadh t' fhonn no t' àilleachd ghlòrmhor	Would your song and splendid beauty take
bhuam-sa gràinealachd mharbh nan dòigh seo,	from me the dead loathsomeness of these ways,
a' bhrùid 's am meàirleach air ceann na h-Eòrpa	the brute and the brigand at the head of Europe
's do bhial-sa uaill-dhearg 'san t-seann òran?	and your mouth red and proud with the old song?

So Eimhir becomes the symbol of every human attachment that provides "bréig a' chridhe shocraich" (the lie of the comfortable heart) to stifle conscience and to rationalize inaction.

What possible aim can MacGill-Eain's prayer have, then; is it to be "an aghaidh m' ùidhe" (against my own desire) in order that his heart be cleansed?

Bho anfhannachd mo ghaoil ghlain ghil,	From the weakness of my pure white love,
an iarr mi spiorad 's e air fhaileadh	will I ask for a flayed spirit
eadhon gum faighear anns a' bhoile mi	even in order that I be found in the madness
cho treun ri Dimitrov no ri O Conghaile?	as brave as Dimitrov or as Connolly?

"Boile" (madness) in this context would seem to be yet another indicator of the poet's sense of ambiguity about causes in general which, alloyed with the emotional turmoil of his love-affairs, constitutes "lìonsgaradh" (fragmentation) — the basis of his perfervid agonizing and uncertainty in the face of the choice between "bàs 'sa' bheatha bhiothbhuan" (death in immortal life), the Christ-like and envied fate of "Cornford agus Julian Bell agus Garcia Lorca/ marbh san Spàinn 'san aobhar naomh" (Cornford and Julian Bell and Garcia Lorca/ dead in Spain in the sacred cause), or the contemptible "beatha bhàsail" (deathlike life) in the flesh-pots. At a more abstract level, the tension subtending the process of choice is between intense commitment to the Republican cause at the emotional level and a thoroughgoing intellectual nihilism/existentialism.

"Death-like life" was his choice because "gum b' fhearr liom boireannach na 'n Eachdraidh fhàsmhor" (I preferred a woman to crescent History). The choice was all the more shameful for him because he has heard and understood the address of mankind in its travail, "thuig is thùr mi fàth an langain" (I sensed and understood the meaning of the cry), but Fate, flying the flags of Evangelical discourse (as I imagine it to be), is invoked to explain the decision:

Chunnaic mi 'n fhuil chraobhach ag éirigh,   I saw the branching blood rising,
tein-aighir an spioraid air na sléibhtean,   the bonfire of the spirit on the mountains,
an saoghal truagh ag call a chreuchdan: the poor world losing its wounds:
thuig is thùr mi fàth an langain   I sensed and understood the meaning of the cry

ged nach robh mo chridhe air fhaileadh.   though my heart had not been flayed.
Esan dh' am bheil an cridhe air ionnlaid   He whose heart has been washed
théid e troimh theine gun tionndadh,   will go through fire without turning;
dìridh e bheinn mhór gun ionndrainn;   he will ascend the great mountain without homesickness;

cha d' fhuair mise leithid de dh' anam   I did not get such a spirit
's mo chridhe ach air leth-fhaileadh.   since my heart is only half flayed.

If the sin of wrong choice has been committed, then the harmony of the universe, or religion, demands just retribution; the loss of the poet's "gaol geal àlainn" (beautiful white love) in 'An Roghainn' provides just that and an opportunity to indulge in some appropriate self-excoriation to boot. His selection of "an t-slighe chrìon bheag thioram ìosal thlàth" (a way that was small, mean, low, dry, lukewarm) obviates the possibility "gun glacainn an rionnag leugach óir,/ gum beirinn oirre 's cuirinn i gu ciallach 'na mo phòc" (that I would grab the radiant golden star,/ that I would catch it and put it prudently in my pocket).

So can we conclude then with the wisdom of hindsight that, given the chance again, Somhairle MacGill-Eain would take his place in the ranks of the International Brigade and leave the affairs of the heart to lesser souls? We cannot. And it is a measure of his integrity that he does not take the easy option of making the 'right' choice in retrospect. Thus, in the final verse of 'An Roghainn' in answer to this question MacGill-Eain expresses a desire whose mood is despair shot through with bravado: if the choice were to be made again, it might be made by a "whole spirit":

Ach nan robh 'n roghainn rithist dhomh   But if I had the choice again
's mi 'm sheasamh air an àird,   and stood on that headland,
leumainn á neamh no iutharna   I would leap from heaven or hell
le spiorad 's cridhe slàn.   with a whole spirit and heart.

The unmistakable implication of this is that somehow the "whole spirit and heart" affords a basis for 'right' choice that is unavailable to a spirit sinking in the bog of duality. But how is such a basis to be achieved? 'A Chiall 's a Ghràidh' gives us a clue in this regard:

Air an taobh a staigh mo ghaol,	On the inside my love,
mo thuigse ar an taobh ghrinn,	my intellect on the elegant side,
is bhristeadh a' chòmhla bhaoth.	and the foolish door was broken.
Is thubhairt mo thuigse ri mo ghaol:	And my intellect said to my love:
cha dhuinn an dùbailteachd:	duality is not for us;
tha 'n coimeasgadh 'sa' ghaol.	we mingle in love.

The point is made with greater intensity in 'A' Chorra-Ghridheach', where "Tràth na mire an tràth shoilleir thig á eanchainn chiar na doille" (The hour of rapture is the clear hour that comes from the darkened blind brain) predates the similar sentiment Yeats expressed in 'Under Ben Bulben':

> Know that when all words are said
> And a man is fighting mad,
> Something drops from eyes long blind,
> He completes his partial mind,
> For an instant stands at ease,
> Laughs aloud, his heart at peace.

Having recovered clarity and wholeness, the Garden of Eden itself, through passion: the passion of violence in the case of Yeats, the passion of love in that of MacGill-Eain, we arrive again, by a somewhat circuitous route, at the shrine of *amour courtois* whose transcendental ideal is precisely that completion of the "partial mind" emphasized by Yeats. The degree to which the ideal may be achieved is not our concern here, but rather it is the ethical dimension of MacGill-Eain's use of the conceit.

Sartre's assertion that "every man who takes refuge behind the excuse of his passions is a dishonest man"[30] is much to the point in this connection. "The Existentialist will never agree", he declares, "that a sweeping passion is a ravaging torrent which fatally leads a man to certain acts and is therefore an excuse. He thinks that man is responsible for his passion".[31]

Like conclusions are not shirked by MacGill-Eain. Thus, in 'Cornford' he refers to "bréig a' chridhe shocraich" (the lie of the comfortable heart) which becomes "an leisgeal" (the excuse) in 'Aig Uaigh Yeats' . But however complex and ambiguous MacGill-Eain's position regarding the relation between this lie/excuse and the requirements of art becomes, as is indicated by the last three lines of the final verse of the latter poem, reproduced below, the ultimate connotation of 'leisgeal' (excuse) in this and most contexts must be pejorative.

Fhuair thusa 'n cothrom, Uilleim,	You got the chance, William,
an cothrom dha do bhriathran,	the chance for your words,
on bha a' ghaisge 's a' bhòidhche	since courage and beauty
's an croinn bhratach troimh do chliathaich.	had their flagpoles through your side.
Ghabh thu riutha air aon dòigh,	You acknowledged them in one way,
ach tha leisgeal air do bhilean,	but there is an excuse on your lips,
an leisgeal nach do mhill do bhàrdachd,	the excuse that did not spoil your poetry,
oir tha a leisgeal aig gach duine.	for every man has his excuse.

Denis Donoghue has said of Somhairle MacGill-Eain: "Remorse is his true vocation".[32] He is on the right track here, but "remorse" hardly seems adequate, surely, in view of the obsessiveness, the sheer bloody ruthlessness with which the Raasay man conducts his self-soundings. Martin Buber, in his essay 'What is Man?' has spoken of 'Existential Guilt', which occurs when somebody fails to respond to the legitimate claim and address of the world, whose foundation he knows and recognises as being those of his own existence and of all common existence. "If a form and appearance and present being move past me," writes Buber, "then out of the distance, out of its disappearance, comes a second cry, as soft and secret as though it came from myself: 'Where were you?' *That* is the cry of conscience".[33] The concept of 'Existential Guilt', understood in this way, fits and indeed informs the extended confessional that is *Dàin do Eimhir*. For the cry of the "fuil 's i reòta cruaidh am bealachan Guadarrama" (blood frozen and hard in the passes of Guadarrama) is answered only by its own echo in the mind and art of Somhairle MacGill-Eain; the poet's sword-arm lies idle. Action in defence of the embattled Spanish Republic is precluded by the demands of more personal and immediate loyalties and beyond these, on a more abstract level, as was said of Tennessee Williams' *A Streetcar Named Desire*, "by doubt and by awareness of the ambiguity of all solutions and motives".[34]

I have discussed earlier and praised fulsomely the 'mediaeval' aspect of MacGill-Eain's work, and indeed the craftsmanship and sensitivity with which he invested the matter of courtly love and the traditional Gaelic love lyric with a modern poetic ambience constitutes a minor miracle in itself. But over and above this, as the latter part of this essay indicates, Somhairle MacGill-Eain has displayed nothing less than the full honesty and courage to admit and express an essential dimension of his own humanity and the age's *Zeitgeist* — "the anxiety of meaninglessness", in Tillich's phrase — and to express it, moreover, with rare psychological acuity and genius. That unanswered cry, which rings insistently in many minds in our affluent western society, is the other, painfully relevant side of the poet's lyrical coin; its articulation in his work raises Somhairle MacGill-Eain from the ranks of the merely accomplished to the status of a major poet.

For all of that, the Raasay man is referred to invariably as a 'Poet of Passion', a *soubriquet* that does honour primarily to the traditional aspect of his achievement. However, on the basis of the perspective I have been seeking to illuminate in this essay, the phrase 'Poet of Conscience' more accurately defines his contribution to the literary culture of our times, however uncomfortably the ex-seceder himself may wriggle on that pin.

TOMÁS MAC SÍOMÓIN

NOTES

1. *Memoirs of a Modern Scotland*, ed. Karl Miller, London, 1970, p. 134.
2. D. de Rougemont, *Passion and Society*, London, 1962, p. 15.
3. *Anthology of Troubadour Lyric Poetry*, ed. & trans. A. R. Press, Edinburgh, 1971, pp. 34-35.
4. *Bardachd Chloinn Ghill-Eathain: Eachann Bacach and Other MacLean Poets*, ed. C. Ó. Baoill, Edinburgh, 1979, p. 112.
5. *Ibid.*, p. 78.
6. *Passion and Society, op. cit.*, pp. 38-39.

7. S. MacLean, 'Realism in Gaelic Poetry', *Transactions of the Gaelic Society of Inverness*, 1934-36, pp. 82-83.
8. *Dàin do Eimhir agus Dàin Eile, op. cit.*, p. 82.
9. *Ibid.*, p. 21.
10. S. MacLean, *Poems to Eimhir*, trans. I. Crichton Smith, Newcastle-on-Tyne, 1971, p. 31.
11. W. Ross, *Songs of William Ross in Gaelic and in English*, (ed. & trans. G. Calder), Edinburgh, 1937, pp. xvi-xxiv.
12. *Memoirs of a Modern Scotland, op. cit.*, p. 127.
13. *Songs of William Ross in Gaelic and in English, op. cit.*, pp. 30-33.
14. *Ibid.*, pp. 58-59.
15. *Ibid.*, pp. 134-35.
16. *Ibid.*, pp. 172-75.
17. *Memoirs of a Modern Scotland, op. cit.*, p. 127.
18. T. S. Eliot, 'Tradition and the Individual Talent', in *Modern Poets on Modern Poetry*. ed. J. Scully, London and Glasgow, 1966, p. 63.
19. *Memoirs of a Modern Scotland, op. cit.*, p. 135.
20. *Ibid.*, p. 127.
21. *Alexander Blok: Selected Poems*, eds. & trans. J. Stallworthy and P. France, London, 1974, pp. 102-103.
22. *Ibid.*, p. 55.
23. J. M. Cohen, *Poetry of This Age*, London, 1959, p. 89.
24. S. MacLean, 'Poetry, Passion and Political Consciousness', *Scottish International*, 10, 1970, pp. 10-16.
25. P. Tillich, *The Courage To Be*, Glasgow, 1979, pp. 138-39.
26. *Dàin do Eimhir agus Dàin Eile, op. cit.*, p. 82.
27. *Lines Review*, 4, January 1954, p. 23.
28. J. P. Sartre, *Existentialism and the Human Emotions*, New York, 1957, pp. 23-24.
29. *Alexander Blok: Selected Poems, op. cit.*, p. 59.
30. *Existentialism and the Human Emotions, op. cit.*, pp. 44-45.
31. *Ibid.*, p. 23.
32. D. Donoghue, *Times Literary Supplement*, 9 Sept. 1977.
33. M. Buber, 'What Is Man?', in *Between Man and Man*, Glasgow, 1979, p. 203.
34. *The Courage To Be, op. cit.*, p. 143.

Note: Translations into English of the section of 'An Cuilithionn'; 'Trì Slighean' and Poem XVII of *Dàin Eile* from *Dàin do Eimhir agus Dàin Eile*, are by the present writer; all other translations are from text cited above.

'The Haunting'

Sorley MacLean:
Continuity and the transformation of Symbols

Of recent years, those who have written and spoken of the achievement of Sorley MacLean have been concerned less with the break with tradition in his work than they have been with tracing the continuity between his work and what went before. It could be argued, for instance, that his war poems are not far removed from the work of John Munro of Lewis. The elegy on his brother Calum is not wholly divorced in form or content from the tradition of *cumha* (lament) in Scottish Gaelic, of which the poet had learned so many excellent examples from his grandmother and his father's sister in his youth. In terms of form, an examination of his verse soon shows up the wide variety of traditional metres — in this respect not unlike the Skye poetess Màiri Mhór nan Òran whom he has so often praised, whose own memory was stocked with a rich repertoire of traditional song before she herself ever began to compose.

John MacInnes, in a characteristically perceptive article in *Cencrastus* (no. 7, Winter 1981-82), has begun to trace the abiding and formative influence of another literature on the mind and voice of MacLean — that of the pulpit, the prayer meeting and family worship. Writing of the Anglo-Welsh writers of Wales, John Ackerman had this to say:

> Made sensitive, under its ever-present influence (i.e. the pulpit's) to the sound of words, such a writer as Thomas found rhythm, incantation, the music of the line (whether in verse or prose) basic aids to expression.[1]

No one who has listened to Sorley MacLean read aloud or even engage in conversation under stress of emotion or deep conviction, could fail to catch an echo of that note of fervent declaration which is heard in the voice of those who preach in Gaelic or lead with freedom in extempore prayer. This characteristic MacLean has in common with a number of writers in Wales and, of course, with W. R. Rodgers in Ireland. Donald MacAulay has acknowledged the power and attraction of these opportunities for self-expression in his poem 'Soisgeul 1955'.[2]

And MacLean, the "giullan Saoir-Chléireach" (little Free Presbyterian boy) who, as he himself tells us, "relinquished Calvinism for socialism at about the age of twelve", listened to many sermons and prayers, and continued to live among, argue and discuss with people for whom the Gaelic Bible and translation of the Shorter Catechism both formed and restricted their intellectual horizon.

It is no surprise, therefore, to find that stretches of Sorley MacLean's poetry are richly furnished with the terminology of that Protestantism in which he was reared and by which he has been surrounded for a great part of his life. The highpoints of its practice appear, for instance, in his use of terms like "latha traisg" (fast-day),

"Sàbaid nam marbh" (Sabbath of the Dead), "ceann-teagaisg" (the text). The
terms used to treat its most profound concerns also appear: for example,
"sìorruidheachd" (Eternity), "Pàrras" (Paradise), "aithreachas" (remorse),
"naomh" (holy), "an Taghadh" (Election), "a' Ghairm Eifeachdach no'n
Dùrachd" (effectual calling or sincerity). It is no surprise to find 'Blind Munro', one
of the great figures of the early nineteenth-century revival in Skye, who organized
the burning of a mountain of fiddles and bagpipes and who was credited with
knowing the whole Bible by heart, bracketed with MacCruimein the piper as the
twin symbolic figures round whom, in tension and identity, the recent poem 'Uamha
'n Òir' [3] is centred.

These terms are used by the poet with an extended meaning. This does not mean
that they are merely ornamental, or extrinsic to the form and texture of his thought,
nor does it mean that they have lost their original meaning.

For example, in the poem 'Urnuigh':

Bha seo aig Cornford òg 'na ghaisge,	Young Cornford had this in his heroism,
eagal smuain a ghaoil bhith faisg air	the fear of the thought of his love being near him
nuair a bha an Spàinn 'na latha-traisg dha,	when Spain was a fast-day for him:
eagal a challa air an duine,	fear of his loss in the man,
eagal an eagail air a' churaidh.	fear of the fear in the hero.[4]

The "latha-traisg" is the Fast-Day which is normally held on a Thursday: it
precedes and helps to prepare communicants for the sacramental celebration on the
following Sunday. John MacInnes has already drawn attention to the provenance of
the opening phrase, "Bha seo aig Cornford òg 'na ghaisge...". This formula
introduces some memorable insight or saying of a godly person from the Evangelical
past: "Bha seo aig té bheannaichte a bha ann an Loch Carrann an toiseach..". (A
godly woman in Loch Carron had [i.e. used to say] this...) Such a godly person
would, of course, belong to that small group of 'Members', or communicants, who
would actually partake of the Sacrament. Young Cornford, together with Dimitrov
and Connolly who appear later in the same poem, is among the secular Elect among
whom the 'unregenerate' might pray eventually to be found.

Another poem of roughly the same period, 'Cornford', begins:

Cornford agus Julian Bell	Cornford and Julian Bell
agus Garcia Lorca,	and Garcia Lorca,
marbh 'san Spàinn 'san aobhar naomh.	dead in Spain in the sacred cause.

The word "aobhar" (cause) itself is one that has strong religious overtones (the
'cause' for which one may arouse scandal or in which one may assist). The cause for
which these young men died is the fight against Fascism; here it is called "an
t-aobhar naomh" (the holy cause) and in the next stanza "an t-aobhar cruaidh" (the
hard cause). For MacLean the political cause is the 'holy' one: as it is in
'Ard-mhusaeum na h-Eireann', speaking of the execution of James Connolly in
1916:

. . . an léine bh' air Ó Conghaile	...the shirt that was on Connolly
ann an Ard Phost-Oifis Eirinn	in the General Post-Office of Ireland
's e 'g ullachadh na h-ìobairt	while he was preparing the sacrifice
a chuir suas e fhéin air séithir	that put himself up on a chair
as naoimhe na 'n Lia Fàil	that is holier than the Lia Fàil
th' air Cnoc na Teamhrach an Eirinn.	that is on the Hill of Tara in Ireland.

The Fast-day then, which prepares the communicant for the annual Communion, has become the purifying time of self-denial in Spain, during which John Cornford was prepared for the sacrifice of his life.

Or one might take the phrase "sàbaid nam marbh" (the Sabbath of the Dead) in the following lines from 'Hallaig'.

Fuirichidh mi ris a' bheithe	I will wait for the birch
gus an tig i mach an Càrn,	wood until it comes up by the cairn,
gus am bi am bearradh uile	until the whole ridge from Beinn na Lice
o Bheinn na Lice f'a sgàil.	will be under its shade.
Mura tig 's ann thèarnas mi a Hallaig	If it does not, I will go down to Hallaig,
a dh' ionnsaigh Sàbaid nam marbh,	to the Sabbath of the Dead,
far a bheil an sluagh a' tathaich,	where the people are frequenting,
gach aon ghinealach a dh' fhalbh.	every single generation gone.

The Jewish Sabbath is, of course, the seventh day of the week, the day of rest and, as such, no doubt appropriate to the condition of the dead. But the word 'Sàbaid' here must surely have added resonances for anyone who has watched the silent, often black-coated figures who say nothing or speak only in low tones as they emerge here and there from their houses and converge upon the church on a Sabbath evening. The use of the word 'Sabbath' prepares us, in fact, for the silence of the vision itself and sanctifies it as does the word 'coimhthional' (congregation) some lines later:

's na h-igheanan 'nam badan sàmhach	the girls in silent bands
a' dol a Chlachan mar o thùs.	go to Clachan as in the beginning.

Or again:

A' tilleadh a Hallaig anns an fheasgar,	coming back to Hallaig in the evening
anns a' chamhanaich bhalbh bheò,	in the dumb living twilight,
a' lìonadh nan leathadan casa,	filling the steep slopes,
an gàireachdaich 'nam chluais 'na ceò.	their laughter a mist in my ears.

A third example, this time a term from the very core of theological discourse, is 'An Taghadh' (Election).

In 'Latha Foghair', the enemy shells have killed his six companions and he, alone of the group, has survived:

Ghabh aon Taghadh iadsan	One Election took them
's cha d' ghabh e mise,	and did not take me,
gun fhoighneachd dhinn	without asking
có b' fheàrr no bu mhiosa:	us which was better or worse:
ar liom, cho diabhlaidh coma	it seemed as devilishly indifferent
ris na sligean.	as the shells.

However robust and reassuring the doctrine of Election may have been in the hands of an Augustine or, for that matter, of Martin Luther and the first generation of sixteenth-century reformers, in the hands of the Calvinist orthodoxy of the following century (to which the Free Presbyterians, among whom MacLean grew up, strictly adhere), it had become a terrifying doctrine, underlining the terrible and arbitrary power of the Deity. According to this doctrine, not only had God, in accordance with His eternal decrees, elected some to eternal life, but He who "for His own good pleasure had foreordained whatsoever comes to pass", had also foreordained some to eternal damnation, good and bad works notwithstanding.

The lines, "Ghabh aon Taghadh iadsan 's cha d' ghabh e mise" (One Election took them and did not take me), which surely echo *Luke* 17, 34-6 ("Bidh dithis dhaoine anns a' mhachair; gabhar aon dhiubh agus fàgar am fear eile..."), derive their force from the poet's long-standing rejection of this doctrine. The poem begins and ends with the grim, inexplicable presence of the six corpses. That is the verifiable reality —

Sianar marbh ri mo ghualainn	Six men dead at my shoulder
latha foghair.	on an Autumn day.

No theological or other rationalisation which is not itself devilish, can explain the randomness of their fate and his escape. MacLean's use here of the term "Taghadh" (Election), a central term from a rejected theological system, serves only to heighten the expression of bewilderment and deepen the pessimism.

This term appears again later in that remarkable poem of shadow and half-light, 'Anns a' Phàirce Mhóir'. The poem is at once a kind of 'Song of Experience' and a 'Song of Innocence' expressing the happiness of those mild harvest nights in the full moon where now and again the clouds blot out the moonlight and the children play hide and seek among the stooks. The poem also captures the half-frightening delight of hiding and being found in the shadows of a field that seemed limitless: "'s gun fhios....cia mhiad adag a bh' air an raon" (when no boy or girl knew how many stooks were in the plain). When the stooks are safely harvested, the field is ploughed again for another crop. Straight parallel furrows cut into the surface of the field and never meet. The destiny of each of those carefree children becomes manifest later in all its loneliness (just as the surface of the field changes from the ripe harvest under the moonlight to the bare furrows of the plough).

Oidhche 'n deireadh an fhoghair	A night in late Autumn
'n uair a bha an Taghadh nas ciaire	when the Election was dimmer
's mu'n robh an saoghal 'na sgrìoban	and before the world was
cruaidhe dìreach giara.	hard straight furrows.
'S gun fhios aig gille no nighinn	When no boy or girl knew
cia mhiad adag bh'air an raon,	how many stooks were on the plain,
a h-uile h-adag fhathast dìomhair	every stook still mysterious,
mun robh an t-achadh 'na chlàr maol.	before the field was a bare expanse.

The word 'fhathast' (still) in the penultimate line cited, warns us that the children's destiny is already at hand, waiting merely to unfold itself. The poet who, at an early age was made to learn the catechism answers to questions concerning Election and God's eternal decrees, adds two lines to those already cited:

Cha robh an Taghadh cho soilleir	The Election was not so clear
is sinne anns a' Phàirce Mhóir.	to us in the Big Park.

Perhaps there is a touch of irony in the recollection of how facilely as a child he could have trotted out the orthodox answers to these perennial mysteries of fate and destiny.

It has already been acknowledged that biblical and homiletic language runs under the surface of MacLean's poetry in rich veins, often coming up into the light like out-crops of rock and always serving to give the poetry a firmness and strength.

Aside from those already mentioned by John MacInnes or those used in this essay, there are two or three examples in the poem 'Urnuigh' which may serve to encourage the reader to search for himself above and below the surface of the poet's language, as in:

Ciamar a sheasas mi ri 'm marc-shluagh,	How will I stand up against their cavalry
's gun mo chridhe ach leth-fhailte?	since my heart is but half-flayed?

The question concerns the poet's fear of the catastrophes that lie ahead, which will be more terrible than anything he has experienced so far. It is scarcely fanciful to hear in the background an oracle of that daring and harassed prophet, Jeremiah: "Ma ruith thu leis na coisichean, agus gun do sgìthich iad thu, cionnus idir a nì thu strì ri eachaibh?" (If thou hast run with the footmen and they have wearied thee, then how canst thou contend with horses?) (*Jeremiah* 12, 5). The verse continues:

....agus ann am fearann sìth, ged robh	....and if in the land of peace wherein thou
agad dòchas, gidheadh ciod a nì thu ann	trustedst, they wearied thee, then how wilt
an onfha Iordain?"	thou do in the swelling of Jordan?.

which may well find an echo in:

Dé 'n t-eagal a bhios ormsa	What fear will I have
roimh thuiltean aognuidh an onfhaidh...?	before the chill floods of the surge...?

In 'Urnuigh', the poet also speaks of those who have already been granted that purity of purpose for which he is not sure whether he can yet pray (like the unconverted who do not know whether they even as yet wish to be changed). He writes:

Esan dh' am bheil an cridhe air ionnlaid	He whose heart has been washed
théid e troimh theine gun tionndadh,	will go through fire without turning;
dìridh e bheinn mhór gun ionndrainn...	he will ascend the great mountain without homesickness...

There is surely an echo here of *John* 13, 10: "Thubhairt Ìosa ris (.i. ri Peadar), An tì a tha air ionnlad, chan eil feum aige ach a chasan ionnlad, ach tha e gu h-iomlan glan." (Jesus saith unto him, He that is washed needeth not save to wash his feet, but is clean every whit.) The word 'glainte' (purified) has already been used of the heart on the previous page of the poem.

It is however with themes, rather than with such echoes, that the rest of this essay will be concerned. For, alongside the dogmatic dis-continuity (which is obvious), there is in the poetry of Sorley MacLean a persistent continuity, an abiding involvement with great universal human themes to which the Evangelical movement has in its time given vivid expression.

In addition to MacLean's moral indignation which has its roots in the tradition which informed the speeches, sermons and poetry of the Land League Movement with the rhetoric of the Gaelic Bible and undergirded it with deep convictions about the Creator (as is notable in the work of Mary MacPherson and John Smith of Lewis), I will take three other themes, namely *Suffering*, *Time* and *Decision*.

No one in this century has given more devastating expression to the half-guilty bewilderment of those who maintain their health and creativity while others, who love them, die in pain. No one has so sensitively expressed the paradoxical realization that poetry could be born of that pain. Before the imponderable devastation of illness, suffering and loss MacLean is as agnostic and as baffled as all must be.

But it is another vein in his poetry which I wish to explore — those poems in which the suffering is explicitly or implicitly set in a social or political context. No one who has read through the compassionate quatrains of 'Ban-Ghàidheal' or felt the throb of its restrained anger, has failed to notice that she carried the seaweed in her creel: "tharruing ise 'n fheamainn fhuar chum biadh a cloinne 's duais an tùir" (to feed her children and to pay the Castle). The girl who was kidnapped on the shore at Geusdo and taken off on the ill-fated "Annie Jane", is representative of the hundreds and thousands who were transported during the Clearances. Again and again, MacLean returns to the sufferings, individual and collective, of those who may be comprehended in 'Gaoir na h-Eòrpa':

Gach bochdainn, àmhghar 's dórainn	All the poverty, anguish and grief
a thig 's a thàinig ar sluagh na h-Eòrpa	that will come and have come on Europe's people
bho Long nan Daoine gu daors' a' mhór-shluaigh.	from the slave ship to the slavery of the whole people.

There can be no doubt that what MacLean learned of the early years of Highland history and what he saw of conditions in Lowland Scotland invited a comprehensive analysis in socialist terms.

What is perhaps of particular interest to us here is that, in developing his analysis, MacLean never falls into the ideological trap of minimizing the significance of the suffering which is (perhaps inevitably) to be met with on the way to the defeat of Fascism and the growth of Socialism. It might be worth considering that what might be called his compassionate balance in the treatment of human suffering *is* balanced because it has its roots in his early critique of the preaching he heard so much of as a boy and as a youth.

It could be argued that much of this preaching, in its anxiety to put the Cross at the centre of its concern, has erred in failing (or seeming to fail) to take seriously the day-to-day suffering of men and women, particularly their poverty. A piety which can take credit for giving men and women a sense of their eternal value in the eyes of God, at a time when their material condition seems to suggest they have no value at all, has another side. This form of preaching also tended to suggest that the value of their souls and the lost state of their souls, if they remained unconverted, was of such importance as to dwarf the significance of any effort to ameliorate their social condition. If the landlord was cruel, there was One who would deal with him in due time. Rather than taking the law into one's own hands, it would be better to consider that, without conversion, your own soul might join his in Hell. This line of thought lies behind the explicit criticism in 'Ban-Ghàidheal':

Agus labhair T' eaglais chaomh	And Thy gentle church has spoken
mu staid chaillte a h-anama thruaigh....	about the lost state of her miserable soul....

The poem 'Calbharaigh' is written against the back-drop of a protestantism which spoke at length of the suffering of the world, but, by *failing* to do anything about it, ran the risk of reducing its lengthy reflections on the death of Christ (Coille uaine tìr an sgeòil) to mere pietistic rhetoric. In 'Am Buaireadh', the sufferings of Christ are nothing in emotional terms compared with the glint of his love's smile. He even goes on to say that his love's beauty has cast a film over the poverty of the world, Lenin's anger, his theory and his praxis.

MacLean appears early on to have found the Christianity in which he was reared defective in its treatment of human suffering, too apt to demote this suffering inside a "scheme of salvation". But the interesting thing is that we do not find him falling into the error which too often became characteristic of the Stalinist ideologue, that of relativizing and de-sensitizing oneself to the suffering which inevitably human beings endure on the curve of "crescent history". His critique of Highland Calvinism in this regard may have saved him from that error.

Closely connected with the theme of *Suffering* is that of *Time*, both in Christian and in Marxist thought. In the poem beginning "Chan fhaic mi fàth mo shaothrach" MacLean begins by expressing misgiving as to the significance of his life-work, writing poetry "in a dying tongue", but the poem goes on to suggest that there is a time-scale within which this, and his love and the sufferings of the masses throughout history may have significance. This is what we have been 'given':

Ach thugadh dhuinn am muillion bliadhna	But we have been given the million years
'na mhìr an roinn chianail fhàsmhoir,	a fragment of a sad growing portion,
gaisge 's foighidinn nan ciadan	the heroism and patience of hundreds
agus mìorbhail aodainn àlainn.	and the miracle of a beautiful face.

'Gaoir na h-Eòrpa' counterpoints the claims of political engagement and personal love and commitment, and in doing so startlingly evokes the suffering of Europe under Fascism. But in 'An Roghainn', which is in many ways its sequel, MacLean brings the argument to a resolution: one who avoided direct involvement in the Spanish War was certainly not fit to encounter the "thunderbolt of love". The poignancy of love is for those who accept the political cross:

Cha d' ghabh mise bàs croinn-ceusaidh	I did not take the cross's death
ann an éiginn chruaidh na Spàinn,	in the hard extremity of Spain,
is ciamar sin bhiodh dùil agam	and how then should I expect
ri aon duais ùir an dàin?	the one new prize of fate?

This would have led to suffering and death for the cause. Certainly, the deaths of such figures as Connolly, Liebknecht, John MacLean, Dimitrov and Rosa Luxembourg are seen as 'necessary'. Connolly's death is spoken of specifically in terms of sacrifice, as we have seen. But both his death and Dimitrov's sufferings are presented as those of men whose hearts have been "flayed" and "purified" (glainte), so that, in a sense, there is no cause for mourning.

The irreversibility of Time and its irretrievability form the central theme of 'Hallaig'. Whatever else is to be said about that unbelievably rich and complex poem, it can be said that it affirms, in a way that invites comparison with MacDiarmid's 'Island Funeral', the capacity of loving imagination to transcend and to redeem the betrayals and irretrievable wrongs of history. The deer, which symbolizes Time, is struck by a bullet from the gun of Love and "goes dizzily, sniffing at the grass-grown ruined homes" of the deserted townships of Raasay. Thus it appears that we have also transcended political hope and entered an altogether higher realm of thought.

But where is the eschatology which will comprehend the running sore of Ulster, the war in Vietnam, the atrocity of Auschwitz and the aching beauty of the world? In 'A' Bheinn air Chall' the end towards which human history moves is itself shrouded, or seen only in tantalizing glimpses through the trees as we climb (we hope) towards the summit.

The sense of mystery, tinged with a certain melancholy hope concerning the end towards which we move, had already characterized the poet's teleology in the closing stanzas of 'Coilltean Ratharsair'.

But in 'A' Bheinn air Chall', while conceding its meaningfulness to a minority, MacLean rejects the eschatological vision of Dante's *Inferno* or that vision as mediated by the eighteenth-century Rannoch schoolmaster, Dugald Buchanan, in his 'Là A' Bhreitheanais' (Day of Judgement).[5] In that momentary glimpse of himself in childhood, MacLean speaks of the child's reflection on received eschatology and the apocalyptic, when once faced with the terrible possibility of perdition and separation from God or Paradise without the majority of his own people:

Pàrras gun Phàrras a chuideachd,	Paradise without the paradise of his own people,
imcheist a' ghiullain Shaoir-Chléirich:	the perplexity of the little Free Presbyterian boy :
a ghearan is a dhiùltadh sàmhach	his complaint and silent refusal
'nan toibheum an amhaich Sineubha;	blasphemy in the throat of Geneva;
agus an amhaich na Ròimhe—	and in the throat of Rome—
ged tha Purgadair nas ciùine—	though Purgatory is gentler—
an robair eile air a' chrann	the other robber on the tree
is Spartacus le armailt chiùrrte.	and Spartacus with his tortured army.

There is no speculative vision, but a certain specification is laid down — its comprehensiveness will include both the first robber and, of course, Spartacus, the leader of the slaves' revolt.

What is true of Time is also true of the significance of Nature in MacLean's poetry. The indifference of the natural world to the sorrows and joys of mankind is a recurrent theme, for example in 'Am Fuaran'. The mountains, springs and trees 'achieve' significance insofar as they are present and participant in the process of human history. The trees of the cleared eastern townships of Raasay are at once the setting, the personification and the continuing presence of the dead emigrant generation ('Hallaig'). One is reminded of Vernon Watkins' remark in the introduction to his edition of the letters received over many years from Dylan Thomas:

> Natural observation in poetry meant nothing to us without the support of metaphysical truth..[6]

The same could be said of the authors of many of the psalms, the Book of Job and the oracles of Isaiah. MacLean might wish to gloss the word 'Metaphysical', but he would (I suspect) be content to admit that this is also true of himself.

The third and final theme to be examined is *Decision.*

It is the nearest thing to an anomaly existing in the practice and preaching of the strictest Highland presbyterianism that, although committed to a thoroughgoing doctrine of Double Predestination, it nevertheless exhorts 'decisions' and makes tireless calls to the unconverted, as though human will had a more significant role to play than presbyterian theory allows. In a religious practice which distinguishes clearly between the converted and the unconverted, the Highland unconverted are allowed a certain freedom to engage in 'worldly' activities, such as piping, singing, dancing and so on. The price they pay is the acknowledgement that they are unregenerate sinners on the way to perdition. They may resign themselves to this status, or they may accept it with occasional pangs of guilt, or they may throw themselves perversely into the unregenerate life and enjoy the fruits of sin for a season. Whatever the reaction (or whatever mixture of the three possibilities), the conscience is bound to be open to frequent and sometimes painful scrutiny.

The presbyterian Highlander is one of an articulate, religious group of people, among whom the introspective, puritan and (at its most fertile, perhaps) divided conscience has made its home. Much has been written about the internal struggle documented in the *Dàin do Eimhir* poems: it has not often enough been discussed in terms of the refinement of the puritan conscience. It might prove worthwhile, in another place, to examine the tension which can be traced in MacLean's work from 'An Roghainn', through 'Urnuigh' to 'Uamha 'n Oir'. This tension is created by the antithesis between the inexorable movement of history (of which the poet is a tiny part) and the role of individual decision in the purification of the will. If my thesis is correct, this tension also remains unresolved in Highland Calvinism.

TERENCE McCAUGHEY

NOTES

1 J. Ackerman, "The Welsh Background", in *Dylan Thomas, A collection of critical essays,* ed. C. B. Cox, Englewood Cliffs, N.J. 1966, p.35.

2 *Nua-bhàrdachd Ghàidhlig, Duanaire Dà-theangach,* deas. le Domhnall MacAmhlaigh, Dùn Éideann 1976, p.193.

3 Parts I — III are published in *Chapman,* 4, no. 3, pp.6-13.

4 This line is an echo in Gaelic of the last line of the second quatrain of John Cornford's poem to Margot Heinemann:

> Heart of the heartless world,
> Dear heart, the thought of you
> Is the pain at my side,
> The shadow that chills my view.

> The wind rises in the evening,
> Reminds that autumn is near,
> I am afraid to lose you,
> I am afraid of my fear.

This poem (see *Poetry of the Thirties,* ed. R. Skelton, London 1964, p.146) was translated into Gaelic by Sorley MacLean in 1980 (see *Seven Poets,* Glasgow 1981). Also see Peter Stansky and William Abrahams, *Journey to the Frontier,* London 1966, p.351 *et passim.*

5 *Dàin Spioradail le Dughall Bochanan,* Glasgow 1946, pp.15ff.

6 V. Watkins, *Letters to Vernon Watkins,* ed. with introd. by Vernon Watkins, London 1957, p.64.

'Tree of Strings'

Language, Metre and Diction
in the Poetry of Sorley Maclean

In the history of Gaelic poetry no voice is more distinctive than that of Somhairle MacGill-Eain. Although readers who have some knowledge of Gaelic poetry in translation may well give an immediate assent to that, realism demands that we base the judgement on a knowledge of the Gaelic poetic tradition in its entirety and in the original language. This is no doubt as much of a commonplace as it is to observe that thematic power, brilliance of imagery, and the various other qualities that distinguish a writer, can and do make their own impact even in translation. But it becomes something more than a mere truism when the original language and the language of translation are as far removed from each other as are Gaelic and English, in nature, in history, and in status. It is not merely that English and Gaelic are inherently, both structurally and phonologically, so very different. There is also the question of cultural and historical perspective. Somhairle MacGill-Eain restored to Gaelic poetry the scope and amplitude of a mature, adult voice. His work is not only the product of his own genius but is shaped, controlled and energised by tradition. Gaelic literature has developed over some fifteen centuries: a rich, dominating, hierarchical literature which expresses the manifold experience of a people who eventually, between Ireland and Scotland, divided into two nations. It has its aristocratic and plebeian aspects; its literary, sub-literary and non-literate streams. As a living language with an immensely large working vocabulary, rich and flexible in the usages of its oral verse-making and story-telling, supported by vigorous traditions of expository prose in writing and extempore eloquence in the Church, Gaelic had by no means lost contact with its former greatness during Somhairle MacGill-Eain's formative years. It is true that by that time Gaelic poetry had in some respects become attenuated, but the language could still cope with an astonishingly wide range of human experience. In none of its registers could it be called a 'peasant language', no matter how poor many of its speakers may have been in terms of this world's goods. A large part of Somhairle MacGill-Eain's greatness as a poet lies in his restorative work: this can properly be celebrated as a triumph of regeneration. His poetry is intensely Gaelic even when it is so different from anything else in Gaelic; his art, even at its most personal, draws upon so much of the inherited wealth of immemorial generations. What is perhaps more difficult to convey to a non-Gaelic reader is that this sense of the restoration of our heritage to its proper place plays a fundamental part in our assessment of his poetry. We experience a shock of excitement as we read him. Naturally this cannot be separated from his art and craft, or from the pain and joy of his poetry, from its subtlety and passion. Yet it is logically, and, perhaps more important, psychologically distinct. There is pessimism in MacGill-Eain's poetry: much of it, indeed, is tragic. But his voice, in my sense of the term, is at the same time optimistic and resurgent and these sentiments are conveyed to at least the same degree as his pessimism. If that is a paradox or a mystery it cannot be helped. The point is that it is true.

How does Somhairle MacGill-Eain achieve this? How did he revolutionise Gaelic poetry? What resources did he have at his disposal in native Gaelic? What did he borrow? What were his strategies? How colloquial or dialectal, literary or artificial, is his language? How different are the formal structures of his verse from those of the poets who preceded him? To deal with any of these questions adequately would require much greater scope than that of a short chapter. All I can hope to do here is to indicate some of the answers and warn non-Gaelic readers of certain pitfalls.

To begin with a general point. Simply by reading an English translation, no one could ever guess at the nature of MacGill-Eain's Gaelic diction. There is nothing very difficult — nor, in purely linguistic terms, anything very egregious — in the English. By contrast the original Gaelic exhibits virtually an entire spectrum of language. Transparent simplicity is to be found side by side with a formidable density of verbal texture. A full linguistic commentary must await another occasion; for the moment it is enough to say that practically all the available registers of Gaelic, ranging in quality from the demotic to the arcane, are included at some point or another. There are times, naturally, when the ordinary reader requires industry combined with ingenuity to unravel the meaning. This fact alone would give added value to the poet's authoritative translations. Personally, and in spite of the author's modest disclaimer, I regard these translations as poems in their own right. Of course they make a very different impression from their originals. Perhaps because in English they do not administer quite the same shock of modernity, or because they are easier, or for some other related reason, bilingual readers may occasionally prefer the translation. MacGill-Eain may be the "Bard of his people", as he has been described, but one must understand that this is a specialized use of the word 'bard'. In mediaeval and later Gaelic society the bard was a fairly simple praise-singer.

There are undoubtedly misconceptions held about some aspects of his work. I have heard him referred to as a Romantic who consistently uses strict Classical forms. This is at best a partial judgement. I have heard it said also that his originality is restricted to the content of his poetry: that he has not brought to Gaelic verse much in the way of metrical innovation. His art has been described as essentially that of a maker of songs, with the corollary that their true quality could only emerge with the support of a musical setting. This last point may display a confusion concerning 'lyricism' or it may be connected with the fact that in Gaelic tradition almost all poetry, including non-lyrical poetry — what we, from a modern Western European point of view, would certainly call poems not songs — was linked with melody or performed in chant.

It is only fair to add that none of these observations has appeared in print, in serious criticism. Rather they are all the kind of comment which one may hear in discussion, made by people who have at best an imperfect knowledge of Gaelic or who have failed to read the poems very closely. One can often see what gives rise to such judgements but there is not a great deal of substance in any of those I have cited. In what follows, I am keenly aware that much of what I say about MacGill-Eain, especially on the subject of his technical achievement, cannot be demonstrated to a non-Gaelic reader. This is unsatisfactory but unavoidable. Matters of technique, and rhythm in particular, require direct knowledge of a language, or an unconscionable amount of space. But a good deal of the argument is really concerned with cultural background and that at least can be checked.

It is obvious from the content of his poetry that MacGill-Eain is a contemporary European poet. What then are the resources that are available to a modern Gaelic writer whose horizons are as wide as that, and what are their limitations?

First, Gaelic is a major European language, drawing as it does on the oldest literary tradition in Europe outside Latin and Greek. But it is not a 'modern' language in the sense that English, French or German are modern languages. The processes of history — which for us have been also processes of ethnocide — have disposed that the terminology of the modern sciences, for instance, is not represented in the Gaelic vocabulary. To put it succinctly: there is a word for atom but only a recent coinage for molecule. On the other hand, largely because of a continuing theological tradition, it is possible, without creating an unduly large number of neologisms, to discuss philosophy, literary criticism and the arts in general.

But the major Gaelic contribution to scientific enquiry is in the field of language. In Europe in the Middle Ages, Gaelic poets and men of letters were unique in the analysis of their own language. Their approach was not based on the model supplied by the grammatical categories of Latin alone, and using a fresh and independent eye, they developed attitudes that are strikingly similar to those of modern linguistic science. The potential of the language for coping with linguistic analysis is therefore clear enough; how easily it can be used in other fields of intellectual and cultural activity has been demonstrated in the twentieth century. Irish Gaelic, which has a roughly similar history, is used in all the disciplines of university curricula; in Scotland, too, Gaelic has been shown to be perfectly adequate for dealing, for instance, with mathematics and biology. But these contemporary experiments apart, the learned vocabulary of Scots Gaelic has on the whole remained substantially that of a mediaeval European language.

Secondly, the Gaelic poetic tradition is one that takes us back almost 1500 years, and this literary tradition does not divide, at any rate in its higher reaches, into its distinctively Scots and Irish streams until the seventeenth century. Throughout the stages and vicissitudes of that long history, formal characteristics of structure and rhythm, alliteration, rhyme, elision, and all the other properties that can be an integral part of the statement of a poem, engrossed the attention of Gaelic poets and linguistic scholars alike. For instance, rhyme, when it emerges in the poetry of the seventh century, is carried not only by the vowels and diphthongs of the language but also by the consonants, which were analysed phonetically and organised in distinct categories for that purpose in the schools of rhetoric. So strong is the Gaelic fascination with the refinements of literary form (and the fascination still exists) that in the 'Dark' Ages high-class men of letters, as a leading Irish scholar, Professor James Carney, has argued, not only concentrated on the most difficult and impressive metres: in the early period these élitists went so far as to avoid vowel rhyme altogether, preferring the subtler and more sensitive, but much more demanding, consonantal rhyme. Such craft could only exist in a sophisticated written literature. At a lower level, so to speak, oral poetry and song followed their own ways, from time to time borrowing, as elsewhere in the world, from the writers. To take one example, although Gaelic is a 'stress-timed' language, the Gaelic *literati* of the Middle Ages evolved a metrical system in which symmetry is achieved not on the basis of the heavy stresses of the verse line but on the number of syllables within it — no matter where the stresses fall. The visual pattern of such strictly 'syllabic' lines is, however, disrupted in speech or song by the inherent rhythm of the language itself, since regularity of stress predominates. What emerges in this kind of poetry then is an overall symmetry which may involve varying degrees of light and heavy stress, wrenched accents, or even silent stresses. Any tendency to preciosity in these 'Strict Metres' was removed when oral poets took over and modified the exacting syllable-count of the writers. Indeed, what are faults from a scholastic point of view seem to me, from the viewpoint of modern Gaelic sensibility, often to be positive virtues. The verse becomes loosened but the subtle rhythmic complexities remain and are still conspicuous in certain areas of Gaelic poetry.

Although the *quasi parlando* style characteristic of some traditional Gaelic singing may be of different or diverse origins, its subtleties are comparable with those just described. Even in the songs that accompanied communal labour (such as the well-known Waulking-songs) there are similar variations in movement, although they can hardly have developed from written poetry. The fact of the matter is that a feel for complexity of rhythm — for the freedom of speech-rhythm, for instance, pitted against the demands of strict form — is one of the most special and sensitive graces of Gaelic verse in general. At one extreme it can be found in dance-songs, particularly the older *puirt-a-beul*, which preserve their regularly accented dance rhythms over against a variably stressed text. The result is a form of syncopation.

But from about the mid-nineteenth century the mainstream of Gaelic poetry failed to draw upon this astonishing rhythmical abundance. For the most part the rhythms commonly used by poets whose work was published tended to be regular, and rather mechanical, stressed patterns. Paradoxically, the technical resources of Gaelic verse had become much more depleted in what was then appearing in print, and in the songs that enjoyed a vogue among the *émigré* Gaels of Lowland cities, than in the still vigorous oral poetry of the Gàidhealtachd itself. MacGill-Eain had free access to this area of poetry — it was a living tradition within his own family — just as much as he had to the entire body of published Gaelic verse. Because he had these advantages, both sides of the Gaelic poetic inheritance contributed to his own metrical restorations and innovations. In that process MacGill-Eain may be said to have slowed down the pace of Gaelic poetry, enlarged its metrical scope and created verse techniques that were capable of coping with the demands of a modern sensibility. In this connection it is interesting to note that one or two earlier poets, notably the Lewisman John Munro, a young graduate of Aberdeen who was killed in action in 1918, had also felt the need to break the constraints of traditional form. It is evident that Munro was influenced by English metrics. MacGill-Eain, of course, also had the freedom to choose from English metrics, but his strategy was different. In essence most of MacGill-Eain's metrical patterns are derived from Gaelic or are a very subtle compound of English and Gaelic forms. The latter offers a range that stretches from the free verse of charms and incantations to the strict metres of the learned poems.

While MacGill-Eain has not cultivated these 'Strict Metres' in the way that George Campbell Hay has done, his technical virtuosity is based on his awareness of what non-literate poets have done in the development of these same forms. Writing about the great anonymous songs of the sixteenth, seventeenth and eighteenth centuries, he himself has this to say: "Technically they are simple but adequate, their metrical basis being the old syllabic structure modified by speech stress"; and significantly he adds: "I think that is the most permanently satisfying basis for Gaelic metrics".

Technically, MacGill-Eain's own verse is anything but simple. It is true that he is not averse to the use of couplets, quatrains and other well-established traditional forms. It is true, too, that some poems can appear to traditionalist readers to be more complex technically than they really are. The syntactical patterns may be unexpected, and grammatical inflection much more strictly imposed than in any variety of colloquial Gaelic; but the stanza-forms and rhymes will remain quite regular. And it is probable also that the brilliant, novel imagery combined with traditional form can give the impression of a new technique. But these are not the poems in which MacGill-Eain's technical originality best manifests itself.

While, as I have suggested, he may have restored a slower pace to Gaelic poetry, MacGill-Eain also writes in metres that stride and surge and alter speed in much the same way as he changes the shape of the stanza and the trajectory of his rhythms from one section of a poem to another. In 'Coilltean Ratharsair' this protean quality is obvious to anyone whether he reads Gaelic or not. In 'Cumha Chaluim Iain Mhic-Eain', which has a unique structure in Gaelic poetry, the stanzas vary from four to twelve lines; and the rhyming lines vary more or less in the same unpredictable way. There is a long, untranslated poem, 'Craobh nan Teud', the elements of which may, technically speaking, all be derived from Gaelic tradition but which are combined in new relationships. (The title 'Tree of Harpstrings' — or of any stringed instrument — is taken from the pibroch 'The Lament for the Tree of Harpstrings'. It may be a corruptly transmitted name, but even if it is a corruption, it is still a remarkable metaphor. MacGill-Eain uses it as a kenning: it is 'the tree of poetry', 'the tree of art', and I shall refer to it briefly in another connection at a later stage.)

'Craobh nan Teud' opens with a section of short-lined octaves:

Air cruas nan creag	On the hardness of the crags
tha eagar smuaine	there is precision of thought;
air lom nam beann	on the bareness of the mountains
tha 'n rann gun chluaine:	there is an undeviating verse;
air mullach beò	on a living summit
tha treòir nam buadhan:	the energy of [mental] gifts;
air àirde ghil	on a shining height
tha 'n lios gun luaidh air.	is the garden that is not spoken of.

After eight declamatory stanzas in which both rhymes and rhythms vary their pattern, there comes a section of ten quatrains of longer lines.

Chunnacas fo sgàil craobh na dòrainn	...beneath the shadow of the tree of agony,
ag coiseachd sràidean Phàrais gu lòghmhor	walking the streets of Paradise radiantly,
na seann siùrsaichean beaga breòite	I saw the little, old, infirm harlots
a chunnaic Baudelaire 'na ònrachd.	whom Baudelaire saw in his loneliness.

Between the fourth and fifth quatrains, an octave, in basically the same metre as the first section, interrupts the progression; the last two stanzas of the second section are also octaves which again reflect the metres of the first section. Each of these has its own individual properties of rhythm and rhyme. These permutations are repeated (though never identically) with an extraordinary exuberance and virtuosity, in diction as well as metre, until we come to the end of the poem.

The sensuous effects which the poet achieves here through rhymes and contrasts of sound, through sustained and cumulative rhythms, and through alternating and contrastive rhythms, are of course utterly impossible to reproduce in translation. I can only offer the suggestion that the intensity and complexity of emotion which are evident even in translation find a counterpart in these 'formal' aspects of the original.

Earlier I drew attention to the fascination that Gaelic poets had, right from the beginnings of our literary history, with the very substance of language and the ways in which its strength and richness and delicateness may be exploited to make an impact upon the senses. MacGill-Eain's concern with the auditory properties of his medium puts him securely in that tradition: it is partly what makes him a Gaelic poet. Yet although at times there is almost an excess in this side of his writing, he can just as easily compose in other styles.

Most of MacGill-Eain's poems have an abundance of traditional rhymes, both internal as well as end-rhymes. A few have only minimal or unconventional rhyme. Many poems are in traditional rhymed quatrains; others are in irregular paragraphs. There is no definite linear development to be traced from any one of these positions to another. His two earliest published poems 'A' Chorra-Ghridheach' and 'A Chiall 's a Ghràidh' are in markedly different styles: the first in rhyming quatrains, of strong but varied rhythm, which shows a number of departures from strict conventions of rhyme; the second in an unusually bare and sensuously meagre *vers libre*, the lines of which are grouped in threes. Certain features of the design of both these poems appear and develop throughout his work.

MacGill-Eain employs the traditional Gaelic system of internal as well as final rhyme very freely. Technically, this ornamenting device, as I shall call it for the moment, is perhaps his most conspicuous link with the traditional past. The internal rhyme is the most distinctive marker of what the modern Gaelic speaker regards as 'traditional' technique (end rhyme is of course taken for granted) and it remained the leading ornament in the diminished verse tradition of the late nineteenth and twentieth centuries which I alluded to earlier. It is sometimes implied that this cross-rhyming is a difficult art. It is not. The fact of the matter is that the Gaelic imagination is so dominated by the design that it is almost impossible to avoid it. Connected with that fallacy is another. We sometimes hear it said that unless we bring a conscious awareness of these aural patterns to bear upon the poems or songs that contain them, our appreciation of the poetry is limited. This is almost the reverse of the truth. If the ornamentation obtrudes, the poem remains no more than an artefact — either that or we ourselves are guilty of focussing on the craft at the expense of the poetry. It is only when we take the craft for granted, and the aural sensuousness works upon us subliminally, that total communication takes place. Furthermore, because of the tyranny of mechanical rhythm and predictable rhyme, it is a more difficult art to break the hold of these metres than to follow their rules. But perhaps even more difficult is to combine old and new in such a way that neither neutralizes the other. This poetry never lets us forget that it is extending the tradition in which it is so obviously rooted.

If Somhairle MacGill-Eain's poetry were subjected to a mechanical analysis in terms of all its rhetorical techniques, we could show that its author is a master in the use of traditional ornament. But the 'ornament' is an integral part of a dense fabric of speech. At other times the senses are jolted because the reinforcement of an expected rhyme is suddenly withheld. The effect is physical and the meaning is altered as well. Those who care to test any of these statements can find the proof almost anywhere in his poetry. One good example is the beautifully designed, wistful poem 'Gleann Aoighre'. It is a sad, exquisite poem of great rhythmic poise and delicateness, with rich textures of vowel contrasts and harmonies, none of which is external to the meaning. Later poems, 'Aig Uaigh Yeats' to take an example at random, on the whole tend towards a looser weave of sound; in this poem the lack of rhyme in expected places and the sudden occurrence of rhyme, as well as the asymmetry of its three stanzas (8 lines; 9 lines; 8 lines), are quite as much part of the meaning as the aural tapestry of 'Gleann Aoighre'. Another late poem 'Creagan Beaga' has a completely different design: three quatrains with regular 'ab' end-rhyme and no internal rhymes.

Tha mi dol troimh Chreagan Beaga	I am going through Creagan Beaga
anns an dorchadas liom fhìn	in the darkness alone
agus an rod air Camus Alba	and the surf on Camus Alba
'na shian air a' mhol mhìn.	is a sough on smooth shingle.

The use of 'agus' (and) at the beginning of a line (where traditionally Gaelic would nearly always use the connective "s') has a strangely unsettling effect. It checks movement and gives the scene a kind of stillness — unremarkable as the word 'and' may seem in translation. The word 'agus', however, is used in various other places in MacGill-Eain's poems in a normal colloquial way but none the less not in the way of colloquial Gaelic in poetry. On each occasion it makes a special impact. The last line of the verse "'na shian air a' mhol mhìn" has a magical effect, achieved by the vowel contrast, of realising the sound of the surf on a shingle beach, and the effect is made intensely real and intensely local by the use of the word 'rod' which is localised in the Gaelic of Raasay and parts of Skye.

Of course one can find in various areas of Gaelic poetry manifestations of a comparable art. In some verse forms the full panoply of rhyme and other devices is mandatory and if the pattern is broken the art is flawed. Other forms allow considerably more freedom. MacGill-Eain uses all the possibilities and uses them together. No other Gaelic poet has produced an art which gives the impression in such a remarkable way of playing constantly fluctuating movement against stable forms. No Gaelic poet has a richer or more delicate or more varied auditory imagination. Yet at no time are we in danger of being seduced by that. It is what he says, not how he says it, that arrests the attention. The reasons why the labels of 'romantic' and 'classical' have been applied respectively to the content and form of his poetry are easy to see but like any other major artist he is not to be restricted by them. Integrity, not formalism, is the distinguishing feature of his poetry. Thus he will introduce stanzas in different metres, or alter their lengths or their rhyme-schemes, according to the demand of the moment and still create a sense not of formal ineptitude but of artistic inevitability.

It ought to be clear even from the brief sketch I have given of the metrical resources of Gaelic that the modern poet has almost an embarrassment of riches to draw on. But because MacGill-Eain's complex music is verbal, not melodic; since the great bulk of what he has written is poetry and not song and has a self-contained existence in speech or on the printed page; it is undoubtedly different in kind from the music-and-verse that precedes him. Does this difference in kind then mean that he has borrowed from English or other metrical traditions? One of the problems in tackling that formidable question is that although Gaelic has unique metrical forms, it also shares a common Western European literary heritage. Specifically with regard to Somhairle MacGill-Eain, one may single out a given structure and find its parallels easily enough in other literatures; sometimes, however, one can more easily find them in earlier Gaelic. Take an example: the fundamental metric of 'A' Bhuaile Ghréine'

Do m' shùilean-sa bu tu Deirdre   To my eyes you were Deirdre
'S i bòidheach 's a' bhuaile ghréine   beautiful in the sunny cattle-fold

is the same as W.B. Yeats's 'To Ireland in the Coming Times'

Know that I would accounted be
True brother of a company

Of course each poet realises the metre in his own individual way. The young Yeats (of the 1890's) lacks the sophistication, the varied pace, of the young MacGill-Eain (of the 1930's); Yeats's later rhythms often remind one, quite irresistibly, of the movement of MacGill-Eain's poetry. Even the sequences of rhyme used by both poets have sometimes a good deal in common. MacGill-Eain tells us (although the statement is not necessarily about metrics) that he "did not know the middle and later poetry of Yeats until well on in the thirties, but from then on it affected me considerably".[1] He has also declared, in a completely different context, that "metrically Gaelic can do anything English has done, but the metric of the great bulk of Gaelic poetry is impossible in English".[2] We must guard against facile comparisons and facile inferences alike.

In any event, there are in Gaelic more than one species of metric in what may generically be called choral songs (waulking-songs and the like) which yield a pattern not unlike that of 'A' Bhuaile Ghréine', 'An t-Eilean', 'Coin is Madaidhean-Allaidh', 'Nighean is Seann Orain' and one or two others.

Waulking-songs are sung (to put it in the simplest terms) in couplets or single lines. When these are written down without their choruses of vocables, we find in some of them a paragraphic structure of irregular lengths, each paragraph division being indicated by change of rhyme. The change usually marks a change in thematic treatment or in subject-matter. There are a few songs (I cannot think of more than half-a-dozen in the whole of Gaelic literature) which appear to have been sung in these irregular paragraphs, not in the lines or couplets of the waulking-song tradition. One of the best known in print is an address to the famous seventeenth-century warrior, Alasdair Mac Colla (Alexander Colkitto):

Alasdair a laoigh mo chéille
Có chunnaic no dh'fhàg thu 'n Eirinn

(Sàr Obair)[3]

The poems I have cited — 'A' Bhuaile Ghréine', etc. — are certainly not replicas: they all tend toward couplet rhyme, here and there extended beyond the couplet, but they do give the same sense of rhythmic drive and energy. This traditional paragraphic structure probably affords one of the best starting points for adapting a Gaelic metre to what we may call, for brevity's sake, a non-traditional sensibility. This opens up an interesting line of speculation, seeing that the metre is native and ancient and that some of the poetry composed in it has a positively surrealistic character. For MacGill-Eain has his own vein of surrealism: 'Coin is Madaidhean-Allaidh', among other poems, exemplifies it. Almost at every turn, the critic is forced to adopt a Janus attitude. Furthermore, Gaelic poetry, in which the oral element is so strong, frequently displays the paratactic style associated with oral poetry throughout the world. The stanza, or even the line, is usually self-contained, in sense as in syntax. In MacGill-Eain's work in general what we find is the normal thematic development of literary poetry. This is not a matter of adding one idea to another, line after line. But when there is a tendency to make the line or couplet autonomous in meaning, the reader frequently has a sense of being poised between the old Gaelic poetry and the new. That feeling is inescapable even if the explanation suggested here is wrong. At all events, the modern revolution in Gaelic poetry is to a large extent centred on thematic development. A new concept of poetic structure has been introduced to Gaelic literature and English poetry certainly provides a wide enough field in which to seek its source. Yet when all background influences on MacGill-Eain's poetry come to be investigated, these vivid, passionate songs, with their flexible paragraphic structure, cannot be left out of account. They have their own kind of thematic sequences which use an antithetical, cumulative or climactic mode of expression.

How did Somhairle MacGill-Eain solve the problem of creating a 'modern' diction from the resources of his native language? First, so far as I am aware, there is not a single neologism, strictly speaking, in the whole of his poetry. "An ceathramh seòl-tomhais" (the fourth dimension), might seem to qualify for the label of neologism but "seòl-tomhais" (a mode of measurement), is colloquial enough: 'seòl' in such compounds is still productive in Gaelic. An English reader, finding the word 'synthesis' in the translation, might well suspect that the original is a modern coinage. But 'co-chur' (better 'cochur': it is stressed on the first syllable) is a well-established item in the vocabulary of Presbyterian theology and preaching. In that context it has a slightly different meaning: its elements nevertheless are precisely equivalent to the Greek elements which form the word 'synthesis'. The fact that the poet can find what he needs in the working vocabulary of the language is a comment on the extraordinary wealth of Gaelic and its capacity for survival in spite of the ethnocidal policies of centuries. MacGill-Eain draws on every area of Scots Gaelic, sometimes using obscure and little-known words, whether from literature or from the living language. It may be that certain of the 'literary' words are now obsolete in speech but it is dangerous to dogmatise about obsolescence in Gaelic, as anyone who has devoted a reasonable amount of time to the study of dialects and oral tradition will appreciate.

A rare, if not obsolete, word is 'drithleann' (sparkle, gleam, etc.), which occurs, for instance, in the very early 'A' Chorra-Ghridheach': "luasgan is cadal gun drithleann" (unrest and sleep without a gleam); "ciùrrte, aon-drithleannach" (wounded, with but one sparkle). The adjective 'drithleannach' is used in a striking image of a piper's fingering in a seventeenth-century song by the Blind Harper at Dunvegan. Noun and adjective alike, however, are rare even in literature. Another very rare word is 'diùchd', (appear, manifest (oneself)). So far as I know, only two poets have used it before MacGill-Eain: Uilleam Ros and his maternal grandfather Am Pìobaire Dall, from whose poetry Ros possibly learnt it. If it is short — 'diuchd' and not 'diùchd' — it may still be known in speech, though in a somewhat different sense. There is actually some doubt as to the quantity of the word: MacGill-Eain writes it with a long vowel.

Interestingly enough, a number of words exist in Gaelic which certain writers, from about the second half of the eighteenth century, have lengthened unhistorical-ly. Some of these are part of the same Presbyterian and theological vocabulary as 'cochur'. For instance, MacGill-Eain takes 'éire' (burden) from established ecclesiastical usage: it occurs in 'Coilltean Ratharsair':

'S e gu bheil iad ag éirigh	It is that they rise
as an doimhne thruaigh reubte	from the miserable torn depths
tha cur air beanntan an éire...	that puts their burden on mountains...

We know from the song tradition, however, that the word is short (e.g. "Och a Rìgh gur trom m' eire / Nochd 's mi 'n eilean a' chaoil", where rhyme fixes the quantity). Although some academic critics may feel that words like these are solecisms, and that it is an aesthetic and linguistic lapse to prolong their existence, this is surely far too austere a view. MacGill-Eain is perfectly justified in choosing words from this particular literary register of Gaelic just as he is justified in taking words from any area of living Gaelic speech. Words are public but far from impersonal entities and frequently have a private life in individual imagination. When an author (who is perhaps more likely to be a writer rather than a non-literate composer) succeeds in transmitting his individual perception of a word — its sound, its appearance on a page, or a latent meaning — to the public context of his work, a hitherto unrealised potential is made available. In that creative process a writer puts his own impress on a word: it can never be quite the 'same' word again. Its position in the language has shifted; its status has been enhanced and its meaning extended. A major writer alters the language itself. MacGill-Eain uses the Gaelic lexicon in such a way that literary Gaelic will never be the same again. The context of his poetry gives the common currency of Gaelic, as well as the antique and unusual words, the quality of newly-minted coin. Recurrent words — among them words that express degrees of brightness, unrest, unattainableness, transience, suffering, pride — form his unmistakable signature. An individual reader will, of course, have his own predilections in choosing the words that sign a poet's style. Some readers may agree that the word 'lì' ('sheen, tinge' in spoken Gaelic) has a distinctive place in the group: normally in MacGill-Eain's poetry it is the sheen of beauty or just 'beauty' itself. 'Àrdan', another key-word, is in common usage 'pride' in a pejorative sense, a tendency to take offence easily. MacGill-Eain emphasises rather its sense of "proper pride, fierce pride, proud anger". Of the various words for 'jewel' in Gaelic, he chooses the interesting and fairly rare 'leug'; adj. 'leugach'. Historically it is interesting, if only for the fact that it has been described as "a false 'literary', 'southern' [Highland] restoration".[4] Although this judgement is unduly dismissive, the word is probably to be regarded as a literary coinage. It is certainly one of the lexical markers of MacGill-Eain's poetry: "Mo leug camhanaich is oidhche" (My jewel of dawn and night); "Agus fodham eilean leugach" (And under me a jewel-like island); "Ciamar a smaoinichinn gun glacainn / An rionnag leugach òir" (How should I think I would seize the radiant golden star); "Agus fo reultan Africa / 's iad leugach àlainn" (And under the stars of Africa, / jewelled and beautiful). A few poets have used 'leug' in the past but it now exists in a wholly new dimension.

From the poet's own translations it is evident that he sometimes focusses sharply and individualistically on a particular point in the semantic range of a word. 'Labhar', for instance, in its general import 'loud', is almost always translated 'eloquent'. This meaning is known neither in literature nor in contemporary spoken Gaelic. But it may have been used in that sense in certain contexts in the past: Dwelly's Dictionary gives 'eloquent' as the fourth sense of the word. This development, too, may have come from ecclesiastical usage. Wherever such extensions of meaning may have their source, they are to be regarded as an enrichment of the language. Even if Somhairle MacGill-Eain is only making accessible what is already latent in Gaelic, his claim to originality is high in this sphere also. No doubt if this poetry were written in Lowland Scots, it would have been celebrated or criticised long before now for its 'synthetic' diction. But if there is any parallel, on a purely linguistic level, between MacDiarmid's treatment of Scots and MacGill-Eain's treatment of Gaelic, the cultural perspectives of Gaelic makes for a fundamental difference of approach on the part of Gaelic readers from that of the critics of 'synthetic Scots'.

Gaelic poets of the past, literate or non-literate, were frequently eclectic. The non-literate Màiri Nighean Alasdair Ruaidh in the seventeenth century, composing in the vernacular, borrows directly or at one or more removes from Classical Gaelic poetry. In the eighteenth century the highly literate Uilleam Ros sought what he required in the living dialects. And there are many other examples. As a general observation, one may say that in Gaelic tradition (where fame and linguistic versatility are closely allied) no poet of note has been, in the strict senses a 'dialect poet'. Even with this background, however, the linguistic authority and arbiter of usage that MacGill-Eain constantly cites is the Church — in his case the Free Presbyterian Church, of which his family were adherents. I have written about this elsewhere (*Cencrastus*, 7) and do not intend to repeat the arguments now. I may, however, add that time and time again I have heard MacGill-Eain back up his discussion of linguistic usage with the phrases: "Chuala mi 'san eaglais e" or "Dh'fhaodainn a bhith air a chluinntinn 'san eaglais" (I (could have) heard it in church).

If English translation cannot possibly transmit a sense of the variety and luxuriance of MacGill-Eain's Gaelic or convey the impact of a rare word in a new and contemporary setting, much less can it suggest the 'ambiguity' which a complex of associations creates. The following lines occur in 'Aithreachas': "A Dhia, 'se bòidhche a' ghàrraidh . . . . nach fhan ri buidheachas an fhoghair" ('O God, the beauty of the garden . . . . which will not stay for the yellow gratitude of autumn'). 'Buidheachas' is gratitude; 'buidhe' is yellow. These words are unrelated and are not normally linked in the mind of a native speaker of Gaelic. The present context, however, inevitably evokes the image of ripening corn. (At a deeper level of analysis, still another word 'buidhe', which belongs with 'gratitude' not with 'yellow', and survives in some stereotyped phrases, where it is in fact linked with 'yellow', would also come under scrutiny. This is the 'buidhe' of the line "bu bhuidhe dhomh na do na h-eòin" (the springtide 'more golden to me than to the birds') in 'Reothairt'. Another example of ambiguity may be found in the opening line of 'Am Mùr Gorm': "Mur b'e thusa bhiodh an Cuilithionn / 'na mhùr eagarra gorm". Here the two words, again unrelated, are 'eagarra' (precise) and 'eag(ach')' (notch(ed)). The translation, "But for you the Cullin would be / an exact and serrated blue rampart", has perforce to put the two elements on the same semantic footing. The original Gaelic allows the primary sense to remain dominant. In his English translations, of each of these citations the poet has succeeded in conveying the scope of the images by making them fully explicit. Even if some subtlety is lost they are still powerful.

Occasionally an image or a statement seems, indeed, to make as great an impact in English as in Gaelic. One of these is the marvellous line in 'Hallaig': "Anns a' chamhanaich bhalbh bheò", translated "in the dumb living twilight". 'Balbh' is primarily 'dumb, without speech', but is also the normal colloquial Gaelic for 'still, hushed'. In Gaelic 'beò' (living) is as unexpected as 'dumb' is in the brilliant translation which selects the primary meaning of 'balbh'. When the native element is combined with a concept that is Romantic (in the sense that Wordsworth's 'living air' is Romantic), the resulting compound image is a microcosm of the blend of sensibilities that makes MacGill-Eain the kind of poet that he is: modern, sophisticated and Gaelic.

I am therefore not implying in anything that I have written that the non-Gaelic reader is cut off from his poetry. What I am emphasising is the need to assess his work against the background, and within the perspectives, of Gaelic literature as a whole, if those aspects to which translation gives us access are to be understood in all their richness. A number of topics which still require to be interpreted in that light come to mind. For instance, an entire essay could be devoted to his use of place-names; another to the sea as a source of imagery. Place-names occupy a central place in Gaelic literature. The sea is one of the great themes of Gaelic poetry, particularly the song-poetry of the Hebrides and the North Western seaboard. In MacGill-Eain's poetry these and other themes make comparisons and contrasts with the poetry of the past.

The wonderful celebration of mountains in 'Ceann Loch Aoineart' is unique as a nature poem in Gaelic in the way it brings together visual, aural and tactile images in a multi-dimensional style. This can certainly be said to be a poem of Romantic sensibility; it is also a poem which is probably quite as effective in English translation as it is in Gaelic. For all that, a Gaelic reader recalls other celebrations of famous mountains: Donnchadh Bàn Mac an t-Saoir's panegyric to 'Beinn Dobhrain', for instance, or Domhnall mac Fhionnlaigh nan Dàn's passionate evocation of the mountains of Lochaber. Certainly a contrast of sensibilities exists between 'Ceann Loch Aoineart' and 'Beinn Dobhrain', whatever terms we may find to express it. Curiously enough, there is more of a bond between the Romantic in MacGill-Eain and the sixteenth-century hunter-poet Domhnall Mac Fhionnlaigh nan Dàn as he views the mountain he shall never climb again while it "will not descend until doom". More than a gap of centuries, however, separates Domhnall Mac Fhionnlaigh's unclimbable mountain and "the mountain that may not be climbed" of MacGill-Eain's 'Nighean is Seann Orain'. And yet at a much deeper and more obscure level one can sense a relationship between, say, "the full, bare mountain" (a' bheinn làn lom) in 'Craobh nan Teud' and the mountains of the wilderness that appear in Gaelic song more than once under the name of 'A' Bheinn Mhór'. Symbolically, the mountain is a place of ritual mourning: "ascending and descending the mountain". It is also equivalent to the Greenwood of Love: "on the peaks of the mountains . . . . . in the track of the belling deer". The mountain and the wild moor symbolise the anarchic energies and activities of human life set in contrast with the regulated life of the settled community. At times one feels that this is an archetypal image: that the 'great mountain', the 'forbidding mountain', the 'mountain of mist', and so forth, are all partly a reflection, no matter how faint, of the cosmic mountain which features in art and culture throughout the world. How much of that is directly relevant to the mountain symbol in MacGill-Eain's poetry ('A' Bheinn air Chall', for example; or 'the shifting mountain of time') must be left in the realms of conjecture. The point is, once again, that the Gaelic reader is aware of the tradition no matter what the sources of the poet's inspiration may have been.

Something of the same kind is true of the image of the tree. Gaelic poetry is full of kennings and metaphors of trees. They are to be found in love poetry and in eulogies composed for the warrior, the 'tree of battle', the 'tree of slaughter'. In a mid-seventeenth-century poem Gaelic warriors are described as "trees of good lineage from fairy hills". The fairy mound or 'sìdhein', the abode of the ancestral dead, is also the local focus of the Otherworld in pagan Gaelic cosmology. An image such as that continues to draw upon a primitive source of energy. The seventeenth-century poet was no doubt well versed in the ancient lore of the great sacred trees of Gaelic mythology which are themselves representatives of the Tree that grows at the axis of the world. For those who know that lore and the kennings of Gaelic poetry, 'Craobh nan Teud', with its 'tree of poetry'; 'the beautiful heroic tree'; 'tree of ecstasy'; 'the love-tree'; the 'great tree of the high mountains' develops a familiar rhetoric even if the development is new and extraordinary. Nevertheless, these particular metaphors actually lead us away from the mythopoeic universe. We return to it in 'Hallaig':

...'s tha mo ghaol aig Allt Hallaig	...and my love is at the Burn of Hallaig,
'na craoibh bheithe, 's bha i riamh	a birch tree, and she has always been
eadar an t-Inbhir 's Poll a' Bhainne,	between Inver and Milk Hollow,
thall 's a bhos mu Bhaile-Chùirn:	here and there about Baile-chuirn:
tha i 'na beithe, 'na calltuinn,	she is a birch, a hazel,
'na caorunn dhìreach sheang ùir...	a straight, slender young rowan...
Chunnacas na mairbh beò...	The dead have been seen alive...
na h-igheanan 'nan coille bheithe,	the girls a wood of birches,
dìreach an druim, crom an ceann.	straight their backs, bent their heads.

'Hallaig' is a twentieth-century poem and contains images of its time. Setting these aside, I have the feeling it is also a poem that would have been understood a thousand years ago and more. The mandarin caste of mediaeval society who were the keepers of ancient wisdom and learning, and whose name 'fili' originally meant 'seer', might not find 'Hallaig' as mysterious as some modern readers do. 'Coilltean Ratharsair' would be far more baffling.

These of course are opinions that depend upon a knowledge of Gaelic poetry throughout history. Much more accessible are the synchronic aspects of MacGill-Eain's poetry: the inner relationships that exist between individual poems and the deployment of certain leitmotifs. Within the limits of this essay I can only draw attention to one or two examples of what I mean. In spite of the fundamental difference between the symbolism of 'Craobh nan Teud' and 'Coilltean Ratharsair', we can sense here and there an underlying connection in imagery, as if parts of each poem had the same matrix. 'Craobh nan Teud' has:

Gealach is dubhar uaine choilltean,	Moon and green shadowiness of woods,
Cùirneanan an driùchd 'na boillsgeadh,	Beads of dew shining in its light,
briodal sùgraidh nan òg aoibhneach,	Tender love-talk of the happy young,
'nan leugan òirdhearc 'na loinn ghil.	Splendid jewels in its bright elegance.
Suaimhneas sneachda nam beann	Snowy tranquillity of sun-lit mountains...
grian-laist'...	

Compare that from 'Craobh nan Teud' with this from 'Coilltean Ratharsair':

. . . . . sàmhchair choilltean,	. . . . . the peace of the woodlands,
ceilearadh shruthan is suaineadh aibhnean,	the bird-song of rivulets and the winding of burns,

ciùine reultan buidhe a' boillsgeadh,
lainnir a' chuain, coille-bìonain na
                                    h-oidhche.

the mildness of yellow stars shining,
the glitter of the sea, the phosphorescence of
                                    night.

'Nuair dhòirt a' ghealach na crùin shoilleir

air clàr dùghorm na linne doilleir...

When the moon poured the bright crown
                                    pieces
on the dark blue board of the sea at night...

..... Sgurr nan Gillean...
.... sgiamhach le ghile,
le ghile sneachda 'na dhrithleann,
ciùin agus stòlda 'na shitheadh...

Sgurr nan Gillean .....
..... in its whiteness,
in its snow whiteness sparkling,
calm and steadfast in its thrust...

Coille uaine . . . . .

Green wood . . . . .

It is only a trace and I have to mutilate the verse in order to focus on it. The
next example is somewhat different. *Dàin do Eimhir* LII reads:

Do m' dhùr-amharc bha thu 'nad reul
's tu leat fhéin 's an iarmailt:
is thugadh dhut an dà leus
le m' aigne thorrach 's m' iargain.

To my steady gaze you were a star
all alone in the skies,
and you were given two rays of light
by my fertile mind and my longing.

'S an uair sin bhoillsg thu le trì
an aon leus dìreach trianaid;
ach cha robh 'nam leòis dhian fhìn
ach clann do lìthe 'n iargain.

Then you shone forth with three
in a single direct effulgent trinity,
but in my intense rays of light
there were only the children of your beauty
                                    yearning.

Bha mi feitheamh ris a' bheum
a mhilleadh do réim le chrìonadh;
ach thug mi dhut na trì dhut fhéin
an ceann réis deich bliadhna.

I waited for the stroke
that would impair your power and wither it;
but I gave you the three for yourself
at the end of a space of ten years.

Oir nam b' iad mo leòis gin fhìn
a bheòthaich lì 'nad lias-sa

For had they been of my own begetting,
those rays that kindled beauty in your
                                    brightness,

bu chinnt gun cailleadh iad am brìgh
le glasadh tìm deich bliadhna.

they would surely have lost their power
through ten years of time's greying.

A shuilbhireachd 's a chridhe chòir
's sibh lòghmhor ann an aodann:
a mheallaidh cridhe 's a mheallaidh sùla
ur n-ìomhaigh rùin a h-aogas!

Affable nature and kind heart,
you are radiant in one face —
beguiling the heart and beguiling the eyes —
beloved image of her appearance.

Cha b' ann fada bha an tòir
a thug còrr 's deich bliadhna
an uair a bha an fhaodail còrr
's na dh'fhóghnadh dòchas sìorruidh.

It was not long, the pursuit
that took longer than ten years,
when the treasure-trove
was more than enough for eternal hope.

If this is compared with 'An Sgian', it is clear that both are metaphysical poems,
twin poems though not identical; and both immediately recognisable as the
offspring of one intellect. Finally, from 'Craobh nan Teud' again come these images:

Eibhneach anns a' mheangach bhlàthmhor
suaimhneas geal an aodainn àluinn,
leugach anns a' chumadh-fàire
fiamh ulaidhe an rainn neo-bhàsmhoir.

Joyful in the flowering branches
White tranquillity of a beautiful face,
Jewelled in the horizon's shape
The precious gleam of immortal verse.

Mar a.reachadh i na b'fhaide	The farther it moved away
's ann a theannadh i na b'fhaisge,	The nearer it approached,
's mar a thrialladh i am fadal	As it travelled into the distance
's ann a mhiadaicheadh a h-aiteal.	So would its light increase.

In passing we may note the resemblance of the first verse to the last stanza of 'Am Mùr Gorm':

Agus air creachainn chéin fhàsmhoir	And on a distant luxuriant summit
chinn blàthmhor Craobh nan Teud	there blossomed the Tree of Strings,
'na meangach duillich t' aodann,	among its leafy branches your face,
mo chiall is aogas réil.	my reason and the likeness of a star.

There are other connections, some simple and some complex, between 'Coilltean Ratharsair', 'Craobh nan Teud' and the short poem 'An té dh'an tug mi . .', with its images of "dim wood", "slender branching" and "her beauty like a horizon opening the door to day". The second verse contains precisely the same kind of metaphysical conceit as we find in the fifth stanza of 'An Sgian':

Mar a rachadh i an àireamh	As it increased in number
nam bruan geàrrte prann,	of cut and brittle fragments,
's ann a ghabhadh i aonachd	so it took unity,
'na h-aonar cruaidh teann.	alone hard and taut.

The intellectual groundwork of 'Craobh nan Teud' is quite different from that of *Dàin do Eimhir* LII and of 'An Sgian', yet both display quite clearly a leitmotif of MacGill-Eain's metaphysical poetry. There are naturally very many finer threads of connection, through the themes of time's destructiveness, for instance, or the unattainability of human desire. But to demonstrate these connections would require a much closer examination of MacGill-Eain's vocabulary.

My register of techniques and formal relationships would not be complete without some illustration of the way in which rhythmic patterns become a vital part of the meaning. I shall take two examples. In 'Hallaig', "The girls a wood of birches / . . . . in silent bands / go to Clachan as in the beginning / and return from Clachan / from Suisnish and the land of the living; / each one young and light-stepping, / without the heartbreak of the tale":

O Allt na Feàrnaibh gus an fhaoilinn	From the Burn of Fearns to the raised beach
tha soilleir an dìomhaireachd nam beann	that is clear in the mystery of the hills,
chan eil ach coimhthional nan nighean	there is only the congregation of the girls
ag cumail na coiseachd gun cheann.	keeping up the endless walk.

In the last line two conflicting rhythms, one the natural speech rhythm of the phrase, the other the rhythm dictated by the verse form, operate at the same time, each inhibiting the other. The result is that the line seems to be suspended: metrically it is in absolute accord with the meaning of the words. The other example comes from 'Cumha Chaluim Iain Mhic Gill-Eain'. If we read the last line of the sixth stanza "Nan tigeadh tu a nall" (if you were to come over) with elision of the 'obscure' vowel written 'a' — in other words, according to the normal pattern of Gaelic speech — a remarkable metrical effect is produced:

Nan robh thu anns a' Chlachan eile	If you were in the other Clachan
Tha bhos ann an Loch Aills,	that is over here in Lochalsh,
Bhiodh am fear treun ud dhe do shìnnsre,	that brave man of your ancestors
Ruairi Beag a' chlogaid dhrìlsich	Ruairi Beag of the glittering helmet,

Moiteil 's e dèanamh gluasaid	would be proud to move
Gu do leigeil-sa ri ghualainn —	to let you to his shoulder —
Nan tigeadh tu (a) nall.	if you were to come over.

The verse has overall a dominating, progressive movement which builds up over six lines. In the last statement that flow is suddenly checked. This gives the impression of a counter-current starting up against the main stream. The effect on the meaning is that the affirmation of the preceding lines is abruptly nullified. There are other examples of equal metrical delicateness but none of greater poignancy in the whole of MacGill-Eain's poetry.

If the subject of this book is a revolution in Gaelic poetry we might reasonably expect that the architect of the revolution had a plan of campaign. Yet this does not appear to be the case. We can, of course, infer the strategy from the evidence of the poetry itself; but nothing that MacGill-Eain has said or written allows us to state that he set out deliberately to change the course of Gaelic poetry. It was the realisation, during his undergraduate years (when he was still writing English as well as Gaelic verse) that the latter was far superior, that made him confine himself to Gaelic. This does not mean that he had not prepared himself: from his teens, according to his own account, he had been reading Gaelic poetry obsessively. In another context I have drawn attention to the relevance of T. S. Eliot's 'Tradition and the Individual Talent': "Tradition...cannot be inherited, and if you want it you must obtain it by great labour. It involves, in the first place, the historical sense...[which] involves a perception, not only of the pastness of the past, but of its presence... And it is at the same time what makes a writer most acutely conscious of his place in time, of his own contemporaneity". Few people know the corpus of Gaelic poetry, published and unpublished, as intimately as MacGill-Eain knows it. Yet he hardly ever draws directly on the highly developed, involuted and sophisticated verbal code which constitutes the traditional diction of Gaelic poetry. In one of the sub-codes of that diction there is a phrase "thall 's a bhos" (here and there), usually followed by "mu" (around, about). In itself no more than one of the inconspicuous pinning-stones of speech, it is used in lyrical poetry with overtones of tragedy, loss and grief. In a famous seventeenth-century song, a party of the hapless Clan Gregor are apparently scattered as fugitives "here and there around Loch Fyne"; in the lament of Campbell of Glen Faochain's widow in 1645 (after Inverlochy): "Here and there about Inveraray women wring their hands, their hair dishevelled". It is as if Auden's "altogether elsewhere" had the backing of centuries of usage. When MacGill-Eain writes in 'Hallaig': "Here and there about Baile-chuirn" these resonances are unmistakeably there. But this type of borrowing is very rare indeed.

MacGill-Eain has invented his own diction. As a poet who is secure in his tradition, "acutely conscious of his own contemporaneity", he has, pre-eminently, a sense of the presence of the past. He is a magisterial writer who is totally in charge of his language and the techniques of his poetry; he is never controlled by them. There are times when he appears to be pushing Gaelic to its limits. There are times, indeed, when he gives the impression of being positively cavalier in his attitude towards the language. At any event he makes no concession to his readers. From that point of view it is perfectly legitimate to call his poetry élitist. Or rather, since the term may be taken to imply conscious intention, the poetry would qualify for that description were it not for the fact that, as he says himself, "I was not one who could write poetry if it did not come to me in spite of myself, and if it came, it had to come in Gaelic".

And it comes, one may add, in spite of what the poetry declares of a division between heart and intellect, as the utterance of an entire person. In other words it has artistic sincerity.

The poetry registers such a range and intensity of emotion that even when its language is most literary and most elevated, it still speaks with affective directness and a simple passionate immediacy. There is no artifice. There are simplicities and difficulties; tenderness, delicateness and a rough-hewn quality; exquisite purity, and here and there an almost stumbling innocence; and immense sophistication. It is truly astonishing that only Gaelic, when it had already been driven so much into decline, could have provided a poet with the passionate eloquence to express that integrity. Somhairle MacGill-Eain needed Gaelic and Gaelic needed Somhairle MacGill-Eain.

JOHN MacINNES

NOTES

1. 'Some Gaelic and Non-Gaelic Influences On Myself', in *The Celtic Consciousness,* ed. R. O'Driscoll (Toronto, 1981), p. 500.
2. 'Aspects of Gaelic Poetry', *Scottish Art and Letters,* 3 (1947), 37.
3. John Mackenzie, *Sàr Obair nam Bard Gaelach* (Edinburgh, 1841), pp. 56-57.
4. John Fraser, 'Varia 2. *leug* "(precious) stone" ', *Scottish Gaelic Studies,* 5 (1942), 161.
5. 'A Radically Traditional Voice: Sorley MacLean and the Evangelical Background', *Cencrastus,* 7 (Winter 1981-2).

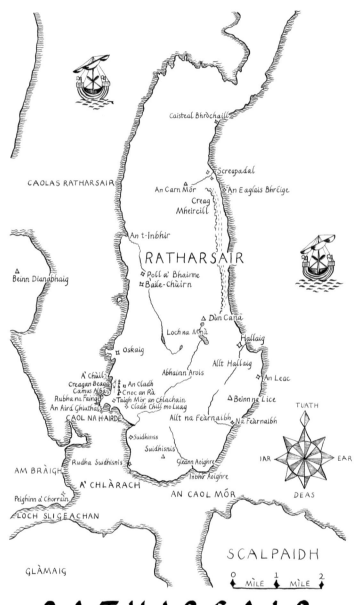

CAISTEAL BHRÒCHAILL

Caisteal Bhròchaill

Screapadal

CAOLAS RATHARSAIR

An Carn Mòr · An Eaglais Bhrèige

Creag
Mheircill

An t-Inbhir

RATHARSAIR

Beinn Dianabhaig

Poll a' Bhainne
Baile-Chùirn

Dùn Cana
Loch na Mnà

Hallaig

Oskaig

Allt Hallaig

Abhainn Arois

An Leac

A' Chùil
Creagan Beaga · An Cladh
Camus Alba · Cnoc an Rà
Rubha na Fainge
An Aird Ghiuthais
CAOL NA HAIRDE
Taigh Mòr an Chlachain
Cladh Chill mo Luag

Beinn na Lice

Allt na Feàrnaibh

Na Feàrnaibh

TUATH

Suidhisnis

Suidhisnis

IAR

EAR

Rudha Suidhisnis

Gleann Aoighre

AM BRÀIGH

Inbhir Aoighre

DEAS

A' CHLÀRACH

AN CAOL MÒR

Peighinn a' Chorráin

Loch Sligeachan

SCALPAIDH

GLÀMAIG

0   1
MÌLE ◆ MÌLE 2

RATHARSAIR

Celebration of a Tension

Sorley MacLean's poetry seems shot through with an awareness of various tensions, within the individual, within society, and within the natural world as a whole. From what one can gather of 'An Cuilithionn' there was to be a resolution. MacLean, overwhelmed by the agony of his *moral* awareness in face of the sufferings of humanity, would appear to have accepted an answer in terms of Promethean political action:

Bha uair ann a shaoil mi
nan tigeadh an t-Arm Dearg
tarsainn na Roinn-Eòrpa
nach biodh a' chòmhdhail searbh:
nach b' ann le teine-aighir
mar chunnacas ann am Pràg,
's nach b' e an curaidh oileanaich
a rachadh suas 'na smàl,
ach connadh crìon an airgid—
b'e falaisgir an àigh—
le ola bhréig nan uachdaran
'ga sgliamadh air gach bàrr.

There was a time I thought
if the Red Army came
across Europe
the tryst would not be bitter;
that it would not be with a bonfire
as was seen in Prague,
and that it would not be the heroic student
that would go up in smoke
but the brittle fire-wood of money
— a splendid heather-burning —
with the lying oil of rulers
daubed on every tip.

That poem from the late 1960s refers obviously to the self-immolation of the Prague student, Jan Palach, who martyred himself in a Prague square in protest, announcing that he was willing to die to oppose the Russian defeat of the humane and open regime which Dubcek had sought to introduce by reforming the politics of Czechoslovakia. Obvious too is the poem's recollection of MacLean's own past, of what seemed to be his last hope in a Europe dominated by totalitarian power. For MacLean, however, the recollection goes deeper. One could not envisage him writing an equivalent of the Ecclesiastical sonnets of Wordsworth, with their implicit forgetfulness of the lessons of early experience and poetry. The desire to climb, to attain awareness rather than contentment, is with him even when "there is not much hope" on 'Creag Dallaig', even if "the brain has no foothold / to lower a rope to my heart". Wordsworth felt no need for a rope that late in his career, even if perhaps he needed the excuse of a map to show how high he thought he had climbed. For MacLean, the opening of one of the published fragments of 'An Cuilithionn' leads to the following statement addressed to the mountain:

Gun tigeadh dhomhsa thar gach àite
bhith air do shlinneanan àrda,
a' strì ri d' sgòrnan creagach sàr-ghlas,
mo ghleachd ri t'uchd cruaidh sgorrach
                bàrcach.

My place above every place would be
to be on your high shoulder-blades,
striving with your rocky stark-grey throat,
wrestling with your hard-peaked heaving
                chest.

The identificatory metaphor of the fourth line above is unusual in MacLean, as if temporarily he did desire to be the mountain, and, by means of the poem, to offer the reader a peak from which to see the spectacle. This again argues an overwhelming force, the desire to demonstrate, but a force, in the poem's context at least, not innocent of Promethean *hubris*.

Yet the recollection of the climb is complex beyond the mere level of the 'objective correlative', or metaphor of a feeling. It is an invocation, or an evocation: the images of throat and thorax are parts of anatomy of great importance to both singer and climber; the images build a climb in song. MacLean's poetry is inter-woven and multi-faceted. The climb meets not only physical obstacles but observations, perceptions, and recollections. The fire-wood and heather-burning imagery of 'Palach' have a like function. The "place above every place" recalls Muir's journey-place antithesis: on a metaphysical level, it is a state of himself at his best. It is a metaphorical point on the graph of the height-imagery which MacLean uses in his poetry: praising MacDiarmid for eschewing a "mean, low, dry way" in one instance, but reinforcing that there is a real height which is not to be confused with any physical or other 'high'. These false, euphoric states can be achieved with a sense of power, inflation, "the rope itself a bellows" when, subservient to authority, someone who climbs a peak by rope-ladder is no better than a lying braggart.

Climbing the Cuillin of the fragment quoted, MacLean's spirit rises till it

gu 'n glac e fàire do chóigimh bidein,	grasps the sky-line of (the mountain's) fifth pinnacle—
far am brist air ceann na spàirne	where will break on the struggle's head
muir mhór chiar nan tonn gàbro . . .	the great grey sea of gabbro waves . . .
cuan 's a luasgan teann an creagan,	an ocean whose welter is tight in rocks,
a chraosan maireann an caol eagan,	its yawning mouths permanent in narrow chasms,
a spùtadh sìorruidh anns gach turraid,	its spouting everlasting in each turret,
a bhàrcadh biothbhuan anns gach sgurra.	its swelling everlasting in each sgurr.

The weaving of sea-imagery with natural landscape also appears in 'Resolution and Independence'. The geological term 'gabbro' is fortuitous, meaning the rock shaped by the contact of lava with water during the remote volcanic era. The flow of the poem is shaped by recollection in a like manner. Thus one sees sea-imagery consonant with mounting feeling, mounting recollection. His body is moving upwards towards a physical peak, one made by a physical conflict in a remote geological era. His whole body rises until

chì mi 'n sàr eilean 'na shiantan	I see the noble Island in its storm-showers
mar chunnaic Màiri Mhór 'na h-iargainn;	as Màiri Mhór saw in her yearning,
's an sgaoileadh ceò bho cheann na Gàrsbheinn	and in the breaking of mist from the Garsven's head
ag ialadh air creachainnean fàsa,	creeping over desolate summits
's ann dhiùchdas dhomhsa càs mo chàirdean,	there rises before me the fate of my people,
eachdraidh chianail an eilein àlainn.	the sad history of the lovely Island.

This is no 'pathetic fallacy' but a vision, something which cries out with importance, almost bursting with it. The island has risen out of the sea, and on the island the cultural reference to Màiri Mhór symbolizes the meaning of her poetry. There is no orgasm of mysterious rapture in the culminating two lines but rather a heightened moral awareness which is integral to the height to which MacLean has ascended. From the opening invocation, "The Sgurr Biorach is the highest Sgurr", MacLean builds towards a peak of anamnesis, through which the metaphysical motif is expressed very dramatically.

One can trace this motif very usefully in Wordsworth, where in the first two books of 'The Excursion' he presents the image of a cottage and garden. All is well, the forces of nature, weather, growth and decay operate in harmony with the efforts of the householder and his wife. The fabric of the house is maintained; the garden is kept up; the wife gives travellers a drink from a wooden bowl.

But economic circumstances compel the husband to depart. The woman can no longer manage, and she also leaves. Finally the cottage is falling in, weather and decay breaking it down; the gardening is no longer done and the place becomes overgrown, sinking into the landscape; the wooden bowl lies in the bed of the stream, slowly rotting, merging with the flow of water. From the fruitful tension of humanity with nature, overwhelming forces of an economic source have deprived man of power. What ensues is in effect stagnation.

This extract from 'The Excursion' can be related directly to 'Hallaig'. The "vehement bullet" in 'Hallaig' announces man's presence in the landscape in the same way as the same imagery does in Duncan Bàn Macintyre's 'Moladh Beinn Dobhrain'. MacLean, no doubt, here remembers that poem, and certainly both it and 'Hallaig' make a statement about life's very real conditions. Reminiscence makes it plain that the scene described in 'Hallaig' cannot be called an idyll, in the pejorative sense of the word. Whether or not Mandelstam ever read Arnold, both he and Eliot agree with the earlier critic in singling out the image from Dante, *Inferno* XV:

> o si ver noi aguzzevan le ciglia,
> come vecchio sartor fa nella cruna.

Compare this to:

| Tha bùird is tàirnean air an uinneig | The window is nailed and boarded |
| troimh 'm faca mi an Aird an Iar | through which I saw the West |

as introducing and *defining* a poem of inwardness.

MacLean's abiding moral concern sustains the motif and intensifies the definition of his poetry as something of more than psychological application. Whatever may be said of the extract from 'The Excursion', MacLean reaches yet another level of universality by using the clear reference to his Gaelic past, and specifically to the Clearances. One now knows why the window is nailed and boarded. In terms of the motif the tension has been overwhelmed, as it might be by a tempest or a blight, or by the action of a landlord.

Power that can overwhelm features strongly in MacLean's poetry, as it does in Highland experience. Reading Czeslaw Milosz's account of his and MacLean's generation, in *The Captive Mind*, the last picture of the best Polish poet of that generation brings a well-known Highland image to mind. The poet was at a street-corner firing a machine-gun at the height of the Warsaw uprising; he was destroyed by a German tank against which he was powerless. Reflecting on the scene, Milosz finds something simply and profoundly inadequate in that extreme moral passion. Instead he seeks another explanation and despite the difference between his poetry and MacLean's, both the title 'Child of Europe', and the subject-matter are similar, although expressed in a different way. Milosz writes that there can be no justification in believing that one is better than those who did not survive; the question we should ask ourselves is not "Why me?", but "Why not me?".

MacLean's passion partakes of the same inadequacy, as inadequate as the kilted figures in the hackneyed picture of Culloden. Any Highlander can be proved inadequate in certain circumstances, like the Polish poet who faced the German tank. Nobody should be judged on those terms; many have been. The Promethean force of technology ensures that more will be, and that the bias of power will jeopardise the spiritual force, climbing to the peak irrespective of what lies in the path. Gaelic and Màiri Mhór, and all that they alone stand for, will be forgotten.

The thought is almost intolerable, but must be borne. It is not that technology should be abandoned for some hayseed pastoralism or a return to primitivism, that caricature of the anti-technology lobby into which many have stumbled. It is the thought of the duty of conflict which has brought MacLean, like Edwin Muir, to meet moral demands which are deeper than rather crude, short-term humanitarianism. One can be an exile in one's own land too, and even if the duty of remembering is displaced in an emergency it will still continue in some, and be a sore need in others:

Tha fuil dhòirte is feòil reubte   Spilt blood and torn flesh
mu na Tighean Seara 'g éigheach   shout about the Easterhouses
's a' mùchadh le sgreadan cruaidhe   and stifle with hard screeches
guth nam martairean truagha.   the voice of the poor martyrs.

MacLean would conspire to no such stifling, or laying down of the burdens which conscience bids him bear. There is nothing which he "has already taken into account", for the accounting and the conflict continue; that phrase is but another euphemism for apathy, for moral and intellectual stagnation: for the lack of love.

And love, which cannot take bomb or tank as its object, is the central theme of MacLean's work. Here is an *amor intellectualis* akin to that of Nicholas of Cusa, which Ernst Cassirer describes in the following passage:

(It) includes knowledge as a necessary element and a necessary condition. No one can love what he has not, in some sense, known. Love by itself, without any admixture of knowledge, would be an impossibility. Whatever is loved is, by that very act, considered good . . . This knowledge of the good must spur on and give wings to the will.

In 'A Chiall's a Ghràidh', for instance, MacLean defines love itself by reference to its object or objects. The desire to love does not conflict with hard experience and cold reason in a battle to the death: they exist through conflict. Love of his people, of the big men of Braes with whom he identifies in terms of a moral ideal, of the composers of the Old Songs with whom he identifies in poetry and humanity, and of others, implies the 'knowledge' which is indisseverable from the cultural reference. The height of love is described by MacLean as a burden taken on in what Muir called "free servitude":

'S e 'n gaol ginte leis a' chridhe   The love begotten by the heart
an gaol tha 'n geimhlich shaoir   is the love that is in free chains
an uair a ghabhas e 'na spiorad   when it takes, in its spirit,
gaol eanchainn air a ghaol.   a brain love of its love.

                                                              ('An Sgian')

Cassirer adds that "the essence of the good itself remains inaccessible to knowledge". It can only be discerned by means of a *visio intellectualis*, which I take in the present context to be one prime justification for the reading of MacLean's poetry. It offers such a vision and, based on his experience of the feeling of love, asks: "What is the Good?"

The question can be discerned in an outline of the peak of love where feeling for "the fate of my people / the sad history of the lovely island" is higher than the peak from which breathtaking scenery can be seen. Increased knowledge in love can beget more love. Hell is to be able to say:

An té dh' an tug mi uile ghaol	She to whom I gave all love
cha tug i gaol dhomh air a shon;	gave me no love in return;
ged a chiùrradh mise air a sàilleabh	though my agony was for her sake,
cha do thuig i 'n tàmailt idir.	she did not understand the shame at all.

Attending to what the poet has said, rather than to the background of the poem, the dilemma is revealed as a classic one; the weight of the lines is far greater than in the kind of love-songs anybody can write. This image should not go over the cliff. If it takes a woman to make a man feel that way, then imagine the speaker of that quatrain as the hounded and impoverished MacDiarmid of the 1930s, and the woman as Scotland. MacLean shared the condition of imposed inadequacy. One might say of an interpretation of that poem in symbolic terms, that MacLean had been shown a *visio intellectualis* of the Good, and had been torn apart for bringing these aspects of his vision together in love, exactly what one might say of MacLean's most extreme statements concerning flaw and wound. The real horror is in the possibility that these statements might be true in the symbolic sense of the *visio intellectualis*. "She" could be Gaelic, Scotland, all humanity — and so far gone that even helplessness before Rommel's guns and tanks would be no plight beside that of finding her depraved and a liar. MacLean has known the thought that all human aspirations, all the feelings and the beauties of the Old Songs, might be a betraying illusion: humanity a lie, love also a lie.

The force of that negative vision brings things, thoughts and ideas into definition. It is, as it were, the brain's foothold. The observation or experience which breaks or relieves the encircling tightness of having that vision, "lowers a rope to the heart", even the heart stuck in the morass. MacLean's eyes have lighted

...air a' chàthar,	... on the morass
air a' bhoglaich oillteil ghrànda	(and) on the ugly and frightful marsh
's am bheil gach dòchas 'ga bhàthadh.	where every hope is being drowned.

The bog, morass, is a symbol of stagnation. It represents a state of life impenetrable to eye and mind, and to direct working of love. It represents too a condition of the self or person, which disables his eye and mind from seeing clearly, from perceptiveness. There is a failure to see what is to be seen which besets the dehumanised spoiler of human beings; and the indifferent drifter who is the spoiler's fellow-traveller; and also, be it known, the being who has resigned thought and judgement, and is narrowly following the line laid or let down by the lying braggarts, rope leaders, false authorities MacLean exemplifies in 'Eadh is Féin is Sàr-Fhéin'.

'When I speak of the face' expresses boldness of heart, a state of being inspired, emboldened, also aware of one's own capacity of awareness because *aware* in a sense beyond the division into qualitative and quantitative. That state is the condition necessary to a specific experience, but also to an overall awareness of experience. To be able to sing his love over the horrendous decay MacLean must know

...seirbheachd gheur an spioraid	...the sharp bitterness of the spirit
na 's fheàrr na aoibhneas luath a' chridhe.	better than the swift joy of the heart.

The alternative may be close to a base thing and a lukewarm.

Perhaps MacLean excluded 'An uair a labhras...' from *Selected Poems 1932-72* because of doubts about the validity of the *feeling* the poem embodies. Yet it would after all be a difficult poem to balance within a representative selection of fixed length. Other things have to be borne in mind beside it — which can be offered not as a reader's guide but as a message *in* MacLean's poetry. The closing lines nevertheless carry much weight, in the observation that joy is activity and pain is fixed. This is of relevance throughout his work too. 'She to whom I gave ...' continues:

Ach tric an smuaintean na h-oidhch'	But often in the thoughts of night
an uair bhios m'aigne 'na coille chiair,	when my mind is a dim wood
thig osag chuimhne 'g gluasad duillich,	a breeze of memory comes, stirring the foliage,
ag cur a furtachd gu luasgan.	putting the wood's assuagement to unrest.

In 'Eadh is Féin is Sàr-Fhéin', MacLean assaults positivism by suggesting that to accept its ever more twisty explanations necessitates admitting that loved things and persons, works of love and works of imagination are simply his own idle fancies reducible to 'psychological laws'.

The wood is language too, the symbolic language of the *visio intellectualis*. In its symbolic sense, as in the straightforward sense of being in a wood, MacLean endows it with a freedom, the antithesis of dullness and inarticulacy. By contrast the firewood and heather-burning in 'Palach' are low and lifeless.

But as the mind's movement dims, that astounding image comes "stirring the foliage":

Agus bho dhoimhne coille chuim,	And from the depths of my body's wood,
o fhriamhach snodhaich 's meangach meanbh,	from sap-filled root and slender branching,
bidh eubha throm: carson bha h-àille	there will be the heavy cry: why was her beauty
mar fhosgladh fàire ri latha?	like a horizon opening the door to day?

MacLean's poems, like the Old Songs, may have their biographical or autobiographical elements, but one should not play Freud or the positivist at the expense of losing symbols "over the escarpment",

sùil saoi air friamhaichean céine;	sage eye on distant roots,
uirigh 'sa' chreig chais uaibhrich	his ledge in the steep proud rock,
a' toirt neo'r-thaing do choille 'n luasgain,	defying the restless wood,
do'n choille fhìrinnich ìochdraich,	the truthful subject wood,
do'n choille iriosail 's i air laomadh	the humble wood that teems
le luibhean searbha dathte mìlse.	with bitter variegated sweet plants.

These poems exhibit sincerity of vision. They matter because they afford insights into the human mind, to situations and to feelings whose validity is universal.

Insight interacts with insight when a man suddenly does something very different from what one expects on the basis of past observation of his conduct. Concerned to understand him, one is confronted by tension. MacLean did not go to Spain in the 1930s, because of his love or in a specific instance because of family obligations. Had he gone, he should have gone because of his love. Love and the Good are to be understood in terms of those statements. Joy, as opposed to sharp bitterness, or sourness, is to be understood in terms of that tension, and a discernment of questions, things, persons and facts to be taken into account as important. MacLean's later poems are part of the process of coming to an understanding of these things. Where one party might assert that poetry's duty is to heal, MacLean may not be so far from Gyula Illyes, whose poem on Bartok affirms every man's right to his own wounds.

A list of these things which were important to MacLean would include: love, the Old Songs, the poems/statements of his own he would stand by, his uncle's ability to "see a world in a grain of sand", the too early death of his brother Calum, the miracles shown forth in Calum's life, and the list of atrocities piling up in 'A' Bheinn air Chall'. MacLean lives by, in, and through these and other considerations which quicken, define or criticize his activity of love.

MacLean questions his own unhappiness by hymning the happiness of his uncle, a happiness which was a gift to MacLean himself. What is a man able to do? How can a man do Good? He had written in 'Am Mùr Gorm':

Mur b'e thusa bhiodh an Cuilithionn	But for you the Cuillin would be
'na mhùr eagarra gorm	an exact and serrated blue rampart
ag crioslachadh le bhalla-crìche	girdling with its march-wall
na tha 'nam chridhe borb.	all that is in my fierce heart.

MacLean's 'love' may have been like a horizon opening the door to day, a foolish door may have been broken, but the discovery of something he could live by was one which closed off or diminished certain satisfactions as necessarily incomplete in relation to that *amor intellectualis.*

That human suffering has been made presently real to him; the horror at the oppression and cruel death of people has swelled into a yearning to change all that, to make of 'A' Bheinn air Chall' MacLean's 'Prometheus Bound'. For all his great regard for Shelley, and a Shelleyan identification of his inner state with that of the external polity, MacLean's relation here is to the Classical and Romantic figure treated in less heterodox fashion by Hölderlin and his contemporaries in interpreting rather than rewriting Greek myth. MacLean is Promethean in the extent of his moral striving. He has given fire to himself and with MacDiarmid said, "To Hell with my *own* happiness": he would send nobody out to be shot, but like his Polish contemporary and others has risked being shot himself.

In 'Hallaig' MacLean ventures a picture of what is good in being a man. Earlier he had also written the stanza in 'Am Mùr Gorm':

Agus air creachainn chéin fhàsmhoir	And on a distant luxuriant summit
chinn blàthmhor Craobh nan Teud,	there blossomed the Tree of Strings,
'na meangach duillich t' aodann,	among its leafy branches your face,
mo chiall is aogas réil.	my reason and the likeness of a star.

Beside the climax to 'An Cuilithionn' that presents the natural growth which the poet holds dear, the tree of strings may be the source of poetry, the Romantics' Aeolian harp, the coincidence of the object of desire with what is right. The face symbolism seems congruent with Muir's. It refers to the individual person, to something of clear definition seen by an eye which sees clearly. It leads like a star, it guides; will, reason and love are at one. It is distant, as 'An Cuilithionn' reaffirms, beyond so much, on the far side of sorrow.

Thus, with the force of

Mairg an t-sùil a chi air fairge   Pity the eye that sees on the ocean
ian mór marbh na h-Albann   the great dead bird of Scotland

one comes on the 'dead souls' image of 'A' Bheinn air Chall' with equal horror.
That the poem can to some extent be paraphrased is not a criticism of it, for not
only is the poem memorable as the Aristotelean 'esoteric' poem is, but the
symbolism permits the relation of tension-interaction with earlier poems.
The mountain is lost. Others may be noble because they have risen from terrible
torn depths, but this one is lost in the lost wood above which it rises. The lost wood
denotes something near the unthinkable; bearing 'Screapadal' in mind, that most
recently published poem also has its feet on the brink of the unsayable. Whatever
truisms there are about nobody being alive to speak or hear after the bombs go off—
truisms which should not be forgotten — MacLean is in the same depths as in the
early love-poems: what he can hardly bear to say, and can hardly say. The symbol of
"our sun" as stretching us in torture is potent. The sky hems all in, space is no longer
felt as a positive.
    Wordsworth and Hölderlin are recalled, the former's "new road" and the latter's

                        Aber bös sind
                Die Pfade. Nemlich unrecht,
                . . . gehn die gefangenen
                    Element' und alten
                    Gesetze der Erd.

Air chall ann an aomadh na coille   Lost in the decline of the wood
iomhaighean iomadhathach ar spéis   the many-coloured images of our aspiration
a chionn 's nach téid na sràidean ciùrrte   since the tortured streets will not go
'sa' choille mhaoth an cochur réidh.   in the wood in a smooth synthesis.

The indication intended here is of MacLean's scope. If what has happened is
lawless, and to some poets seemingly counter to divine edict, then the conduct which
has led to this overwhelming of the poet's powers has been an overwhelming of the
tension of human thought in those leaders whose rule led to the horror. Something
let loose has taken shapes which cannot be accommodated. Remembering Muir's
exposition of archetypal mountain-symbolism in Journeys and Places, "Auschwitz
of the bones" seems to be the site of a new stack. "Fresh rich trees / pins on
mountains of pain": this is the torment of the Prometheus of ethics. This should be
compared to the poem which begins "Let me lop", in which MacLean is
contemplating the divided state of man, meaning the species. Works of love do
nothing but add to the agony. "Heartbreak is about the mountains . ."
    The true Promethean longing, bound, is a despair of all that lives, and "the grey
nonentity of the dust / a withered brittle comfort". And the love which tears this
Prometheus can be traced back to

Pàrras gun phàrras a chuideachd,   Paradise without the paradise of his own
                                                                                people
imcheist a' ghiullain Shaoir-Chléirich.   the perplexity of the little Free Presbyterian
                                                                                   boy.

Spartacus on the cross is an image from Dàin do Eimhir, and the great torment of
'A' Bheinn air Chall' can be traced back by recalling the original leap MacLean
made when very young, to the ethics of socialism. He has found himself at one point
in middle age tormented by inhumanity world-wide, and he has been chained to the

rock, torn by the talons of the horror expressed in the poem. The extent of the crime which some would see in the child's "complaint and silent refusal" is mirrored by the man's sense of the world's ills.

In *Selected Poems* MacLean follows up 'A' Bheinn air Chall' with the elegy for his brother. After the opaqueness of the comprehensive horror, the transformation is from inner intellectual-moral preoccupation to a presence and memory he must recall and serve. The tension in the elegy lies between the continued existence of beauty and the fact that his brother is dead. There is also that different state, that level of awareness, which exists in MacLean's consciousness of his brother's life and wonderful qualities. Between this poem and the opaqueness of 'A' Bheinn air Chall' there is a tension. Between the elegy for his uncle and 'A' Bheinn air Chall' there is a greater tension, expressed as a question by the *visio intellectualis*.

If the last line of 'A' Bheinn air Chall' recalls MacLean's early poetry and *Dàin do Eimhir*, the switch throughout the poem could be seen as being from middle age to boyhood to young manhood. 'Palach', several pages earlier in *Selected Poems*, comes equally out of chronological succession. MacLean thinks back to the 1930s, to the opinions he then held, and also to his symbolism:

Tha corra shamhla cnocaireachd
mu 'n Bhealltainn seo fo ghruaim.
Bha peileirean 'sa' Phère Lachaise
ag cnagadaich 'nan suain. . .

There is a ghost or two hill-walking
about this Beltane in gloom.
Bullets in the Père Lachaise
were crackling in their sleep. . .

In the student unrest of the late 1960s, in the pyre of Palach's small body, MacLean sees the strength of the human spirit as he seems not to see it in 'A' Bheinn air Chall'. Had 'Palach' been printed after 'A' Bheinn air Chall' there would have been one obvious link with

ged tha 'n fhuil mhear gu luaineach
air mire bhuadhar 'san òigridh.

though the restless sportive blood
rages triumphantly in the young.

One could have seen Palach as Chiron to MacLean's Prometheus, willing to surrender his immortality, to die, to release the imprisoned heroic figure from the punishment of his *hubris*.

MacLean's approach to Chiron is not as a divine figure, nor as a poet, nor as a teacher. Palach was a student, as were the "dozen Palachs in France", railing against stagnation and an authority which was not worth even scant respect. What is important? Who are the 'Heroes'?

Chunnaic mi gaisgeach mór á Sasuinn,
fearachan bochd nach laigheadh sùil air,
cha b' Alasdair á Gleanna Garadh—
is thug e gal beag air mo shùilean.

I saw a great warrior of England,
a poor manikin on whom no eye would rest;
no Alasdair of Glen Garry;
and he took a little weeping to my eyes.

The obvious and dramatic force of MacLean's poetry should not be read as a hymn to those qualities. What sustains it to the end, and sustains MacLean, is the passionate marriage of *love* with *knowledge*, which is not always a comfortable one when speaking Gaelic and living in the world. He claims no exalted role other than by his actions:

Ach thugadh dhuinn am muillion bliadhna
'na mhìr an roinn chianail fhàsmhoir,
gaisge 's foighidinn nan ciadan
agus mìorbhail aodainn àlainn.

But we have been given the million years,
a fragment of a sad growing portion,
the heroism and patience of hundreds
and the miracle of a beautiful face.

ROBERT CALDER

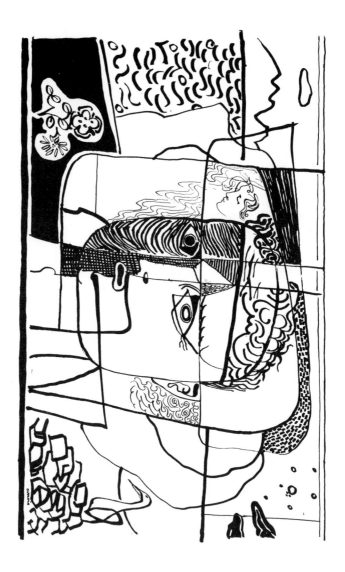

'Multitude'

The Ghost Seen By The Soul:
Sorley MacLean And The Absolute

Có seo, có seo oidhche chridhe?	Who is this, who is this in the night of the heart?
Chan eil ach an nì do-ruighinn,	It is the thing that is not reached,
An samhla chunnaic an t-anam,	the ghost seen by the soul,
Cuilithionn ag éirigh thar mara.	a Cuillin rising over the sea.

These lines from the conclusion to 'An Cuilithionn' announce with great immediacy and directness a theme which is central to the poetry of Sorley MacLean. The heroic striving for the unattainable goal of human aspiration represents a value which underlies the love-poems and others which are thematically related to them, and expresses a temperament and cast of mind for which the absolute, and nothing less than the absolute, is the measure of spiritual worth. In this essay it is suggested that a great part of the stature of MacLean's work derives from the tension arising from the collision between the ideal and the actual, between aspiration and limitation, between the finite and the infinite. It is this conflict which is the occasion for the creative confrontation between intellect and passion which has often, and rightly, been noted as characteristic of the poet. For the author of 'Calbharaigh', 'Ban-Ghàidheal', and the great war-poems is clearly not one who merely has his head in the clouds. On the contrary, MacLean is remarkable above all for his clear-sightedness, for the straightness, realism and directness with which he fixes his gaze on whatever is before his eyes; and moreover he admits to a constitution which is naturally pessimistic. The bracing qualities of MacLean's poetry derive largely from the co-existence in tension of polar opposites, a co-existence which reflects an inherent law of nature.

In 'Gleann Aoighre' the sense of the limitation imposed by external circumstances upon the questing spirit is expressed as "a wall between joy and my harsh little croft, a boundary that would not be changed to set joy free". Yet the check upon the poet's desire, which means that "I would not get the thing I wanted", has its ultimate source within, in "the divisive passion of my spirit", for "I could not stand on Blaven and stay in the garden where fruits were growing richly". What frustrates the fulfilment of desire is, paradoxically, the limitless nature of the poet's aspiration:

Agus ged dhìrichinn Blàbheinn	And though I were to climb Blaven,
nach robh innte ach beinn shuarach	it was only a mean mountain
bho nach fhaicinn saorsa chluaintean,	from which I would not see a freedom of grasslands,
agus m' ùidh air Kilimanjaro,	when my desire was on Kilimanjaro,
a' Mhatterhorn is Nanga Parbit	the Matterhorn and Nanga Parbit,
agus àirde Everest.	and the height of Everest.

The vision of freedom evoked in the third line indicates that the scaling of the peak has an end beyond itself, and this suggestion reappears in 'Nighean is Seann Orain', a poem whose rhythms and imagery wonderfully communicate, even in translation, an intense poignancy of longing. When the girl sings the old songs which give voice to "the unattainable stricken thing / that our people fashioned in obscurity", it is

. . . mar gun crathteadh dhìot an sgìos ud	. . . as if there were shaken off you that weariness
Th' anns a' bheinn nach gabh a dìreadh,	that is in the mountain that may not be climbed,
'S nach fhaicear a mullach lì-gheal	and whose gleaming white summit is not to be seen
Leis a' cheò air creachainn sìnte.	for the mist on high top stretched.

The poem ends with an image of unattainable rest, a ship in the sea of Canna which, like the deer in 'Hallaig', frozen by the gun of love, is fixed eternally in a voyage to no shore:

No có chì long 'sa' Chuan Chanach	who sees a ship in the sea of Canna,
Nach eil a strì ri sgrìoban geala,	a ship that does not strive with white furrows,
Nach eil ag iarraidh gus a' chala	that does not seek the harbour
Nach ruig té seach té r'a maireann,	that no one will ever reach . . .

In *Fear and Trembling* Kierkegaard provides the *locus classicus* for the analysis of the spiritual state which finds expression in Sorley MacLean's love poetry. The case is that of the 'Knight' who makes the inner movement of 'infinite resignation' in renouncing his love:

> Spiritually speaking, everything is possible, but in the world of the finite there is much which is not possible. This impossible, however, the knight makes possible by expressing it spiritually, but he expresses it spiritually by waiving his claim to it. The wish which would carry him out into reality, but was wrecked upon the impossibility, is now bent inward, but it is not therefore lost, neither is it forgotten.

In 'Coilltean Ratharsair' MacLean speaks of "the single-minded love unattainable, lost, unspoiled": the love is lost, but not the wish. In this movement of infinite resignation, which "is the last stage prior to faith", "there is peace and rest and comfort in sorrow". Kierkegaard's insight strikingly illuminates the motif of self-sacrifice which is prominent in MacLean's love-poems: the waiving of the claim is an essential element in the metaphysical movement "which in its pain reconciles one with existence". In this process, a kind of resolution of intractable conflicts is achieved by re-stating them at a higher level. The specific unattainable object — in the love poetry, a woman — is assimilated to a generalized, undefined object of aspiration, as in the finale of 'An Cuilithionn'; that is, the goal is ultimately religious, though the movement of faith is not made. Psychologically this process is sublimation, and this fact is not lost on the poet:

'S gum b'e siod an aisling chonnain	That was the lustful dream
a bh' aig mo spiorad riut 'sna neòil	that my spirit had with you in the clouds,
's tu laighe mar rium anns na speuran	you lying with me in the skies
nuair thréig an tairbhe bha 'nad fheòil.	when the profit of your flesh had failed.
	('Am Mac Stròidheil').

Aesthetically, however, it involves the maintenance of opposites in a state of tension. A synthesis is not possible in the finite world, as a stanza from *Dàin do Eimhir* XXIII (in Iain Crichton Smith's translation) strikingly states:

Cha dèanar a' cho-chur de 'n chàs,	Such synthesis is dream indeed —
glòir agus ànradh na cruinne,	of the planet's glory and its pain,
an éitig fhiabhrais 's Pàdraig Mór,	the hero's feverish death and you,
daorsa, Beethoven 's thusa.	Beethoven and the slave's chain.

Iain Crichton Smith, in the introduction to his translations of *Poems to Eimhir,* points out that one is aware "that this is the record of a real love-affair which confronted the poet with real choices in a real world". That may be so, but the important point about these poems is rather their re-statement of the conflict at a higher level. We are reluctant to believe in the reality of what Blake calls "mental fight": as Kierkegaard puts it, "People believe very little in spirit, and yet making this movement depends upon spirit". The struggle which is expressed in the poems of conflict in the early part of the *Dàin do Eimhir* sequence arises in the mental world, however closely it may be related to choices in the 'real' world between, for instance, private love and social conscience. Thus the verbal mood which prevails in 'Gaoir na h-Eòrpa' is the conditional throughout, and the dilemma treated in 'Reic Anama' is, for all the passion with which it is confronted, a hypothetical one:

Ach thubhairt mi rium fhìn, 's cha b' aon-uair,	But I did say to myself, and not once,
gun reicinn m' anam air do ghaol-sa	that I would sell my soul for your love
nam biodh feum air bréig is aomadh.	if lie and surrender were needed.
Thubhairt mi an deifir sin gun smaointinn	I spoke this in haste without thinking
gum b'e an toibheum dubh 's an claonadh.	that it was black blasphemy and perversion.

In 'Urnuigh', the tortuous brilliance of whose language John MacInnes has shown as deriving from the linguistic traditions of the sermons and prayers of the Free Presbyterian Church (*Cencrastus* 7, Winter 1981-82), the theme is the internal self-division of the spirit, which leaves the 'single brain' turning restlessly in every direction in its vain efforts to impose a synthesis upon the conflicting desires of the 'split heart'. But although the poet condemns himself for having "preferred a woman to crescent History", the issue is not, essentially, whether or not he should go to Spain: it is whether or not he can reach a state of wholeness of spirit in which one passion does not interfere with the other in terms of *inner* commitment. So in another poem we find him exhorting himself to exclude from his poetry the graces lent to it by his love's beauty, in order to "put the people's anguish in the steel of my lyric". It is clear that this quenchless thirst for undividedness is another facet of MacLean's search for the absolute:

Esan dh' am bheil an cridhe air ionnlaid	He whose heart has been washed
théid e troimh theine gun tionndadh,	will go through fire without turning;
dìridh e bheinn mhór gun ionndrainn;	he will ascend the great mountain without homesickness;
cha d' fhuair mise leithid de dh' anam	I did not get such a spirit
's mo chridhe ach air leth-fhaileadh.	because my heart is only half flayed.

When love comes to dominate the poet's spiritual landscape without division, it is celebrated because it promises to make the ideal actual and to confer form and content upon the formless movements of inner experience:

'S 'nad fhaisge tha a' chòmhail	And with you the meeting

a th' agam rium fhéin	that I have with myself
cho dlùth rium re smior mo chridhe	is as near me as my heart's marrow
's e falbh air binnean céin.	when it goes on a far-off peak.

('Irisleachd')

In the poetry the tendency is, however, for the human love to become a boundless metaphysical entity, an image of the absolute which scrutiny by the intellect serves only to make more unassailably ideal. This is the theme of 'An Sgian', in which the dissection of the stone of love by the knife of the brain paradoxically results in an all-embracing and yet adamantine unity, an authentic symbol of the self:

Bha a' chlach a fhuair a gearradh	The stone that was cut
á m' aigne chumhang fhìn	out of my own narrow spirit
air a bearradh gus a' mhórachd	was clipped to the greatness
a thoilleadh domhain-thìr.	that would contain the land of the world.

It must be of the sublimation of natural love into such a symbol that MacLean speaks in the same poem when he writes that

'S e 'n gaol ginte leis a' chridhe	The love begotten by the heart
an gaol tha 'n geimhlich shaoir	is the love that is in free chains
an uair a ghabhas e 'na spiorad	when it takes, in its spirit,
gaol eanchainn air a ghaol.	a brain love of its love.

In the poems just discussed it is the intellectual vitality, the vigorous tension of the ideas and (the non-Gaelic speaker must rely here on the testimony of others) the richness and complexity of MacLean's resources which provide the bones of the poetic structure. In more lyrical poems, something more is needed to counteract the tendency of MacLean's subject-matter to encourage abstraction of language, and two main elements are decisive here, both drawing their strength from the poet's topographical and cultural roots: the imagery of landscape, and the concept of the hero and the heroic. These factors (which are moreover related, since the landscape of Skye and Raasay on which MacLean mainly draws for his images and symbols is itself a heroic landscape, both by its physical nature and through its cultural associations) serve to mediate between the finite realities of the physical world and the ideal realities of the spiritual. Mountain, loch, glen and wood, sea, shore and headland, the rhythm of the tides, the action of wind and weather, the movements of the heavenly bodies: these natural things by their solid physical presence anchor the poetry to the finite and to the natural world, but by their infinite symbolic suggestiveness they point towards the ideal and towards metaphysical and spiritual truth. The idea of the heroic, similarly, which bears witness to the continuity of MacLean's poetry with a traditional society in which an ideal value was the yardstick for moral choice and moral judgement, tends constantly towards penetration of the mundane by the ideal.

The function of the imagery of the natural world in the love-lyrics is most often to evoke the enormity of the sublimated love. This can be done in a number of different and sometimes contrasting ways. In 'Lìonmhoireachd' (which takes up an idea found in the first stanza of 'Am Buaireadh') it is not the vast "golden riddle of millions of stars" with their cold, distant and impersonal beauty which lights up the interior universe of the poet's mind, but the human miracle of the loved one's face. In 'Camhanaich', however, instead of putting nature in the shade, the girl *becomes* the beauty of the material world:

Bu tu camhanaich air a' Chuilithionn	You were dawn on the Cuillin
's latha suilbhir air a' Chlàraich,	and benign day on the Clarach,
grian air a h-uilinn anns an òr-shruth	the sun on his elbow in the golden stream
agus ròs geal bristeadh fàire.	and the white rose that breaks the horizon.

'Am Mùr Gorm' gives us another variation: here the existence of his love alters the poet's relation to the natural symbols that are all around him, imposing upon them "an edict above my own pain".

Mur b'e thusa bhiodh a' ghaineamh	But for you the sand
tha 'n Talasgar dùmhail geal	that is in Talisker compact and white
'na clàr biothbhuan do mo dhùilean,	would be a measureless plain to my expectations
air nach tilleadh an rùn-ghath.	and on it the spear desire would not turn back.

'Tràighean' employs a marvellous sequence of conceits to put love into relation with eternity by imagining the poet and his loved one standing together for ever amid the space and solitude of the shifting scenes which are evoked — all of them actual shores in the Hebrides and on the west coast of Scotland. MacLean's conceptual inventiveness and powers of sensuous evocation are at their most miraculous here, as repeatedly he finds in the imagery of sea and sand and rock a fresh and vivid metaphor for limitless ideality. It is seldom in Sorley MacLean's poetry that natural features stand for nothing beyond themselves; an exception is 'Ceann Loch Aoineart', really a verbal sound poem, but even here we feel that the thrusting mountains are striving towards consciousness, or at least towards animation:

Onfhadh-chrios mhullaichean,	A surge-belt of hill-tops,
confhadh-shlios thulaichean,	impetuous thigh of peaks,
monmhar luim thurraidean màrsail,	the murmuring bareness of marching turrets,
gorm-shliosan Mhosgaraidh,	green flanks of Mosgary,
stoirm-shliosan mosganach,	crumbling storm-flanks,
borb-bhiodan mhonaidhean àrda.	barbarous pinnacles of high moorlands.

This poem has something in common with 'Coin is Madaidhean-allaidh', the eerie dream-poem in which MacLean's as yet unwritten poems are imagined as lean, questing beasts surging across the snows of eternity in pursuit of "the deer of your gentle beloved beauty". It is through a landscape of wintry and forbidding grandeur that "the mild, mad dogs of poetry" take their relentless course, and such a heroic landscape is perhaps most typical of MacLean's use of natural imagery. Sometimes, though, by contrast, he will produce an image from nature of the most delicate poignancy, like that of the spring, in the poem of that name, whose waters retain for ever the likeness of his love who had once bent her head to it; or, conversely, the smells of honeysuckle and bog-myrtle which remain in the poet's memory when her words have vanished ('Abhainn Arois'). The imagery of nature thus enacts a kind of dialectic, an argument between finite and infinite in which neither has the final word, the creative dynamics of the poetry being most intimately involved in the tensions between them. When, rarely, MacLean draws his metaphors from another source we are somewhat taken aback, for instance at the technological weapon-imagery of 'An Ceann Thall' (which is daringly juxtaposed with the traditional image of a mountain journey and an analogy with the story of Deirdre and Naoise):

Cha d' rinn tancan do dhualchais	Neither the tanks of your heredity
no gunnachan móra do rùin	nor the big guns of your desire
no luingeas-adhair do dheagh-ghean	nor the aeroplanes of your goodwill
an éifeachd bu neoinithe do d' dhùil.	had the most infinitesimal effect on your expectation.

The poems in which a symbolism of natural features is most schematically developed are the conclusion of 'An Cuilithionn' and 'Coilltean Ratharsair', and it is here too that the theme of the striving for the unattainable is brought to its most complete development. I have discussed these poems at some length in *Lines Review* 61 (June 1977) and here I must limit myself to emphasising the central place which they occupy in the history of Sorley MacLean's 'quest of the absolute'. The two works were composed only a few months apart and are closely linked in both theme and imagery. Compared with a poem of mental struggle like 'Urnuigh' both have great emotional lucidity, but of the two 'Coilltean Ratharsair' is considerably more complex. The Cuillin symbol in the poem which bears its name (or rather in the finale, which apparently stands rather apart from the unfinished and largely unpublished long poem which it nominally brings to a conclusion) represents a trinity comprising "the blue Cuillin of the island, . . . the Cuillin of ancient Scotland and the Cuillin of mankind". In its last-named function it stands essentially for the heroic values which rise triumphant above human misery, imaged as a "black ooze on the rock face". These values appear first as "the red rose of hero courage aflame above the mountain summit", but they soon emerge as attributes of the mountain itself:

Neòr-thaing chithear an Cuilithionn	Nevertheless the Cuillin is seen
'S e 'g éirigh air taobh eile duilghe,	rising on the far side of agony,
Cuilithionn beadarrach nan saor,	the lyric Cuillin of the free,
Cuilithionn togarrach nan laoch,	the ardent Cuillin of the heroic,
Cuilithionn na h-inntinne móire,	the Cuillin of the great mind,
Cuilithionn cridhe garbh na dórainn.	the Cuillin of the rugged heart of sorrow.

It is however the impassable distance which separates the poet from the longed-for peak which lends the symbol its numinous power. For the Cuillin lies "beyond the seas of sorrow, beyond the morass of agony", and between him and it lie "the lochs of the blood of the children of men" and the swamps and pitfalls of every human evil and wretchedness. The lonely "journeying one" is ever seeking that distant summit and never reaching it, for it is indeed but "the ghost seen by the soul", a spectral projection of the ardent longings of the human heart. As an ideal spiritual construct it forms a bulwark against despair, but the poet's realism involves the clearest recognition that it does not belong to the finite world.

In 'Coilltean Ratharsair' the ideal concepts emerge slowly and inevitably from the world of nature. It is the poem's great strength that it is grounded in the natural world, the symbolic meaning taking shape from the gradual, animistic evolution of the natural images into intellectual and spiritual forms, a development analogous to a psychological movement from unconscious to conscious life. The wood, mysterious, beautiful, ambiguous and paradoxical, is at one level a symbol of the unconscious, a role which it takes in several other MacLean poems, notably 'Eadh is Féin is Sàr-Fhéin' and the lyric beginning "She to whom I gave all love . . . "; as such it also represents Nature and the feminine principle. Over against it stands the Cuillin, which in its massive thrustingness, its singleness and definition, stands for the differentiating consciousness, and hence for the spiritual and the male principle. Beyond that, of course, it symbolizes once more the aspirations of the poet and their unattainable ends, and, as with 'An Cuilithionn', it is in the nature of the symbolism that the seeker and the sought are not clearly distinguishable. This is psychologically correct, for what is sought is finally the inner wholeness of the individual, of which the external goal is only a projection.

In 'Coilltean Ratharsair' there is held out for a fleeting moment the vision of the unreachable thing all but within the grasp:

'S e bhith creidsinn le feòil	To believe with flesh,
le eanchainn 's le cridhe	with brain and heart,
gu robh aon nì coimhlionta	that one thing was complete,
àlainn so-ruighinn.	beautiful, accessible.

This thing is love, and the heart of the poem is reached with the question "What is the meaning of giving a woman love . . . ?" Receiving no answer, the question moves out of the finite and into the infinite. The perfection of this love, "unhesitant, undoubting, hopeless, sore, blood-red, whole", indicates to us that by its nature, by the very necessity to believe in it, it belongs to ideality and cannot be realized in the finite world:

ged bheirteadh an gaol do-labhairt	though the unspeakable love were given,
cha bhiodh ann ach mar gun cainte	it would be only as if one were to say
nach b' urrainn an càs tachairt	that the thing could not happen
a chionn gun robh e do-labhairt.	because it was unspeakable.

This is exactly the situation of Kierkegaard's knight, who has "no need of the intervention of the finite for the further growth of his love", precisely because "from the instant he made the movement the princess is lost to him". Thus the "single-minded love" is "unattainable, lost, unspoiled": unspoiled just because it is lost and unattainable. However, it is the inescapable nature of humanity to cling to the finite. Even when we seek to make it infinite, we nonetheless desire, paradoxically, to retain the thing under its finite form. This paradox is expressed in lines which bring us to another major theme in Sorley MacLean's poetry:

nì a sheachnadh allaban	a thing that would avoid the travail
na colainne 's a' chruaidh-chàis,	of the flesh and hardship,
nach millteadh le meapaineadh	that would not be spoiled by the bedragglement
time is buairidh.	of time and temptation.

This is the theme that is developed at length and with extraordinary poetic inventiveness and intellectual passion and tenacity in 'An Tathaich'. The face of a girl says to the poet's heart "that a division may not be sought between desire and the substance of its unattainable object"; in other words, as I understand it, the object of desire must be stripped of its finitude and made infinite as the desire itself is infinite. The problem is the one that Hopkins confronts in 'The Leaden Echo and the Golden Echo': how to find the means "to keep back beauty, keep it, beauty, beauty, beauty, . . . from vanishing away". For like Kierkegaard's knight again, the poet is "too proud to be willing that what was the whole content of his life should be the thing of a fleeting moment". MacLean's answer is to invoke the philosophical idea that what has once been is preserved for ever in eternity:

a chionn gum bheil i 'n dràsda	because it now is

gum bi 'cruth 's a bith gu bràth ann
agus nach urrainn caochladh
a h-aonachd a mhàbadh.

that its form and being will always be,
and that change cannot
maim its unity.

The tension and greatness of the poem arise, however, from the fact that the poet cannot wholly believe this: arise, that is, from the conflict between his belief and his unbelief. Not trusting his subjective intuition that finitude is annihilated by the relativity of time, he casts around this way and that without rest in his efforts to find some way of perpetuating the beauty of his love's face, of "checking this hour and holding it in the sand of change with the fluke of an anchor". All of his imaginative invention, however, cannot establish such a certainty:

O aodainn a tha 'gam thathaich,
a mhìorbhail a tha labhar,
am bheil aon phort an tìm dhuit
no balla-crìch ach talamh?

O face that is haunting me,
O eloquent marvel,
is there any port in time for you
or march-wall but earth?

The poem ends where it began, with the eloquent triumph of the girl's face still putting its eternal question.

The preoccupation with time and eternity recurs in 'Nighean is Seann Orain', in 'Ard-Mhusaeum na h-Eireann' — which ends by asserting that the heroic life of James Connolly is not bounded by mortality:

Tha an curaidh mór fhathast
'na shuidhe air an t-séithir,
ag cur a' chatha 'sa' Phost-Oifis
's ag glanadh shràidean an Dùn-Eideann

The great hero is still
sitting on the chair
fighting the battle in the Post Office
and cleaning streets in Edinburgh

— and above all in 'Hallaig', which once more has its life in the tension between the vision of past time subsisting in eternity and the fear that this idea is purely subjective, contained within the poet's imagination and hence limited by his own mortality. The poem establishes this tension in the opening lines, which bring together present desolation and the continued presence of the past within the context of the poet's own life:

Tha bùird is tàirnean air an uinneig
troimh 'm faca mi an Aird an Iar
's tha mo ghaol aig Allt Hallaig
'na craoibh bheithe, 's bha i riamh.

The window is nailed and boarded
through which I saw the West
and my love is at the Burn of Hallaig
a birch tree, and she has always been.

In the vision of the cleared township which follows, where "the dead have been seen alive", the past generations somehow have their present being in the unchanging features of the landscape which they once inhabited, and which is animated by their having lived in it. When time, the deer, is struck by the gun of love and his eye frozen in the wood, this is equivalent to saying that time is annihilated by the eternalizing action of the loving will. This is not, however, an aesthetic event. It is not in art or through art that the moment is eternalized; the poem merely records a mystery which occurs within the human mind itself. Hence "his blood will not be traced while I live": the poem will survive the poet's death, but the vision, it is perhaps being suggested, may not.

We have seen how the heroic ideal functions in a general sense in several of MacLean's major poems as one of the ways in which the absolute can find expression in human terms. There are also, however, a considerable number of poems in which the heroic, or the figure of the hero as traditionally understood in Gaelic society, takes a more specific and more central part, authenticating individual experience and placing the personal within a mythical framework. In 'A' Bhuaile Ghréine', for instance, the poet's love is made absolute by the comparison of his girl with the great heroines of history and legend, a comparison which compels him to the duty of raising in art an image of "the form and spirit of every beauty". But it is in the war-poems that the heroic idea operates most clearly, and with a wide range of application from the very direct to the subtly ambivalent and the bitterly ironic. It is at its most direct and uncomplicated in 'Dol an Iar', where MacLean derives moral sustenance from the invocation of the roll of his heroic ancestry:

Agus biodh na bha mar bha e,	And be what was as it was,
tha mi de dh' fhir mhór' a' Bhràighe,	I am of the big men of Braes,
de Chloinn Mhic Ghille Chaluim threubhaich,	of the heroic Raasay MacLeods,
de Mhathanaich Loch Aills nan geurlann,	of the sharp-sword Mathesons of Lochalsh;
agus fir m' ainme — có bu tréine	and the men of my own name — who were braver
nuair dh' fhàdadh uabhar an léirchreach?	when their ruinous pride was kindled?

In complete contrast, the ideal functions in 'Glac a' Bhàis' as an ironic point of reference lying outside the poem itself, in the note which records its perversion in the words of the Nazi who "said that the Fuehrer had restored to German manhood the 'right and joy of dying in battle' ". Here the ideal, or rather its misuse or misapplication, is subjected to savage scrutiny by the implicit contrast with the reality of the dead boy-soldier who "showed no pleasure in his death below the Ruweisat ridge".

It is 'Curaidhean', however, which embodies the most finely-balanced working-out of this theme. The first stanza places its subject in the company of three great historical examples of physical heroism; in the second stanza both his deviation from the traditional image of the hero and his conformity with the spirit that lies behind it are recorded:

Fear beag truagh le gruaidhean pluiceach	A poor little chap with chubby cheeks
is glùinean a' bleith a chéile,	and knees grinding each other,
aodann guireanach gun tlachd ann —	pimply unattractive face —
còmhdach an spioraid bu tréine.	garment of the bravest spirit.

But if the case of the courageous Englishman suggests a criticism of the ideal by his deviation from it in terms of his appearance, a more radical criticism arises from his conformity with it in deed. For the account of his extraordinary courage is followed by four lines which register a decided dissent from any unquestioning acceptance of the ethos of a heroic society in the context of modern warfare:

'S có dhiubh, ma sheasas ursann-chatha	And at any rate, if a battle post stands
leagar móran air a shàilleabh	many are knocked down because of him,
gun dùil ri cliù, nach iarr am meadal	not expecting fame, not wanting a medal
no cop 'sam bith á bial na h-àraich.	or any froth from the mouth of the field of slaughter.

The final stanza holds all these ambiguities together in a delicate tension, the qualifications not detracting from the soldier's heroism, but the whole making only a modified endorsement of the heroic value. That is the point of the final line, "and he took *a little* weeping to my eyes": the lament for Alasdair of Glen Garry which it echoes makes no such qualification.

This theme has at any rate remained of great importance to MacLean in his later poetry ('Dà Dhòmhnallach' provides an obvious example), and it is prominent in the unfinished long poem 'Uamha 'n Oir', in which the figure of the second piper who goes into the cave, not expecting ever to return, embodies the value of self-sacrifice. Where it differs from the early poetry is in its pessimism, the sense of the loss of what MacLean often calls 'expectation', and especially the loss of social hope. The piper sees "the great horse of his aspirations bridled and tethered by the past", "his loved stallion a poor gelding under the whips of the unseen lord", and "the old community broken". Yet though he goes into "the mouth of death" believing his sacrifice to be unavailing and indeed no sacrifice at all, he still values "the courage that would not willingly surrender" and remembers that "he would not be the worse of leaving the name of hero in Borreraig and the Dun". There is a suggestion, too, that the by-products of the quest can compensate for its failure, for the piper understands

. . . ged nach robh feum san t-sireadh	. . . though the quest was useless
Nach biodh an ealain gun treòir.	that the art would have its strength.

The destruction of the roots of political and social hope overshadows the later poetry, and personal aspiration no longer mitigates the agony of the times.

'Twenty-Five Years from Richmond 1965' (*Contemporary Scottish Verse*) expresses an acceptance learned painfully on the field of battle and in the defeat and despair which followed victory, and gives us perhaps the saddest lines in MacLean's poetry:

Ma théid mi lath-eigin a Richmond	If I go someday to Richmond
'S gum faic mi 'n Caisteal cuimir làidir,	and see the shapely strong Castle,
Cha toir e orm ach snodha-gàire	it will only make me smile
Mas cuimhne liom idir mo chràdhlot.	if I remember my agony at all.

It is a certain, bleak, clear-sighted purity of acceptance which makes the black pessimism of some of the later poetry sadly moving rather than intolerably depressing: poems like 'Eadh is Féin is Sàr-Fhéin', which mourns the loss of the symbols and images on the great plain; 'A' Bheinn air Chall', "lost in the wood that is lost" when the horrors of contemporary civilization can no longer be synthesized with the glories of the natural world in any "eternity of the mind"; 'Creag Dallaig', which begins "Expectation and hope are changed, and there is not much hope"; and 'Screapadal', which envisages the destruction of the beauty of the beloved Raasay landscape by the hydrogen and neutron bomb. For all that, even in 'Uamha 'n Oir', the old images reappear and reassert their power, stating that only in the spirit can the evils of the world be overcome and despair made good:

Agus an teine tha san spiorad	. . . the fire that is in the spirit
A' streap ri mullach reòta ghràidh,	clambers up the frozen summit of love,
Far an loisgear iomadh miann	where many a desire is burnt
A th' ann am binneinean na colainn	that is in the peaks of the body
Gus am bi an spiorad fhéin	until the spirit itself is
Air a' bhiod nach ruig an aiteamh.	on the pinnacle unreached by thaw.

The piper is therefore a true mythological hero in the sense indicated by Jung in *Symbols of Transformation* when he writes: "The hero is a hero just because he sees resistance to the forbidden goal in all life's difficulties and yet fights that resistance with the whole-hearted yearning that strives towards the treasure hard to attain, and perhaps unattainable — a yearning that paralyses and kills the ordinary man''.

The quest of the absolute which this essay has attempted to chart is a Promethean undertaking, for as Thomas Merton once wrote, ''The longing of the restless spirit of man, seeking to transcend itself by its own powers, is symbolized by the need to scale the impossible mountain and find there what is after all our own''. In Sorley MacLean's case this deeply rooted and unappeasable longing has expressed itself in work of a spiritual grandeur which is possibly unmatched in modern poetry.

JOHN HERDMAN

CALBHARAIGH

Poem: Somhairle MacGill-Eain
(translated by Douglas Young)

Music: Ronald Stevens

NOT TOO SLOW; FREELY, SIMPLY, QUIETLY

Cha n-eil mo shùil air Cal - bha-raigh_____ no air Beth-le - hem an
My een are nae on Cal - va - ry_____ or the Beth - le - hem they

aigh_____ ach air cùil ghrod an Glas-chu_____ far bheil an lo - - bhc
praise,_____ but on shit-ten backlands in Glas-ga toun_____ where grow-an life_____ de

fàis_____ a - gus air seò-mar an Dùn-éi - deann, seò-mar boch-dainn's cràidh-
cays,_____ and a stair-heid room in an Em-bro land, a chal-mer o puir-tith an skaith_____

far am bheil an nao-idh_____ ean creuch - dach_____ ri
whaur mo - nie a shil - pet bair - nie kie gaes smoor - - - -

ao - na-graich gu 'bhàs.
- - - it doun til daith.

Repeat the whole song very softly.

MacLean: Musician manqué
(and a composer's collaboration)

My initiation into Gaelic song happened when I was 30. The year: 1958. The occasion: a Scottish Arts Council tour of Argyll, mainly the Isle of Islay in the Inner Hebrides. I was solo pianist and accompanist. Our troupe also included a violinist, an 'elocutionist' (a surviving phenomenon of Edwardian culture) and a singer, Evelyn Campbell from Lewis. She sang a mixed repertoire of accompanied songs and unaccompanied Gaelic folk songs. While she sang in Gaelic, I eavesdropped in the wings. The audience very softly joined in the choruses. From my vantage-point I could see they also gently swayed as they sang; and I could hear them keeping time with the music by quietly tapping their feet to emphasize the main rhythmic beats.

The general mood of the music was characterized by a low, melodious moan. Few of the songs were humorous or spirited. I later realized that this ratio of much sweet melancholy, some stoicism and a little spirited humour was basic to the moods of Sorley MacLean's poetry; and to the great body of Gaelic poetry, excepting the satire of, say, a Rob Donn.

A few years later, one evening sometime in the early sixties, Hector McIver sang some Lang Psalms of Lewis to me in the Abbotsford Pub, Edinburgh. I have written of this elsewhere.[1] Here, suffice it to say that this was my initiation into the intricacy of rhythm in Gaelic song; intricacies similar to those observed in some of MacLean's poetry.

Another Joycean epiphany: in the late seventies the Gaelic poet from Skye, Aonghas MacNeacail, took me along to hear Flora MacNeil from Barra singing in the Highland Church Hall, Edinburgh. In her unforgettable Barra Boasting Song ("you black besom") I again experienced the musically intricate rhythm germane to some Gaelic songs: just *how* intricate, I discovered later, when trying to notate this song from Flora's recording of it[2].

All these experiences were relevant to the musical ethos and the metrical sophistication of MacLean's poetry.

In 1966 I broadcast a 'self-portrait' as composer on Radio 3, with a spoken introduction to a selection of my music. This broadcast elicited a letter from Mr. W. Grant Kidd, conductor of the Greenock Gaelic Choir. He wondered whether my commitment to Scottish music extended to *Gaelic* music. If so, he would like to commission me to compose some choral music for his choir, set to Gaelic words. My reply begged time to consider this.

Visiting my fellow-composer, William Wordsworth (descended from the poet's family) in Kincraig, Inverness-shire that summer, I met a former BBC employee, then a school-teacher in Kincraig, Mr. John Russell. He was a friend of Sorley

MacLean and a self-taught Gaelic speaker. I mentioned the possible Greenock Gaelic Choir commission and he tape-recorded for me his reading of some poems from MacLean's *Dàin do Eimhir*.

I chose three poems: 'Ceann Loch Aoineart', 'Calbharaigh', and 'Lìon-mhoireachd': the first sings of nature's majesty in the Scottish Highlands; the second laments human misery in the Lowland slums; and the third contrasts the remote beauty of the cosmos with the only true miracle of human love. I set the poems as a choral cycle, giving it my own Gaelic title: 'Anns an Airde, as an Doimhne' (In the Heights, from the Depths).

First (in 1967, I think it was) I submitted the texts to the committee of the Greenock Gaelic Choir. They requested a meeting with me. I invited them to my home. A faction of the committee disapproved of the text of 'Calbharaigh'. One of them protested: "Mr Stevenson, we know there are slums: we don't want to sing about them". While not wishing to underestimate the often sterling work achieved for the cause of Gaelic by An Comunn Gàidhealach (The Highland Association), I do believe this response to MacLean's 'Calbharaigh' typifies an all-too prevalent attitude fostered by the choral repertoire sung at the National Mod. I hasten to add that this attitude was not shared by Mr. Grant Kidd, the choir's conductor. He, indeed, gave me stalwart support. But I needed diplomacy in dealing with his committee. I explained: because the poem has so many dissonances ("... a foul-smelling backland in Glasgow, where life rots as it grows", for example), some people may fear that my music for it would be replete with discords and thereby prove difficult to sing. I continued: precisely because the poem was so shot through with pain, that was the very reason why I considered the music to it as very still and contained, to allow the words to speak. If the image is not too pious or flowery, all I wanted to do was to enhalo the poem in melody. Finally, the committee realized that they were not functioning as commissars and that a composer could only set to music poetry with which he could identify. My diplomacy prevailed. It was amusing that, when the choral cycle was eventually performed,[3] it was the central song, 'Calbharaigh', that was sung with the greatest conviction and received with most appreciation.

I composed the cycle in 1968. In the same year I visited MacLean at his home in Plockton and played the work for him on his upright piano. He approved the setting of his words, apart from one detail that was easily corrected. When he read the three poems to me — I requested a slow reading, so that, music score in hand, I could check every rhythmic detail — I noticed that I had omitted one *svarabhakti* vowel (that residual Sanskrit vowel inserted in Gaelic between two consecutive consonants, as in "Al-a-pa", the pronunciation of 'Alba' — Scotland).

On my visit to Plockton, the poet's daughter Catriona sang songs handed down from Mary MacLean (née Matheson), the poet's grandmother. After one song, Sorley, in a characteristic gesture — hand over eyes, to aid recall — said (with his idiosyncratic repetition): "Ah, Catriona, Ca - tri - o - na, it is not ... it is not ... not ... not ... just as it should sound." The poet, who has described himself as a musician *manqué*, evidently treasured every phrase, each note, all the nuances of these folksongs from Skye, Kintail and Lochalsh, whose preservation, in some cases, was unique to the MacLean family. These songs are the *fons et origo* of the phenomenon of MacLean, the musician-in-words. In a literary *milieu* in which verbal music has been virtually silenced in much twentieth-century poetry — or at least minimized — MacLean is a lone exemplar of the art of the singing word.

In 1970 the Scottish tenor, Duncan Robertson, commissioned me to compose a song-cycle. The work that resulted was 'The Infernal City', a setting of five MacDiarmid poems and MacLean's 'Calbharaigh' in the metrical Scots translation by Douglas Young.[4] While metrical, this translation does not preserve the metre of the original Gaelic, adding a few more feet to the line. As I used the same melody (my own, not a borrowed folksong, though based on Gaelic melodic idioms) this necessitated the addition of some notes (monotones — reiterated notes) to the original tune. The absorption of Gaelic words into Scots is more widespread than is generally realized : likewise, Gaelic melodic idioms are frequent in Lowland folksongs; and it was this factor that determined my use of the same melody for both Gaelic and Scots words. Sometimes Gaelic and Scots own a common allegiance, a mutual source in Latin-rooted words, as in the line from 'Calbharaigh':

> agus air seòmar an Dùn-Éideann,
> seòmar bochdainn 's cràidh.....

which is translated by Douglas Young as:

> and a stairheid room in an Embro land,
> a chalmer o puirtaith an skaith......

Here 'seòmar' and 'chalmer' both derive from the French *chambre*. Young's Scots is coarser, cruder than MacLean's Gaelic. For example, MacLean writes:

> ach air cùil ghrod an Glaschu.....

whereas Young writes:

> but on shitten backlands in Glasga toun.

'Cùil ghrod' literally means 'a putrid nook'. 'Shitten' is strong in meaning, but fortunately the 'sh' is soft in sound. I say 'fortunately' not out of prudery, but out of concern for the hush of the song, its still intensity. I attempted to match the coarser element in the Scots by using a few harsher discords in the harmony of the accompaniment, which I had not done in the original Gaelic setting.

Another stroke of luck for the composer was that the soft sound of MacLean's ending of 'Calbharaigh' , 'gu bhàs' (till death), is translated into Scots also with a hushed sound — 'til daith'. (Here I remember that James Joyce — and no writer has been more concerned with, more aware of, the music of words than he — said somewhere that at the end of his *Ulysses*, and again in the non-end of his *Finnegans Wake*, he attempted to take language to the threshold of silence: in the one, the last word is 'yes' (the sibilant approaching a whisper); in the other, the last word was 'the' (without a full-stop). Joyce felt the word 'the' was even nearer to silence than the word 'yes' was).

Eager to try out my setting of 'Calbharaigh' in different versions, I have more recently had it performed by solo (unaccompanied) voice. This emphasizes the poem's remorse. And I have written a simple clarsach accompaniment for it. In this setting, it sounds like a distant Hebridean memory of a soul-scarring experience in the Lowlands. I also used it on solo violin, as a song without words, in the film music which I wrote for Granada's TV tribute to Hugh MacDiarmid on his 85th birthday in 1977. The violin (really thought of in this context as a street fiddle) played the background music to a Glasgow slum scene sequence in the film. Such was the potency of MacLean's words that had printed itself indelibly on my melody, that, even when the 'Calbharaigh' tune was played without the words, their spirit pervaded it.

In 1979 I addressed myself again to setting MacLean's poetry to music. This time I chose 'Tràighean'. I compared the original Gaelic with the English translation by MacLean and by Iain Crichton Smith. I must say in this instance that I infinitely preferred MacLean's. I set out an excerpt for comparison:

MacLean:

> And if we were together
> on Calgary shore in Mull,
> between Scotland and Tiree,
> between the world and eternity,
> I would stay there till doom
> measuring sand, grain by grain.

Crichton Smith:

> And if the two of us were together,
> on the shores of Calgary in Mull,
> between Scotland and Tiree
> between this world and eternity,
> I'd stand there till time was done
> counting the sands grain by grain.

MacLean's version is essential, laconic, drastic: Smith's loose, prosaic, almost conversational. I had no doubt which suggested music. Smith's use of a consecutive sibilant and consonant in "this world" is awkward to sing; MacLean's version — "the world" — is singable. Also, the sea-like sibilants in MacLean's "measuring sand" are preferable to Smith's "counting the sand". I only set to music the second stanza of MacLean's poem: the three long stanzas would have made a very long song. This is 'composer's licence': to set only an excerpt of a poem, if he chooses. It has been practised throughout music history, however it may offend the poet's sense of propriety (and maybe his sense of property, too!). Besides, I was setting the poem as a wedding gift for friends, and the opening image of the complete poem — "If we were in Talisker on the shore where the great white mouth opens between two hard jaws" — was not suitable for an epithalamium; whereas the second stanza was perfect for this. The fact that this second stanza begins with a conjunction — 'agus' (and) — did not deter me in the least; for didn't Ezra Pound begin his *Cantos* with the word 'And'? Also the second stanza's mention of Tiree was particularly appropriate as it held memories for the bride dedicatee of my song.

I composed my setting to MacLean's English translation but kept an eye cocked on the original Gaelic, so that I could make it into a Gaelic song afterwards. Gaelic has subtleties that make the noble English language appear poor in comparison. To give only one instance, the last image of the stanza I chose was:

> the sea draining drop by drop.

'Drop by drop' in the Gaelic is 'bruan air bhruan'; the Gaelic word for drop
undergoes a mutation, the 'bh' is pronounced as a 'v'. If I had set the English words
without a glimpse at the Gaelic, I might have set the repeated word 'drop' on the
same note. The mutation in the Gaelic made me choose a different note.

Whilst composing my MacLean song 'Tràighean', I enlisted the help of Aonghas
MacNeacail. I got him to read the poem in the Gaelic. I compared his reading to that
of MacLean in the same poem[5]. MacLean's reading is extremely idiosyncratic. For
example, he emphasizes and prolongs the *svarabhakti* vowel: Listen to him say
'Alba': it comes out as 'a - laaa - pa'. No doubt there is the early influence of the
incantatory tones of Calvinist ministers on the poet's native isle of Raasay; but there
is assuredly also a highly personal approach to the sonics of language as well,
overlaying it.

To return to the above criticism of Crichton Smith: it applied to a specific
instance; it was not a general criticism. Indeed, Smith has worked a minor miracle in
some of his translations from MacLean: he has actually managed to sound a Blakean
note which is like the lingering echo of the Blake influence on the young MacLean to
which the poet has confessed. Compare the following MacLean/Crichton Smith and
William Blake:
MacLean/Smith:

> let me burn away each leaf
> that grew joyfully from my grief . . .

> (from the poem on Liebknecht's death)

Blake:

> O! he gives to us his joy
> That our grief he may destroy. . .

> (from 'On another's sorrow').

I too as a young man confessed Blake as a major influence (and still do): so major
that I set to music all his *Songs of Innocence* before I was 21. Were I to set Crichton
Smith's MacLean poems (those in the mood of Blake), their music might well be like
that of my Blake songs.

MacLean's poem on Liebknecht's death (Liebknecht was a German Spartacist,
murdered with Rosa Luxembourg in 1919) is symptomatic of one of the poet's
unique achievements, which is to fuse politics and lyricism in his verse. He has set
this out as his purpose in the lines:

> loisgeam gach meanglan craoibhe
> a dh' fhàs aoibhneach thar duilghe,
> 's cuiream diachainn an t-sluaigh
> an iarunn-cruadhach mo dhuain.

The first two lines have already been quoted in Crichton Smith's superb translation.
Smith's version of the last two lines is as near as English can get to both the meaning
and the spirit of MacLean and are the very core of his creed:

> And let me hammer the people's wrongs
> into the iron of my songs.

MacDiarmid, too, wrote political poetry and some love verses (very few in his voluminous corpus) but never coalesced them as MacLean does in one and the same lyric. MacDiarmid's voice becomes exhortatory in his political verse; the lover never exhorts. MacDiarmid in fine lyrical mood can write:

> Better ae gowden lyric
> Than the castle's soaran waa.
> Better ae gowden lyric
> Than onythin else avaa.

And then he comes down with a bump in the next stanza:

> Better ae gowden lyric
> Than Insurance, Bankin an Law.

I have set to music that first stanza: the second is unsettable, except in Kurt Weillian irony, which contradicts the rapt first stanza completely. Ah, you might say, this alienation was MacDiarmid's point. That may be so. It has nothing to do with music.

Busoni put his finger on the problem, in his opuscule *A New Aesthetic of Music* (1907):

> Is it possible to imagine how a poor, but contented man could be represented by music? The contentment, the soul-state, can be interpreted by music; but where does the poverty appear, or the important ethic problem stated in the words 'poor, but contented'? This is due to the fact that 'poor' connotes a phase of terrestrial and social conditions not to be found in the eternal harmony.

Yeats, too, like MacDiarmid, wrote political and love poetry; but, again like MacDiarmid, never achieved a fusion of both. He wrote his 'Ballad of Roger Casement' in an entirely different 'tonality' from that of his love verses to Maud Gonne. MacLean is a Yeats who writes about his own 'Maud Gonne' in the same poem which laments the Spanish Civil War. And not only in *one* poem: he does it again and again. Incidentally, the parallels between MacLean and Yeats are many and significant. Both Celtic nationalists; both great lyric poets writing from unfulfilled love; both incantatory readers of their verse.

Which brings me to what I may perhaps term the *specific resonance* of MacLean's poetry. Basic to this concept is the fact that, unlike nearly all non-Gaelic poets writing in Britain today, MacLean's work is not rooted in the printed page but in a still-living oral tradition. The public readings by poets whose work is based on the soundless world of writing are lifeless in comparison with the live memory of orality.

Underlying any specific resonance is the primacy of rhythm. One of the most penetrating insights I have ever had of MacLean's sense of rhythm was on that visit to him in Plockton, to which reference has already been made. I asked him what qualities he valued most in MacDiarmid's poetry. Among many, the first he mentioned was MacDiarmid's rhythm. The example he gave was:

> I' the how-dumb-deid
> O' the cauld hairst nicht

— intoned in a strongly marked, deliberate, almost morose measure and baritone pitch-range. His reading was, at one and the same time, performance and analysis. I became more keenly aware of the function of the trochee introducing the spondee, which itself (with the inexorability and inevitability of the tide) slowly pushed on to break on the rock of the last word of each of MacDiarmid's lines. And this new awareness disclosed a revelation: insight into the ancient meaning of the trochee — the movement of feet; — and the spondee — two long quaffs, the rhythm of a solemn toast. I realized how MacDiarmid's rhythm was felt by MacLean as archetypally funereal. Indeed, I was vividly reminded of the actual rhythm of the funeral march on the death of a hero, from Beethoven's *Piano Sonata*, opus 26.

It is also possible, metrically, to hear the MacDiarmidian rhythm, in the lines quoted, as *pyrrhic* (short-short) and *molossus* (long-long-long). Even in this interpretation, the root meanings of the pyrrhic metre (a war song about a costly war) and the molossus (a triple growl of a dog) their baleful expression would appeal to MacLean. His labours for a moribund language might well make him echo Pyrrhus after the Battle of Asculum in Apulia: "One more such victory and we are lost." And a growl, an heroic moan, is often heard in MacLean's public readings.

I also remember MacLean's enthusiasm for Britten's word-setting in his *Serenade* for tenor, horn and strings: particularly the Tennyson setting, 'The Splendour falls on the Castle walls', with its incantatory, falling repetition of the words "the Echo...dying....dying....dying......dying".

The tenor of MacLean's poetic voice is threnodic; the form it takes is fundamentally elegaic. The *timbre-palette* of that voice draws upon mainly bituminous tone-colours, the sound-spectrum of his deep pessimism.

The specific resonance of his poetry vibrates in the rhythmic, myoritic space of the high tablelands and deep lochs of his native Western Islands and in the vibrancy of his humanity.

RONALD STEVENSON

NOTES

1. R. Stevenson, 'The Emergence of Scottish Music' in *Memoirs of a Modern Scotland*, ed. Miller, London 1971.
2. Tangent Records, TGS 124: Flora MacNeil, *Craobh nan Ubhal.*
3. Première: The Orion Singers (conductor: W. Grant Kidd), in St Cecilia's Hall, Edinburgh, 10 December 1976, presented by the Saltire Society with the assistance of the Scottish Arts Council (Isobel Dunlop Memorial Concert).
4. Première: Duncan Robertson (tenor) and the composer (piano), in the Purcell Room, South Bank, London, 28 February 1971.
5. Claddagh Records, CCA 3, Sorley MacLean, *Barran agus Asbhuain.*

'Calvary'

The Poet as Critic

My purpose in contributing to this volume is to emphasize an area of Sorley MacLean's literary activity which has attracted less critical attention than his poetry, but which deserves a wider audience than it has so far enjoyed. Dr. MacLean's writings on Gaelic literature not only represent a substantial and pioneer achievement in their own right, but also contribute significant insights into the mind of the poet.

These critical writings consist of essays and lectures published from the late Thirties to the present. Many of them were delivered first to the Gaelic Society of Inverness and appeared subsequently in the latter's *Transactions*. Several are to be found in other Highland and Scottish literary journals, and a couple in collections of critical essays.[1] Their subject matter embraces two main categories: the works of individual Gaelic poets from the seventeenth, eighteenth and nineteenth centuries; and aspects of the anonymous song-poetry whose roots go back much further, but which left a rich legacy in the sixteenth and seventeenth centuries before entering into decline with the fragmentation of traditional Gaelic society in the Jacobite period. Some of these essays were composed for a Gaelic-speaking audience – indeed some of them are *in* Gaelic – but they draw their insights from the whole range of Western literature, and are of the utmost interest to anybody with more than a passing curiosity about Gaelic literature.

In what follows I shall seek to show how MacLean has, by means of these writings, brought off a remarkable feat of ordering and definition, of demolition and resurrection, and blazed a critical trail worth following, in a manner directly comparable (*si parva licet componere magnis*) with the breakthrough achieved by his poetry. In order to measure his achievement it will first be necessary to look back briefly at what had passed for Gaelic literary criticism before MacLean's day.

It is not too much to say that the bulk of writing on Gaelic poetry before the present century, and a depressing proportion down to the present day, has been quite unsatisfactory from the literary point of view, whatever claims may be made for it in other respects. This is not the place to enter into detailed explanations; but it may be observed that the seeds of self-conscious criticism of Gaelic literature were sown at a time when, on the one hand, the tradition was constitutionally weakened through the disintegration of the society that had supported it and been supported by it; while at the same time the 'Ossianic' compositions of James MacPherson had ensured that Gaelic poetry would be exposed to the glare of powerful and persuasive, but largely alien, expectations and values.

Inevitably, stresses and distortions occurred. In particular, published criticism tended to be in English (i.e. directed towards non-Gaels or 'ex-Gaels'), and to be deferential to the alien values and expectations, both in the categories it selected for coverage and in what it said about them. It tended to be defensive in tone and obfuscatory in effect if not in intention. Even the Gaelic scholars tended to be accomplice to a greater or lesser extent, whether by devoting their energies discreetly to the firm rock-faces of Celtic philology, or by adding their own refinements to the myth: few indeed were able or, if able, disposed to make a clean break. When Alexander MacDonald in 1751 became the first Gaelic poet to publish a printed collection of his poems, and called it *Ais-Eiridh na Sean-Chanoin Albannaich* ('The Resurrection of the Old Scottish Tongue'), he could hardly have envisaged the complex-ridden contortions to which the new medium would expose Gaelic poets and their interpreters in the ensuing century and a half.

The rot had set in, of course, at the top end of the social scale, where favourable conditions were provided by the coincidence of several interests with a motive for perpetuating such concepts as the noble warrior past of Gaeldom, together with a resigned nostalgia for the same. The ordinary folk of the Highlands were relatively less prone to infection at this ideological level, though they might be exposed to it intermittently through the ministrations of teachers and clergymen, and would encounter it more than intermittently if they developed ambitions to 'make good'. Moreover, the period of the land agitations in the 1870s saw the belated coming of age of an alternative model for the interpretation of recent Highland history, and with it the possibility of a more self-confident attitude towards the Gaelic language and its orally-preserved literary and musical heritage. And, as is now more widely recognised, recitation and discussion of Gaelic poems and songs had always taken place in households and céilidh-houses throughout the Highlands, forming an indigenous tradition of criticism quite innocent of the Celtic Gloom which Gaels were supposed (according to the myth) to inhabit.

Despite all this, there was precious little systematic guidance at the written level for someone of MacLean's generation who happened to be curious as to the real strengths and weaknesses of Gaelic poetry through the ages, or even as to its range; and there were plenty of seemingly authoritative sources which in fact perpetuated misapprehensions and errors. That MacLean was able to surmount these obstacles in the way he did is in the last resort testimony to the intellect, vision and great-heartedness of the man. In more immediate terms, his writings indicate, both explicitly and indirectly, some of the particular sources of strength he drew on; and it is worth dwelling briefly on some of these weapons in his armoury.

When certain Scottish poets were asked, some years ago, to contribute an exposition of their 'relationship with the Muse' to a volume of *Chapman*, MacLean's account of why he was a poet began, and continued for several pages, with a discussion of his family and forebears.[2] This gambit is revealing as an example of the thoroughly Gaelic view of a man's forefathers as being part of his identity; but the facts given by MacLean are even more illuminating, since they enable us to confirm and explain a sense of continuity and belonging which we receive throughout his essays – and indeed in his poetry – whereby his 'people' are a constantly supportive presence and a reference point for judgement and action. In other words he is part of something larger than himself – a self-sufficient, self-confident entity, deeply rooted in Raasay and Skye, mindful of its members' doings and achievements, and long of memory. Its 'mythology', as rehearsed in his youth, included direct experience of, and involvement in, all the great social, political and religious events of the nineteenth century – the trauma of clearance, famine and emigration; the radical politics of the Crofters' Wars; and the great issues and debates of Highland Presbyterianism. Moreover, Sorley MacLean's forebears and relatives also numbered amongst them exponents of poetry and song, both as composers and as outstanding tradition-bearers; and, as he makes clear, he grew up in a household where the native brand of literary criticism alluded to above was a flourishing concern.[3]

From his earliest days, then, MacLean enjoyed a direct and intimate access to the Gaelic oral tradition of his own people. Many of the poets of earlier centuries would have been three-dimensional characters to him, even if he had never opened a book of poetry. As his perspectives widened and his ideas formed, his interest in and appreciation of this traditional legacy became more self-conscious, but it did not lose its immediacy. (It is worth recalling here his brother John's abiding interest in the *piobaireachd* tradition, and the fact that his brother Calum went on to become a folklorist of international reputation.)[4] While his passion for English and world literature, history and philosophy continued through his school and university career and beyond, there is, extraordinarily, no evidence at any stage for a dissociation of the Gaelic dimension from his intellectual development: the Gaelic *seann òrain* and the court poetry of Mary MacLeod and Mairearad Nì Lachlainn found their place beside Donne and Valéry and MacDiarmid, the muckle sangs and the makars, just as the Highland Clearances were to be seen as an integral part of the fabric of world history. It should be clear even from what has been said above that this landfall could not have been achieved without a rare and formidable combination of single-mindedness and judgement.

Fortunately for students of Gaelic, MacLean's indignation at a 'great injustice in the world' and his instincts as a scholar and teacher combined to ensure that his insights were shared. It was in keeping with his sense of priorities that his first concern was to set the record straight for his fellow Gaels. In the series of studies which began with 'Realism in Gaelic Poetry', delivered to the Gaelic Society of Inverness in 1934, he proceeded to spell out his own account of Gaelic poetry – 'from the inside', as it were. That account is selective rather than exhaustive; it contains *idées fixes* and hobby-horses and recurrent attempts to pin down certain elusive qualities; and there are, not unnaturally, some changes of ground over the years. But there is an overall coherence of philosophy and vision; and the tenor and direction of subsequent writing on Gaelic poetry shows that his main emphases and perceptions have weathered well.

The outstanding qualities in MacLean's criticism, and those which give even his earliest papers a continuing relevance down to the present day, are, in my opinion, uncompromisingly honest first-hand judgements, a consistent philosophy of poetry (e.g. his unshakeable belief in the universality of artistic endeavour), sympathy bordering on empathy with the creators of the poems he deals with, and a coherent vision of the Gaelic literary tradition as a whole. It is appropriate to mention some specific aspects of his work in slightly greater detail at this point.

MacLean has pretty definite views on poetry in general, as on other matters of importance to him. They are manifestly the product of independent thought stimulated by catholic reading in ancient and modern criticism and aesthetics. Although he has never published a systematic account of his theory of literature, his essays on the Gaelic tradition frequently require him to make general statements drawing on his conception of the nature of poetry and the function of art. Thus, for example, he would insist on the other-ness of poetic discourse, and on the need for a harmonious engagement of intellectual and sensual faculties if that otherness is to be attained. He praises realism (though not naturalism) in poetry, and believes that 'most really great poetry is tragic or suffused with the *lacrimae rerum*'. The medium best fitted to convey this supreme distillate is the short lyric poem, where 'lyric' signifies poetry having a musical dimension, or suggesting song.[5]

These axioms of MacLean's criticism naturally apply to Gaelic poetry as to any other. Indeed, one could ask whether the development of his views on poetry in general might not have been coloured by his prior experience of Gaelic literature and song; and it may be that some subtle osmosis has taken place at that level.[6] At all events Gaelic literature would have offered plenty of scope to someone with MacLean's critical *points d'appui*; and it is undeniable that his treatment of it opened up its strengths and weaknesses in a penetrating and convincing way.

The most important single departure in MacLean's writings on Gaelic has been his tireless advocacy of the anonymous tradition of popular song-poetry – or 'the old songs' (*na seann òrain*) – as supremely embodying the intense feeling, realism, lyricism and sensuousness he desiderated in great poetry.[7] Conversely, much of the previously exalted 'Augustan' poetry of the named poets of the eighteenth century seemed to MacLean to be over-stated and under-powered, with a tendency to vacuousness which was realised all too frequently in their nineteenth-century successors.

MacLean was thus undeterred by literary reputations: even the most illustrious were put firmly in their place if they failed to live up to his standards – e.g. by over-reliance on technical virtuosity or by loss of concentration or seriousness. That is not to say, however, that the four-square *amhran* metre employed most exclusively by these poets was *per se* incapable of producing great poetry in MacLean's terms. Admittedly, its sheer expansiveness contained a temptation to indulgence on the part of a tradition whose modes of poetic communication had been nurtured on less lush verse-forms; and the high degree of convention demanded in subject matter encouraged the more ambitious poet to concentrate his efforts on the 'medium' – the word-music – to the detriment of the 'message'. Yet some of these poets turned the constraints to strengths, and MacLean's general preference for the terser, starker world of the 'old songs' does not leave him insensible to the merits of the 'Golden Age' poets or their successors when they do achieve this breakthrough.

Thus MacLean defends William Ross against possible charges of self-indulgence and over-elaboration, recognising the tumultuous seas which Ross was negotiating in his love-songs, and regarding his *Oran eile* as a 'cry of anguish expressed in language almost as stately as a Greek sculpture or a MacCrimmon *piobaireachd*... almost unaccountable in its blend of emotion and art.'[8] By contrast, Rob Donn is found lacking in intensity and passion;[9] and even Alexander MacDonald's highest achievements lack what MacLean terms the 'duality' present in the old songs – the extra plane of artistry provided by the 'ineffable' melodies associated with the latter.[10] Naturally, there are fewer examples of first-rate poetry amongst the works of those later and lesser men who were content usually to stand in the shadow of the great eighteenth-century figures. But even here MacLean is quick to detect and praise what is poignant, spontaneous, direct and personal, however unpromising the source might appear. His quest for poetic beauty and strength takes him into all corners of the literature, and the only areas where he consistently fails to find it are those where Gaelic poets have allowed their senses to be dulled by exotic myths about their literature and selves – i.e. by Celtic Twilight, mist or tartanry.

To revert to the old songs, it is worth commenting briefly on the reasons for

MacLean's insistence on their merits, by which he sought to raise them from relative obscurity to become the principal jewel in 'perhaps the greatest peasant culture the world has ever seen.'[11] The starting point would seem to be MacLean's acute sensitivity to verbal music and rhythm, which led him to demand harmonious union of mental and sensual communication between poet and audience before a work can be termed successful at the highest levels. ('To me no poetry, whatever it has of intellect or passion, or of delicacy and subtlety of perception, is great poetry unless it also has an auditory effect in proportion to one or more of its other qualities.')[12] It has often been observed, of course, that Gaelic poetry in general makes much use of word-music as an aural enhancement; and that in some Gaelic poetry the word-music becomes an end in itself, functioning independently of the verbal 'message' and the mood of the poem. This disjunction (which can be found in bardic syllabic verse, and in some 18th-century *amhrain*) counts as a weakness by MacLean's reckoning: it is the engagement of sensual and conceptual levels that is desirable.[13] Part of the miracle of the old songs was that he found this harmony of rhythms and sounds with content overwhelmingly present in them.

Harmony of another sort was involved too. When one deals with traditional Gaelic poetry it must be borne in mind that a very high proportion of it was (and still is) composed to be sung. To MacLean melody, as well as melisma, is an integral part of the complex, contributing by its excellence and fittingness to the stature of the whole song-poem. In this musical respect the 17th-century tradition either represents a peak of achievement, or else preserves the tail-end of a richer and more creative tradition than survived later on. In either event, MacLean's 'old songs' are notable for their richly variegated musical structure, rhythm and melodic line, by comparison with which the tunes associated with later compositions can appear rigid and predictable. MacLean's assertion of the interdependence of words and music is fundamental: in 'Old Songs and New Poetry' he goes so far as to claim that the poet is a musician manqué, and that the converse is also true.[14] Insofar as the artistic chasm can be bridged, he argues, it has been bridged by the old songs, which may accordingly be regarded as the 'supreme hermaphrodites' of words and music. As he puts it, the tunes 'seem like exhalations from the words, as if the very words created the tunes.' Or again, bearing in mind our ignorance of the actual circumstances of composition of most of the old songs, 'The words created the tunes – or seem to, which is the ultimate test.'[15]

MacLean's insistence that a prospective critic of Gaelic song-poetry should tackle it in the round may seem unsurprising nowadays; but when he first started to make these points the received wisdom of the time was to play down or ignore the musical dimension of Gaelic poetic texts. Even W. J. Watson's excellent and influential *Bàrdachd Ghàidhlig* may be faulted in this respect, both in its tendency to exclude the more popular strands of the Gaelic literary tradition, and in its policy of presenting the song-texts chosen for inclusion in a way which obscured their musical dimension. By reinstating their multi-dimensional character and linking it to his concept of poetic unity, MacLean made it possible to take the old songs as seriously as they deserved to be taken, and offered fresh criteria to explain and judge their effect.

This new rationale was also applicable, and again to a greater extent than was generally admitted, to other categories of Gaelic verse text composed to be sung. Thus, for instance, one of the last metrical-musical developments before the post-Culloden crisis paralysed the innovative confidence of Gaelic poets was the importation of the ground and variation structure of the classical pipe music, with its varying phrase-patterns, tempi and rhythms, as a means to escape from the limitations of the unvarying stanzas of the *amhran*. So far as we know, Alexander MacDonald's 'Moladh Móraig' was the first, and Duncan Bàn Macintyre's 'Moladh Beinn Dóbhrain' the second example. Critics over the years have debated the respective merits of the two, with more recent judgements coming down on the side of MacDonald qua innovator, and for his linguistic virtuosity and inventiveness. MacLean, however, has adduced a powerful argument in favour of Macintyre's poem, based on the essential appropriateness – the 'organic necessity' – of the relationship between form and theme in Macintyre's treatment of the mountain, beside which the undenied brilliance of MacDonald's poem on Mórag comes to appear more as a *tour de force*.[16]

Again, considerable discussion has taken place in recent years regarding the composition and origins of the *òrain luaidh*. Strictly speaking, this term means 'waulking songs' – i.e. songs sung as a functional adjunct to the communal labour of waulking the tweed. However, many waulking-song texts share common ground with or are clearly the same as songs of the sort we have been calling the 'old songs'. What is the relationship between the two genres in cases like these? MacLean's verdict on the waulking versions is unhesitating: they are the secondary ones. Although the custom of communal hand or foot waulking undoubtedly helped to preserve many old songs that might otherwise have been lost, the functional requirements of the waulking process meant that 'their rhythms and timing were quickened and made less poignant and subtle, and . . . verbal accretions . . . lessened the intensity of their poetry.'[17]

In neither of these two cases would MacLean claim to have terminated debate. He is well aware that 'Moladh Beinn Dóbhrain' has weak sections as well as strong ones, and that this unevenness would have to be taken into account in a full assessment of Duncan Macintyre's great work. Similarly, it is clear that the rhythmic characteristics of the waulking songs are not merely negative and degenerate features. But by taking as his starting point the most insistently oral and musical end of the tradition, and evolving a critique to evaluate it in its entirety, he has established a perspective which cannot be ignored, and whose relevance extends to the more 'literary' strands in Gaelic poetry as well as the obviously 'folk' poetry.

During the course of his campaign to evangelize the old songs MacLean has had to find at least provisional answers to a series of questions which includes some of the thorniest problems of Scottish Gaelic literature. Not least was the question of how to specify the *seann òrain,* given that the songs he was concerned with are not the only 'old songs' in Gaelic, and that thematic and structural considerations do not by themselves lead to clear-cut criteria in this case. In a sense, calling them 'the old songs' is merely a shorthand for something like 'certain mostly anonymous lyric or dramatic song-poems of uncertain provenance, apparently composed earlier than the eighteenth century, with certain thematic and metrical-musical characteristics yet to be defined'. It is easy enough to cite clear-cut examples, but the limits and articulation of the genre or genres involved have been obscured by the passage of time since such songs were actively composed. Amongst other difficulties, the native metrical and musical vocabulary has become very confused over the last couple of centuries, and offers little help, especially at sub-literary levels. MacLean seems to feel that the critical factor is the music, on occasion calling them 'the songs with ineffable tunes' or similar with an almost definitional force.[18] This may well turn out to be a sound instinct at the end of the day, though one has to be prepared to encounter examples where the tune which has been preserved does not match the quality of the text associated with it or vice versa, and though a number of the texts one would want to include in this class on literary grounds are contained only in sources which do not provide tunes at all.[19] At all events, MacLean's perception of a unity based on the artistry of this group of song texts provides a criterion that will have to be taken into account by scholars and critics approaching the vernacular Gaelic tradition from other standpoints.

MacLean also attempts to define the special powers of the old songs – partly as a question of aesthetics and partly in response to the tendency of some earlier critics to equate 'oral' and 'folk' with 'simple', and 'simple' with 'artless'. His views on this matter may be summarised as follows. It is fully accepted that the language of the songs is 'simple' (i.e. uncomplicated and direct), that they abound in such oral-popular features as repetition and formulaic phraseology, and that they are metrically simple – at least when viewed as printed texts shorn of vocables, refrains and other musical 'complications'. At the same time, the degree of simplicity in their language or metre is immaterial if, as MacLean consistently maintains, they are capable of communicating all that has ever been communicated of human experience by whatever means: linguistic and formal complexity are all too often symptomatic of diffuse thought or deficient matter, and the Gaelic songs should not be denied credit for having an art that conceals art. Insofar as they lack anything expressed by (say) 20th-century English verse, they may be said to lack 'the complexity of explicit thought', a product of 'the troubled, mixed modern mind'.[20] Again, such oral-traditional features as verbal or conceptual formulae and repetitions are to be seen as integral to the dialectic and rhetoric of the genre, and as making an important contribution to the resonance of the songs themselves. In other words, 'allusive' may be fairer than 'simple' as a description of the old songs; the hearer who is *au fait* with the tradition 'supplies' part of the complexity, and the articulation of the song *as sung* (i.e. the pattern of line-repetition employed, and the alternation of text-line and vocables) is geared to help him do so. Hence MacLean may voice fears that some day nobody will be able to appreciate the old songs fully, but he has no doubts about the validity of their claims as literature, and he proceeds to account for their undoubted spell in a perceptive and illuminating way.

A similar point needs to be made with regard to the apparently 'simple' circumstances of composition suggested by song texts. In certain cases it can be shown that such texts mask complexity and irony, and the possibility must hence be borne in mind that in other cases we may be missing the full import through inability to fill in the unsaid spaces between lines, or by failing to pick up the full significance of what is being said, either through ignorance of the historical background or even, at the purely linguistic level, through inadequate understanding of the semantic history of words used.[21] Although there are very many cases in which we simply cannot get behind the bare text, literary and historical detective-work can sometimes cast light on such questions, and should be allowed to where possible. MacLean himself is no mean historian, and practises what he preaches. Striking examples, with both literary and historical implications, include his reflections on the wisdom imputed to Alasdair Dubh of Glengarry by Sìleas na Ceapaich in her elegy for him, and on the 'image' of the Campbells projected by the MacDonald poets, in the context of Iain Lom's 'terrible' verse on the Campbell women after the battle of Inverlochy.[22]

Again, his investigation of literary theories formulated outwith the Gaelic context, and perhaps also his experience as a practising poet, alerted him to a problem posed by the sheer intensity of the grief, passion, jealousy, anger, and so on to which so many of the songs bear witness. To put it crudely, they argue emotional states to the exclusion – or so it would seem – of tranquillity. How could such art be compatible with such passion? MacLean struggles valiantly with this question, which clearly exercised him greatly. Was there something especially sustaining about the tradition in which these 'old, unknown composers' worked – 'composing unconsciously in a great oral tradition of technique' – which enabled their 'tragedy of circumstances' to be transmuted into great songs? Or was there something about the age itself which permitted poetry two or three hundred years ago to sustain a greater 'intensity of emotion' than it can now? Or should we simply marvel at the finesse implicit in this poetry's manifestation of 'supreme passion held at the shortest arm's length compatible with art or the longest arm's length consistent with passion'?[23]

There is another possible way of resolving this question of art and passion, though it carries further difficulties. For it may be asked whether a song like *A' bhean iadach*, which purports to be the *cri de coeur* of a young wife and mother lured on to a tidal island and left to drown by a jealous woman who hopes to steal the first woman's husband, could really have been composed by the victim – especially if, as the tradition states, the ploy was successful; or whether it is not more likely to have been composed by somebody else, either after the event or *in vacuo*, as an act of pure imagination. To assume the latter would require us to recognise artistry of a quite different kind from what has normally been envisaged for these songs.[24]

Now there would certainly be some advantages in postulating a definite class of song-makers to account for some of the sustained literary and musical features characteristic of the old songs. For instance, there is at least a suspicion of paradox involved in talking of a high level of artistic achievement consistently attained by the unconscious artistry of individuals who happen to be affected by momentous personal events, as MacLean is forced to do.[25] Nor would such a hypothesis of itself require us to abandon the traditional ascriptions born by some of the songs; for who is to say that 'Beathag Mhór' or 'Fraser of Reelig's daughter' – i.e. the names associated with certain particular songs in oral tradition – could not have been members of the proposed class of song-poets, or indeed typical of it?

It has to be said, however, that in the present state of knowledge we lack the external corroboration needed to settle the question. That is, our only practical starting point is the power and beauty we may find in the songs themselves. To adapt MacLean's conclusion regarding the composition of the tunes of the songs, if the lyrics convey the speaker's devastation or exultation (or whatever) in an overwhelmingly convincing way – i.e. so that they are *as good as* composed by someone in the grip of the circumstances they imply or state – then for present and practical purposes we can do no better than accept what we are offered. Even where the speaker is someone about to be drowned by the rising tide, refusal to suspend disbelief can only distract us – lacking, as we do, the possibility of such fresh insights as might be gained from pondering the autobiographical dimension in a modern novel, or considering 'Ulysses' as a work of Alfred, Lord Tennyson.

A different set of problems is generated by recognition of the part played by prolonged oral transmission of literary texts. This 'weathering' is common to all classes of Gaelic song, but is most insistently present in the songs preserved by the waulking tradition. Here we meet what at times becomes an almost kaleidoscopic effect, whereby a given song (at least as sung in this century) may present abrupt changes of subject-matter and mood, and some sequences of lines which have an obvious unity crop up almost verbatim in other, quite different songs – and yet the song in question can impart a sense of identity and substantiality at odds with the incoherence implicit in its 'amoebic' tendencies. In some cases one can isolate the cause of this present coherence defying potential chaos, and express it in practical critical terms, as MacLean does for *Gur e mise chunnaic iongnadh*; but the larger questions raised by the phenomenon are by no means finally resolved.[26]

MacLean's main general contributions to the debate are to show that we need to approach the problem from both ends – i.e. both in historical terms and synchronically, in terms of the songs as we have them – and that the data must take precedence over *a priori* theorizing. One particularly interesting perception of his may be mentioned. In a discussion of the song made by Beathag Mhór to Martin of Bealach, who has been her lover but now rejects her, MacLean detects a change of tone in the course of one text he knows for it. Whereas the main body of the song is distinguished by its intermingling of 'love, regret, and bitterness and a triumph in the existence of the son she had from Martin', one section contains a relatively light-hearted, even slightly malicious diagnosis of the sorts of problem Martin will encounter if he marries a MacDonald or MacLeod wife from the Outer Isles. This reminds MacLean of the inter-clan or inter-island banter that is an identifiable strand in the waulking songs, and their 'sexual bravado', and leads him to wonder whether the section in question may be an accretion to the original text, representing 'an after-the-event extemporisation at a *luadh*'.[27] We need a great deal more of this basic but delicate sorting out of categories.

Finally, while the effects of oral transmission on old Gaelic song-texts have naturally included degeneraton of the sorts familiar from other traditions, manuscript or oral, MacLean was one of the first Scottish Gaelic scholars fully to appreciate the extent to which this negative concept of textual transmission falls short of adequately describing what happens with Gaelic oral poetry. It has in fact been a characteristic of the Gaelic tradition from early times that its scribes and tradition-bearers display a peculiar blend of reverence and familiarity towards the material passed down to them, such as to allow certain sorts of 'positive' changes to occur almost as a matter of course. The precise consistency of this phenomenon will depend upon a number of variables, but I believe it is particularly likely to be widespread when the tradition-bearers are also composers in the same line of succession – as must have been the case for a considerable length of time with the songs we are considering. At all events the old songs display evidence for such 'positive' developments in ways that range from the making good or 'improving' of lines which had come to seem unworthy of the song (perhaps as a result of earlier corruption, or by loss of contact with the original point of the passage in question), through seemingly unmotivated substitutions which do not materially alter the import or texture of the passage at all, to creative additions in the fullest sense. As I say, MacLean is very sensitive to this dynamic element in Gaelic song-texts, to its mechanics, and to its theoretical implicatons for 'the text' of a given song. Thus, for example, his essay 'Old Songs and New Poetry' contains a particularly instructive comparison between the Gaelic songs and the Border Ballads, which bear the scars of oral transmission more openly. And he provides elsewhere an outstanding

example, from the 1570 lament for Gregor MacGregor of Glenstrae (which we are
fortunate to possess in several versions), of an 'obvious corruption' which is 'as
breathtaking as the undoubted original – in total imaginative effect as well as in
rhythm or metre'.[28] This awareness, duly exploited, is by no means the least of
MacLean's contributions to the study of the old songs.

While MacLean's greatest love and attention have always been directed towards
the popular song-poetry he has certainly not ignored the rest of the Gaelic poetic
tradition in his writings, which cumulatively provide a coherent picture of the whole
tradition as he sees it. His interpretation of the larger developments is confident and
convincing, from the interweaving of separate literary strands that gave strength in
the seventeenth and eighteenth centuries through to the emergence of modernism in
the 1930s – from exhilaration and confidence, through the full bloom of technical
brilliance to introspection and escapism, and then on to fresh beginnings. He is
keenly aware of weaknesses as well as strengths, such as the intellectual confusion
and enervation of much of the poetry from the dark days of the Clearances; but he is
equally clear about the smothering forces which nearly extinguished the fires of
poetry at that time, and quick to respond to the occasional flickers of illumination
that burst out in isolation and against the odds.[29]

As regards individual poets (i.e. those known by name, with a more or less
traceable biography and identifiable *oeuvre*), MacLean's essays contain numerous
appraisals, ranging from extended studies to passing judgements, on both major and
minor figures. Amongst those receiving extended treatment are three women poets:
Sìleas na Ceapaich (Julia MacDonald of Keppoch), Mairearad nighean Lachlainn
(the Mull poetess Mary Maclean, née MacDonald), and Màiri Mhór nan Oran
(Mary MacPherson, the Skye poetess of the Land League period).[30] The amount of
poetry preserved in the case of the first two, who flourished in the late seventeenth
and early eighteenth century, is considerably less (under 1000 lines each) than that
of Màiri Mhór (over 9000 lines), and a great deal more is known or ascertainable
about the latter's life and times than is the case with Sìleas and Mairearad. (This is
partly a matter of the passage of time, and partly due to the decline of Gaelic
tradition in Strathavon and in Mull by comparison with Skye.) Again, when
MacLean wrote these essays the poems of Sìleas and Mairearad were scattered in
18th- and 19th-century collections, unedited, while Màiri Mhór's poems had been
collected by a Gaelic scholar from her own lips and published in her lifetime. As a
result MacLean's approach could not be the same in all three cases: for Sìleas and
Mairearad a high proportion of spade-work was necessary, involving such scholarly
chores as the establishment of a corpus and chronological framework for their
poetry. (Since he wrote Sìleas has received a Scottish Gaelic Texts Society edition,
but Mairearad's work has yet to be edited.)

Nevertheless, the questions which exercise MacLean most with regard to poets
and poetry are pretty constant, and his efforts to find answers to them have the effect
of bringing out or even creating a basis for comparison and literary appraisal. (It is
doubtless also true that his choice of poets to study depended largely on the interest
of the testimony they could furnish with regard to his own preoccupations.) As
regards the three women poets, one notes the strong sense of redoubtable individual
personality – by no means to be taken for granted in traditional poetry – he is able to
demonstrate in the works of each. Thus he stresses the intimate, conversational style
and poignant grace of Sìleas in her poems for members of her family. By contrast,
Mairearad achieves the 'true voice of the whole clan' in her elegies for what is in

effect the world of her people, disintegrating under pressure from the Campbells, and imparts a new power to the traditional forms by her verbal restraint, subtly original movement and lively imagery. (MacLean concludes his essay on Mairearad by apologising for having failed to capture her special gift; but he has certainly located it with some precision.)

While Mairearad spoke for his own clan, and he tells us elsewhere that he had been profoundly affected by the sense of desolation he encountered in Mull during his period as a teacher there, Màiri Mhór was closer to him in that she distilled the experience of the people of Skye in his parents' and grandparents' day. Indeed, one senses even closer sympathies when he comes to discuss the store of oral-traditional poetry she carried in her head and its subtly transformed echoes in her own songs, or her struggles to reconcile her love of it with the doctrines of the Revival, or the merging of images and symbols in her descriptions of Skye, or her fusion of social and private passion. He is also well aware of the unevenness of some of Màiri's poetry – and, in his 1975 article on her, of the imputations of banality that have been levelled at her; but he is prepared to argue in her defence that 'any big body of poetry that is at the same time social, confessional, discursive, with passionate criticism of life, is bound to be sometimes trivial in content, inconsistent in diction and conventional in imagery'; and 'the fire of passion in some words, lines or verses has a way of burning up the clichés in and around them so that the very clichés are weed-killers of the precious and contrived.'[31] Possibly there is an element of Skye solidarity here (he remarks elsewhere that 'of course, it is difficult for any Skyeman . . . to speak coldly of Màiri Mhór'[32]); but there is no doubt whatsoever about the absolute merits of Màiri's best work, about the efficacy of her poetry in the longstanding tradition of poets as public commentators for Gaelic communities, or about the fervour and great-heartedness of her commitment to the cause of the Highland crofters.

A bond of sympathy through common purpose may be discerned between MacLean and the nineteenth-century Islay poet William Livingston.[33] Livingston is best known nowadays as the author of the powerfully moving *Fios thun a' bhàird* (described by MacLean as 'the last word on the theme of the Clearances'), but his works also include a series of quasi-historical epic poems (now mostly unread) on themes of heroic conflict set in the Roman or Viking period or during the Wars of Independence, as well as a substantial number of contemporary poems in which a burning indignation at the desolation of the Highlands predominates – though not so exclusively as is sometimes assumed. A self-educated working man, Livingston seems to have sought personal relief from the 'heavy burden of love of country', and a deeper understanding of the ills that had overtaken the Highlands, in an obsessive study of Scotland's past. The quality of the sources available to him, and the prejudices which he reinforced by reading them, together resulted in a highly idiosyncratic brand of Gaelic nationalism; but MacLean rightly insists that Livingston is not to be dismissed as an 'egocentric crank with a merely antiquarian feeling for Scotland'. Through the 'overkill' of interminable battle scenes and generals' harangues, the historical naiveté and the intellectual inconsistencies – not to mention the unsuccessful metrical gambles – one can perceive a sustained, indeed heroic attempt to assert a set of values and a sense of continuity – in short to create a Caledonian mythology – which may have been foredoomed by his practical limitations, yet requires us to see him in the same tradition as Alasdair Mac Mhaighstir Alasdair – and, one may add, of C.M. Grieve and Sorley MacLean. MacLean also shows that for Livingston, as for Màiri Mhór, there is a great deal still to be said about the relationship between the individual Gaelic poet and the store of orally preserved poetry and tradition available to him.

It is noticeable that MacLean's studies of individual figures do not (so far at least) include the most famous of the 'big names' of Gaelic poetry – Iain Lom, Alexander MacDonald, or Duncan Bàn Macintyre, for example. Naturally, they appear in discussions of points of technique and artistry in his more synoptic papers, and they are frequently cited for comparison with the poets whom MacLean does treat at length, from which it is possible to infer his general respect and particular preferences.[34] Such references are always apposite and illuminating and argue an intimate acquaintance with the works of the poets in question. That MacLean should have eschewed full-length studies of these major figures – for example, of William Ross, for whose best love-poems he has the utmost love and admiration – was perhaps partly dictated by the consideration that there would have been more to say about them than could be comprehended within the compass of the type of essay he favoured. At the same time, it is clear that one of his overall aims all along has been to publicize the merits of more neglected areas of Gaelic poetry; and also that, in the last resort, none of the 'big names' seem to him to reach the highest peaks of lyric expression to the extent that his beloved 'old songs' do.[35]

In the same way, it is to be noted that MacLean has not had a great deal to say about the twentieth-century intellectual poets of the 'Gaelic Renaissance'. Possibly he feels such comment would be premature, or considers himself to be too close to the movement to be able to comment properly or usefully on it. He does, however, give some very interesting insights into the relationships between contemporary Gaelic poets (including himself) and traditional Gaelic poetry, and into the concatenation of circumstances which permitted some Gaels of his generation to open their eyes to the true strengths of their native tradition, together with the stimulus to creativity and critical discrimination which sprang from that liberation. It is worth quoting one such description:

> In the Thirties . . . something happened to articulate Gaels which had not happened for 100 years before. It was as if a French child of some peasant family near Chartres or Rheims, after being inside these cathedrals, had been taken away to some English industrial town where the only Gothic architecture was a few Gothic churches; as if he had lived there and had never seen a picture of a French or English medieval church, until, in his late teens, he went back to the French cathedrals. In 1920 the 'image' of Gaelic song was to almost all articulate Gaels only as mediocre Victorian Gothic is to the Gothic of the 12th or 13th centuries. By 1930 there was beginning to be a difference, and as the Thirties went on, more and more Gaels were boldly proclaiming where the real artistic glories of their people lay.[36]

Even if this Renaissance were to be 'the last glimmer of the Gaelic sun before it goes down forever', it had to refresh it a fountain of native inspiration newly purified by genuine research, cutting through the encrustations of Celtic Twilight and the corrosion of the nineteenth-century loss of spirit.

Taking MacLean's critical writings as a whole I would suggest that his most fundamental objective has been to identify what is best in Gaelic literature and draw it to the attention of Gaels and lovers of good poetry. This has necessarily involved an element of evangelizing, and sometimes dogged campaigning against entrenched misconceptions, especially in his advocacy of the claims of neglected areas like the old songs. I believe it can truly be said that he has pursued these ends without fear or favour. If he has had less to say about poets whose reputations are safe and whose merits are well-known, he has taught us to look out for the rare moment of lyric perfection in more obscure sources, and not to doubt it when we find it.

Indeed, some of his most valuable insights of all concern such revelatory moments in unexpected corners. Thus, for example, when discussing the 'mixed blessing' of adjective-packing (a sort of 'aureation' indulged in by, amongst others, the composers of the literary *amhrain* in the seventeeth and eighteenth centuries), he adduces as a triumphant counter-example to his general criticism of the practice the line from the love-song 'Am buachaille bàn'

An cridhe geal fialaidh aotrom aighearach òg

where the girl's fair-haired lover is characterized as 'the heart' (an cridhe) that is 'bright, generous, light, cheerful, young'.[37] Or again, when discussing the lack of pity in Duncan Bàn Macintyre's songs of hunting, he recalls the lines of the sixteenth century poet of the chase, Domhnall Mac Fhionnlaigh nan Dàn, who, in the midst of a sequence of verses in praise of the deer and the hunting way of life containing such verses as

> Sweetest music of all music
> is the voice of the big hunting-dog as he approaches,
> a stag jinking down a glen
> with hounds at his throat and haunches

comes out with the extraordinary lines:

> Nimbly would you run up
> the hard, steep mountain face;
> let everyone else praise the dog –
> I praise the wretch that is getting away.

There were worlds beyond Duncan Bàn's perception.[38]

MacLean is capable of breathing new life into his subject by taking it in unexpected directions, sometimes right out of the Gaelic context. When discussing Dugald Buchanan's evangelical poetry he compares the position of the Calvinist poet, who is committed to the belief that '90 per cent of humanity, including nearly all that one loves most, are to spend an eternity of spiritual and physical torment', with that of a 'modern' poet believing that 'the world may soon be turned to rubble by the atom bomb'.[39] This idea occurs in a paper in which he also suggests an equally bold comparison between the 'terrible clarity and intensity' of Buchanan's 'Calvinist passion' and the 'inhuman sexual passion' of the old song to Ailean Dubh:

> You burned my stackyard of oats and barley,
> you killed my father and my husband,
> yes, and my three young brothers;
> though you did that I rejoice that you are alive.
> I like dark Allan from Lundy,
> my love the brown-haired, coated Allan,
> I like dark Allan from Lundy.

Is this so far removed, he asks, from Buchanan's 'expression of human love pitted in acceptance against a pre-conceived theistic view of the universe'?[40] It need hardly be said that MacLean's readiness to see links between different periods and genres of

Gaelic poetry and, perhaps even more important, between Gaelic poetry and the 'outside world', was as novel as it was salutary, and as salutary as it was critically effective.

MacLean would be the last, I am sure, to claim that he has said the last word on all or any of the subjects he has touched on in his essays. Quite apart from those areas where there is room for difference of opinion in matters of interpretation or critical judgement, and those where he himself has revised his opinions over the years, he is often at pains to signal a provisional quality in his findings, especially where he is feeling his way towards a working critique to cope with the oral-traditional element in Gaelic poetry in general, and the 'old songs' in particular. He is uncompromisingly honest, and when he talks of the 'indefinable graces' of Sìleas na Ceapaich and Mairearad nighean Lachlainn, the 'unaccountable' blend of emotion and art in William Ross, the 'ineffable tunes' of the old songs or the 'incomprehensible tragedy of passion' contained in them, he means what he says: he has done his utmost to define, account for, put into words or comprehend, and taken matters as far as he humanly can at that juncture. It should be clear from the preceding discussion just how far he has carried the torch, and over what rough and varied terrain.

In a nutshell, he has both broadened and deepened Gaelic criticism in a much-needed and profoundly liberating way. He has added breadth not only by adding the popular songs to the corpus of material to be reckoned with in any serious treatment of Gaelic literature, but also by his insistence that there is no oneness of Gaelic poetry, thus laying the demeaning myth of a single quality or objective or tone that can characterize it once and for all, and by identifying and unravelling some of the strands that go to make up the complex fabric of the real thing. He has broadened it in another sense too, by showing in a natural and unforced way that specific Gaelic poems and poets can be compared fruitfully with something other than similar Gaelic poems and poets, whether that something be Wordsworth or Homer, Byron or Verlaine – or indeed, since this is integral to MacLean's view of artistic creation, with non-verbal art-forms such as music, architecture, sculpture or painting. As to depth, it is not too much to say that he has done a major service towards making Gaelic poetry accessible to serious modern criticism and rescuing it from irrelevance, mysticism and evasiveness, by showing what were the right tools for the job and demonstrating how they could be applied to it. No less important, he established the areas where additions to the existing range were needed, and made considerable progress towards filling the gaps. Here his original perceptions on the creative process in an oral-musical context in a traditional society not only suggest ways forward to a more complete understanding of the art of the old songs, but also have the power to enhance our appreciation of the rest of Gaelic literature.

The tone and style of MacLean's essays are individual. To some extent, I suppose, this is to be connected with the fact that most of them were written to be delivered orally to a largely non-specialist audience. They are pretty free of technical jargon, though he is incapable of 'talking down', and though some terms attain a new technical status in his discourse. His intuitions and perceptions are underivative, and stand unencumbered by the hedging and disclaimers of scholarly justification, though the rigour of purpose, the justness and the clarity of expression are scholarly in the best sense. There is an evangelical fervour when it comes to doing justice by the old songs, and he frequently cites the greatest of them by name in a sort of litany. On at least one occasion he remonstrates with himself, 'Sometimes I feel that people like myself ought to shut up about the old songs'.[41] But he has an axe to grind: having won his own way free from the undertow of misconceptions about Gaelic poetry he is continuously aware of the need to throw lifebelts to others who are still struggling.

The upshot of all this is a highly readable, original, stimulating and important body of writing. When one takes account of the humanity and authority that inform what MacLean has to say it is no wonder that his essays have been inspirational amongst Gaelic scholars, and it is encouraging to know that they are now available to a wider audience in collected form.[42] He has restored and tuned a harp which it behoves us to play.

WILLIAM GILLIES

NOTES

1. Those cited specifically in this paper are, in order of original appearance, as follows:
   'Realism in Gaelic Poetry', *Transactions of the Gaelic Society of Inverness*, 37 (1934-36), 80-114.
   'The Poetry of the Clearances', *TGSI*, 38 (1937-41), 293-324.
   'The Poetry of William Livingston', *TGSI*, 39/40 (1942-50), 1-19.
   'Aspects of Gaelic Poetry', *Scottish Art and Letters*, 3 (1947), 37-42.
   'Mairearad Nighean Lachlainn', *TGSI*, 42 (1953-59), 30-46.
   'Notes on Sea Imagery in 17th Century Gaelic Poetry', *TGSI*, 43 (1960-63), 132-149.
   'Silis of Keppoch', *TGSI*, 45 (1967-68), 98-112.
   'Old Songs and New Poetry', in *Memoirs of a Modern Scotland*, edited by Karl Miller (London, 1970), pp. 121-35.
   'Some Raasay Traditions', *TGSI*, 49 (1974-76), 377-97.
   'Màiri Mhór nan Oran', *Calgacus*, 1 (Winter, 1975), 49-52.
   'On Poetry and the Muse', *Chapman*, 16 (Summer, 1976), 25-32.
   'Some Thoughts on Gaelic Poetry', *TGSI*, 52 (1980-82), 302-17.
   These and other items appear together in the recently published collection of MacLean's prose writings referred to below (note 42).
2. 'Poetry and the Muse', pp. 25-27; see also 'Raasay traditions', pp. 377-80.
3. 'Poetry and the Muse', p. 26.
4. For this 'family' dimension to MacLean's commitment to traditional Gaelic poetry, see 'Old Songs', p. 121; compare John's 'Am Pìobaire Dall', *TGSI*, 46 (1951-52), 283-306, and Calum's 'Traditional Songs from Raasay and their Value as Folk-literature', *TGSI* 39/40 (1942-50), 176-92.
5. See, e.g., 'Realism', pp. 80-87; 'Poetry and the Muse', pp. 27-28; 'Some thoughts', pp. 314-15. On 'lyric' see especially 'Old Songs', pp. 122, 134.
6. Compare 'Aspects', pp. 37-38.
7. The term 'old songs', which I shall follow MacLean in using, is a convenient label, though not a satisfactory solution to the terminological problem discussed on p. 190.
8. See 'Realism', p. 105; cf. 'Some thoughts', pp. 315-16.
9. 'Some thoughts', pp. 314-15; cf. 'Realism', pp. 102-103.
10. 'Old songs', p. 125; cf. id., p. 121.
11. 'Realism', p. 97.
12. 'Old songs', p. 131; cf. 'Poetry and the Muse', p. 28.
13. See 'Sea imagery', p. 140, for an interesting discussion of the sorts of

sensuousness – auditory, visual, tactile and dynamic – whch MacLean discerns in Gaelic poetry and song.

14. 'Old songs', p. 127; cf. 'Some thoughts', p. 304.
15. 'Some thoughts', p. 302; cf. 'Old songs', p. 131.
16. See 'Some thoughts', pp. 310-11; cf. 'Realism', pp. 100-101.
17. 'Some thoughts', p. 303.
18. E.g., 'Some thoughts', p. 309.
19. E.g., 'Some thoughts', pp. 304, 310; 'Old songs', p. 131.
20. See 'Old songs', pp. 127, 134.
21. E.g., 'Some thoughts', pp. 306, 313.
22. 'Some thoughts', pp. 307, 313.
23. 'Realism', pp. 94, 97, 112; 'Old songs', pp. 127-28.
24. 'Sea imagery', pp. 144-45; 'Some thoughts', pp. 307-8. The tradition associated with *A' bhean iadach* makes the treacherous sister hear the song and repeat it in the husband's hearing, leading to her unmasking: we are not the first to have been exercised by this point. It should be noted that a relationship has been claimed between *A' bhean iadach* and the theme of The Two Sisters as found in 'Binnorie': see further Margaret Fay Shaw, *Folksongs and Folklore from South Uist* (London, 1955), pp. 254-57. If that were correct the case for imaginative composition would be strengthened, which could have implications for other songs of the 'woman's dramatic monologue' type, though this would not be a necessary inference.
25. Compare Seán O Tuama's treatment of the similar problem presented by the Irish popular love songs: *An Grá in Amhráin na nDaoine* (Dublin, 1961), pp. 263 ff.
26. See 'Sea imagery', p. 146. The wider problem is best expressed by Dr. J. MacInnes, 'The choral tradition in Scottish Gaelic songs' (*TGSI*, 46 (1969-70), 44-65), who goes on to argue that 'this "incoherence" is intrinsic', and that 'it is precisely these abrupt transitions from image to image . . . that release the creative energy'.
27. 'Some thoughts', pp. 306-8.
28. See 'Old songs', p. 129; 'Raasay traditions', pp. 389-90.
29. E.g. 'Realism', pp. 111-13.
30. See especially 'Silis of Keppoch', 'Mairearad nighean Lachlainn' and, for Màiri, 'Poetry of the Clearances' and 'Màiri Mhór'.
31. 'Màiri Mhór', p. 52.
32. 'Poetry of the Clearances', p. 320.
33. See especially 'William Livingston'.
34. E.g. 'Some thoughts', pp. 310-15; 'Realism', pp. 83-84; 'Aspects', p. 42.
35. Cf. 'Realism', p. 98; 'Old songs', p. 127.
36. See 'Old songs', p. 122 and passim. (In the passage quoted '1920' appears as '1930', which cannot be right; '1920' is my conjecture.)
37. 'Some thoughts', p. 310.
38. 'Some thoughts', p. 312.
39. 'Old songs', p. 133.
40. 'Old songs', p. 126.
41. 'Old songs', p. 132; cf. p. 121.
42. Published by Acair Ltd., under the title *Ris a' Bhruthaich* (Stornoway, 1985).

Questions of Prestige:
Sorley MacLean and the Campaign for Gaelic

In assessing the contribution he has made to our cultural treasury, it is entirely proper that we lay most emphasis on the literary achievements of Sorley MacLean. No doubt it pleases him, or at least does not offend him, that he should be so honoured, although the ceremonial honours so far conferred on him – Doctorates from the Universities of Dundee and Edinburgh and the National University of Ireland – in no way reflect the extent of the recognition which he now receives in informed circles.

Yet when he himself recollects past achievements, it is not to the poetry he refers but to the part which he played in the campaign for the provision of a Higher Leaving Certificate examination paper specifically designed for learners of Gaelic. Not, at first glance, the most likely object of pride to our greatest living poet, but the "Learners' Paper" had deep symbolic significance for MacLean.

Few will dispute that his poetry establishes Sorley MacLean as the greatest bard in the records of Gaelic literature, a foremost Scottish 'makar', and a major poet of our time by any measure. Nor has his reputation, tribal, national or global, yet reached its full magnitude.

That reputation rests on a published corpus of poems written entirely in a language which today is spoken by no more than 80,000 people. Of that number, only a small minority are fully literate, and of those an even smaller proportion are likely to have any great interest in modern poetry.

Here we may consider further ironies. The first is that most of MacLean's working life as a schoolmaster was spent teaching not the language of his infancy and of his art, but that of the intrusive culture, English. The second and perhaps deeper irony, in that it would shape his consciousness both as poet and as teacher, can be presented most simply in decadal figures, beginning with the year of his own birth: 1911 – 202,398; 1921 – 158,779; 1931 – 136,135; 1951 – 95,447; 1961 – 80,978. These numbers, recognizable to any Gaelic activist are, of course, the census figures for Gaelic speakers in Scotland. To one as passionate in his commitment as Sorley MacLean, the evidence that his native language and its attendant culture were rapidly sliding towards extinction must have been an agony.

As a poet he could do little directly to reverse the process although, if Gaelic survives, it will be possible – and plausible – to argue that the prestige accruing to Gaelic, through the recognition of the greatness of his poems, contributed an important element to changes in the Gaels' attitude to their own language. As a teacher, he was in a somewhat different position. Practical action became a possibility in a number of ways. It was also a necessity.

So many other Gaels in education, who like MacLean were aware of their circumstances, apparently accepted the decline of Gaelic as irrevocable. The question as to why a positive response mattered so acutely to MacLean may be partially answered by reference to his background. Both sides of his family provided rich sources of tradition and a view of the world through a Gaelic lens that was not at all narrow. The music, the song and the poetry, legends, the histories of clan deeds and of the Clearances were readily available from parent, uncle, aunt or grandparent. Political discourse with uncles and aunts made him a socialist at the age of twelve. The language in which all this knowledge was transmitted to the young MacLean was, of course, Gaelic.

School not only taught a different history, but was itself moulded by a specific continuum which was, and remains, essentially hostile to vernacular knowledge; not only indigenous languages and dialects but the entire cultural strata of communities are largely disregarded by the formal education system.

Over three hundred years of constitutional hostility to Gaelic, much of it documented in the recent past by J. L. Campbell and K. M. Mackinnon, came to an end with the passing of the 1872 Education Act. Those centuries may be regarded as the first, albeit protracted, stage in the continuum.

Introducing the second, as yet unfinished, phase, the Act of 1872 established the basic structure of compulsory education throughout Scotland. It was probably the first piece of legislation embracing education in the Highlands which contained no clause hostile to Gaelic. In fact, it omitted any reference to Gaelic, thus placing the language in a grossly disadvantaged position from the start. Gaelic was, in effect, locked outside the gates of legitimate education. Any remedial progress could only come in the form of piecemeal concessions, which would have to be fought for.

Agencies did exist with mandates to involve themselves in such campaigns. The Gaelic Society of London had been established in 1777 to secure the repeal of the Disarming Acts which had proscribed Highland dress and bagpipes after the '45. Its objectives achieved, the Society remained – and remains – in existence to promote activities in other areas of Gaelic life and culture, including education.

In 1871, the Gaelic Society of Inverness was founded to enable articulate Gaels in that town to speak on behalf of their less advantaged brothers and sisters in the homelands. Soon they were actively campaigning for provisions to be made for Gaelic in Highland schools.

An Comunn Gàidhealach, aspiring to speak for all Gaels, came into existence in 1891. Seldom without its critics within Gaeldom, Sorley MacLean among them, An Comunn nevertheless devoted much energy to the cause of Gaelic in education. That energy seems, all too often, to have been dissipated. For example, the questions which Sorley MacLean would address with passionate intensity in the mid-sixties were raised in the recommendations of a committee which reported to An Comunn on Gaelic in education in 1936. That report was already advocating that "more trouble should be taken to teach Gaelic to non-native speakers", and "in Secondary schools, even outwith the Highlands, it should be given equal status with any other language within the curriculum". Due to the campaign waged by MacLean and others in the sixties, Gaelic has, technically, achieved equal status with other languages, and is being freely taught to non-native speakers where the facilities (i.e. teachers) are available.

In 1872, then, Gaelic had, for educational purposes, officially ceased to exist. By the time Sorley MacLean became a teacher, some small steps towards recovery had been made. In fact, the most significant changes had been achieved before he began his formal schooling. In the early years of the twentieth century, a Lower Grade paper, with no formal status as a qualification for University entrance or for anything else, was made available. It was clearly aimed at pupils with a fluency in the language. So also was the Higher Grade paper which eventually appeared in 1915.

After various forms of pressure, including a petition containing 20,000 signatures, a clause was added to the 1918 Education Act, which compelled Local Authorities to make "adequate provision for teaching Gaelic in Gaelic-speaking areas".

As it neither defined "adequate provision" nor "Gaelic-speaking areas", it became a clause that could be honoured as much in the breach as in the fulfilment. Its continuing potential for controversy was clearly revealed in the recent past, when Donald Stewart, M.P., tabled a Private Members' Bill which sought to make precise definition of Gaelic-speaking areas. The bill was defeated.

When MacLean took charge as Headmaster of Plockton Secondary School in 1956, he was no doubt confronted with the full ironic force of the ambiguities underlying the 1918 mandatory clause. The catchment area for his new school would in 1918 have qualified as a Gaelic-speaking area without question. By the mid-fifties it is doubtful if it would have qualified as a borderline case. Demographic shifts, as much as basic losses within the community, were among the major factors, but while the emigration of Gaels and the immigration of non-Gaels certainly contributed to the change, there was also evidence that the language was not always being transmitted to the rising generation.

This, of course, was not a new phenomenon, nor was it confined to Wester Ross. Lacking educational prestige, or social status, Gaelic had also been declining in, among other places, Skye, where MacLean had received his secondary education and where he later began his teaching career, in the same school in Portree.

When he transferred from Portree to Tobermory in 1938, he entered an area where the stagnation of Gaelic was already at an advanced stage. He has described the experience as traumatic: the "historical associations of the Clearances that had been widespread in the island during the nineteenth century made it a heart-breaking place for a man who bore the name MacLean". He goes further in referring to the "terrible imprint of the Clearances" on Mull, which "made it almost intolerable for a Gael" (*Chapman* 16, Summer 1976). His impressions of the state of things on the island were not totally negative, however. He was later to recall the impact made on him by the discovery that the Gaelic teacher at Tobermory was teaching classes where upwards of 75% of pupils were non-native speakers of the language.

At the beginning of 1939 he moved again, to Boroughmuir Secondary School in Edinburgh, with which he would be associated, apart from war service, for the next seventeen years. Throughout this time as teacher of English, and later as Principal teacher of English, he maintained a passionate concern for his first language, the steadily, unbearably declining language of his art, and of his history.

The extent to which Sorley MacLean, teacher as much as poet, is a product of that history, is partially revealed in his explanation for his choice of English as a specialist subject at University, and in his later attempt to extend his Gaelic qualification to Honours level. Quite simply, his main reason for choosing English was that a degree in Gaelic would have represented too great an economic gamble for a person in his circumstances. At the time he entered University, his family were, like many others in the Highlands and Lowlands, suffering considerable hardship, and in need of an assured income from some quarter. There would always be openings for teachers of English, in the Highlands and elsewhere.

Boroughmuir was far from the heartlands of Gaeldom and, although there were many exiled Highlanders in Edinburgh, none of the Edinburgh schools offered classes in Gaelic. Though he had not been able to obtain his hoped-for qualification to teach Gaelic, the plight of his language and the need to do something to staunch its wound, prompted him to offer to teach voluntary Gaelic classes (outside school hours). These classes, which ran for a number of years, were successful enough to meet with official approval, to the extent that the Headmaster, the Director of Education and City Education Committee were prepared to grant a request from An Comunn Gàidhealach that the classes be formally absorbed into the curriculum. The fourth essential element, parental support, was unfortunately not forthcoming.

While MacLean was at Boroughmuir he was aware that Gaelic was being taught in schools in Argyll and Glasgow to non-native speakers who would eventually sit an examination which had been set with native speakers only in view. One of the teachers involved was Donald Thomson, who will be remembered by most Gaels from his appearances at National Mods as a rather conservative figure; a stocky, kilted Lewisman with a voice like a rasp-file. Although Thomson was a man of intense commitment, he was not, in later years, one who presented an image of visionary radicalism; yet it was Donald Thomson who pioneered the teaching of Gaelic to non-native speakers in an attempt to halt the decline of the language in Argyll. Since the mid-thirties, his classes at Oban High School had in theory been open to any who wanted to study Gaelic. But, in practice, only A-stream pupils willing to forego French got into Thomson's classes.

As MacLean had observed when he taught at Tobermory, non-Gaelic speaking children in Mull were being encouraged to study Gaelic there. This was also true of the Junior Secondary schools in Islay, Tiree and Lochgilphead, all of which fed pupils into Oban High School – into Donald Thomson's classes and those of another Lewisman, Donald Morrison.

In 1946 provision for the teaching of Gaelic was made in the Glasgow schools at Woodside and Bellahouston. Twelve years later Greenock High School and Norton Park in Edinburgh offered similar facilities. In each case, the provision would have been made primarily for children of Gaelic background. In fact, the majority of those who opted for Gaelic had no such background. And in all those cases, we have to remember that students in Scotland were required to perform the equivalent of sitting a paper in French that had been set for Parisians, or a paper in German for Berliners.

It might seem odd that we should be asked to regard as pioneers a handful of teachers who aspired to bring pupils with no prior knowledge of a language to a degree of proficiency equivalent to that of the native speaker. The fact that they were given no additional time, nor special facilities, at a time when resources for the native-speaker were themselves grossly inadequate, only serves to highlight the madness of the venture. Most absurd of all, particularly for those pupils resident in Argyll, was the fact that this mysterious language was still spoken naturally and daily by a significant proportion of the community in which they lived. Yet both teachers and pupils can rightly be regarded as pioneers and MacLean certainly regards them as such.

Perhaps the more curious question is why there was apparently no sustained agitation for a change in the status of Gaelic in order to include a separate syllabus for learners which would put it on the same basis as French and other languages. The answer is that there was a continuing campaign which was waged more or less entirely through 'official channels'.

When in 1950 John MacLean, Sorley's brother, became Headmaster at Oban, he discovered the great efforts Donald Thomson and his junior colleague, Donald Morrison, were making to give non-Gaelic pupils access to the language, up to certficate standards, and he immediately gave his support to a campaign of 'in-service' agitation. A great many representations from the headmaster and the Gaelic Department to the Scottish Education Department followed, which were supplemented by pleas and exhortations at educational conferences. The objective was to make available a certificate examination for learners of the language.

A course was eventually conceded, no doubt as reluctantly as previous concessions to Gaelic had been made. This course was to Lower Grade standard only, which did not count for University entrance until 1962 (the year Ordinary Grades were introduced). This recognition was granted only after Sorley MacLean made what he calls "a bit of a row". The ultimate objective, however, remained the elevation of Gaelic to the same status as other languages. This could only be done by removing it from the ever-decreasing ghetto of 'native-speaker studies'.

For the first six years of his headmastership at Plockton, MacLean had only been able to devote a small portion of his time and energy to matters relating to Gaelic. It was very much a rural establishment. In order to provide the full range of subjects, the versatility of the teachers was fully tested. MacLean himself taught most of the English and history classes, teaching for thirty-three periods out of forty, while also having to perform his administrative role as headmaster. For his first three and a half years, he was also without secretarial assistance. For sixteen years MacLean was acting as Assistant Teacher of Gaelic, and for one year he taught almost all the Gaelic.

There was, however, no problem about introducing the idea, and the practice, of teaching Gaelic to non-Gaels. At the school there was already an excellent teacher, one Catherine MacRae, able, in every sense of that word, to teach practically all subjects on the curriculum, except French and Latin. Adding the Gaelic learners' stream to her workload meant shifting some of her previous obligations in science, geography and mathematics onto others, including the headmaster himself.

Those who are primarily concerned with Sorley MacLean as poet should not be surprised that his creative output during this period was sparse. A glance at the acknowledgements page of *Reothairt is Contraigh* would suggest that no poem was published between 1954 and 1970. Whether any were written during that time is debatable. The school was his predominant concern, with, in their seasons, extra-mural activities that included supplementary classes for pupils approaching the Higher examination in History, and coaching the school shinty team.

For most of his first ten years at Plockton, the Gaelic class was part of the routine, an important part certainly, but capably dealt with by Ms MacRae, who coached her pupils, native-speaker or learner, according to their needs. At the end of the day the two streams met in the examination room.

Occasionally an opportunity arose to take issue with the authorities. In 1964, Jordanhill College of Education and Inverness-shire Education Committee brought together, at a conference at Inverness, representatives from those Education Authorities which included Gaelic on their curricula. These included Inverness-shire itself, Ross and Cromarty – the county which employed MacLean – and

Argyllshire. The Plockton headmaster seized his chance and with the able support of Dan Morrison, Donald Thomson's assistant at Oban High School, raised an "unholy row" on the question of the Higher paper for learners. The resulting dispute was essentially an in-service event though, and, as far as those in authority were concerned, conflicts which developed there ought to be containable. The conference dispersed and Sorley MacLean returned to the frequently arduous routine of running his school in Plockton, where his concerns always included the need to ensure that the teaching of Gaelic, both to native-speakers and to learners, flourished in the face of continuing official indifference.

In 1965, however, a small bomb exploded in MacLean's consciousness which would send blast-waves rippling out far beyond Plockton. What detonated his indignation was the difference between two examination results in the Higher Gaelic paper of that year. His response was to involve himself directly in the campaign for a separate paper for learners of Gaelic. Three documents composed between the summer of 1965 and the spring of 1966 testify to the intensity of his feeling, and of his commitment to battle. The first text, a letter to the Scottish Education Department, presents the respective performances of the two pupils, a native speaker who passed the examination, and a learner who failed.

While such results might otherwise seem predictable, the comparison in this case is between a learner who is a "very able and hard-working pupil who passes in Higher Latin, Higher English, Higher Mathematics and Higher Science, and fails in Higher Gaelic due to not being a Native Speaker", and a native Gael "who came to Plockton school as a Junior Secondary pupil and who was not fit to sit any other Higher except English, in which a bare pass was obtained, and gets a Credit pass in Higher Gaelic because this pupil is a Native Speaker". In the letter he exonerated the teacher from any blame. The parents of the learner, non-Gaels themselves, he commended for their patriotism, while he felt that children from such a background "whose environment makes it impossible that they should be Native Speakers ought not to be put at such a disadvantage". Had the "school been one where it was possible to study the difficult language Russian, this pupil would certainly have passed it".

"A result like this", he concluded, "is bound to disquiet and exasperate the most admirable of all Gaels *qua* Gaels, those teachers who are teaching Gaelic to pupils who do not already know it".

That he did not receive an answer which afforded any satisfaction may be inferred from a reading of the next document. This was a letter, dated November 1965, to the Gaelic Society of Inverness. We may also detect a raising of the psychological temperature.

> I wonder if you have thought of a chief for this year. I think it ought to be Donald Thomson, both for his own sake and for the sake of the tiny group of whom he is the pioneer and the most noted: those teachers who are teaching Gaelic to pupils who do not already know it. One of my own bitterest regrets is that I have been so late in raising my voice on their behalf and on behalf of the patriotic parents who are encouraging their children to take Gaelic in secondary schools when their environment makes it next to impossible that they should be Gaelic speakers.

> In the next few months there is going to be much agitation in favour of those parents and teachers, especially in order to hasten the provision of a Learner's paper in Higher Gaelic.

He continued that the society could support this effort by making Donald Thomson chief.

It should, perhaps, be noted that Donald Thomson had been actively involved in An Comunn Gàidhealach since the mid-Thirties – more or less since he had commenced teaching learners alongside native Gaels. He had, in the summer of 1965, completed his three-year tenure as President of An Comunn Gàidhealach.

Curiously, when Sorley MacLean reminisces on this period, he inveighs most caustically against "Urracha Mór a' Chomuinn" which could be translated as the 'Comunn Hierarchy', or more literally as the 'nobility – or bourgeoisie – in An Comunn'. The barb is not directed at the likes of Donald Thomson, whose commitment to Gaelic was total, but at those whom MacLean elsewhere referred to as "Place Gaels or Platform Gaels" or, more graphically, as "sentimentalizing, hypocritical Quislings, who make a profession of supporting Gaelic in education provided it is contained beyond the Kyle of Lochalsh and the Minch, where it cannot clog the wings of their own children, who frequently enjoy the benefits of rocket-propulsion in the rat-race supplied by the snob-contact schools of the south". It may, nevertheless, be asked why Thomson did not use his position as President of An Comunn to make a public demand for that small concession to Gaelic in education which he and Sorley MacLean, among others, so dearly sought. Two answers present themselves. Firstly, he may have felt circumscribed by the fact that as a teacher of Gaelic he was laying himself open to the charge that he sought personal aggrandizement in promoting such a course. Secondly, after preparing non-Gaels for thirty-odd years to sit an examination designed for natives, he may have begun to take it for granted that there was no alternative. MacLean was certainly under no such illusions, nor did he feel in any way constrained by position. By the spring of 1966, he had decided that the debate should be made public in a way that would persuade, or provoke, as many influential citizens as possible.

The venue he chose was a meeting of the Gaelic Society of Inverness, where, as honorary Bard to the Society, he had previously read many papers on themes of his own choosing, usually literary or historical topics. This time the subject was contemporary, the title innocuous enough: "Problems of Gaelic Education". Appeals through 'official channels' had not brought a resolution to the problem which most concerned MacLean. He has recalled being told in 1964 by what might be termed a 'well-informed source' that the S.E.D. would "never grant a Higher paper for Gaelic learners". His response then had been to warn his informant that the Department might expect to be "kicked in the teeth if they don't". The paper which he presented to a stunned audience of Inverness Gaels provided that kick. It may have been aimed ultimately at the S.E.D. but it caught, and deliberately caught, in its swing a number of his fellow Gaels, including some who were in his audience. The impressive flow of invective quoted above in respect of "Place Gaels or Platform Gaels" is but an example of the flyting with which he sought to shame into action those who were in a stronger position than he to influence the attitudes of government. But the paper was not simply a torrent of excoriation against those "socially ambitious ... Gaels on the make" who had "almost without exception acted as if Gaelic were surely dying, and the sooner dead the better". It provided a serious analysis of the state of Gaelic in education at the time, seeing it clearly in the context of its history.

Contemporary attitudes to other languages were also examined:

We all know the intrinsic difficulties of a language can be eased for learners by an easing of academic standards. Russian is probably for Scots people a more difficult language than Gaelic is, but it was very recently possible for a student at a Scottish University to start Russian *from scratch and take the degree examination in it*.... I am sure that such a student of Russian cannot at all have the same knowledge of Russian as the native speaker from Moscow of comparable ability has. It is obviously government policy....

Many schools in Holland, he noted, made it possible for individual pupils to study as many as five languages including Dutch, while in Bavaria it was common for pupils to take at least three languages besides German.

It ought therefore to be well within the scope of a great number of pupils in Scottish secondary schools to do three languages besides English, and surely it is not expecting too much of Gaelic patriotism to demand that Gaelic should be one of the three?

Questions like the need to update vocabulary and the need to standardize spelling were seen in the wider context of what was being done with Irish, Hebrew and Welsh. The possibility that lack of suitable text-books, audio-visual aids, and so on might be used as an excuse for inaction was challenged by his experience of Bavaria where he "saw the marvels done in the teaching of English without audio-visual aids, with the minimum of text-books, with gross overcrowding and with teachers innocent of Colleges of Education". The pupils who studied successfully under such conditions "did not spend any time on texts such as Shakespeare's tragedies, as we used to do on Corneille and Racine.... their English study was confined to modern colloquial prose". At the time he spoke, learners of Gaelic in Scotland would have been confronted with the works of Donnchadh Bàn, Mac Mhaighstir Alasdair and Màiri Nighean Alasdair Ruaidh among others. The eighteenth century was the high watermark of Gaelic poetry before MacLean himself: the range and force of its vocabulary presented considerable problems for native speakers. It must have been totally impenetrable to many learners.

The main thrust of his argument was to stress the status of Gaelic in secondary schools, the need to give the language prestige at national level, and, above all, the need for a separate paper for learners. Why, he inquired, had the S.E.D. for years been "deaf to appeals made to it... why had the new Examinations Board not immediately produced a suitable paper for learners?" Was it, perhaps, because "the existence of such a paper would shame professing Gaels into making their own children or grandchildren take Gaelic in Secondary Schools"? Whatever the answer, he placed a moral obligation on the Gaelic Society of Inverness to make a full commitment to the campaign.

Following his appeal to the Society is a passage which nicely illustrates the subtly wounding element in his technique. His reference is to an allegedly bilingual scheme which had been introduced in certain schools in Inverness-shire during the mid-fifties. There is good reason to assume that the prime objective of that scheme was not language maintenance, but the least psychologically troublesome language shift. MacLean certainly questioned its value, as the passage referred to shows.

It would be far more proper for the Gaelic Society of Inverness to do what it can to ensure that there is such a paper in the S.C.E. exams.... It would be far more proper for the Gaelic Society of Inverness to do that than to allow its annual dinners to be a platform for the glorification of the much publicised but relatively unimportant Inverness-shire scheme which, though genuine enough, in effect envisages Gaelic as fit only for the lesser breeds beyond the Kyle of Lochalsh or the Minch.

Variants on this barb recur throughout the paper as do references to "snob-contact schools in the south". Such allusions are obviously pointed, but nowhere in the text are they more explicit than those quoted above. Inverness-shire at the time included Skye and the southern half of the outer Hebrides, and was, therefore, by a small margin still the most Gaelic-speaking of Highland counties. It was also the one which made little, if any, provision for learners of Gaelic in its secondary schools. What was most offensive to MacLean was that publicly "professing Gaels" should privately betray the language. His demand that they support the introduction of a Learners' paper, coupled with his determination to expose them as traitors who undermined their own language, created a neat and unanswerable logical twist. If they lived within range of a school where Gaelic was taught, but sent their children elsewhere, they were caught. Whether they opposed or approved of the Learners' paper they were vulnerable: opposition could be counted betrayal and approval hypocrisy. Enraged though they might have been we must assume that it was less painful to be a hypocrite than a betrayer, as a Higher paper for learners, with the same status as other languages, appeared not long after.

To what precise degree MacLean's address to the Gaelic Society of Inverness swayed the Scottish Office in acceding to the demand for the full status for Gaelic in schools, we cannot be certain. It was *de jure* a significant victory for the Gaelic language. *De facto,* the machinations of bureaucracy have ensured that its impact has not been as widespread as it could have been. The 1918 Act can still be used in obfuscation to prevent Gaelic, Scotland's oldest language, from being taught throughout the land. MacLean claims no credit for initiating the campaign to introduce a separate syllabus for learners of Gaelic. He has, as already quoted, expressed his bitter regrets that he was so late in joining the struggle. I hope that this brief contribution has shown that when he did act, it was with characteristic feeling and an impatience with talk for talk's sake. Words were wasted unless they led to action. The words he delivered to the Gaelic Society of Inverness on the subject of "Problems of Gaelic Education" were designed to ensure that there would be action, of one form or another.

There were, in fact, several responses. His prime objective, to publicise the debate and effect change, was achieved, but not without cost. He had expected to alienate some, but there was also some fall-out in unintended directions. Another surprise awaited when, as was customary, he submitted his paper to the publications committee of the Society, for inclusion in the next volume of *Transactions of the Gaelic Society of Inverness.* In an act of censorship unprecedented within the Society, the committee rejected the paper. Undeterred, and still determined that the questions he had raised should be as widely aired as possible, MacLean sought alternative outlets. In due course the radical nationalist magazine *Catalyst* obliged, and his paper appeared as a two-part essay within its pages.

Perhaps MacLean ought not to have been quite so surprised at such reactions. The combination of philosophical examination and polemic made for a volatile mixture. In looking back on the period, however, he touches on those animosities only in passing. What most concerns him is that he and his colleagues in what he calls "that tiny band of pioneers" achieved their declared objective. In the piecemeal progress of Gaelic in education it is up to others now to take the campaign onward to further objectives.

In considering the way in which MacLean confronted that dichotomy which can too often arise between word and achievement we are afforded, I believe, a glimpse of the way in which he sees himself. His precise stature as a man of letters is for others to assess. It is a matter of crucial importance to himself that he played an active part in effecting a change which would be beneficial not only to the vitality of his own language and culture but potentially to the cultural life of Scotland as a whole.

AONGHAS MACNEACAIL

Some Aspects of Family and Local Background: An Interview with Sorley MacLean

This contribution comes directly and almost totally from a series of tape-recordings made in Edinburgh in September 1982.[1] These conversations — sometimes almost monologues — so far exceeded my hopes and expectations as to take over and completely transform the original scheme which was to use the tapes as a quarry from which material could be extracted. I had known that information and tradition of this kind, interacting with much else, had been revolving and evolving in Somhairle MacLean's mind for many years. This was obvious enough from some of his poetry, from other written work of his own such as the admirable paper on Raasay traditions in the *Transactions of the Gaelic Society of Inverness* (1977) and from his fascinating account of himself as a writer in *Chapman* (1976), both of which publications ought, ideally, to be read in conjunction with this piece.

A. Well, I am Somhairle mac Chaluim 'ic Caluim 'ic Iain 'ic Tharmaid 'ic Iain 'ic Tharmaid. That's as far back as we can go with certainty in Raasay.[2]

Q. And did your own people know that genealogy right back like that?

A. Oh yes. You know, there's a song that a woman composed to my great great grandfather who was called Tarmad Mór Iain 'ic Tharmaid to the same tune as 'Mhic Mhaoilein a shaorainn,'[3] but I've only got two verses of it that I heard from my father's sister Peggie MacLean.

> A Tharmaid Iain 'ic Tharmaid
> 'Se d'sheanchas a leòn mi
> Bhith cuimhneachadh do shùgraidh
> Gun dùil ri do phòsadh.

> A Tharmaid a' Chaolais
> Nan gorm shùilean bòidheach
> Cha d'aithnich thusa raoir mi
> Seach maighdeannan Osgaig.[4]

Anyway, we've been in Raasay for at least seven or eight generations.

Now the MacLeans: my father was a very fine singer, and he was a very fine piper, though he never played competitively. My brother Seonaidh used to say that he could recognise his father's playing anywhere. And my uncle Alasdair was a piper too, and my father was a very good singer. He used to sing the songs of Uilleam Ross.[5] I have never heard anyone who was as good at the song 'Gur mis' tha fo mhulad san am'[6] as he was, and, indeed, I hardly like to hear that song sung by anyone else. He was also marvellous at 'Crò Chinn t-Sàile',[7] the pibroch song. I remember him singing Rob Donn's 'Marbhrann Eóghain'[8] and the tune he had for it was the same as the tune of 'Mhic Dhughaill 'ic Ruairidh',[9] and I don't know if there's anyone alive who sings Rob Donn's 'Marbhrann Eóghain'.

He was well acquainted with the poetry of Iain Lom[10] but I don't think he was acquainted with the poetry of Alasdair mac Mhaighistir Alasdair,[11] though I remember him quoting that thing . . . him telling about what the Aireach Muileach[12] said of Alasdair mac Mhaighistir Alasdair:

> Cha b'e 'n creideamh ach am brosgal
> Chuir thu ghiùlan crois a' Phàpa.[13]

Anyway, my father was a very fine singer and my grandmother, my father's mother who died in 1923, was then about eighty-six and was living with us — in our home. She was Màiri Matheson. Her great grandfather came from Lochalsh . . . Màiri Iain 'ic Sheumais 'ic Dhòmhnaill Ruaidh.[14] Dòmhnall Ruadh came from Lochalsh as a miller to Steinnseal in Staffin[15] . . . She was born in Staffin. Dòmhnall Ruadh, her great grandfather, had the mill there and so did Seumas her grandfather, but her father Iain did not. They were cleared out of Staffin because her father had built a good house. They were on Major Fraser's estate and he was the worst proprietor in Skye at that time. She was about seven when they left Staffin and came to the Sgor, opposite Portree, outside Penifiler. Now I'm not sure what happened to the people in the Sgor — whether they were cleared from there or whether they left of their own accord — but they went to Braes. That's where her father died, Iain mac Sheumais. And she married my grandfather, Calum, and went to Raasay.

Now she was a very fine singer. In my early memories, she used to sing splendid old songs like 'Cumha Iain Ghairbh' ('S mi nam shuidhe air an fhaoilinn)[16], 'Tha na Féidh am Bràigh Uige'[17], 'Mo Shàth-ghal Goirt', by Màiri Nighean Alasdair Ruaidh,[18] 'Milis Mórag'[19] and 'Crò Chinn t-Sàile'. Oh, what didn't she sing, and it seems that she — the family — had brought songs from Lochalsh and Kintail. They had got songs when they were in Iochdar Thròndarnais,[20] for when Dòmhnall Ruadh came from Lochalsh to Staffin, he married another Matheson from a family that was in Skye already. She was from Peighinn Sóbhraig near Uig and so she had the songs of Iochdar Thròndarnais, such as there were, and the songs of Lochalsh and songs that they had around the Sgor and these places, and in Braes. She had a splendid memory. My mother's brother Alasdair[21] used to come across specially to write down songs that she had. She was confined to bed for the last four years of her life, but that didn't stop her singing. That didn't stop her singing and though she was of the Free Presbyterian Church, you know, that didn't hinder her at all. My uncle Alasdair used to take down the names of herbs and that sort of thing from her too. It seems she was tremendously knowledgeable.

And they say that she was very good looking herself. It seems that her nickname was Siùcar Iain 'ic Sheumais.[22] And her sister Caitrìona Mhór Iain 'ic Sheumais was married to Somhairle Neacail, Gille Dubh a' Bhràighe.[23] She [Caitriona] was a big woman and they say she was as strong as two men.

Q. And did they say that your grandmother was strong too . . . that there was strength in that family?

A. Oh, I think so. I think there was, right enough. Now, the MacLeans we belonged to, it seems . . . In Eilean nam Fear Móra,[24] in Raasay, there was Tarmad Mór Iain 'ic Tharmaid as he was called and his brother was called

Calum Mór and another of them was called Eachann Mór Sgreapadail,[25] the older brother, and another of them was called Niall Mór. But Tarmad Iain 'ic Tharmaid married a very small woman. She was a MacLeod. And his son Iain married another one after him. And so the MacLeans of Raasay got rather . . rather small! Well, my father's brother Alasdair was about six feet tall. My father was just about my own size.

Q. Now, before they called someone "Mór", he had to be a pretty big man, I suppose?

A. He had to be in Raasay — for there were very big men in Raasay. You know "Eilean nam Fear Móra" was not just an [idle] word. I can remember when I was young myself and I was at funerals in Raasay, I used to wonder at the size of the men — MacLeods and Nicolsons most of them. Oh there were others — others too . . .

Well, now, she [my grandmother] was full of old songs. She learned a lot from my grandfather. He was a fisherman and he had a smack, but he died of pneumonia when he was just fifty-two and she was a widow for much of her life. It seems she was a terribly good worker, and it seems that she was great at *speuradaireachd*, you know, forecasting what the weather would be. Oh, she was an able woman.

Q. And do you still remember the words of these songs you used to hear from her?

A. Oh goodness yes! I can't forget them somehow. I remember when I heard others singing 'Luinneag Mhic Leoid'[26] . . . and how different it was in comparison . . . she sang it so slowly . . .

Now my father's sister Peigi was the eldest of the family. She was ten years older than my father. Peigi used to come to stay with us for a month every year. She was working in Glasgow or . . in London pretty often. And we had to go out fishing with her. I used to go out, and I was terribly keen on boats, and Peigi, she'd get up at about eleven o'clock and away out to fish. We'd come back home for dinner and out again after that, and again in the evening, out to fish for saithe. I used to go out alone with her, and it was all songs. She was full of old songs. I used to threaten to go on strike unless she sang songs! I remember one day when everyone else had gone to the Portree Games, I stayed behind to take her out fishing. What fights and arguments would be going on about politics. You know, she had become a Tory about that time because of the First World War, though she had been a Socialist and a Nationalist and a Suffragette before the war — the First War. Yes. Oh yes . . she was a tremendous woman was Peigi!

My father's sister Floraidh was married to a Uistman so she wasn't in Raasay very often, but she was good at the songs too. She had a sort of refrain to 'Na Féidh am Bràigh Uige' that I never heard from anyone else in the world. It was curious, in a way: Peigi had things that her mother didn't have, as far as I can remember. I think it may have been from their father they got it, for he was a sort of bard, my grandfather Calum MacLean, though I don't know a single word of poetry he composed.

Q. Now when you mentioned the way Floraidh had the refrain of 'Tha na Féidh am Bràigh Uige', is this the way your own daughter Catriona has it?

A. Oh yes.

Q. And it was you yourself who taught it to her?

A. Between myself and Seonaidh. The most part of what Catriona has of the songs of Raasay, it was Seonaidh and I who taught her.

Well now, my mother, she was Ciorstaidh Shomhairle Mhóir Iain 'ic
Shomhairle Phìobaire 'ic Iain 'ic Eóghain.[27] That's as far as I can take it. Now
. . . my grandfather was . . . Somhairle Iain 'ic Shomhairle Phìobaire.
Somhairle Pìobaire was a piper in Spain and he got his hands damaged . . . the
frost got him and his fingers stiffened and he came out of the army. He was at
Corunna [1809] and it was on the retreat to Corunna that that happened to
him. It seems he was a very handsome man, Somhairle. There is a *port á beul*[28]
about him.

He was big and he was fair-haired but he married . . . It's in the *port á beul*
that he married *"An té bheag dhubh a mhill an fhuil".*

Q.   Oh, how does the *port* go? I don't think I've ever heard the *port*.
A.   Somhairle na Pìobadh
                               An gille grinn a bha Holm
                               Somhairle gun chomhairle
                               Gun tarrainn thu ó hó
                               Somhairle na Pìobadh
                               An gille grinn a bha Holm.[28]

Now, you know, there was something coming into it . . . a variation about
"An té bheag dhubh a mhill an fhuil".[29] She was a MacDonald . . . but,
Donald, I must admit she was a Nic Cuidhein![30]

And that Somhairle, Somhairle na Pìobadh, he was Somhairle mac Iain 'ic
Eóghain, and they say that his grandfather [Eóghan] was quite closely related
to Nicolson of Sgoirebreac[31] and that he was evicted from good land that he
held at the Bile near Portree for his part in helping in the escape of Prince
Charles, but I don't know about that.

Now when the people were cleared from Sgoirebreac, Somhairle Pìobaire
came to Braes, as an old man, and he was in Camus Tianabhaig and in Gead an
t-Sailleir. And I don't think there was much music in these Nicolsons, though
he was a piper, Somhairle Piobaire. And Iain mac Shomhairle, my great
grandfather on that side was married to another Nicolson in Braes, of another
line. And my mother's mother, she was called Iseabail Dhòmhnaill Bhàin.[32]
My grandfather Somhairle Mór Iain 'ic Shomhairle Phìobaire married
Iseabail MacLeod, daughter of Dòmhnall Bàn. These MacLeods were from
Raasay. They were in Torra Mìcheig and they came to Braes when the people
were cleared from Torra Mìcheig — where the golf course is, in Sconser. It was
Dòmhnall Bàn mac Alasdair 'ic Iain 'ic Ailein Ruaidh[33] they called him, and
Alasdair the father of Dòmhnall Bàn is buried in Raasay, but I don't know how
many generations they were in Skye, but Ailean Ruadh was in Raasay and
some say that it was from Lewis that Ailean Ruadh came ... no, not Ailean
Ruadh himself ... but his forebears, I suppose. Others say it was from Gairloch
or from Coigeach.

Now my grandmother, Iseabail Dhòmhnaill Bhàin, died when she was only
about fifty, in 1910 I think it was. It seems that though she was an adherent of
the Free Presbyterian Church ... she wasn't a communicant but she was, you
know, pretty circumspect. She was a very fine singer too and my mother's
people learned songs from her. Now my mother couldn't sing but her sister,
Ceit, was very good.

It seems their mother was a very fine singer and they got songs from her. My mother's brother Alasdair got songs from other people in Braes, especially from Màiri Iain 'ic Caluim.[34]

Now, my mother's sister Ceit left Portree School when her mother died and from then on she kept house for her father and one or two of her brothers. Teaching in Braes at the time of the First World War was Magaidh Chrìsdein, sister of Ailean Chrìsdein, the famous doctor, and Ceit got songs from her.[35] It was from her that Ceit got the tune and the words of 'Mo Robairneach Gaolach'.[36] Seumas Campbell[37] learnt it from my Aunt Ceit.

Now Dòmhnall MacLeod, Dòmhnall Bàn [32] as they called him, was married to Caitriona Iain Stiubhairt[38] and the Stewarts, so it seems, had brains — more brains than most people had. My great-grandmother's brother Aonghus was the first witness to give evidence before the first Crofters' Commission. But the Stewarts had no music in them. And Iain Stewart was a bard.

These Stewarts were in Peighinn a' Chorrain in the Rent Roll in 1733.

Well, now, that's . . the Nicolsons and the MacLeods and the Stewarts.

Q. And so there was music coming in from every side.

A. Yes. Yes. I think from every side — from every side.

Q. And now what about memory? You know, you've got an outstandingly good memory yourself, Somhairle, in many ways.

A. Well . . . It seems that Caitriona Iain Stiùbhairt, my great grandmother, had a tremendous memory and I know that my father's mother had a tremendous memory: Màiri Iain 'ic Sheumais[39] — Matheson. . . . But I didn't have the memory Seonaidh had . . . Oh, he had a marvellous memory, my brother Seonaidh. You know, books of the Iliad, he had them off by heart without ever trying to learn them and they say there were seventy pibrochs — he could tell if he heard three notes from any one of them, which it was from. And he was late starting piping. It was in Cambridge he took up piping properly — though he used to play the chanter when he was a boy. But I think for Gaelic poetry, the old songs, that my own memory was every bit as good as his. It was as if I couldn't forget one word of them, well, until a few years back. I'm not quite as good now.

Q. Was it just as easy for you to remember something you had read as something you had heard from oral tradition — or did the two things go together?

A. Ah, it was pretty good, you know, for something I read when I was young. Even now when I wonder about my memory, whether it's deteriorated, I have a try at the 'Birlinn'[40] and I never heard the 'Birlinn' in oral tradition. Now the second last year I was in Plockton, I had to start teaching Latin. The lady who taught Latin was off ill for a whole year. And I remember the second book of the Aeneid — I almost had it off by heart. But oh, we were taught Latin so well in Portree.

I think, the thing was, I couldn't sing as most of my people could, so I got tremendously keen about a lot of the old Gaelic songs. And so, though I couldn't get the pitch right, it used to drive spears through me almost, the rhythm, the movement and the time, when I heard something I thought was wrong.

Q. And so you can still keep the two things apart — the way you heard it from one person and the way you heard it from another?

A. Oh yes. Oh I think I can. I think I can . . .[41] Well, that's how it was, but my memory is going now.

Well, I think I told you about Caitriona Iain Stiubhairt, that her memory was famous. And my grandmother — my father's mother, Màiri Iain 'ic Sheumais. But there was also on the MacLean side, my grandfather's brother Tarmad. He was famous in Raasay for his memory and for how precise he was about things. Dr. Galbraith made a map of place-names in the south of Raasay and it seems he got almost all the names from Tarmad. Tarmad was born in Sgreapadal and then he lived in the Fearna, then in Bailechùirn and then in Osgaig. When people used to come from Luib or from Applecross with funerals to Raasay, it was Tarmad who used to tell them if they didn't know where their people were buried. Now Tarmad died the same year as my grandmother Màiri Iain 'ic Sheumais, in 1923, in the autumn. Everyone said of him that anything he said would be so accurate and if he said something wrong, he thought it was just like telling a lie. That's the sort of man he was.

Q.   You have what some people might call an upper register, an extra register of the language that you would not have had if you did not have a Biblical and religious background?

A.   Oh, there was no doubt at all about that. And also it gave you a knowledge of variants — dialectal variants — because at communion times you might have a minister from far away with a very different Gaelic, and elders speaking on the Fridays also with a very different Gaelic. One was also rather aware of how certain words were in different registers in different parts of the country, which is very important and which often is a stumbling-block to literary critics of Gaelic at the present day because they don't know, so many of them, how registers can vary dialectally.

Q.   I know that you have registers derived from a very wide reading of all sorts, but would you say yourself that possibly most of the language you use in your own poetry you knew naturally?

A.   I would say the *great* bulk of it I knew naturally. Perhaps there is a word here and there that I actually picked up in my teens from the reading of Gaelic poetry or from hearing it. But I would say the great bulk, almost without exception, comes naturally. I've invented a neologism once or twice, but very few.

      I think, you see, that the long preachings and prayers in Gaelic at the Free Presbyterian Church and the Free Church, combined with our family's richness in oral tradition on more than one side, had a very considerable effect on me; and the fact, for instance, that my father was so very well versed in Gaelic — in Gaelic poetry and song, and so were some of my mother's people. Because, you see, there was a considerable difference, for instance, between Raasay and the Braes district and Tròndarnais district, and Raasay was in some things more like Applecross in Gaelic. And I think that as far as vocabulary went, I was in a particularly favourable position because I was brought up in a Free Presbyterian environment with an awful lot of Gaelic preaching and, also, that my family, in such an environment, were unusual tradition bearers, especially of song, and, to a certain extent, of tales too.

Q.   So you had a combination of all these strands.

A.   I think I had. And, of course, I'm perfectly sure that my father had not only a wonderful ear for music but that he had a very unusual linguistic sense, and an interest in it. I used to hear arguments on this between my father and my mother's eldest brother Alexander, Alasdair Nicolson, the man who made the

Gaelic grammar and the *History of Skye*. For instance, on the Friday of the communion, you might be in church, or usually you were outside because there was no room in the church, from half past eleven until four o'clock. And you might hear anything up to twenty elders "speaking to the question". And the variety of Gaelic could be immense.

Q. Perhaps we'd better explain "speaking to the question" [bruidhinn *or* labhairt air a' cheist.] This took place on the Friday; communion went on from Thursday till Monday.

A. Till midday on Monday.

Q. Yes. And that was twice a year, wasn't it?

A. Well, sometimes it was only once a year but sometimes it was twice a year . . . The Thursday was the Fast-day: there would be a sermon in the morning: two sermons.

Q. But you can't remember any traditions of people actually fasting on the Thursday.

A. No. None whatsoever of fasting, of actual fasting. But it was considered in some way almost a Sunday — the Thursday. Now Friday was the day on which somebody proposed a text and as many elders as could, from all over, different places, spoke on it, and delivered a miniature sermon. I think they knew beforehand what it was going to be, and very often, of course, they couldn't all be called — there would be perhaps up to twenty of them. Of course, they would be from different parts of Skye and the mainland opposite, Gairloch, Applecross, Lochalsh.

Q. And this, in effect, would be a debating session bringing in theological ideas?

A. It would vary from a purely theological discussion, to a giving of their own particular experience and of course you would hear so much, even long quotations transmitted orally from people as far back as Maighistir Lachlainn, Maighistir Ruairidh, Céit Mhór Loch Carann, 'Blind Munro', the woman called Bean a' Chreideamh Mhóir,[42] and so on. And, as I use in one of the poems, you would hear a phrase like "somebody had this", meaning that some point had come home to him and he had illustrated and so on . . . And the fact that our family were, I think, for their place, unusually rich in oral tradition, meant that our vocabulary was extensive. Then, of course, I took Gaelic in Portree School at quite a young age where I read every bit of poetry I could come across, and, of course, as I have often said, I made up for my lack in pitch in music by having an inability to forget the words of any Gaelic song I liked, even if I heard it only once. And . . . words became as it were second nature to me.

Q. On the subject of taking communion, the ordinary person was more or less forbidden, wasn't he? It's only those who were in a 'state of grace' who took communion, wasn't it?

A. Oh, of course. It's said very strictly in the Shorter Catechism — only a very, very small minority — I don't think five per cent of the congregation, and most of them would be old people.

Q. Would you say that this set the seal on you having turned your back on the 'vanities of the world'?

A. Oh, completely. Yes, it did. There's been an awful lot of exaggeration of a kind of self-righteousness, because those people were not self-righteous. I mean, in all fairness, there might have been some cases of hypocrites and all that, but there would be in anything. So you see . . especially in the Thirties when a lot of people were talking and finding all the faults of Scotland in Calvinism, I was saying, "What the devil do all these people, writers and all those, know about Calvinism?"

Q.   And this despite the fact that you had turned your back on Calvinism?

A.   Oh yes, one has to be fair. Among those people, there are so many I know who were saintly, just saintly men.

Q.   You might reject part of the philosophy but you were still . .?

A.   Yes. I was sympathetic in the sense that I didn't find those people hypocrites. Because the whole business of this sinfulness, the desperate wickedness of the human heart precluded self-righteousness.

Q.   Then there was the Monday, of course, which wound the whole thing up in a way. Didn't it?

A.   Yes, the Monday service was called Latha a' Chàinidh[43] in which there was a denunciation of . . Well, it didn't mention the Catholic Church, that was beyond mention. The Episcopalians weren't worth mentioning. The Church of Scotland was hardly worth mentioning. The concentration was on the backsliding "so-called Free Church of Scotland". And they wound up with scientists, spiritualists and socialists. But that was some ministers . . . And, of course, then, there were very different people. You see there was the wonderfully human Ewen MacQueen. A preacher with a wonderful register was Ewen MacQueen, a marvellous Gaelic . . with the kind of ability to change the registers and to use the local colour, to use everything. He was a wonderfully human man: he was even amusing in telling of the depths of depravity to which in his unregenerate days he had sunk, such as drinking whisky out of an envelope! Time and place specified!

Q.   He had a very great charisma, hadn't he?

A.   Oh, wonderful, wonderful charisma, and, I've said this, that if his sermons could have been recorded *in toto* you would have a Gaelic prose amazing in its richness, variety and raciness. Well, there were others, but, of course, my experience is limited pretty well to when I was young, and to Free Church and Free Presbyterian.

Q.   What of the influence of landscape?

A.   Well, you see, I'm very much affected by what one calls physical beauty. I think I have always been, and Skye, of course, is an island of an amazing variety of beauty, but, above all, apart from the great sea cliffs of Biod an Adhar in Diùirinnis and the cliffs of Bioda Ruadh and of Minginnis and so on, you get the great winding sea lochs and you get a lot of the high green, like the green dome of the Storr suddenly plunging into pretty well perpendicular cliffs of 500-600 feet and then, but above all, the Cuillins. It's a very, very spectacular landscape and it is the kind of landscape that easily resolves itself into what you might call heroic symbols. Now, Raasay has a wonderful situation in relation to Skye and the mainland of Wester Ross, which is very beautiful too. And Raasay has this great geological variety, hence a great variety of scenery within it. What fascinated me especially was the kind of semi-limestone belt from the Fearns to Screapadal including Hallaig: the rocks . . most of them being what they call inferior oolite which is something to do with limestone and sandstone mixed, and the kind of narrow valleys, the great shelter, this geological variety and the tertiary and mesozoic rocks, two thirds of it in the south, then the Torridonian, north about Brochel and so on, and then the Lewisian; also, the woods of Raasay which, apart from the native birches, hazels, rowans and so on, are now nearly all recently planted conifers. When I was young there were not only conifers and Scots firs, but almost every conceivable deciduous tree and other kind of trees, in the two woods planted from about 1870 or 1875 onwards, which made the landscape of Raasay a great contrast to the Cuillins and also to the Red Hills, the so-called Red Hills, of Skye. And, of course, we had the great landscape, granted from most parts of Raasay we could only see part of the Cuillins, the Sgurr nan Gillean to Bruach na Frìthe group, but you have the great landscape of Blàbheinn and the Garbhbheinn further to the south-east. Also the fact that Raasay was such a wonderful centre-point, from which you had such views, from most of Raasay, from the coastline of Skye, from Beinn na Caillich in Broadford to Rudha nam Bràithrean in Staffin and a very spectacular coastline. And I think there must be very few stretches of water, of seawater in the Highlands, more spectacular than the south part of the Sound of Raasay which is called the Clàrach. And this, I think, had . . Oh, I'm sure of it, had a very big effect on me.

I was also keen on the sea and boats, but became less keen when, in my early twenties, I went to teach in Portree School and started going to the Cuillins. In those days I could get very few people to go with me, practically nobody in those days, and I used to wander about alone on them, ridge-wandering and doing some rock-climbing to avoid detours and being there in all kinds of conditions. To me the whole thing was bound up with the history of Skye and Raasay, as I knew it. Because, you see, I was of that, in every way, except that I knew that my paternal grandmother's people had come from Lochalsh perhaps 250 years before that. And also, you see, even at my youngest and most . . . what you might call politically radical time of my life, I had this sense of continuity. And when I was up on the top of the Cuillins or on Dùn Cana I mean, it wasn't just a case of scenery, but it was always very much intermingled with the people.

I came to maturity at the time of the great symbolist movement in European poetry, which you've got in Yeats, Eliot, MacDiarmid, Blok in Russia and Paul Valéry in France, and my symbols came mostly from my immediate environment, because in many ways my immediate physical environment was very varied. The Cuillins naturally became a symbol of difficulty, hardship and heroic qualities as against, as it were, the softness and relative luxury of the woods of Raasay with all their own contradictions.

So you see, all this was so much associated with what I knew from oral tradition, song and even stories. The fact, for instance, that you remembered in an old story that the boulders of Mol Stamhain were thrown up on dry land the day that Iain Garbh Mac Gille Chaluim was drowned. Oh, there were other stories too which involved not storm but witches, about the death of Iain Garbh Mac Gille Chaluim.

When I was younger, I wasn't affected so much by colour as I was by outline in landscape, and, of course the outlines of Skye are spectacular and even heroic, and, well, perhaps you've got even greater variety of colour . . in Raasay, but there is the atmospheric colour to remember, too. I remember an evening being on Sgurr Alasdair, a summer evening, and seeing glitter — the glitter of the sun, west of Barra. And another day, for instance, being on the

Cuillins, with swirling mist on the narrow top of Sgurr a' Ghreadaidh, and the mist suddenly clearing and there was a glint of sun on the wings of a golden eagle standing on a ledge about twenty feet below me. I grew up at that time, when symbolism was such a thing in European poetry and I was affected a lot by .. people, more by MacDiarmid and Yeats, and my symbols almost automatically became the landscape of my physical environment. But, of course, that was always affected, blended with what I knew of the history of my people.

DONALD ARCHIE MACDONALD

NOTES

1. These tapes, now SA1982/150-57 in the archives of the School of Scottish Studies, may be consulted by prior arrangement with Somhairle MacLean and D. A. MacDonald. The archives also contain a video recording of an interview with Dr. MacLean.
2. "Somhairle son of Calum, son of Calum son of Iain son of Tarmad son of Iain son of Tarmad." Somhairle is often 'anglicised' as Samuel, Calum as Malcolm (from the older Maolcoluim), Iain as John, Tarmad/Tormod as Norman. The MacLean family are almost certain that they were originally from North Uist, of the family of the MacLean tacksmen of Boreray. The late James MacLean, Yr. of Glensanda, lecturer in History at Edinburgh University, apparently said that Tarmad, the most distant name in the above genealogy, was the son of Iain who was the son of Neil, the first of these MacLeans to come to the MacLeod lands in Skye. He also stated that this Iain was the first of the family to go to Raasay. Somhairle MacLean does not know the source of James MacLean's information. Catherine MacLean (Caitriona Uilleim), a fine local tradition-bearer in Raasay, held that her own family and Somhairle MacLean's were the same people. This family, of whom the famous Pipe Major William MacLean of Kilcreggan was also a member, had a tradition that the first of them to come to Raasay was called Iain Mór Buidhe ("Big Yellow John") and that he was a son of a MacLean of Boreray. See also Somhairle MacLean's article in *Transactions of the Gaelic Society of Inverness*, 1977, pp 377-8.
3. "MacMillan I would excuse you": mock love-song by a Kintail bard called MacCulloch *alias* An Tàillear Crùbach, "The Lame Tailor".
4. Tarmad son of Iain son of Tarmad

    > It was your words that wounded me
    > Remembering your love-talk
    > With no hope of marrying you.

    > Tarmad from Caolas
    > Of the bonny blue eyes
    > You did not acknowledge me last night
    > Ahead of the maidens of Osgaig.
5. William Ross (1762-90), the famous Skye and Gairloch bard.
6. "I am full of sorrow at this time".
7. Traditional: 'The Crò of Kintail'.

8. 'Elegy for Ewen', by the famous Sutherland bard Rob Donn Mackay, "Brown-Haired Rob" (1714-78).
9. Traditional lament (17th Century?): "Son of Dughall Son of Ruairidh".
10. Iain Lom MacDonald, "Bare John", the famous Lochaber bard (*c.* 1620-1710).
11. "Alasdair son of the Rev. Alasdair", probably the most famous of the eighteenth-century bards (*c.* 1700-*c.* 1770).
12. "The Mull Herdsman".
13.   It was not faith but flattery
           that drove you to carry the Pope's Cross.
This refers to the fact that Alasdair Mac Mhaighistir Alasdair became a Catholic convert, the implication being that this was a flattering gesture to the Jacobite cause. Elsewhere in these recordings (SA 1982/151A) Somhairle MacLean has pointed out that the fact that his father did not seem to be well acquainted with MacDonald's poetry may have been due to prejudice against him in Presbyterian areas for his change of religion, perhaps also for his scurrilous satire 'Di-moladh Móraig', 'In Dispraise of Morag'.
14. "Mary daughter of John son of James son of Red Haired Donald".
15. Here and *passim* I have translated An Taobh Sear as "Staffin", which is the usual practice in Skye. An Taobh Sear is on the east side of Tròndarnais.
16. 'The Lament for John Garbh' ('As I sit on the raised beach'). Traditional lament for "Stalwart John" MacLeod, Chief of Raasay, drowned in 1671. The composition is usually attributed to his sister.
17. 'The Deer are in the Braes of Uig'. Traditional lament.
18. 'My bitter fill of weeping' by the famous bardess Mary MacLeod (*c.* 1615-1707), 'Mary daughter of Red-Haired Alasdair'.
19. 'Sweet is Morag'. Traditional love song.
20. "Lower Tròndarnais", i.e. the north-east wing of Skye.
21. Alexander Nicolson, Lecturer in Gaelic at Jordanhill College of Education, Glasgow.
22. "Iain mac Sheumais' sugar".
23. Caitriona Matheson: "Big Caitriona daughter of Iain mac Sheumais" was married to "Somhairle son of Neacal (Nicol), the Black Lad of Braes", a famous strong man. He was a Nicolson.
24. "Island of the Big Men".
25. "Big Eachann (Hector) of Sgreapadal".
26. 'MacLeod's Ditty' by Mary MacLeod (Màiri Nighean Alasdair Ruaidh).
27. "Christina daughter of Big Somhairle son of John son of Somhairle the Piper son of John son of Ewen".
28.   Somhairle of the Pipes
           The handsome lad who was in Holm
           Somhairle ill advised
           I would grab you o ho!
           Somhairle of the Pipes
           The handsome lad who was in Holm.
A *port á beul* ("mouth-tune"/"mouth-music") is a diddling type of song, usually a dance tune. Holm is north of Portree.
29. "The little black one who spoilt the blood".
30. The surname MacCuidhein is often anglicised as MacQueen or MacQuien,

but in Skye always MacDonald. It was relatively common for lesser-known surnames to be replaced by one of the better-known Clan names.
31. These Nicolsons, Clann 'ic Neacail Sgoirebreac were an important tacksman family located for centuries at Sgoirebreac (Scorrybreck) near Portree.
32. "Iseabail Daughter of Fair-Haired Donald".
33. "Fair-Haired Donald son of Alasdair son of John son of Red-Haired Allan".
34. "Mary, daughter of John son of Calum".
35. "Allan son of Christopher" and "Maggie daughter of Christopher"; the well-known singer and doctor in Skye, Dr. Allan MacDonald, and his sister Maggie MacDonald.
36. Roughly "My beloved bonny lad".
37. The late J. C. M. Campbell of Kintail and London, a well-known Gaelic singer and friend of Somhairle MacLean.
38. "Caitriona daughter of John Stewart".
39. "Mary daughter of John son of James".
40. 'Birlinn Chlann Ràghnaill' ('Clan Ranald's Galley') by Alasdair Mac Mhaighistir Alasdair.
41. Quotes a verse heard from his grandmother and a variant from another source.
42. "The Woman of Great Faith".
43. "The Day of Scolding".

Register of Gaelic Placenames
in the Poems of Sorley MacLean

Translations are given where place-names are currently transparent to Gaelic speakers. Many Highland place-names, especially in the Hebrides, are partly or wholly Norse in origin, and are hence at least partially opaque. Nevertheless, the most commonly recurring Norse elements may carry some meaning, if only at the intuitive level of association with certain natural features or with other names containing the same element. Originally Norse elements found in the following list include the suffixed elements -*aidh*/-*eidh* 'island', -*(bh)aig* 'settlement', -*(bh)al* 'steep hill, cliff', -*(e)art*/-*ort* 'fjord', -*dal* 'dale' and -*n(a)is* 'promontory'.

A

Abhainn Arois: Aros Burn. Raasay. It flows south-west from Loch na Mnà near Dùn Cana and enters the sea at Inverarish.

Abhainn Chluaidh. The River Clyde.

Adharc an Sgurr Dheirg. 'The Horn of the Red Peak'. One of the Cuillin peaks, Skye. It is known as the 'Inaccessible Pinnacle'.

An t-Aigeach. 'The Stallion'. A steep hill on Neist point at the western tip of Diùrinis, Skye.

An Aird Ghiuthais. 'The Promontory of the Pine'. The peninsula to the west of Raasay House, Raasay.

Aird Mhór Shrath Shuardail. 'The Great Promontory of the Strath of Swordale'. Strathaird from Torrin to Elgol, Skye.

Allt Éire: Auldearn. 'The Stream of Éire'. Eighteen miles east of Inverness, on the Moray Firth (Nairn). Here Montrose and Alasdair MacDonald defeated a Covenant army on 9 May, 1645.

Aodann Bàn: Edinbane. 'The White Slope'. At the head of Loch Greshornish, south of Loch Snizort, Skye.

Aoighre: Eyre. Township in the south of Raasay.

Arasaig: Arisaig. On the west coast of the mainland between Morar and Moidart, Inverness.

B

Baile Chùirn. 'Cairn-Township' (?). Two and a half miles north of Raasay House, Raasay.

Barraidh: Barra. An island in the Outer Hebrides, south of Uist. A rich source of traditional lore.

Beinn Dianabhaig: Ben Tianavaig. Mountain south-east of Portree, Skye.

Beinn Dubhagraich: Ben Duagraich. A mountain to the east of Bracadale, Skye.

Beinn Li: Ben Lee. A mountain to the west of Braes and north of Loch Sligachan, Skye. In 1865 the common grazing was let to a tenant and not till 1887 did the crofters of Braes win the right to graze their stock on the mountain.

Beinn na Gréige. 'The Greek Mountain'. Used by the poet to denote Mt. Olympus or Mt. Parnassus.

Beinn na Lice. 'The Mountain of the Flagstone'. In the south-east of Raasay, between Hallaig and Na Feàrnaibh.

Bhatarnais: Waternish. One of the four divisions of Skye made by the Norse, with Diùrinis, Tròndairnis and Minginis.

Bhatarsaidh: Vatersay. An island to the south of Barra, Outer Hebrides.

A' Bheinn Mhór. 'The Great Mountain'. In South Uist, Outer Hebrides.

A' Bhuaile Ghréine. 'The Sunny Fold'. Deirdre's retreat at the head of Loch Etive in Argyll, to the north-east of Oban.

Am Bidein. 'The Pinnacle'. One of the Cuillin peaks, Skye. At the western end of Druim nan Ràmh.

Am Bioda Ruadh. 'The Red Point'. A rocky point south of Talisker, Skye.

Blà Bheinn: Blaven. A mountain to the east of the Cuillins, Skye.

Boraraig: Boreraig. In the north of Diùrinis. Traditionally the site of the MacCrimmons' piping school 1500-1800, Skye. The MacCrimmons were the hereditary pipers of the MacLeods of Dunvegan.

Am Bràigh: Braes. The district between Ben Dianabhaig and Loch Sligeachan, Skye. In 1882 there was a battle between crofters and policemen, which led to the appointment of the Crofters' Commission in 1883.

Bràigh Aoineart: Brae Eynort. The uplands on the north side of Loch Eynort, Skye.

Bràcadal: Bracadale. The whole district round the east side of Loch Bracadale, Skye.

Bruach na Frithe. 'The Brae of the Deerforest'. One of the Cuillin peaks, Skye.

Brunnal. On the eastern shore of Loch Eynort, about one and a half miles south of Grùla, Skye.

Am Buta Leódhasach: The Butt of Lewis. The northernmost tip of the island of Lewis, Outer Hebrides.

C

An Càrn Mór, or **An Càrn.** 'The (Large) Cairn'. A hill to the west of Screapadal in Raasay.

Caisteal Bhròchaill: Brochel Castle. In the north of Raasay. In ruins. Built for MacSwan or MacLeod of Raasay. Visited by Boswell and Dr Johnson in 1773, when it was already uninhabited.

Calgaraidh: Calgary. In the north-west of Mull, Argyll.

Camus Alba. 'The Bay of Scotland'(?). Raasay. A small bay north-west of Raasay House, with white shingle and sand.

An Caolas: The Kyle of Barra. The strait between Barra and South Uist, Outer Hebrides.

Caol Ile: The Sound of Islay. Between Islay and Jura, Inner Hebrides.

Caol na h-Airde. 'The Strait of the Promontory'. The Narrows of Raasay, between the promontory in Braes and An Aird Ghiuthais in Raasay.

Ceannachnoc. 'The Top or Head Hill'(?). At the head of Glen Morrison, above the southern end of Loch Ness, in the Grants' country, Inverness.

Ceann Loch Aoineart: Kinloch Ainort. 'The Head of Loch Ainort'. Opposite Scalpay, Skye.

Ceann Loch Nibheis: Kinloch Nevis. 'The Head of Loch Nevis'. Between Knoydart and Morar, in the land of MacDonell of Glengarry, Inverness.

An Caol, or **An Caol Mór.** 'The (Great) Kyle'. The Sound between Raasay and Scalpay.

Clachan. 'Village containing a Church, Kirkton'. The principal village of Raasay, containing Raasay House, and the old cemetery of Cill mo Luag. The other Clachan is the Kirkton of Loch Aills. See **Loch Aills.**

A' Chlàrach. The stretch of sea between Caol na h-Airde and An Caol Mór. See **An Caol Mór.**

A' Chreag or **Creag Mheircil.** 'Meirceal's Rock'. It runs north parallel to the east coast of Raasay, from Dùn Cana to Screapadal.

A' Chomraich: Applecross. In full Comraich mo Ruibhe, 'The Sanctuary of St Maol Ruibhe'. The mainland area opposite Raasay, Wester Ross.

A' Chùil. 'The Recess'. A little bay about half a mile north of Camus Alba, Raasay. See **Camus Alba.**

An Cladh. 'The Cemetery'. "Dà chladh saoibhir leth mo chinnidh" (The two rich graveyards of half my people) in 'Coilltean Ratharsair' are Cnoc an Rà and Cill mo Luag, where the MacLeans and MacLeods are buried. The poet's mother's people, the Nicolsons, are buried in Sròn Dhiùirinis or on the Meall of Port-righ. See **Sròn Dhiùirinis.**

Cnòideart: Knoydart. The mainland area between Morar and Glenelg, opposite Sleat, Skye.

Cnoc an Rà. 'The Hill of the Fortress'. (?) A ridge running about three quarters of a mile northward from Raasay House. The cemetery is on the eastern slope. The older cemetery of Cill mo Luag is in Clachan. See **Clachan.**

Cnoc Hàllainn: Hallin Hill. Near Daliburgh in South Uist, Outer Hebrides.

Coire Lagain. 'Corrie of the Hollow'. In the Cuillins, about half a mile west of Sgurr Alasdair, Skye.

Coire Mhadaidh. 'The Dog's Corrie'. In the Cuillins, facing north-west, at the foot of Bidein Druim nan Ràmh, Skye.

Coire Monaidh: Corriemoney. 'The Corrie of the Moor'.(?) At the head of Glen Urquhart, about nine miles west of Loch Ness, Inverness.

Corcal: Corcul. A small area about half a mile west of Plockton, Wester Ross. See **Am Ploc.**

Còrnaig. In Tiree, Inner Hebrides.

Creagan Beaga. 'Little Rocks'. A ridge above the road between Camus Alba and A' Chùil, with trees on the slopes, Raasay.

Creag Dallaig. 'The Rock of Dallag'. A rocky, precipitous hill to the south of Plockton, facing north, Wester Ross. See **Am Ploc.**

Creag Mheircil. See **A' Chreag.**

Crò, Crò Chinn Tàile: The Cro of Kintail. 'The Sheep-Pen at the Head of the Salt-Water'. A valley, containing a circular fort, at the head of Loch Duich, Ross & Cromarty, which was the home of John MacRae (Iain Mac Mhurchaidh), who went to Carolina in about 1770, and became a United Empire Loyalist.

Cruachan Suidh-Fhinn. 'The Stack of Fionn's Seat'. A mountain southwest of Portree, Skye.

Cuan Canach: Sea of Canna. The open water to the south of Skye.

Cùil-Lodair: Culloden. 'The Back of the Little Pool'.(?) On Drumossie Moor, about five miles east of Inverness, where Prince Charles Edward Stuart was defeated in 1746.

An Cuilithionn. The Cuillin Hills, Skye.

D

Diùirinis: Duirinish. A district in Skye: see **Bhatarnais.**

Drochaid Aonachain: Spean Bridge. At the foot of Glen Spean in Lochaber, Inverness, about three miles before the River Spean flows into Loch Lochy.

Druim Buidhe: Drumbuie. 'Yellow Ridge'. South-west of Plockton, Wester Ross. See **Am Ploc.**

Dùis MhicLeoid. 'The Country of MacLeod (in Skye)', i.e. Diùrinis, Bràcadal and Minginis.

Dùn Bheagain, An Dùn: Dunvegan. 'The Fort of Beagan'. Ancestral home of the chiefs of the MacLeods of Skye, said to have been first built in the ninth century.

Dùn Cana. The highest mountain in Raasay.

Dùn Éideann. Edinburgh.

Dùn Sgàthaich: Dunscaith. 'The Fort of Sgàthach'. In Sleat, Skye. The ancestral home of the MacDonalds of Sleat. Famous in early Irish literature as the site of a school for warriors where the hero Cuchullin learnt the tricks of battle from the queen, Sgàthach.

E

An Eaglais Bhréige. 'The False Church'. A great rock on the eastern shore of Raasay, opposite the northern end of Creag Mheircil.

Earra-Ghàidheal: Argyll. 'The Border Region of the Gaels'(?). The West of Scotland from Ardnamurchan southward to the Mull of Kintyre.

Eige: Eigg. An island of the Inner Hebrides. It consists of two ranges of hills joined by a neck of low-lying ground.

An t-Eilean Sgitheanach: The Isle of Skye. 'The Winged Island'(?); also known as Eilean a' Cheò, 'The Island of the Mist', or simply as An t-Eilean, 'The Island'.

Eirisgeidh: Eriskay. An island between Barra and South Uist, Outer Hebrides.

An Eist Fhiadhaich: Neist Point. 'The Wild Stallion'.(?) The most westerly point of Skye, in Diùirinis.

F

Faoileann Aoighre. 'The Raised Beach of Eyre'. Above Inver Eyre, Raasay. See **Aoighre.**

Na Feàrnaibh: Fearns. 'The Alder-Trees'. Crofts south of Beinn na Lice in Raasay.

An Fhionna-Choire. 'The Fair Corrie'. A corrie on the northern edge of the Cuillins, below Bruach na Frìthe, Skye.

G

Geusdo: Gesto. At the northern end of Loch Harport, Skye. The ancient house, now in ruins, was the home of Captain Neil MacLeod of Gesto, who made a collection of pibrochs in the old syllabic notation, of which he published twenty in 1828.

A' Ghàrsbheinn: Garsven. A peak in the south of the Cuillins, Skye.

Glàmaig. A conical peak south of Loch Sligachan, Skye.

Glaschu. Glasgow.

Gleann Garadh: Glengarry. 'The Valley of Garadh'. Runs westward from the Great Glen towards Knoydart. The land of the MacDonalds of Glengarry.

Gleann Aoighre: Glen Eyre. 'The Valley of Eyre', Raasay. See **Aoighre.**

Gleann Dail: Glendale. 'The Valley-dale'. In Diùrinis, Skye. Home of John MacPherson who led the crofters there in the 1880s.

Gleann Da Ruadh: Glendaruel. 'Valley of the Two Red Ones'(?). In Cowal, Argyll. One of the places where Deirdre and Naoise lived in Scotland.

Gleann Eite: Glen Etive. The valley around upper Loch Etive, Argyll. See **A' Bhuaile Ghréine.**

Gleann Ruaidh: Glenroy. 'The Valley of the Roy'. Enters Glen Spean above Spean Bridge, Inverness (see **Drochaid Aonachain**). Montrose led his troops down the 'Parallel Roads' of the valley to attack Inverlochy in February, 1645.

Glinn nan Granndach. 'The Valleys of the Grants'. Glenmoriston and Glen Urquhart, north-west of Loch Ness, Inverness.

Grimeasaidh: Grimsay. An island between Benbecula and North Uist, Outer Hebrides.

Grùla. Township at the head of Loch Eynort in Minginis, Skye.

H

Hàclait. In Benbecula, Outer Hebrides.

Hallaig. Deserted township north of Beinn na Lice in Raasay. Cleared after 1846.

Hòmhstaidh: Homhsta. Between Tigharry and Griminish Point in North Uist, Outer Hebrides.

I

An t-Inbhir. 'The Estuary'. The rivers that drain the high lands to the west and north-west of Dun Cana in Raasay enter the sea at An t-Inbhir, Raasay.

Inbhir Aoighre: Inver Eyre. 'The Estuary of Eyre', Raasay. See **Aoighre.**

Inbhir Chéitein: Inverkeithing. In Fife, close to the northern end of the Forth Bridge. Here, on 20 July 1651, a detachment of Leslie's Royalist army was defeated by Lambert. Nearly 700 MacLeans were killed.

L

An Leac. 'The Flagstone'. Township on the east side of Beinn na Lice in Raasay.

Lionacro: Linicro. Tròndairnis, Skye.

Liondail: Lyndale. At the head of Loch Snizort, Skye.

Loch Aills: Lochalsh. On the mainland, opposite the eastern tip of Skye, Wester Ross. The poet's Matheson ancestors originally came from the Loch Aills district.

Loch Harport. A long inlet stretching from Bracadale into Minginis, Skye.

Loch Shlaopain: Loch Slapin. A sea-loch east of the Aird of Strath, Skye.

Loch Shnigheasort: Loch Snizort. Between Bhatarnais and Tròndairnis, Skye.

M

Am Màm. 'The Round Hill'. North of the Cuillins, at the head of Glen Brittle, Skye.

Mararabhlainn: Mararaulin. A marsh north of the Cuillins, Skye.

Minginis: Minginish. One of the Norse divisions of Skye north of the Cuillins.

Mol Steinnseil Stamhainn. 'The Pebble-beach of Stenscholl in Staffin'. In Tròndairnis, Skye.

Mórair: Morar. The area to the south of Knoydart, Inverness.

Mosgaraidh: Mosgary. Mountainous area west of Loch Ainort and south of Glàmaig, Skye.

Mùideart: Moidart. The area to the south of Morar, Inverness.

Muile: Mull. The land of the MacLeans. The Clearances of the nineteenth century desolated the island. Described as, "ane grate rough isle" by Dean Munro.

P

Pàislig: Paisley. The adopted home of the South Uist poet, Donald Macintyre (Dòmhnall Ruadh).

Peigh'nn nan Aoirean: Peninerine. Home of the story-teller Duncan MacDonald in South Uist, Outer Hebrides.

A' Phàirce Mhór. 'The Big Field'. South of Oskaig, the poet's birthplace in Raasay.

Am Ploc: Plockton. On the southern shore of Loch Carron, west of Strome Ferry, Wester Ross. The poet was Headmaster of the Secondary School there from 1956 to 1972.

Poll a' Bhainne. 'Milk Hollow'. A little to the north of Baile Chùirn, Raasay. See **Baile Chùirn.**

Port-righ: Portree. Popularly explained as 'The King's Harbour' and associated with James V, who anchored in the bay in 1540. The chief town of Skye.

Priseal: Preshal. The name of a rocky hill above Talisker in Minginis, Skye.

R

Ratharsair: Raasay. East of Skye, 14 miles long, 27 square miles in area. After the '45, nearly all the houses were burnt, and the sheep, cattle and boats removed or destroyed. Dr Johnson calculated that it might have 900 inhabitants (1773). It was cleared in the late 1840s. The population is now around 200.

Ròmasdal: Romisdale. In the middle of Tròndairnis, Skye.

Rònaidh: Rona. An island between Skye and the mainland, north of Raasay. Now deserted.

An Ros Muileach: The Ross of Mull. The south-west promontory of Mull, Inner Hebrides.

Rubha na Fainge. 'The Promontory of the Sheep-pen'. Raasay, west of Camas Alba.

Rubha nan Clach. 'The Promontory of the Stones'. North of Talasgar in Minginis, Skye.

Rudha an Dùnain. 'The Promontory of the Little Fort'. South-west of the Cuillins, Skye. A nearby dun used to be the fort of the MacAskills.

Rudha Hùnais: Rudha Hunish. The northernmost tip of Skye.

S

Scarral. Two hills north-west of Grùla. See **Grùla.**

Screapadal. Township in North Raasay. Cleared after 1846.

An Sguman. A peak of the Cuillins, near Sgurr Alasdair, Skye.

Sgurr Alasdair. 'Alexander's Peak'. The highest peak in the Cuillins, Skye. First climbed in 1873 by Sheriff Alexander Nicholson and named after him.

Sgurr Biorach. 'The Pointed Peak'. Another name for Sgurr Alasdair, Skye.

Sgurr Dubh an Dà Bheinn. 'The Black Peak of the Two Pinnacles'. In the Cuillins, Skye.

Sgurr nan Gillean. 'The Peak of the Lads'. In the Cuillins, Skye.

Sgurr Urain. A mountain on the eastern side of Glen Shiel in Ross and Cromarty. One of the 'Five Sisters of Kintail'.

Sléite: Sleat. The southernmost wing of Skye.

An Srath: Strath. 'The Strath'. The district around Broadford in south central Skye, including Scalpay and Pabbay. Once the land of the MacKinnons.

Srath Shuardail: Strath Swordale. In Strath, Skye. See **An Srath.**

Sòghaidh: Soay. South of the Cuillins, Skye.

Sròn Bhiornaill: Strone Vourlinn. The northernmost end of the great ridge of Tròndairnis, Skye.

Sròn Dhiùirinis: Stron Dhuirinish. 'The Headland of Diùirnis'. The 'new' cemetery of Portree, about three quarters of a mile south on the road to Broadford, Skye.

Struighlea: Stirling.

Staolabhal: Staolaval. A mountain in South Uist, Outer Hebrides.

An Stòr: Storr. A great rock, over 2,000 ft high, about seven miles north of Portree, Skye.

Suidhisnis: Suishnish. A point at the south-west corner of Raasay. Also the name of the nearby township and hill.

T

Taigh Mór a' Chlachain. 'The Big House of the Village'. Raasay House. Built in the 1740s for MacLeod of Raasay (see **Clachan**). After being entertained in Raasay House, Dr Johnson wrote: 'In Raasay, if I could have found an Ulysses, I had fancied a Phœacia'.

Talasgar: Talisker. On the western shore of Minginish at the foot of Priseal Mór, Skye.

Teacal: Hecla. A mountain in South Uist, Outer Hebrides.

Na Tighean Seara. 'The East Houses'. The poet's rendering of Easterhouses, a housing scheme in Glasgow.

Tìr an Eòrna. 'Land of the Barley'. Poetic name for Uist, Outer Hebrides.

Tìr Mhic Ghille Chaluim. 'The Land of MacLeod of Raasay'.

Tìr Mhic Ailein. 'The Land of Macdonald of Clanranald'. This included the island of South Uist, Outer Hebrides, and Morar, Arisaig, Moidart.

Tiriodh: Tiree. An island of the Inner Hebrides.

Tròndairnis: Trotternish. The northernmost 'wing' of Skye. See **Bhatairnis.**

U

Uamha 'n Òir. 'The Cave of Gold'. At the end of Harlosh Point in Loch Bracadale, Skye. Associated with the MacCrimmons.

Uamha 'n Fhuamhaire. 'The Giant's Cave'. On the east coast of Rona, north of Raasay.

Uidhist: Uist. North and South Uist are two of the principal islands in the Outer Hebrides.

DOUGLAS SEALY